Praise for Steve Knopper's

MJ

"Veteran journalist Steve Knopper balances the musical and the personal, packing the four hundred pages of MJ: *The Genius of Michael Jackson* with fascinating anecdotes, covering every stage of the singer's career in vivid detail. . . . The section on Jackson's childhood is especially gripping . . . an authoritative account of a world-changing force of nature."
—*Rolling Stone*

"Steve Knopper has done something very difficult: He's written a fair-minded, musically comprehensive biography of the weirdest superstar in pop history. This is the clearest, most objective portrait of Jackson I've read."
—Chuck Klosterman, *New York Times* bestselling author of
Sex, Drugs, and Cocoa Puffs and *I Wear the Black Hat*

"A rich and thorough examination of one of music's most riveting, mystifying, incandescent figures. Steve Knopper brings insight and clarity to the chaos of Michael Jackson's tragic final years, but—maybe more importantly—fleshes out the powerful and brilliant performances that transfixed the world."
—Alan Light, author of *Let's Go Crazy:*
Prince and the Making of Purple Rain

"The definitive Jackson biography."
—*The Denver Post*

"Steve Knopper is on a rescue mission: To restore Michael Jackson's legacy as a significant artist. . . . Through reminiscences and observations Knopper gathers from more than four hundred interviews, MJ deftly recounts the familiar aspects of the story. . . . Knopper shows similar critical and reportorial savvy in assessing Jackson's creative peaks and valleys. . . . Among the book's many answers that can't be questioned is the resonating impact of Jackson's boundary-shattering talent."

—*USA Today*

"Extensive interviews with the multitudes who crossed Jackson's path, from record executives to studio personnel to video directors, set Knopper's effort apart, and the portrayal shies away from sensationalism. What emerges is a thoughtful look at an artist who grew up in a segregated mill town and who, for the rest of his life, made music to bring down walls."

—*Chicago Tribune*

"[Knopper] takes a journalist's approach to the story, chronicling M.J.'s journey from a working-class family, in Gary, Indiana, to unequaled fame and riches."

—NewYorker.com

"Michael Jackson's story is well-known, but journalist Steve Knopper's meticulously researched book avoids sensationalism and hyperbole to create a rich, fair-minded portrait of Jackson and his unique artistry."

—*Buzzfeed*

"Very powerful."

—*Booklist* (starred review)

"Reminds us why Michael Jackson was, indeed, a 'genius' entertainer."

—*Newsday*

"Amazing."

—Maxim.com

"Superb . . . [a] fascinating, fair-minded account of Jackson's dazzling rise to the pinnacle of pop music and his ignominious fall. We learn the backstory of the moonwalk, the military jackets, white socks, glove, plastic surgery, skin whitening and more, all of it scrupulously documented with multiple sources."

—Associated Press

"Tracing Jackson's life and career, from his upbringing in Gary, Indiana, to the Jackson 5, solo fame, and through his death, [Steve Knopper] reveals a complicated, workaholic, tortured, sensitive soul, a peerless performer. . . . Knopper writes with verve not only about the music business, but also about music and performance."

—*Kirkus Reviews*

"Knopper rewards readers with surprising, apt, and copious details. . . . Knopper handles his prodigious subject with a reporter's imperative of impartiality but a music fan's spirit of appreciation."

—*Boulder Daily Camera*

"A book on Jackson that treats him fairly and shows his life wasn't black and white."

—Examiner.com

"The first narrative biography to deconstruct Jackson's inimitable dance steps, live performances, songwriting method, and studio sessions in fine detail."

—RollingStone.com

"A fascinating account of the tortured artist's tumultuous life that will be an invaluable resource to music historians and fans alike."

—*Publishers Weekly*

"More than rehash the well-known arc of the dysfunctional Jackson clan, Knopper targets the details that turned a child star into the King of Pop."

—*5280: The Denver Magazine*

ALSO BY STEVE KNOPPER

Appetite for Self-Destruction:
The Spectacular Crash of the Record Industry in the Digital Age

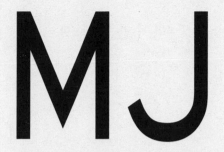

MJ

THE GENIUS OF
MICHAEL
JACKSON

STEVE KNOPPER

SCRIBNER

NEW YORK LONDON TORONTO SYDNEY NEW DELHI

For Melissa and Rose

Scribner
An Imprint of Simon & Schuster, Inc.
1230 Avenue of the Americas
New York, NY 10020

First Scribner trade paperback edition June 2016

SCRIBNER and design are registered trademarks of The Gale Group, Inc., used under license by Simon & Schuster, Inc., the publisher of this work.

For information about special discounts for bulk purchases, please contact Simon & Schuster Special Sales at 1-866-506-1949 or business@simonandschuster.com.

The Simon & Schuster Speakers Bureau can bring authors to your live event. For more information or to book an event, contact the Simon & Schuster Speakers Bureau at 1-866-248-3049 or visit our website at www.simonspeakers.com.

Designed by Jill Putorti

Manufactured in the United States of America

10 9 8 7 6 5 4 3 2 1

Library of Congress Control Number: 201500868

ISBN 978-1-4767-3037-0
ISBN 978-1-4767-3038-7 (pbk)
ISBN 978-1-4767-3039-4 (ebook)

CONTENTS

PROLOGUE

The trouble began when a janitor forgot to unlock the auditorium doors at Emerson High School, in Gary, Indiana, on September 26, 1927. A crowd gathered in the hallway and waited for first period to begin. Then two African-American students walked by. A white kid blurted out: "Let's get out of here until they get rid of the niggers."

Within hours, six hundred white Emerson students, some on the football team, were parading down the streets of northern Gary, chanting, "Strike! Strike! Strike!" and "We won't go back until Emerson's white!" Strikers in cars drove in circles, honking horns, disturbing the peace, frightening passersby. The local *Post-Tribune* sensationalized the crisis, printing bold headlines: 'E' STRIKERS VOTE TO REMAIN 'OUT.'

It seems William A. Wirt, the superintendent who had run the Gary schools since the city had opened for business twenty years earlier, had miscalculated. Before the semester began, he realized Gary's black schools didn't have enough space to accommodate the three thousand African-American students enrolled in the fall, so he relocated fifty of them to a handful of white schools. Emerson received eighteen. (It wasn't Emerson's first influx of black students, but school officials had carefully screened the few earlier kids for what they considered high intelligence, good manners, and light skin, so as not to attract too much attention.) The superintendent insisted segregation did not belong in Gary, but he took no action against the strikers.

The students' ringleader, Winfield "Junior" Eshelman, was a member of the swim team who wore a blue-and-white athletic sweater and calmly delivered his demands to the press and school officials. "The strikers are firm in their belief that a colored line must be drawn, and Emerson made a white school," Eshelman said. Facing mayoral pressure to resolve the problem, Wirt and Gary's city council compromised. They granted the strikers "excused absences." They transferred fifteen of the eighteen black students to temporary schools. They set up a temporary school facility for blacks with $15,000 in city money. And they agreed to allocate $600,000 to build a permanent all-black school, far away from Emerson. The *Post-Tribune* was euphoric: STRIKE OFF; ALL HAPPY.

Gary, Indiana, had not been built for African-Americans. Once a region of swampy marshland and sandy dunes, Gary's location on the lower shore of Lake Michigan attracted oil and steel companies at the turn of the twentieth century. In 1907, oilmen bought nine thousand acres of land and announced plans to spend $65 million on massive plants. U.S. Steel would provide living quarters for loyal workers.

The steel giant's Gary Land Company built 506 houses and quickly added more, but at fourteen dollars per month, even the cheapest homes were too expensive for the mill workers, who made 16.7 cents an hour. By 1911, overcrowding was a problem. Garbage was everywhere. Barely born, Gary was quickly segregating into two cities, for rich and poor. The former, on the north side, contained tony establishments such as the Binzenhof pub and the Hotel Gary. The latter would attract two hundred saloons over three years, with names like Jack Johnson's Gambling Joint and the Bucket of Blood. Executives and skilled workers called this southern part of town the Patch, or the Other Gary.

The all-black Roosevelt High School, created from segregation, opened in the heart of the Other Gary on April 19, 1931. Eighteen years later, across a narrow alley from Roosevelt's track field, a one-story house would appear on the corner of Jackson Street and West Twenty-Third Avenue. It was roughly thirty feet long and twenty-five feet wide, with ten tall windows, impeccable white siding, and a brick chimney at the top. The address was 2300 Jackson Street. Within a couple of years, Joseph Jackson, a construction worker, would use his savings and some money from his new wife's stepfather to buy the tiny house, as well as a refrigerator, a stove, and a bed. Joseph and Katherine would raise nine children—six boys and three girls. The oldest boy would play baseball for Roosevelt High. He and four of his brothers would sing "My Girl" at a talent show in the Roosevelt auditorium. One of the youngest brothers would spin around and around and around, mesmerizing the audience.

Years later, Michael Jackson argued with Rupert Wainwright, director of one of his short films—a teaser video for the *HIStory: Past, Present and Future, Book 1* album. Michael wanted to display a four-hundred-foot statue of himself in the film. Wainwright gently pushed back: "Some people might think it's slightly vainglorious," the British director told him. They went back and forth. "Verbal fisticuffs," is how Wainwright describes it. He assured MJ he'd be happier if the image were abstract, as opposed to the King of Pop celebrating his own legend. Michael disagreed. It had been thirty years since Michael had been the kid from the segregated Gary neighborhood who'd barely seen Chicago, much less the rest of the world. He'd spent his first five or six years on the planet with nothing but walls and boundaries, and by 1995 he wanted no limits at all. He refused to let race, gender, musical styles, family, even his own facial structure constrict him. Every time somebody tried to define him, he literally shifted his shape, altering his music, his clothes, his image, his nose. On albums, he wanted sounds that had never been made before. He wanted to sell more records than any musician, ever. He could heal the world, make it a better place, comfort the sick, save the environment, bring the children into his home, turn their fears and anxieties into joy. "With These Words," he wrote in the liner notes to *HIStory*, "I Lovingly Dedicate This Album Of My Music To All The Children Of The World." The capital letters were not vainglorious. They were just how Michael Jackson thought. He was bigger than the world, and he used his powers for good. Why not a four-hundred-foot statue?

Jackson told Wainwright the statue wasn't so much a representation of himself as it was a "symbol of music." Wainwright said that was worse than a statue. Michael called him dumb. Wainwright said maybe he was. How many records had Wainwright sold?

"You have lots of statues where you're from," Michael finally told the director.

"I live in LA," Wainwright said, confused.

"In England, you have statues. You have statues of *that woman* all over the place."

"Which woman?"

"The queen."

CHAPTER 1

By training, Joe Jackson was a craneman. His job in East Chicago, Indiana, was to sit in a metal cab about the size of a freight elevator, twenty or thirty feet off the ground, using the huge jaws of his crane to move heavy ingots onto buggies. He had no choice but to work in the mills. Almost every African-American man in the Gary region did back then, unless he was lucky enough to find work as a schoolteacher or had enough entrepreneurial gumption to open a radio station or record store. "It was said there were only three outcomes to life in Gary: The Mill, prison or death," Joe's son, Jermaine, would say.

Joe was lucky—crane operator wasn't especially tough work. But in the shower at the end of every day, Joe dreamed of show business. He wanted to be an actor.

Joe had arrived in Gary in the late forties. He was from the South, and he took a train to get there, like the six million African-Americans who were part of the Great Migration. Blues musicians such as Muddy Waters, Howlin' Wolf, John Lee Hooker, and Buddy Guy were part of this exodus, which lasted from 1910 to 1970, hauling their guitars in beat-up cases, carrying vague visions of changing music forever, or at least making a few bucks.

Joe's route north was more indirect. Born July 26, 1929, Joe grew up in the tiny fishing town of Dermott, Arkansas. Slavery complicated his lineage. Joe's great-grandfather, July "Jack" Gale, a Native American medicine man and a US Army scout, married a black slave named Gina during the years before the Civil War. Their first child, Israel, was born a slave, too. Israel—known as "Nero, son of Jack," which evolved into Nero Jackson—was "light-skinned and tall, with high cheekbones and small, twinkly eyes," as Joe wrote in his autobiography. He was eventually sold to a Louisiana plantation, where he was forced to eat from a trough. When Nero tried to escape, the plantation owner clamped his nostrils with hot tongs until he fainted.

After the Civil War, Nero became a free man and bought nearly three hundred acres on a farm in Amite County, Mississippi, where he found and married a woman named Emmaline and raised fifteen children—the rare African-American couple in Mississippi able to raise a family on their own land. "He could probably pass for white, the way his picture looked," says Thomas Jackson III, one of his descendants. Nero was known for his singing, and on Saturday evenings he performed Choctaw war dances at the center of town, prompting occasional sheriff visits for disturbing the peace. In 1920, oilmen apparently realized Nero's land was sitting on top of oil reserves; the Jacksons leased a portion of their land for $200 a year. But Nero, sadly, never saw the profits. He died in 1924, and his heirs sold his Mississippi plot during the Depression to pay taxes. Joe Jackson, always one to lament a lost fortune, estimated drilling rights would be worth $100 million today.

Nero's youngest son, Samuel, went on to earn bachelor's and master's degrees from Alcorn University, then walked two hundred miles to apply for a teaching job in Ashley County, Arkansas. Professor Jackson, as most locals called him, fell in love with one of his students, Chrystal, who had a "radiant smile, a loud laugh and a lively personality," and married her when she turned sixteen. He built a house by chopping down trees; he borrowed a horse to pull a plow, and raised vegetables in a huge garden. Samuel and Chrystal had six children. Joseph Walter was the oldest. They were strict and not above corporal punishment. "My mom put the spanking on me, and my dad put the spanking on me," recalls Joe's younger brother Martin Luther Jackson. "He said, 'Boy, you gotta stay out of jail.'"

Joe attended Dermott, an elementary and high school hybrid, where beatings were routine. Stumbling home with welts on his back, Joe dreamed of fame. One day, during a class talent contest, he picked a spiritual he'd heard from his father, "Swing Low, Sweet Chariot," and nervously stood up to sing despite jeering and laughter from the other kids. "I was so scared that I sang faster and faster, in order to finish and sit down again," Joe recalled. Finally, he slunk back to his seat, humiliated. But his teacher took him aside and insisted they were laughing because he was nervous, not because he was bad.

Joe's little sister Verna Mae was smart and precocious, a "little housewife" who made the beds and dusted all the rooms before her mother came home from work. At age seven, Verna Mae read stories to Joe and his younger brother Lawrence by kerosene lamp. Then she developed a mysterious illness. She became so weak she couldn't hold a spoon. Doctors couldn't figure out what was wrong, and her condition worsened every day. But she remained cheerful, even at the end: "Everything's fine," she kept telling her family. She died when Joseph was eleven. "As far as my understanding goes," Jermaine Jackson said, "that was the last time he shed a tear."

In 1942, when Joe was in sixth grade, his parents, both devout Christians, split up after eleven years of marriage. Chrystal had devastated her husband by having an affair with a soldier—she married him and relocated to Pine Bluff and, later, East Chicago, outside Gary.

Samuel fled to Oakland, California, where he switched careers, find-ing work in a Bay Area shipyard. "When I stopped crying, I wrote to him as often as possible," Joseph said. "Occasionally, he answered me."

For a while, Joe took a bus to Oakland to visit his father. "I con-stantly traveled back and forth between Mom and Dad, trying to make them both happy," he said. "I felt like a ping-pong ball." Finally, he moved to East Chicago for good.

By the early fifties, when he was in his twenties, Joe was working at Inland Steel, when he spotted a young woman riding her bicycle in the street. Their eyes met. He called out. She stopped. Her name was Katherine Scruse, and she was visiting her mother. She lived in Indiana Harbor, about ten miles away. Her parents were divorced, too.

Born May 4, 1930, in Barbour County, Alabama, Katherine also knew from cotton fields. Her father, Prince Albert Screws, had been a railroad worker and cotton farmer; her mother, Martha, was a house-wife; and she had one sister, Hattie, a year younger, tougher and more athletic. (Prince Albert would change "Screws" to "Scruse"—Kath-erine's maiden name.) When Katherine was eighteen months old, she developed polio, which forced her to wear a brace through ado-lescence. She always walked with a slight limp—one that made her self-conscious and inclined to avoid public gatherings. She managed to skip high school, earning her diploma from equivalency courses. She listened on the radio to the plaintive country ballads of Ernest Tubb and Hank Williams.

A dreamer, Katherine aspired to be an actress, like her heroines Kathryn Grayson and Barbara Stanwyck, or a singer, as she'd trained in her Baptist church and junior high choir. She found saxophone play-ers sexy, and while Joe Jackson did not play the saxophone, he had an electric guitar and was leading his own five-man blues band, the Falcons, which scored the occasional gig at a party or nightclub. His younger brother Luther was also in the band. This was a crucial time in the development of American music, when bluesmen who'd come up from the South were spinning their teary acoustic ballads into more aggressive, electric songs. While Luther played in a separate blues band and idolized electric guitarist Jimmy Reed, Joe composed songs in his head while operating his crane at the mill—he insisted he wrote something called "Tutti Frutti" a year before Little Richard came out with his famous hit by the same name.

Joe invited Katherine to the movies, and they arranged a second date at a party. "Not only did I think that Joe was handsome, I liked his manner," Katherine said. "He was on the quiet side, kind of cool-acting." She was characteristically self-conscious, but Joe, fortunately, had enough confidence for both of them. "We have the floor to ourselves, Katie," he told her. "Let's keep dancing."

Too poor for a wedding, Joe and Katherine went before a justice of the peace in Crown Point, Indiana, a small town south of Gary that must have seemed like another world. Almost no African-Americans lived in Crown Point, even though it was just a twenty-minute drive from Gary in Joseph's brown Buick. They were married on November 5, 1949, and started having kids, beginning with Rebbie in 1950.

After Rebbie came Sigmund Esco (Jackie), a year later, followed by Tariano Adaryl (Tito), in 1953, Jermaine in 1954, La Toya Yvonne in 1956, Marlon David in 1957, Steven Randall in 1961, and Janet Dameta in 1966. Between Marlon and Randy, on August 29, 1958, was Michael Joseph Jackson.

From the first child, the household was chaos. After Michael was born, Katherine added roughly twenty dollars a week to the family budget from her part-time job as a cashier for Sears in downtown Gary—which is to say, the white part of the city. The family had to make choices, buying a freezer instead of a television or new car. Katherine froze pinto beans, pinto soups, egg sandwiches, mackerel with rice, and tons of chicken. "We ate so much spaghetti that I can't stand pasta today," Jermaine recalled. Joseph grew potatoes, string beans, cabbage, beets, and peanuts in a community garden plot not far from the house. The boys slept in a three-level bunk bed, with Tito and Jermaine in the top rung, Jackie anchoring the bottom, and Michael and Marlon in between. The girls shared a living-room sofa. The cramped quarters fit with Katherine's keep-everybody-together philosophy. "It wasn't much bigger than a garage," she said.

Joseph began to grow into a hard, uncompromising man, with thick, fierce eyebrows. His kids would say repeatedly that he was difficult to really know. In the fifties, he was becoming more and more desperate as his obligations increased. Northwest Indiana's steel mills were thriving, but jobs available to blacks were dangerous and depressing. One of Joe's early mill jobs was in the blast furnace, where he used air hammers to remove cinders from stone walls and floors after the oven had cooled down for a day. "It was hot as hell. Nobody could stay in there more than ten minutes, and only the most robust workers could manage that. The weaker men had to leave right away," Joe said. "When I came back out, I was covered with greasy black soot. . . . Some of the workers fainted."

Every day, Joe put on a jacket with an L-shaped rip in the back, which repeatedly tore open despite Katherine's attempts to stitch it up. He had upgraded from the Buick to a beat-up family passenger van and commuted thirteen miles from the family home in Gary. Joe and his colleagues were given just twenty minutes for lunch every day, but Joe couldn't afford to bring a lunch, sometimes reluctantly accepting tacos from coworkers.

Joe Jackson responded to stress by drawing closer to his family, insisting on protecting his boys from the increasingly dangerous Other Gary. They would always be "winners," he vowed, over and over. "I was strict," Katherine said. "Joe was stricter." The kids left home only for school and sports, and returned home on time. "When he arrived home . . . the air in the house stiffened," Jermaine recalled. When Joe became angry, which was often, wrinkles and creases would form in sharp angles all over his face. "Clean the house!" he would shout to his kids, who dropped everything and reported for duty. "Wait for me in your room!" he would say, indicating an impending wallop from a leather belt. The standard amount of "whops," as Jermaine referred to them, was ten.

Michael did not escape this abuse. As a child, he was soft-spoken, an animal lover who secretly fed a mouse in the kitchen, and was shy and reserved, like his mother. He craved candy, and when he got it, he eagerly shared it with the neighborhood kids. He also had a rebel streak. At eighteen months old, he threw a bottle at his father's head; at four years old, he escalated to a shoe, prompting a severe spanking. When Michael was three, Joe finally caught him feeding his mouse and took off after him. Michael tried to hide in his bedroom, but Joe dragged him out and spanked him. As an adult, Michael would at first complain, vaguely, that Joe "has always been something of a mystery to me" and "one of the few things I regret most is never being able to have a closeness with him." Later, Michael elevated those claims to an alarming level of specificity, sobbing as he spat out memories of Joe beating him with iron cords, throwing him hard against the wall, as Katherine screamed, "Stop it! You're going to kill him! Stop it!" His kids called him Joseph, not Pop or Dad or Father or even Joe.

Joe would dismiss the abuse charges—from several of his children— as standard parenting practices of the time. "I whipped him with a switch and a belt," he clarified, regarding his treatment of Michael. "I never beat him—you beat somebody with a stick." Besides, his kids needed the harsh punishment to avoid getting into trouble. "They didn't have to go out there in the streets," he said. "They wasn't locked up like so many other people, or robbing people—they never did any of that stuff."

It wasn't just Joe's strictness that made the Jacksons so insular. In

1960, Katherine went through a spiritual crisis, having been frustrated with her Baptist faith when she learned her church minister had been having a relationship with a neighborhood woman. She switched to a Lutheran church, with the same result. So when a Jehovah's Witness knocked on her door one day, talking Scriptures and the encroaching Armageddon, she and Joe agreed to convert, although Joe, who liked his nightlife, soon lost interest. Katherine held Bible studies every day for her children, who were paying closer and closer attention to her religious transformation. She was baptized at the Roosevelt High swimming pool in 1963, and continues knocking on strangers' doors for the Witnesses to this day, or so she told Oprah Winfrey not long ago. Michael also went door-to-door well into his adulthood, even, crazily, at the peak of his fame. Still, while early church experiences informed the music of soul masters like Ray Charles, Aretha Franklin, and Sam Cooke, in the case of Michael Jackson, they mostly illustrated the differences between his religious mother and his uninterested father.

The Jacksons entertained few guests outside the family circle, other than Uncle Luther and his three Falcons band mates, who still showed up with beer to fuel the late-night blues jams. "The Jacksons didn't come out much. They were pretty much a close-knit family," says Reynaud D. Jones, who lived half a block away. One of the few extracurricular activities Joe allowed was Little League baseball, and Reynaud was on the same team as Jackie, who was around his age. Soon Reynaud was becoming close not only to the Jackson boys but to Joe himself.

Jones* found himself regularly sitting silently in the Jacksons' fam-

---

*Reynaud Jones would forever brand himself an enemy of the Jackson family when he, with two other people, sued Michael Jackson in 1993 for copying songs without permission that they'd written and sent to him. Reynaud's side lost. However, he says everything's okay with the family, to the point that his old friend Tito Jackson gave him the famous guitar that once belonged to Joe, before a recent concert in Indiana. Several credible sources, including Ronnie Rancifer, Gordon Keith, and Shirley Cartman (in her book), acknowledge Jones was instrumental in the Jackson 5's early development. In his book, Jermaine said Jones "played bass on a couple of occasions," and Michael would say in court that Jones came over on a couple of occasions for "hello—goodbye."

ily room with Jackie, Michael, and his brothers, taking in the Falcons' informal jam sessions. He recalls the elder Jackson fiddling with his electric guitar on songs by Jimmy Reed, T-Bone Walker, and other blues heroes of the time.

When Joe was at work, Tito played his father's prized electric guitar, hidden in a case in Joe's bedroom closet. The Jackson brothers would gather around, harmonizing on Four Tops songs. Katherine, who gasped when she first saw what was happening, let it go on. One morning, Tito broke a string. He carefully put the guitar back in its case, hoping his father would miraculously conclude the instrument managed to break itself. All the boys fled to their bedrooms and waited. "WHO'S BEEN MESSING WITH MY GUITAR?" Joe roared when he returned from work that night. Tito owned up to his crime, then boldly told his father he knew how to play it. Jermaine insisted Joe did not beat Tito, as reported in numerous accounts. Tito himself has been more vague: "He took care of me for it," he says. Either way, Joe's eyes widened as Tito played.

The standard version of this Jackson 5 creation myth involves the Jackson kids practicing, and Joe slowly evolving into a talent manager, pushing them in the right musical direction and maneuvering them to local performances around Gary. But that's missing a step, according to Reynaud Jones. He was a guitarist, too, and, unlike amateur bluesman Joe, the teenager had been keeping up with the musical styles of the times. The hard, industrial Chicago blues sound was giving way to a softer, if just as intense, style that began with street-corner doo-wop groups and had evolved into soul bands such as the Impressions and the Temptations. "Everywhere you went," Jones says of Gary at that time, "you could hear music from somewhere." By the early sixties, the press box at the baseball field down the alley from the Jacksons' house was playing R&B and Motown hits—not Jimmy Reed.

Jones soaked it all in. He had an electric guitar of his own and a separate group, the Epics. They experimented with doo-wop harmonies and harder soul-band arrangements. In 1965, Jones and Tito Jackson bonded over their musical tastes, and soon they were practicing in Jones's basement. Jermaine and Jackie dropped by Jones's house to watch, and they began to sing together—in surprisingly sophisticated harmony. Jones envisioned a newfangled version of the Spaniels, the Gary doo-wop group famous for 1954's "Goodnite Sweetheart, Goodnite," and fantasized about bringing the Jacksons out of his basement and onto a stage, where they could make actual money.

The youngest brothers, Michael and Marlon, showed up one day, and while Marlon struggled to learn the dance steps, six-year-old Michael had no such limitations. "He wouldn't stop," Jones recalls. "He was like a little wind-up toy. . . . At some point, I had to tell him, 'Okay, okay, *okay*, Mike. That's good.'" The Jacksons had splurged for a small black-and-white television set, Jones recalls, and Michael had absorbed all of James Brown's dance moves. Jones waxed the floor of his tiled basement, encouraging Michael to slide in his stocking feet. The group rehearsed for hours, until the Jackson boys heard a familiar car pull up. "We have to go! Joseph will be home!" they declared, and took off.

By this time, Joe Jackson had already discerned his kids' talent, although he wasn't sure what to do with it. Not long after Tito broke his guitar string, Joe came home from work with a new red guitar for his son. In August 1965, Joe picked up the newspaper and spotted a tiny classified ad: ADULT AND TEEN TALENT WANTED OF ALL TYPES. Evelyn LaHaie, who ran a modeling school, had placed it to find musicians and actors who could perform as volunteers for local hospitals and nursing homes. The ad was small, and LaHaie hadn't expected much response, so she was shocked when two hundred performers signed up to audition—singers, go-go dancers, pianists, actors. Evelyn dutifully watched all of them, taking copious notes on a legal pad. The

Jacksons were No. 55, and they rated exclamations such as "terrific" and "AA++." "The very minute I saw that little child, Michael—oh my God! I fell in love with him," LaHaie says. "Even to this day, I see six-year-olds, they're normal children, they can't do anything. But Michael was a star."

The boys were known as the Jackson Brothers, but LaHaie made the crucial suggestion to rebrand them the Jackson 5—and Joe agreed. The gig they signed up for was called the Tiny Tots' Back to School Jamboree, on August 14, 1965, and it centered on a fashion show of LaHaie's creation. "All I remember," Jermaine said, "is seeing a decent-sized crowd of young girls and Joseph telling us after the show to 'get down there and start selling your photos.'"

How the Jackson 5 landed their next gig is open to historical interpretation. In her book *The Jacksons: My Family*, Katherine said the suggestion came from Joe's sister-in-law, Bobbie Rose Jackson. Reynaud Jones, a sophomore at Roosevelt High, belonged to an extracurricular theater group called the Masque and Gavel Organization, which sponsored Roosevelt's prestigious annual talent show. He used his connections, he says, to get the Jackson brothers on the bill. It took Jones three days to convince Joe and Katherine to give permission for their kids to perform. In exchange, he promised them front-row balcony seats.

The band rehearsed the Temptations' "My Girl," James Brown's "I Got You (I Feel Good)," and Robert Parker's "Barefootin'," songs rooted in Joe's blues but with the kids' emerging style of upbeat soul, with a burst of showmanship provided by Michael. When the Jacksons finally performed in September 1965, Michael flung his shoes off during "Barefootin'" and slid across the floor. The audience paid twenty-five cents per ticket to get into the gym, and it was packed. Dressed in white open-collar shirts, cummerbunds, and black slacks, the Jacksons competed against more experienced student groups. Carl Protho, a student at the time, wasn't sure what to make of these little kids in cummerbunds—until they got to "My Girl." "That was the performance that tore the roof off the auditorium," he says. "Until then, [the competition for first place] was a very tight call, with so much talent in Gary. But I'll never forget it—the noise level, the screaming, and how everyone was standing up." Michael and Jermaine were the lead singers, but even then, Michael had evolved into the obvious star of the group. "Jermaine had a few solo parts, as did Jackie, but the main focus was on Michael. He stood out," says Benny Dorsey, one of Michael's teachers at Garnett Elementary School, who saw the show in his capacity as a member of Roosevelt's alumni association. Joseph Jackson stood next to the stage, arms at his sides, staring intently as Michael did his James Brown screeches and skillful whirligigs.

After the exhilarated boys won the talent-show trophy, Joseph calmed them down. "Overall, you did good," he said soberly, "but we've got some work to do."

The Jacksons worked some more in Reynaud Jones's basement until they showed up one day to tell him band practice had been moved to their own living room. Jones continued to rehearse with them. Not long after that, he reported to 2300 Jackson Street, as per usual, and Jackie answered the door. "My dad says you can't come in," Jackie told his friend.

Jones understood. He was not a Jackson. That meant he was not a star.

Once Joe Jackson took control of the family band, the lively little house at 2300 Jackson Street transformed into a barracks for future music professionals. "These boys are going to take me out of the steel mill," Joe wrote to his brother, Lawrence, who was in the air force. Joe insisted Katherine put dinner on the table and the boys ready their instruments by 4:30 P.M. daily. He came home from work, the family ate, and the boys hit the living-room stage. If Joe was late, Katherine pinch-hit. "Sometimes we'd want to, you know, slack off, and Dad would make us practice," Michael recalled. "He'd say, 'Practice makes perfect.'"

As the lead singer of the family band, seven-year-old Michael began to develop leverage over his father. Some days, he didn't feel like singing. That halted the entire operation. When Joe attempted to spank Michael into submission, he withdrew further. To break the gridlock, Michael's brothers would, as their sister Rebbie recalled, "try to laud him on, play to his little ego." Michael fell in line once the band became successful. As they began to win every conceivable talent show, he started to see, like all the boys, that this kind of life was cooler than throwing a ball on a field or messing around the streets.

Slowly, during this time, the Jackson 5 began to take shape. Michael was the natural front man, but Jermaine had a specific skill—he could strain his vocal pitch into a pleading gospel style, like Levi Stubbs in the Four Tops or John Lennon in the Beatles. Jackie, the baseball player, was the ultimate utility man, with a sweet harmony vocal that always seemed to fit just right, especially above Michael's bright and sharp leads. Tito mostly kept to his guitar and occasionally added a baritone in the style of the Temptations' Melvin Franklin. Jermaine also started to play bass guitar. As for poor Marlon—even his mother didn't think he was talented. "His lack of singing ability bothered Joe even more than his dancing," Katherine said. Joe kept trying to drum him out of the group, but Katherine stood up for him. Marlon worked five times as hard as his brothers on dance steps, willing himself into a permanent position with the Jackson 5. His role, though, was eternally ambiguous. "It's a fact that Marlon never sang a word as a member of the Jackson 5 until the boys began recording for Motown," Katherine said.

Joe surrounded the boys' voices with rock 'n' roll instruments—not just guitar and bass, which Tito and Jermaine were handling, but drums. The band's earlier drummer, Milford Hite, had moved to another neighborhood and was unavailable for regular rehearsals. So Joe started to recruit new musicians. Leonard Gault, a drummer, had bonded with Joe at Inland Steel, but he was too old to play with the Jackson boys. He volunteered younger brother Earl as a substitute. Gault showed up for rehearsal and fit in as both a band mate and a friend. "Their voices blended together . . . it was beautiful," the retired railroad worker* recalls by phone from his Merrillville, Indiana, home. "They had it."

The evening rehearsals turned into events, with relatives such as Uncle Luther's five-year-old son, Keith, taking exalted spots on the living-room floor. "All the neighborhood kids used to be at the window wondering what's going on," Keith remembers. Friends and relatives, sensing the beginning of something, opened their dens and basements, too. "They would rehearse in anybody's backyard, anybody's house, wherever," says Johnnie Gault, who lived in the neighborhood and was married to Earl's older brother.

Katherine funded Joe's profligate purchases of new instruments by tapping into the savings she'd gathered over the years through her Sears paychecks, which she had planned to use to remodel the house. "Mom had some doubts about the soundness of this decision," Michael said.

Joe networked up and down Gary and Chicago's nearby South Side. It was a time of racial transition in the US. In 1968, Gary elected Richard M. Hatcher as the country's first-ever black mayor, simultaneously breaking racial barriers and spurring white flight. In moving to the suburbs, whites left behind poverty, crime, gangs, and drugs—but also black-owned businesses, Black Power, black politics, and, of course, black music. "Gary was called Chocolate City—a lot of gambling, a lot of prostitution," recalls Maurice "Mo" Rodgers, a

---

*Gault, who rarely does interviews, says he prefers to be remembered not as a footnote in the Jacksons' biography but as a member of the Seventh-day Adventist Church.

Gary singer at the time who would help form Steeltown Records. "It was jumping, and there was music all over the place, artists and singers and groups." As Joe began to tell everybody he could find about his talented boys, he went deeper and deeper into African-American neighborhoods, hanging around instrument shops and networking with merchants, promoters, producers, DJs, musicians, politicians, and policemen.

Joe made all kinds of deals, some in conflict with each other, but his persistence brought the band before adult Gary audiences—Bird's Pub, the Elks Lodge, and Joe Green's Club Woodlawn, run by a husband-and-wife team that specialized in blues singers and local bands. Club hoppers would start out at, say, Joe Green's, bringing their own liquor and supplementing it with a five-dollar "set-up" tray containing a small bowl of ice, a bag of potato chips, four or five cups, and maybe some Coca-Cola. If they were lucky, they'd catch a major touring act, like Motown's Jr. Walker and the All Stars or Chicago R&B star Tyrone Davis. The Elks Lodge had an after-hours license, so by two or three in the morning, music fans wound up there, among hard-drinking mill workers.

Mr. Lucky's was a sophisticated bar turned club catering to black professionals, serving one-dollar fried tacos. The Jackson 5 showed up regularly, making eight dollars for five sets per night, six or seven days a week. "We were playing between bad comedians, cocktail organists and strippers," Michael recalled. Katherine, raising her kids Jehovah's Witness, was suspicious of the nightly debauchery they were absorbing. Joe didn't care. If Katherine was a Sunday-morning kind of lady, Joe was a Saturday-night kind of guy.

At Mr. Lucky's, the Jackson 5 were finally allowed to play an entire show, rather than a song here and there. They loaded up their sets with hits by James Brown, Sam and Dave, and, of course, Motown. During Joe Tex's "Skinny Legs and All," Michael dropped to his hands and knees, crawled into the audience, looked up women's skirts, then rose up into a dance.* The boys were under-age and technically not allowed to be in any of these clubs, but they helped the bartenders and waitresses sell food and liquor. Proprietors made deals with the cops—they looked the other way as long as the boys didn't drink.

In summer 1966, the Jackson family journeyed 1,600 miles in Joe's cramped Volkswagen van to see his father, whom the boys called Papa Samuel, in Winslow, Arizona, and play a concert at the Old Arcadia Hall. (They didn't stop to sleep, but they did pull off in Oklahoma City to visit a relative, and Katherine and Rebbie made fried chicken and pork and beans during a welcome five-hour respite from the road.) It was a torturous trip—at one point Jermaine watched as Joseph pulled the van to the side of the road and started "vigorously rubbing his cheeks." "Just tired," Joe told his gaping son. Once they arrived, the boys, who had never been outside of Gary, were especially amazed by the color of Arizona's soil. "Michael used to like nature-type stuff," recalls Earl Gault, the drummer who had become close enough to the family to make the trip. "He ended up putting some of that red dirt in this jar and bringing it back." Upon their return to 2300 Jackson Street, Marlon began teasing Michael about his beloved dirt. He did it so often that one of the older brothers, Tito or Jermaine, hollered to Michael from another room, accusing Marlon of pulling all the dirt out of the jar. "And Michael jumped and ran out there," Gault recalls. "They were just joking, but Michael wanted that dirt."

When Gault had to quit the band because his father objected to the travel, Joe acted on a recommendation from Shirley Cartman, a

---

*Jessye Williams, who fixed windows for the Gary Community School Corp., gave me a new perspective on the famous detail that crowds threw dollars and coins and Michael picked up the money while singing. Williams, a neighbor in a rock-and-soul band called the Tempos who regularly shared bills with the Jackson 5, recalls: "When they would finish the song, I'd go throw five bucks, and then everybody would follow suit in the audience." I have no reason not to believe Williams, who died in August 2014, other than people have a tendency to write themselves into Michael Jackson's history.

teacher at Beckman Junior High in Gary, and found the best drummer in the school. The Jacksons claimed Johnny Jackson, then fourteen, was a distant cousin, but his name was a coincidence. Jermaine called him "a bubbly, animated little guy with a cheeky smile" and "the best drummer around for miles, as confident with his skill as Michael was with his dance." He had good timing and a knack for showmanship. In an early black-and-white publicity photo, the first of the Jackson 5 to catch your eye is Michael, holding up an open palm and clutching a microphone in his other hand, staring seriously into the distance. The next is Johnny, in the center, holding a drumstick in mid-twirl above a snare, with a bass drum marked, in crude sticker letters: THE JACKSON 5 AND JOHNNY. Like Earl, Johnny grew close to the family. "We were brothers," he said. "We did everything together."

The Jacksons were slowly becoming regional stars in Chicago and northwest Indiana. They needed records. Joe started to drag his sons, or sometimes just Michael, to studios for auditions. One day in 1966, on Chicago's famous Record Row, Joe brought Michael to One-derful Records for a solo audition. Michael sang Lou Rawls's "Tobacco Road." The lyrics may have resonated. "I was born / in a dump," goes the first line.

George Leaner, one of the label's cofounders, had been wary of working with underage performers, given the expensive complications of touring chaperones and child-labor laws. But in early 1967, he took a chance and signed the band.

Joe kept his boys on a strict schedule. Every day for five months, at five P.M., One-derful professionals coached them on harmonies and chord progressions. Then they'd sing during jam sessions. This mentorship, concludes the *Chicago Reader*'s Jake Austen, helped "transform a talented teen band into an act on the verge of greatness." In the end, One-derful, a small label without any major hits, lacked the resources to give the Jacksons a breakthrough record. The label's founders filed the session away, and the Jackson 5's One-derful single, "Big Boy," written by Eddie Silvers with fifteen-year-old hotshot

Larry Blasingaine on guitar, never came out. This version of the song was unknown to the public until Austen told the story in 2009, after Michael's death.

Not long after the One-derful sessions, the phone rang at 2300 Jackson Street. The caller was a young Gary singer, producer, and raconteur named Gordon Keith. He'd heard about the Jacksons through Shirley Cartman, Tito's junior high orchestra teacher. Inspired by Motown, Keith and three of his best friends had formed Steeltown Records in Gary. "It was tough," recalls Mo Rodgers, one of Steeltown's early principals. "[As] black entrepreneurs, we went up against the typical walls, and the banks and stuff." But Keith knew a phenomenon when he saw one, especially after witnessing Jackson 5 posters all over Gary. Cartman invited Keith to her house, where the boys sang two of her own songs, "The Scrub" and "Lonely Heart," although Keith didn't show up. Instead, he went later to the Jackson's home, where he watched in disbelief as Michael high-jumped Tito's guitar cord, stretched chest-high between a guitar and an amp.

Despite the Jacksons' One-derful contract, Keith signed the band to Steeltown and began recording the band after school days in November 1967. His instinct was to use his usual Gary studio, but he had a feeling about the sessions, so he relocated to a more accomplished one on West Sixty-Ninth Street in Chicago. Morrison Sound Studio was an enclave for African-American musicians in the heart of a white neighborhood. "Most sessions were done late—midnight till two in the morning," recalls Jerry Mundo, a studio singer, organist, and guitarist. "A lot of cats would come in late, get blasted. We'd live on White Castle hamburgers. They'd have a bottle of gin on the floor, and an hour later they'd be gone, and the drummer would get into an argument with the bass player, and they'd get into a fistfight." The nightly ruckus eventually cost the owner his lease, and he'd soon have to relocate the studio to a black neighborhood on the East Side.

The Jacksons, says Delroy Bridgeman, a Gary singer who worked on the sessions, were "very quiet, well-mannered kids." It took about four hours to record a song they'd learned at One-derful and had incorporated into their club sets: "Big Boy." They also came up with "You've Changed," "We Don't Have to Be Over 21," and "Some Girls Want Me for Their Lover," all written by local artists, R&B songs designed for adult listeners. Michael was an accomplished mimic, sounding as smooth as a grown-up. The sessions were long and difficult, and the boys stayed until ten or eleven nightly.

The Steeltown version of "Big Boy" was Michael Jackson's formal introduction to the world. He comes in after thirty seconds, following drums, bass, a trebly blues-guitar riff, and backup harmonies that sound too polished to be Jackie or Jermaine. (Because they weren't—after the Jacksons had finished recording, Keith and his colleagues decided to overdub the boys' vocals, other than Michael, with professionals.)

"Big Boy" is like a house built out of fine materials by a not-terribly-proficient work crew. (Tito plays guitar and Jermaine plays bass, but Keith beefed up their contributions with four or five session musicians.) The song is lazy and flat, with no dynamism—until Michael comes in, effortlessly brassy, stretching out the syllables to the first words: "*faaaaairy-taaaaaalessssssss.*" The single, with its flip side, "You've Changed," came out on January 31, 1968. The Jacksons couldn't believe they finally had a record.

Back then, South Side blues label Chess Records owned an AM radio station whose call letters, WVON, stood for "Voice of the Negro." At a puny one thousand watts, the mostly R&B station became a trusted news source for the growing civil rights movement. (In 1968, when Martin Luther King Jr. was assassinated, the Rev. Jesse Jackson made his first phone call to King's wife. His second call went to WVON.) The station also had a stable of regionally famous DJs known as the Good Guys, who developed a reputation for breaking the best singles. "If you got a hit on WVON—literally, this is not ego—it spread across the country," recalls Lucky Cordell, a retired DJ and manager at the station who still lives in Chicago. WVON put "Big Boy" on the air, and within a month the record went into regular rotation. On March 5, 1968, hallowed Atlantic Records, which had introduced Ray Charles and Aretha Franklin to the world, struck a deal with Steeltown to distribute the single nationwide. "I honestly heard something that I felt was the beginning of something big," Cordell says.

In 1967, while the Jacksons were driving around Gary and Chicago, winning talent shows, Ronnie Rancifer was playing blues and touring at clubs. His band, Little Johnny and the Untouchables, had a floor show—a revue—including snake dancers. One weekend on the road in Alabama, the snake got loose and Rancifer was so freaked out he threatened to jump out the window while speeding down the highway. The band stopped, secured the boa, and resumed.

Rancifer lived in Hammond, Indiana, a mostly white, working-class neighborhood outside Gary. Joe Jackson knew his mother from when the Rancifers and the Jacksons had lived near each other in nearby East Chicago. One day, on a tip from a worker at a music shop in Hammond, Joe called Ronnie's mom. Then he dropped by the Rancifers' house, and the next thing Ronnie knew, he was in the Jackson 5.

The best way to gain national stardom as an African-American musician in those days was to perform at a network of clubs and theaters known as the chitlin circuit—Louis Armstrong, Duke Ellington, Ella Fitzgerald, Nat King Cole, Count Basie, James Brown, Sam Cooke, and the Temptations were among its alumni. Every big city had a theater on the circuit—the Uptown in Philadelphia, the Howard in Washington, DC, the Fox in Detroit, and, of course, the Regal in Chicago. Built in 1927 on the South Side, the 3,500-seat Regal was at first a segregated movie house, but it supplemented the pictures with performances by Armstrong, Cab Calloway, Lena Horne, and others. Crystal chandeliers hung from the ceiling, flanked by silk drapes and floors of Italian marble. Ushers wore full-length capes to lead customers to their seats.

The Jackson 5 were not new to this circuit—they'd already won an amateur talent show at the Regal—but after "Big Boy," they began to land regular slots alongside established performers from James Brown to Etta James to Jackie Wilson. "You'd go in there, you'd do three or four shows a night, come back to the hotel, and be ready to do it again the next night," Rancifer says. "You know what a musician's steak is? A musician's steak is crackers and cheese. Crackers and cheese in a van. And potato chips." Although the Jackson 5 were rivals to the Five Stairsteps, another family band on the circuit, Stairsteps singer Clarence Burke remembers befriending the Jackson boys, particularly Jackie, who at sixteen was around his age. Outside one of the theaters was a basketball hoop, and the two teenagers used to shoot around until Michael came out. Burke tried to put Michael on his shoulders to help him with the shots, but Michael, like any nine-year-old younger brother, insisted on doing it himself—endlessly.

Joe, the Jacksons' driver Jack Richardson, and sometimes Rancifer took the wheel on the road trips. The boys listened to music in the back and tried to out-jive each other. By far, the champion trash-talker was Michael Jackson. "Michael was a very watchful guy. Whatever weak spot on you he saw, he could blow that up and throw it back at you. Say if your socks smelled bad. Then he would get on you about your socks," Rancifer recalls. "If you came around and you had some eyeglasses on that looked real funny, he'd say, 'Oh, God, you got microscopes on!'"

The Apollo Theater, on 125th Street in Harlem, had a distinctive kind of legend. It was in a lively part of town, the street corners jammed with moaning brakes and honking horns, storefronts packed with juke-boxes blaring Ray Charles and Dionne Warwick, and people yelling from shoe-shine parlors, restaurants, and appliance stores. Underneath the Apollo's purple vertical neon sign, stars such as Sammy Davis Jr.

and Jackie Robinson could be spotted chatting with box-office staff and managers about securing front-row seats.

The Jacksons had killed at the Apollo in 1968, winning the Super-dog talent contest, and had been gathering strength and skills on the circuit, but the Stairsteps were the hotter group. They had a *two*-year-old singer, Cubie. They did not, however, have Michael Jackson, who was absorbing technical information from superior singers and dancers at an alarmingly fast rate. "I carefully watched all the stars because I wanted to learn as much as I could," he would say. "I'd stare at their feet, the way they held their arms, the way they gripped a microphone, trying to decipher what they were doing and why they were doing it." He was always looking for mentors. Feeling isolated from his brothers, who were older and able to wander the streets, and not being able to connect with his father, Michael spent most of his time in those days standing behind dusty stage curtains. Headlining a different night at the Apollo in May 1968, blues singer Etta James said Michael freaked her out by watching her set so intently. She told him to scat, and he ran away, wide-eyed, but returned ten minutes later to the same spot. Later, Joe made Michael apologize, and the gruff, hard-living diva was so charmed by Michael's sincerity that she wound up giving him advice while he sat on her lap. "I don't remember what I told him," she said, "but I remember thinking, as he was leaving, 'Now there's a boy who wants to learn from the best, so one day he's gonna *be* the best.'"

It wasn't only Michael Jackson who was learning from the best. Every chitlin circuit band was stealing from other acts in those days. Motown's Temptations actually derived the famous Temptation Walk (". . . put your right foot down, start walking all around") from a doo-wop group called the Vibrations. Best known for "Peanut Butter" and "The Watusi," the Vibrations did fast steps and splits and ran and jumped in the aisles. Carl Fisher, the Vibrations' front man, occasion-ally noticed the Tempts' Paul Williams watching intently from back-stage. Not long after that, Williams's band would be onstage doing one of the same steps. Trained by television, mentored by Chicago studio pros, exposed firsthand to Jackie Wilson and the Temptations, Michael used these chitlin circuit stages as a master dance class.

"Everybody was ranting and raving about how great the Five Stairsteps were," recalls Teddy Young, drummer in R&B star Joe Simon's band, which headlined one night with the Jacksons and the Stairsteps. "So the Jacksons came on. Nobody knew who they were. They did their set the first night. The second night. Then Michael kept asking: 'How'd Jackie Wilson do that dance, and that quick turn he do?' He kept asking, kept asking. Joe Simon is not known for dancing, but Joe actually showed him, while we were rehearsing, before show-time, how to pivot that little turn." By the end of those Apollo dates, Michael was fluent in both James Brown and Jackie Wilson. "Right there, at the Apollo, Michael and the Jackson 5 took the torch from the Five Stairsteps," Young recalls.

Word spread about the Jackson 5. Motown star Gladys Knight, leader of the Pips, happened to catch the group at a Regal performance in Chicago. Like everybody, she was transfixed, especially by Michael and his steadily growing collection of super-smooth dance moves. She invited a few Motown executives to catch one of the band's shows. They communicated their enthusiasm back to the company's president, Berry Gordy Jr.

In July 1968, backstage before a show at the Regal, Joseph Jackson was nowhere to be found. The Jackson 5 were about to open for Motown act Bobby Taylor and the Vancouvers, famous for a rock-and-soul hit about interracial dating, "Does Your Mama Know about Me," and Michael's older brothers were hungry. They wanted to grab dinner out, in Chicago, for the hour they had left before returning to their dressing rooms to prepare for the evening show. Vancouvers' guitarist Eddie Patterson and keyboardist Robbie King were chilling in the green room, which contained bunks, a coffee machine, and a little rehearsal area with some mirrors. They agreed to keep an eye on the younger Jackson boys, Michael and Marlon.

Patterson and King sat around and read magazines while Michael queued up funky tunes on an old record player, practicing his steps in front of the mirror. Michael didn't say much, and Patterson wasn't especially interested in conversing with a ten-year-old.

Later that night, Patterson found himself in the audience, watching the singer he'd just babysat. "Michael was like a little magic kid on a top, just bopping and singing and smiling and dancing," he says. "In his last days, he was awesome. But when he was a kid, he was defying gravity." Like Gladys Knight before him, the Vancouvers' front man, Bobby Taylor, spread the word to Berry Gordy Jr. at Motown.

This time, Gordy listened intently.

CHAPTER 2

The Snakepit was a messy room. Microphones hung from the ceiling. Cables were spread everywhere. A set of drums was in one corner, a grand piano in the other. There was a worn spot on the floor near the mixing board where producers had tapped their feet for a decade. But when the Jackson 5 showed up at Hitsville in Detroit, they didn't care about the housecleaning. They could feel the presence of the singers who'd come before them   Marvin Gaye, the Supremes, Smokey Robinson, the Temptations, the Four Tops. The Jacksons had shown up to cut vocals for their first songs for Motown Records. The Funk Brothers, the label's famed house band, had already laid down the instrumental tracks, and like any discerning singer, Michael Jackson—at ten years old—was self-critical. He didn't like the way he sounded on a few lines, and he wanted to overdub some things onto the tape over an extra hour or two. "He wouldn't let himself get away with anything unless it was right," recalls one of the freelance Motown engineers, Ed Wolfrum.

But Michael's perfectionism was too much for his father. The Jacksons had to pay expenses for every recording session. "Michael, this is advanced against royalties!" Joe hollered as he hit him. "This is costing us a fortune!" Wolfrum had worked with difficult artists, but he had never seen anything like this. He and his fellow engineers intervened. "If you're going to deal with it like that," they told Joe, "then we're stopping the session until you cool down." Wolfrum happened to be studying for the priesthood at the time. "I certainly morally couldn't leave it alone," he recalls, years later. "It really struck me." Bobby Taylor of the Vancouvers, the producer, knew what to do in situations like these. "I wouldn't let Joe Jackson interfere," he said. "I once pulled a gun on him in the studio and told him not to come back while we were working."

The Jacksons told reporters Diana Ross discovered them and brought them to Motown—their debut album was called *Diana Ross Presents the Jackson 5*. Over more than four decades, Bobby Taylor has meticulously corrected the record. Upon spotting the Jackson 5 at the Regal Theatre in Chicago, Taylor called Motown executive Ralph Seltzer. Seltzer had reservations. Stevie Wonder, who'd begun his Motown career at age twelve in 1962, was a once-in-a-lifetime talent, but issues with child-labor laws and chaperones had been almost too much. "I had a reluctance to sign really young people," recalls Seltzer, in his late eighties, by phone from a senior living center in Grants Pass, Oregon. "I felt that I'd rather sign a twenty-two-year-old adult who lives around the corner from our studios and was in high school or Wayne [State] University or whatever. This was five minors—with a father who supervised their career and had to be dealt with."

Seltzer trusted Bobby Taylor, but he needed another opinion. He turned to Suzanne Celeste de Passe. At just twenty-one, she was a rising creative executive at Motown and a confidant of Berry Gordy Jr., the label's founder; in 1968, she listened to the Jackson 5, dubbed them "terrific," and recommended Motown sign them. Gordy responded obstinately. "I don't want kid acts! Do you know how much trouble

Stevie Wonder is?" De Passe snapped back: "Oh, no you don't. Not if they're great."

Days later, Gordy, de Passe, and a few others were in an eighth-floor office.* Dick Scott, Gordy's assistant, had set up a new video camera, a piece of technology rare for 1968. The footage Scott made of the Jackson boys was grainy and black-and-white and eventually leaked to the public. In the foreground, a short-haired ten-year-old Michael Jackson, wearing long pants and a tight long-sleeved shirt, claps his hands and glides from side to side, keeping his upper body still while moving his legs in perfect rhythm, like a tap dancer, to James Brown's "I Got the Feeling." In the background, his brothers provide the music—Tito on guitar, Jermaine on bass, Jackie on tambourine, and Johnny Jackson steady as usual on the drum kit. In the video, the brothers' heads are out of the frame, so you can see only their long, skinny legs stepping in well-rehearsed choreography. Only Marlon, because he's almost as short as Michael, appears in full, albeit briefly. Toward the end, Michael spins with fantastical grace, drops to his knees like Jackie Wilson, snaps back up, grabs his belt, then goes into a long, James Brown–style side-stepping routine.

Gordy recalls giving a brief congratulatory speech at the audition, after they'd finished the Temptations' "Ain't Too Proud to Beg" and "I Wish It Would Rain" and Michael's road-tested version of "Tobacco Road." But the boys were confused. "Uh, Mr. Gordy, does that mean you're gonna sign us?" Jermaine asked. "Yes, yes, it docs," Gordy said. They cheered.

There were contracts. Seltzer, the label's legal specialist, met for nearly two hours with Joe Jackson at Motown's Detroit offices on July 26,

---

*There is some dispute about whether Gordy was, in fact, present for the audition. In his account, he was leading it and making speeches; others recall Seltzer overseeing the recording and sending the film to Gordy afterward.

1968. After haggling over the number of years the band would be signed to the label, Joseph signed. He didn't read the contracts. He didn't have a lawyer. He let Seltzer explain everything. Joe wanted a one-year deal. Motown wanted seven years. Seltzer made a show of granting Joe his wish. It was a mirage. Joe didn't realize the contract forbade the Jacksons from recording for another label for seven years. This type of subterfuge was the way record executives did business in those days, especially with poor and desperate artists who couldn't afford to hire their own attorneys. And Joe wasn't far removed from Gary's steel-mill hell. He saw to it that all the boys signed, too.

Seltzer credited Jackson 5's father on one level. "Most of our artists, we supervised and managed completely, and Joe Jackson, with very good reason, didn't feel he wanted some strangers he'd never met before to walk in and have one hundred percent say about everything," he recalls. He also believed Joe was a rube: "I didn't have gigantic respect for him. Because I thought he thought he knew a lot more about the music business than he actually did."

Bobby Taylor hounded Gordy to let him take over the Jacksons' career. Gordy agreed. Taylor succumbed to the irresistible novelty of Michael Jackson—he could sing like an adult, so Taylor connected the band with adult songs, such as Smokey Robinson's simmering blues "Who's Lovin' You" and Ray Charles's ballad "A Fool for You," as well as a slow burner from their Steeltown Records days, "You've Changed," and Sly and the Family Stone's funky hit "Stand!," which would be something of a blueprint for the Jackson 5's Motown career.

The Jacksons spent weekdays attending school in Gary, then drove the laborious four or five hours to Detroit during weekends and summers, plopping mattresses and sleeping bags onto the floor of Taylor's small apartment. He taught the group how to properly use microphones and not to worry about "projecting" over built-in amplification.

Taylor cut fifteen tracks in all, and when the Jacksons finally joined him in the studio to sing, the revelation was Michael's voice. He could embody the blues just as Ray Charles did, and he had an extra gear that none of his brothers had, an inspired brightness that could overwhelm a song, like when he shouted "I love you!" in the background of the Philly soul classic "Can You Remember." "He got it," Taylor said. "I didn't have to explain, didn't have to analyze. I went in and sang it for him, then got out the way while Michael tore it up. When he got through, there were tears in my eyes."

Contractual issues—mostly thanks to Steeltown, which insisted on waiting for the Jacksons' original agreement to expire—prevented the band from putting out Motown singles until 1969. While they waited, they continued performing, at the Apollo in New York, the Twenty Grand Club in Detroit, and familiar Chicago hot spots such as Guys and Gals and the High Chaparral. To add to all this work, Gordy paraded the Jacksons around Motown. Back then, he lived in a million-dollar mansion on Boston Boulevard in Detroit and brought in the Jackson 5 for a charity event. On this night, Motown stars Smokey Robinson, the Temptations, the Four Tops, and Diana Ross were like kings and queens in Gordy's royal court. And then there was ten-year-old Michael Jackson. "How in the world—'cause this little boy, and he was a *kid*—be so talented? That's what everybody went away talking about," singer Brenda Holloway said. It was at this party that Michael, wide-eyed, met Ross for the first time. Michael reacted with typical subtlety: "DIANA ROSS!" he shouted to his brothers. "I'VE JUST SEEN DIANA ROSS!" Jackie, the oldest, the leader, got them to concentrate. "We was quite nervous," Tito acknowledged.

When Motown signed the Jackson 5, the small record label had been tied to Detroit as intimately as the Ford Motor Company or Al Kaline of the Tigers. It was in Detroit that Berry Gordy had started out as a boxer. He wasn't bad, but he had an epiphany upon seeing boxing and big-band handbills plastered on the same wall: the twenty-three-year-

old boxers looked like they were fifty, while the fifty-year-old bandlead-
ers looked like they were twenty-three. Joseph Jackson had been a failed
boxer, too, but while he channeled his ambitions into fiercely driving
his sons, Berry channeled his into building a factory-style assembly line
in Detroit for hit records.

Motown songs, according to Gordy, had to be short, catchy, and
fun. They had to avoid politics, even when race riots were threatening
to destroy Detroit (although, beyond his control, songs like Martha
Reeves and the Vandellas' "Dancing in the Street" became unofficial
civil rights anthems). With Gordy's hands-on guidance at all levels,
from songwriting to quality control to charm school, the company
released immortal sixties hits such as "Baby Love," "Ain't Too Proud to
Beg," and "I Heard It through the Grapevine."

By the time the Jackson 5 signed with Motown in 1968, Gordy
and Motown were going through a transition. The Supremes (who
hated each other) and the Temptations (whose front men had drug
problems and hated each other) were not the reliable superstars they
had been for much of the sixties. The company's famous songwriting team, brothers Eddie and Brian Holland and Lamont Dozier, had
left the company, then sued Gordy over money. Stevie Wonder and
Marvin Gaye were beginning to envision a world beyond two-and-
a-half-minute singles, plotting albums that would change music for
decades. And, fairly or not, Gordy didn't see much of a future on
Motown's bench, as stars such as Martha Reeves and the Vandellas,
the Contours, and Jr. Walker and the All Stars represented the previous decade rather than the new one. He knew the real clout was in
Hollywood. He bought his first Los Angeles home in fall 1968 and
began to contemplate a company-wide move. The idea was to make
movies with his muse, Diana Ross, but first he needed to consoli-
date his base. For this, he required fresh music stars who'd play by his
rules, stars who would roll off a new Motown assembly line that was
strict and streamlined even by Gordy's standards. Gordy saw in the

Jackson 5 a new franchise player, crucial to Motown's LA future. A group he could fully control.

The new Motown sound, based in LA, would have hints of Motown's familiar "Sound of Young America"—catchy, sophisticated pop melodies set to a steel-beam rhythmic mixture of jazz, R&B, and gospel music. But it would be more scripted, less improvisational, and fully dictated by Gordy and his producers—which is to say, less vulnerable to mutiny by self-determined studio musicians such as the Funk Brothers, Motown's storied in-house backup band throughout the sixties. "Their music was not the R&B that we were typically known for," Martha Reeves says. "When we recorded with the Funk Brothers, the Funks initiated the sound. Jackson 5 were closer to disco than to R&B."

"They thought the West Coast was going to generate a new sound that would perpetuate the company and make it go on and on," adds Clay McMurray, a longtime Motown arranger and quality-control staffer who worked as a Jackson 5 songwriter and producer. "It just worked in the reverse, with the exception of Thelma Houston and Brenda Holloway and the Jacksons. They just never came close to what we did here in Detroit."

Made in Detroit, Bobby Taylor's Jackson 5 recordings were not hits. Gordy could tell that right away. Taylor had to go. "Berry was very, very direct about his instructions," Motown arranger Paul Riser recalls. "He would say, 'I need hits. I don't want anything else.'" In Taylor's place, Gordy installed a team of songwriters—Fonze Mizell, Freddie Perren, and Deke Richards, the latter of whom had just helped write Diana Ross and the Supremes' megahit "Love Child." The trio created an instrumental called "I Wanna Be Free." They assembled all-star Hollywood musicians at the Sound Factory and other studios. These were hired hands, Los Angeles session players paid handsomely (about $105 per session, or double union scale) to record exclusively for Motown. Some, including guitarists David T. Walker and Louie Shelton, were given the freedom to improvise within the context of an established instrumental, while others were on hand for their ability to efficiently read sheet music and play the notes flawlessly. They were not, however, the Funk Brothers, and they knew it. "The Funk Brothers were all jazz musicians who played at night and came to the studio in the daytime. The piano parts were so outrageous and so loose. Genius," says Don Peake, one of the LA session guitarists who would play on numerous Jackson 5 recordings as well as other Motown hits. "On the West Coast, we were a little straighter."

Hype had been building for the Jackson 5 throughout 1969 as the group steadily played gigs. They performed at the Daisy, a posh club in Beverly Hills, with the help of Motown's publicity machine. Diana Ross introduced the band she'd "discovered." "All we needed was a hit," Tom Noonan, the late Motown executive, would say. By August 1969, Gordy sent for Joe and the Jackson boys, including keyboardist Ronnie Rancifer and drummer Johnny Jackson, to join him in LA.

Richards, Mizell, and Perren were thinking Gladys Knight when they assembled their musicians to cut "I Wanna Be Free." The song begins with a piano glissando by moonlighting Jazz Crusader Joe Sample, and every instrument carries its own sing-along hook, from fellow Crusader Wilton Felder's loping, simplistic bass lines to the siren quality of the guitar to the string section (recorded at a different studio) to the omnipresent hand claps.

Satisfied, Richards, Mizell, and Perren booked a flight at the airport, "I Wanna Be Free" tapes in hand, so they could meet Knight in the studio to lay down the vocals. Gordy paged them before they could board. "Don't get on the plane," the boss told Richards. "Come straight to my house." Surprised, they obeyed.

Gordy asked them to rewrite the song to be more teen-pop Frankie Lymon and less Ray Charles, and give it to the Jackson 5. "Direct it towards kids, so they can identify with it," he told his new writers. Thus did "I Wanna Be Free" morph into "I Want You Back."

Michael could sing the hell out of a blues song, but as critic Nelson

George has observed, Motown's immaculate decision was to make the Jackson 5 sound like themselves. Like kids. The LA musicians' more controlled approach fit the Jacksons, who had experience from Joe's relentless home rehearsals and the chitlin circuit, but they needed rules. "The writers were different on the West Coast. The energy was a little different," recalls arranger Paul Riser. "The Jackson 5 were kind of a mechanical group—very, very regimented. The songs are very lock-step. It wasn't as soulful as we did it in Detroit."

Deke Richards recognized the Jackson 5's vocal versatility immediately, and played to each singer's strengths—with Michael being the central, unifying voice. On "I Want You Back," he establishes himself as a superstar the moment he comes in with "Oh-oh-oh-oh, lemme tell ya now." Jermaine's yearning style is a great foil, especially in the dueling "baby!" bursts at the end. Jermaine was useful to Richards. They sang in the same register, allowing Jermaine to pick up Richards's vocal parts and communicate them easily to the rest of the group. The Jacksons worked long hours on vocals. Due to time and labor, the session for "I Want You Back" cost $10,000, which was $7,000 more than Motown had ever spent on any single. They often were in the studio ten to twelve hours a day, five to seven days a week. "I had to stop it," Richards recalls. "They brought in the labor force and it seemed like it was Nurse Ratched that came in with her crochet needles and sat there in the corner and the kids came in and sang for a certain point and they got their ten-minute breaks and they had to leave at a certain time for their schooling." Actually, it was Rose Fine, a tutor and welfare worker, who formed a lifelong bond with Michael. He would later praise Fine as "more than a tutor" and credit her for providing soothing and tenderness when his father, Joe, was incapable of doing so. The sessions became so strict that Richards, who had a habit of listening to playbacks with his eyes closed, once looked up at 3:02 P.M. and found the room was empty.

Joe stayed away, for the most part. Richards kept a sign near the studio phone that said CALL PAPA JOE, and whenever the boys became too wiggly, he merely pointed to it. He never called. Thanks to Jackie's stern hand as the older brother, the boys' mischief rarely went out of control, even when Marlon and Michael couldn't seem to stop poking and hitting each other, Three Stooges style. "When you've got one [song] you have to do over and over again, the monotony brings out the little one-liners and the joking around and silly stuff," Richards says. "They have no idea how close you are to capturing the last part of it. You've found the one spot that you need so badly, and they've picked [that] particular time to go [into] their Disneyland joke arena. It's like, 'Jesus! No, not now!' But you have to be careful. You couldn't talk to them too rough, because then you're going to turn around and the kids are going to rebel—and they get enough of telling them what to do from their dad."

Motown in Los Angeles, from the company's offices near Sunset and Vine in Hollywood to its various studios, including one across the street from a huge park on Romaine Street, became a sanctuary for Michael Jackson. He could, for the most part, escape his father. And inside Motown, the Jackson 5 didn't have to flee from screaming fans or worry about image. "They just felt comfortable away from the public," recalls Russ Terrana, Motown's chief recording engineer. "They could be kids again." But Motown was not a true sanctuary—even top artists complained of exploitation. The Jackson 5 received a minuscule two cents for every album they sold. That was not far from the same low rate that established Motown stars such as Marvin Gaye and the Supremes received—6 percent of 90 percent of the wholesale cost of an album for every sale, only it was divided five ways among the Jackson brothers. "Just about everyone got ripped off at Motown," said Clarence Paul, the late songwriter and producer. "Tunes were stolen all the time, and often credit wasn't properly arranged." In person Berry Gordy seemed like a benevolent father figure, but as fond as he was of Michael, the singer was just another racehorse in his stable.

*   *   *

Back home in Gary, life was getting worse. Richard Hatcher had become a national phenomenon as the first African-American mayor of a major US city, but his aggressive social programs such as Operation Crime Alert and Operation Safe Gary were no match for the decline of the steel mills and white flight. In 1968, the city's crime rate increased by 11 percent. One day, Tito Jackson walked home from school and a kid held him at gunpoint, demanding lunch money. Another time, two rival gangs approached each other at Twenty-Third Avenue and Jackson Street, *West Side Story* style, rumbling as Katherine frantically locked the doors and windows. Joseph once had to yell, "Everyone down!" as a gang fight escalated to the point of gunfire. Jermaine, Tito, Janet, and Marlon would defend their father's violence as necessary discipline to prevent the boys from falling into dangerous lives. "Joseph did rule with an iron fist, but that wasn't abnormal in the neighborhood," Marlon said. "As I got older, I understood why he did certain things." How this translates into Joe Jackson smacking his son within the confines of a recording studio is unclear.

Joe, Tito, Ronnie, and Johnny arrived in Los Angeles via Dodge Maxivan, which replaced Joseph's old Volkswagen van. Michael, Marlon, Jackie, and Jermaine flew out later at Motown's expense. The brothers shared rooms at the Tropicana, a not-exactly-high-class motel on Santa Monica Boulevard. Joseph would attempt to upgrade their homes during their time in Los Angeles, moving them to the Hollywood Motel ("which was nothing special either," Joe said), then a house at 1601 Queens Road. At first the older boys, Jackie and Tito, attended Fairfax High School, while Michael went to Gardner Street Elementary School. Girls started to come around, such as Susan and Sherry, fifteen-year-old twin sisters who met the boys a week before "I Want You Back" came out in October 1969.

"We're from Gary, Indiana. We're part of the Jackson 5," they told the girls.

"Jackson who?" they said.

"And then: boom," Susan recalls.

The boys sent for the rest of the family. They went to the beach. Michael became obsessed with the Hippodrome carousel on Santa Monica Pier. They drove around looking for a vantage point to see the Hollywood sign. They drove to San Francisco and back. Michael developed a love for Disneyland. Between cannonballs into the Tropicana's outdoor pool, they were regular visitors at Gordy's wooden, ranch-style home in the Hollywood Hills. Sometimes they lived with him. They spent hours in Diana Ross's nearby home—"all white and bright, with sumptuous cushions, billowing curtains and shag-pile carpets that we would do our best to ruin," Jermaine said. Although many accounts, including several from Michael himself, insisted he lived with Ross for lengthy periods during this time, Jermaine declared such claims to be Motown hype: "That's not to say we didn't spend good times there. Diana taught me to swim, coaching me in her pool, holding me afloat as I held on to the sides and kicked my legs while Michael and Marlon played ball in the deep end."

Motown's plan to turn the Jacksons into kids singing like kids for kids worked. Although "I Want You Back" hit the pop charts at just No. 90 during the week it came out, within ten weeks, in January 1970, it built to No. 1. That was enough to inspire a full-fledged Motown marketing campaign. Tours were planned. Costumes were designed. The short hair Michael and his brothers displayed in that grainy audition video turned into Afros so huge that you had to wonder how Jackie managed to get through doorways. As for the Jackson 5's biggest star, Harvard scholar Henry Louis Gates Jr. explained: "People responded viscerally to Michael Jackson's beauty." Their first national appearance was on *The Hollywood Palace*, a variety show that ABC hastily added to its schedule after a show featuring Jerry Lewis had tanked. "Every host

was a giant star—Joan Crawford, Bette Davis, Milton Berle, Sinatra,"
recalls William O. Harbach, one of the *Hollywood Palace* producers.
"The Jacksons were darling, and they were cute looking, and Michael
was nine or ten."

As Jacksonmania began to spark on television, the songwriting
group Gordy called the Corporation was thinking about the follow-up
to "I Want You Back." The song that kept sticking in Deke Richards's
head was "1-2-3," an up-tempo, nursery-rhyming soul hit by Philadelphia singer Len Barry. Richards had the LA studio musicians cut the
music, and his working title was "ABC." Gordy didn't like it. He wanted
to change the title and lyric to "1-2-3." They argued about letters and
numbers for days. Finally, Richards cut another version according to
Gordy's specifications and gave Gordy the impression that he'd erased
the old one completely. Gordy heard it and realized immediately he'd
made a terrible mistake. Richards let Gordy sweat, then told him he'd
actually saved a copy of the original. The Motown boss laughed. Richards didn't feel too bad borrowing from Len Barry. Really, the original
"1-2-3" had been an obvious Motown rip-off in the first place.

Richards and the Corporation were desperate for hits and scav-
enged inspiration from everywhere. Richards knew he wanted to do a
Sly Stone–style "bum-ba-bum-bum" breakdown during "ABC," and he
planned to have Michael shout something lively at that point. He had
no idea what that would be. Finally, the group was laying down vocals
in the studio. It was crunch time. Richards flashed back to his days
of playing LA clubs as a rock-and-soul singer and guitarist, to funny
costumes and slathered hairspray. On the last day of a gig, he'd vowed
to jump off the four-foot stage in dramatic fashion. It was hot, he was
sweating, the hairspray was dripping into his eyes, and he couldn't see.
But he jumped anyway . . . and landed in an aisle, bowling over a young
woman on her way to the restroom. "I wiped my eyes real clear so I
could see her, and I sang especially to her," Richards recalls. "I said, 'Sit
down, girl! I think I love you! No—get up girl! Show me what you can

do!' And we did a little dancing." It was gobbledygook in most con-texts, but somehow it made perfectly charming sense when Michael Jackson made the same declaration on "ABC."

Motown's musicians and producers would record 469 Jackson 5 tracks, although the boys sang on only some of them. They did a ver-sion of Lulu's hit "To Sir with Love" and the Supremes' "I Hear a Symphony," and Michael sang a solo cover of a later Supremes track called "Love It Came to Me This Time." The vaults filled up with live tracks (like a version of Sly Stone's "Thank You [Falettinme Be Mice Elf Agin]") and elaborate instrumentals. At first, Motown was stingy about releasing them—by 1974, only 174, or 37 percent, had appeared in record stores—but many have dribbled out over the years, most recently on 2012's thirty-two-song *Come and Get It: The Rare Pearls*. The group's first album, *Diana Ross Presents the Jackson 5*, released in late 1969, packaged "I Want You Back" with some of the blues and R&B material Bobby Taylor had cut early on.

The *ABC* album, five months later, took the same approach, pack-ing filler around the smash title track as well as the band's third hit, "The Love You Save." Jermaine and Michael trade verses in their com-plementary timbres as wah-wah guitar, strings, and bass lines operate beautifully at rhythmic cross-purposes. Plus, as with "ABC," there's an alphabet lesson: "*S* is for 'Save it!' *T* is for 'Take it slow!' *O* is for 'Oh, no!' *P* is for 'Please, don't go!'"

The Jacksons didn't get it at first (although, obviously, they would come around): "God, Deke, that's some real jive stuff," they told Richards.

Gordy's opinion mattered more. "Who came up with this stuff?" he said. "It's genius."

The Jacksons were beginning to find a home on television—they'd performed a pivotal December 14, 1969, performance on *The Ed Sul-livan Show*, which had transformed the Beatles and Elvis Presley from singers into legends. Suzanne de Passe was responsible for the absurdly clashing, psychedelic, form-fitting costumes the boys draped over their

skinny frames throughout the band's Motown career. She started relatively conservatively. On a 1970 *American Bandstand* appearance, most
of the band wore brightly colored dress shirts with subtle floral patterns
and huge collars and dark vests, while Jackie stood out at the center
with a flowing, powder-blue, fringed cape. As the seventies wore on,
de Passe supplemented the Jacksons' growing Afros with over-the-top
pop art. During a Los Angeles Forum performance in 1972, Marlon's
bell-bottoms were three quarters green, one quarter orange, all Day-
Glo, with purple stripes at the knees, while Michael covered his bright-
orange dress shirt with a black-and-white daisy-print vest. Their look
was a hybrid of Parliament-Funkadelic, Black Power, and Andy Warhol, engineered somehow to appear both cuddly and timeless.

Then there was the matter of reproducing the music onstage. No
Jackson ever played a note on any Motown recording—with one
exception. Jackie happened by the studio during the recording of the
band's fourth single, "I'll Be There," and picked up a tambourine. Ironi-
cally, the Jacksons had to learn to play their own music in order to take
it on the road.

De Passe and Motown's agents secured big-time tour dates, beginning with the Philadelphia Convention Center on May 2, 1970. To
the boys' surprise, every arena they played sold out, sometimes setting
attendance records—18,675 at the Forum, 18,000 at the Hollywood
Bowl, 13,500 at the Cow Palace in San Francisco. Basketball star Elgin
Baylor's production company sponsored several shows, reporting gross
profits of as much as $105,000 per event. After all the No. 1 singles,
offers jumped from $2,000 per show to $20,000—and even $25,000, for
one night at the Forum.

Motown royalty money eventually kicked in. In March 1971, Joseph
and Katherine bought a $250,000 home in Encino, in the San Fer-
nando Valley. They picked 4641 Hayvenhurst for its size—eight thousand square feet—and unusual details like a pattern of two dolphins
etched into the bottom of the swimming pool. The one-story ranch

house was nothing special, although its previous owner, Earle Hagen, the Emmy Award–winning composer of the whistling *Andy Griffith Show* theme and other TV hits, had left behind a built-in recording studio. The house was at the center of two woodsy acres, including gardens full of lemon and orange trees, a flagstone patio overlooking the garden, and a basketball court. The Jacksons slept two to a room. Tito and Jermaine handled the vacuuming and laundry; Michael, Randy, and Janet washed windows; Jackie and La Toya mopped floors and raked leaves. The family, especially Michael, accumulated a menagerie of exotic pets—birds were everywhere, from peacocks on the lawn to a yellow-and-green parrot in the study, as well as tigers, lions, ostriches, and two intimidating German shepherds called Lobo and Heavy (in addition to Johnny Jackson's Doberman, whom the drummer mischievously named Hitler). As Johnny and Ronnie Rancifer grew older, they drifted away from the Jackson household, enjoying life on LA college campuses as well as the Sunset Strip, an emerging hangout for rockers.

It was a comfortable life, except for the snake. "I came home one night from partying in Hollywood and a freaking boa constrictor was in the bed," Rancifer says. "I didn't like that. The only boa constrictor in the bed is supposed to be attached to me." Regular Motown drummer Gene Pello visited the house to give Johnny Jackson lessons on how to play a shuffle beat for Jackson 5 shows, and noticed his music stand moving around in a strange way. Michael walked in and asked, "Anybody see my boa constrictor?" Pello soon noticed the snake on his stand, slithering into and out of a hole. "I got to go home," he meekly told the family. The lessons resumed, though, when Michael retrieved his snake.

The boys wound up at the Walton School in Panorama City, where the "liberal attitude better suited our touring requirements and we were treated as equal with everyone else," according to Jermaine. The Walton School, built for Hollywood stars' children, was liberal, all right. Teachers didn't mind when, after family driver "Uncle Jack" Richardson dropped off the Jackson boys in the morning, Tito and Jermaine took off in a young female teacher's powder-blue Chevy Malibu for Hollywood to hang out at the wax museum and the drugstore instead of attending classes. "It was like we had a groupie for a teacher," recalls Mike Merkow, who befriended classmates Tito and Jermaine at Walton. "We loved it—are you kidding? There was no such thing as homework." Once, playing hooky as usual, the boys spent the day exploring Hollywood and managed to lose Michael. After looking everywhere, they finally worked up enough courage to call Joseph, who blew up and alerted all the Jackson friends' parents. Michael was quickly located at Schwab's Pharmacy on Sunset Boulevard, eating candy and reading comic books, but the damage had been done. Everybody was grounded.

"All Michael did every single day, for years, at school, at lunchtime, was just draw and draw and draw," Merkow says.

Walton had a football rivalry with a high school in Beverly Hills. The team secretly sneaked nonstudent Jackie Jackson into uniform as the second-half quarterback, replacing Merkow. "Even our own principal knew!" Merkow says. Jackie was a ringer—the fastest player on the field by far—and Walton ended up winning the big game. Merkow recalls those days, especially for Michael and Marlon, as happy and fun-loving, but Jermaine was sort of the family's angry enforcer. "If you did something Jermaine didn't like, he'd just kick your ass," Merkow says. "When we needed some muscle, he was the first one."

The Jacksons eased into their rich celebrity life. Katherine Jackson bought furniture and a wardrobe. Joseph bought a new van. Jackie bought an orange Datsun 240Z (which he would total near Ventura Boulevard while fumbling for gum behind the wheel and slamming into a parked car). Tito moved out to live with his new girlfriend, Dee Dee, and bought his first car, a Trans Am. Friends of the Jacksons quickly found that if you were "in," you had access to a benevolent kingdom of riches. At one point, Merkow and his wife went to Tito's home to find he had just bought another car. Merkow wondered aloud what Tito would do with his old, Gucci-trimmed Mercedes. "I don't know," Tito said, "What do you think?" "Well, I'll take it," Merkow suggested. Tito tossed him the keys.

But, Merkow adds, "When you had a falling-out with the Jacksons, you're done."

"As they got bigger and bigger and more famous, this one had to have a big house and this one had to have a bigger house and this one had to have a big car and this one had to have a bigger car and this one had to have a Rolls-Royce and this one had to have a Rolls-Royce. And this one's wife had to have a diamond and this one's wife had to have a bigger diamond," recalls Susan Jackson, who married drummer Johnny.

"And," adds her twin sister, Sherry Danchik, who often socialized at Hayvenhurst, "this one had to have two kids and this one had to have three kids."

At Hayvenhurst, Jackie, Michael, and Marlon convened in one room to work on their dance routines. Jermaine, Tito, Rancifer, and Johnny Jackson rehearsed in another room. The Motown songs, especially hits like "I Want You Back" and "The Love You Save," were built on complicated studio arrangements, but the Jackson 5 managed to strip them down so Tito, Jermaine, and Johnny could provide the rhythm and Ronnie could "make it fat" with his organ sound.

As the singles took off, so did the boys. They appeared on the covers of teen-dream publications such as *Right On!* and the more journalistic *Soul* (subtitle: "America's Most Soulful Newspaper"). Fans learned Jackie liked Tom Jones and regarded Jermaine (not Michael, conspicuously) as the group's best singer; Tito was a fan of Chicago Cub Ernie Banks; Jermaine taught himself to play the bass "mostly by fooling around with it"; and mischievous Marlon bothered Michael on a regular basis because, according to Michael, "sometimes he doesn't know when to stop." Michael, in one interview, spoke revealingly of gathering around the family TV set whenever a "good group" is performing. "See, it's not copying. That's not the point," he said. "You've just got to keep up with the different steps and sounds that everyone is coming up with. It's all part of keeping your own act together. We know a lot of groups watch us. And we're very happy they do."

At the end of every Jackson 5 show, teen girls by the dozens rushed the stage, to the point where the brothers had to regularly drop their instruments and run as fast as they could to waiting cars before even finishing their sets. At the Boston Garden, they had to sneak into a Pinto and hide under blankets to avoid fan detection.

It was even worse in Europe. "When we got to the venue, the kids were climbing up on the fence. The fence was very, very high . . . and they were about to break the fence down!" said Jeannie Long, a member of the Sisters Love, a Jackson 5 opening act. "Then after we got to where we were going to be staying, we went to have something to eat. And the kids—the wall of the restaurant was all glass. And it scared me so badly, because it seemed like they were going to break the wall down." Jermaine lost tufts of hair, Michael lost a shoe, and the Jacksons at one point had to give an impromptu rooftop concert to calm a pursuing crowd. Once, Michael made the mistake of wearing a scarf. "They were pulling on both ends of the scarf—choking him," Jermaine said, clearly scared. "He put his hand under the scarf so it wouldn't tighten up on his neck." It was like the Beatles' *A Hard Day's Night*, but with frightened children instead of bemused adults. Only in Japan, where the fans preferred tossing dozens of roses onto the stage rather than chasing and hair grabbing, did the boys get any peace on the road.

The Jacksons' security man, a former Los Angeles cop named Bill Bray, turned the Commodores, another opening act, into Jacksonmania guinea pigs. He set the older band in open limos along the street near the venues. When the Jackson 5 rushed offstage, the screaming girls encountered the Commodores instead of the Jacksons. This bought crucial time for the actual Jacksons to pile into their own limos and drive away. "We got a few nicks and cuts and scratches," recalls Walter "Clyde" Orange, the Commodores' drummer. "But we loved it."

The shows were rigid. All five Jacksons stood in a line—Tito with his guitar, on the left, followed by Marlon, Jackie, and Michael doing their high-step-and-hand-roll moves in the center, then Jermaine with his bass. With their bobbing haircuts, striking good looks, and psychedelic costumes, they had a collective charisma, which Michael amplified when he separated from the pack and strutted around the front of the stage, doing his slides, twirls, and lead vocals. They played all their Motown hits—"I Want You Back," "ABC," "The Love You Save," and "Mama's Pearl." They overreached with Isaac Hayes's "Walk On By," which they turned into a psychedelic-rock workout featuring Tito, then segued into Stevie Wonder's "Don't Know Why I Love You." Michael's rehearsed patter, with his brothers playing straight men, was usually built around the shtick of "Isn't it funny that I'm the lead singer *and* I'm really young?" "I met a girl in the sandbox," Michael would say before "Who's Lovin' You." "We toasted our love during milk break. We fell out during finger-painting."

At the hotels, there were pillow fights and card games, and more grown-up diversions as well. "It's just like rock 'n' roll—there's groupies everywhere," Rancifer recalls. The older Jacksons, particularly budding sex symbols Jackie and Jermaine, began to indulge, sometimes in front of tiny Michael, who would say the way his brothers treated women on the road turned him off from sexual activity for years. Bored, Michael pounded on doors of his grown-up entourage, including Motown's Weldon McDougal III. "Man," McDougal told Michael, "why don't you go and hang out with Jackie and them guys?" Michael said, "Hey, man, they got somebody in their room." McDougal: "Well, how do you know?" Michael: "Because I was listening at the door for about an hour."

When the brothers grew old enough, women threw hotel-room keys onto the stage, which the boys dodged. During one late-period Motown tour, a beautiful blond woman approached manager Samm Brown with a come-hither look. ("She's not here for *you*," Brown had to keep telling himself as he spoke with her.) She asked to be introduced to one of the Jackson boys. Brown interrupted the brother in question—he won't name names—while he was dressing in his room. "Well, what does she look like?" this Jackson asked. "Stunning," responded Brown. The brother instructed Brown to crack open the door so he could check her out, through a mirror on a side wall. Finally he motioned with his hands: "Come in!" Years later, Brown realized the woman had been a *Playboy* Playmate.

"Suffice it to say, it wasn't Michael," Brown recalls. "She was not there to see Michael."

Joe Jackson's presence as tour manager didn't make anybody feel more comfortable. The Commodores, including front man Lionel Richie, used Traffic's rock hit "Feelin' Alright" as an onstage jam, until Joe, one day, inexplicably forbade the opening act from playing it. The Jackson 5 put the song in their own set the same night. Another time, at the Cow Palace in San Francisco, tour roadies "forgot" to bring the Commodores' equipment, including their stage clothes, from the previous show in another city. Joe refused help, so the band improvised, borrowing equipment from nearby friends, forgoing boots and even pants and replacing "Feelin' Alright" with Buddy Miles's hot new blues anthem "Them Changes." The impromptu fashion statement, as Orange recalls, led to rave newspaper reviews the next day. "Nobody really liked Joe Jackson," Orange says.

"Stand still," the studio men kept telling eleven-year-old Michael Jackson.

Michael Jackson couldn't stand still.

When he sang, he danced. When he danced, he jerked his head around. When his head moved forward, he sang too close to the microphone. When his head moved backward, he sang too far from the microphone. He was knocking the vocal sound off track.

Suzee Ikeda walked into the sound booth and gently pushed

Michael's head and neck closer to the mike during the soft part, and pulled it away during the loud part. "It started out like that," she says, "and it became a whole other thing."

Ikeda, twenty-two, had arrived at Motown's Los Angeles offices three years earlier, in 1967. As a girl, she had been an aspiring actress, but she became frustrated with the cattle-call auditions and geisha-girl roles the producers lined up for her. Instead, through her junior high school orchestra teacher, she wound up sitting in on professional recording sessions with Frank Sinatra, Petula Clark, and others, sometimes singing a bit herself. She worked on a Supremes Christmas album and, over time, she impressed influential in-house songwriter Brian Holland, who signed her to a solo Motown contract.

Suzee's talent turned out to be not in her singing ability but in her personality. In her shiny, Diana Ross–like voice, she would record a few singles for Motown, including the desperate "I Can't Give Back the Love I Feel for You." But when she wasn't performing, she was working as a creative assistant at Motown's studios in LA, watching producers, asking questions, learning the business. Eventually, Berry Gordy noticed her hanging around. "Look, I've got enough singers," he said. "But I don't have anybody like you, who knows how to do all this stuff." Ikeda resisted at first—"If I do this, good-bye, singing career," she told herself—but eventually she accepted Gordy's full-time job offer.

Ikeda turned out to be a tender figure for Michael Jackson. She helped him in subtle ways. Musically, she discovered to her surprise, he didn't need much. Most singers had to take a tape of new songs home to "live with it" for a few days, then return with the proper phrasing. Not Michael. Suzee would teach him a song in the studio, give him the tape, and the next day he was ready to go. "He had the fastest ear of anyone I'd ever known," she recalls. "He'd sing a song one time and he knew it."

Suzee and Michael developed a series of hand signals and written notes. Standing next to him in the studio, she'd crook her finger a certain way, prompting him to begin a new vocal run. She'd type out lyrics in advance, triple-spaced. It was not her idea for Michael to stand on a milk crate, covered with a strip of carpet, so he could reach the microphone and stand evenly with Jackie and Jermaine, but she wound up overseeing this crucial piece of equipment. (The crate is still in her house.) She provided paper and Sharpie markers so Michael could doodle cartoons—reverential images of Berry Gordy Jr., Diana Ross, and Ikeda herself, although his rendition of her had such comically exaggerated Asian features that she had to say to Michael, "*Excuse* me?"

Suzee teased him on whether he could understand the grown-up emotions in his love songs—like "Never Can Say Goodbye," with its references to anguish and doubt. Michael insisted he could. When Suzee quizzed him about what a word meant, he would say, "I'll tell you tomorrow." Invariably, most likely after consulting a family dictionary, he'd come back the next day with the correct answer.

Suzee taught Michael how to unplug his microphone so he could speak freely in the studio without the entire production staff hearing him from behind the glass. Through notes and whispers, he appealed to Suzee. "I don't want to do it this way," he wrote. "I don't think that's right." Under her breath, she responded, "Do whatever you want." She understood that Michael Jackson, at age eleven, knew instinctively how to sing a song better than veteran Motown producer Hal Davis did.

Davis could be infectiously enthusiastic. He had a way of saying, "That's a hit!" that suggested whatever artist or songwriter in his presence was the most important person in the world. He could also be reclusive, inscrutable, vengeful. Suzee kept hundreds of Michael's cartoons and doodles in a file cabinet in Davis's office. One day, Berry Gordy informed Ikeda that she would be working in a new song-production group. When it started to look as though Ikeda would have increased access to the all-powerful Gordy, Davis developed an attitude. He dumped the contents of Suzee's cabinet, Michael Jackson doodles and all, into the trash.

With Davis essentially running Motown in Los Angeles, Gordy began to shift his attention away from music. He put his time, money, and creative energy into making Diana Ross a movie star, giving her the title role in his new Billie Holiday biopic. "Berry wasn't even listening to the records then, let's be serious," recalled Barney Ales, Gordy's top lieutenant. "He was going in a new direction. He was all *Lady Sings the Blues* by then."

Still, when it came to Gordy's two biggest acts, Ross and the Jackson 5, he continued his controlling ways. Arthur Rankin, cartoon producer at ABC, met with Gordy at his Hollywood Hills home to go over designs and choreography for a new cartoon series they were discussing on Michael and his brothers. Rankin had ideas of his own. He wanted prominent illustrator Jack Davis to do the artwork. "Bring him over here," Gordy said. "We've got all the stuff we need right here." When Rankin showed up, he was surprised to find Gordy with a room full of technicians standing by to roll tape. Gordy took an interest in design, appearance, and how the cartoon likenesses would move and sing. He was "very much in control of his kingdom," Rankin recalls.

The Jackson 5 were coming off three straight No. 1 hits—"I Want You Back," "ABC," and "The Love You Save"—and Berry wanted a fourth. Originally, the Corporation had agreed, with Gordy's blessing, to divide its lucrative songwriting royalties in such a way that Deke Richards received 50 percent, Mizell and Perren took 20 percent each, and Gordy grabbed 10 for his (minimal) input. "After 'I Want You Back,' he got so excited, and got more involved than he thought he would be," Richards says, adding that Gordy rejiggered the percentages so they were more favorable to himself. The Corporation kept pushing for a

Jackson 5 hit, something upbeat that "bounced and kicked," as Richards says, but Hal Davis was scavenging for hits, too. He found one that had been lying on his desk for months, a ballad by bassist and arranger Bob West. Excited, and not worried that it was late at night, Davis called an experienced songwriter he knew, Willie Hutch, and showed up at his house at 3:45 A.M. Hutch finished the song in ninety minutes. Davis was at Gordy's house by eight. The song, a ballad about peace and love (this was the seventies), was built around the killer line "you and I must make a pact / we will bring salvation back." Gordy loved it, especially the way the word *salvation* fit the song. He instructed Hutch to convert it to a boy-girl love song. The Sound Factory musicians cut the track. The Jacksons launched hit number four: "I'll Be There."

Richards's grand plan for the Jackson 5 at Motown had involved spinning each member of the group into a solo star, with hits created by the Corporation. First would come Michael, then Jermaine, then Jackie, then a Duane Eddy–style instrumental rockabilly album by Tito, then something from Marlon. "I thought [Marlon] was a little bit 'under,'" Richards says. "I didn't know what I was going to do with him, but I thought, 'Jeez, if I could get these other two boys going, there would be enough fans clamoring for Marlon.'" But by the time Jackson solo albums started to come out, beginning with Michael's *Got to Be There* and *Ben*, both in 1972, the Corporation was falling apart. Their most recent Jackson 5 hits, including "Mama's Pearl" and "Sugar Daddy," had failed to hit No. 1, thanks in part to competition from a rival boy band, the Osmonds. The subsequent Jermaine and Jackie solo albums didn't sell well.

Davis, who had been more recently successful than the Corporation with Jackson 5 hits, including the No. 2 "Never Can Say Goodbye," picked Jerry Marcellino and Mel Larson as the group's new songwriters. Marcellino had found a hit novelty tune from the fifties, "Rockin' Robin," and given it to Michael for his first solo album. At first, Gordy, whose Jobete Music didn't own publishing rights, buried the song on the B-side. Radio DJs didn't go along with his plan. "Berry Gordy was actually kind of pissed off because the DJs wanted to play that. They forced out a big hit," Larson recalls. "But he worked with [the other publishing company] and finally got them to agree with some royalty to split."

The Jackson brothers—not counting Michael—began to focus on more personal endeavors. Eldest sister Rebbie had wed in 1968, but Tito was the first of the Jackson band to get married, in 1972, to his girlfriend Dee Dee. (He told reporters she "treats me nice and shows me the same respect I gave her.") A year later, Jermaine married Hazel Gordy, Berry's daughter, in a ceremony that *Soul* estimated to have cost $80,000 to $200,000—the bride wore a white satin dress with a twelve-foot mink-lined train and 7,500 pearls hand-sewn into the fabric; the seven thousand flowers included camellias, white carnations, and chrysanthemums; the menu was papaya with San Francisco bay shrimp topped with Lorenzo dressing; and the happy couple released 175 white doves. Joe Jackson was never a big supporter of his kids' marriages. He felt Tito's betrothed status would deter female fans. And Jermaine's marriage was part of some kind of testosterone-competition triangle between Joe and Berry. Plus, Joe was distancing himself emotionally from his family, cheating on Katherine to the point that one of his girlfriends had a child. Katherine filed for divorce in March 1973. For this, some of her children, including Michael, would forever turn against Joseph. Katherine was more malleable, however, and rescinded the divorce two months later.

The Jacksons, especially Jermaine, Marlon, and Michael, grew up in public. They became skinnier, more lithe, and Michael and Jermaine's voices were lighter and more precious as they changed. (It's possible to identify the point on record when Michael Jackson makes the transition from bright-sounding child prodigy, effortlessly belting out high vocals, to the more nuanced balladeer's voice he would use on "She's Out of My Life" and "Human Nature." It occurred on the band's 1973 album *Skywriter*, via hippie-dippie singles such as "Hallelujah Day" and "Corner of the Sky.") Michael was famous among friends and family for rarely eating, other than the most healthy vegan dishes, and he was distressed when acne broke out on his face when he was fifteen or sixteen. Blotchy photos of him began to appear in teen-beat magazine features.

When Jermaine and Michael brought their urgent acne worries to Motown's Nancy Leiviska, she set them up with an LA dermatologist. "They had really greasy skin, especially Jermaine," recalls Leiviska, head of the company's video operations at the time. "They both had to go to major sessions."

The Jacksons were no longer the cuddly little kids who had been on *Ed Sullivan*. *Skywriter* and its follow-up, *Get It Together*, were full of flat performances and uninspired writing and production—a "mishmash of material," Deke Richards said. It lacked the snap of "I Want You Back" or even "Rockin' Robin."

"It was a searching period," songwriter Jerry Marcellino says, "when you have a lot of different producers coming up with tracks and trying to come up with a newer direction as they got older."

What rescued the Jackson 5's career was an invisible man with stiff arms, uncontrollable legs, and a following of thousands of young dancers in urban nightclubs.

Drummer James Gadson showed up at the studio, sat behind the drums, and waited for the "Dancing Machine" intro to begin. Then, almost uncontrollably, as if he had some kind of rhythmic spasm, he spewed out an impromptu, off-beat *ba-bump-ba-bump*. Everybody stopped.

Oh, no, I'm fired, Gadson thought.

Producer Hal Davis and arranger Arthur Wright conferred for five minutes, then turned back to him. "We want to know something," they finally said, as Gadson sweated behind his drums. "Can you do that again?"

"Dancing Machine" would not only kick off Gadson's accomplished career as a session musician, it would rejuvenate the Jackson 5 and give Michael Jackson his first "what-the-hell-was-that?" signature dance move—the Robot. (Davis and Wright had pointedly engineered "Dancing Machine" so listeners could dance to it, employing a variety of moves, particularly the Robot, in clubs. The "automatic, systematic" lyric was a clue.) Get It Together's title track and first single stalled out at No. 28 on the pop charts in August 1973, but dancers and radio DJs picked up on "Dancing Machine," which Motown then rushed out as a single. The label built an entire new album around it, Dancing Machine, a year later. The single hit No. 2 and became one of the Jackson 5's most enduring songs.

Technically speaking, "Dancing Machine" was not a disco hit, as critic Vince Aletti would define the genre in Rolling Stone: "The music nurtured in the new discotheques is Afro-Latin in sound or instrumentation, heavy on the drums, with minimal lyrics, sometimes in a foreign language, and a repetitive, chant-like chorus." Gadson adds: "What was disco? One hundred twenty beats per minute. That was a little faster than 'Dancing Machine.'" But the hit inspired countless disco singles, and the Jacksons would influence disco culture throughout the seventies—the Bee Gees' "Stayin' Alive" is not so far removed from "Dancing Machine"—while letting it wash over them. Disco would eventually be blamed for destroying the music business, turning the world into polyester, threatening rock 'n' roll, and killing off the sixties. Eventually, MJ would be called upon to help destroy disco—then pick up its pieces for his own purposes—but for now he was content to wear the tightest, brightest, loudest, sparkliest, most open-collared jumpsuits in the entire history of TV. How he was embarrassed by the size of his nose and the blotchiness of his acne but not these incomprehensible, disco-era fashion monstrosities remains one of the greatest mysteries of Michael Jackson's mysterious life.

Joe Jackson soured on Motown after Gordy allowed the Jermaine and Jackie solo albums to flop. He began to learn the terms of his family's Motown contract were more unfavorable than he'd ever realized. In court documents, Joe's own lawyers would acknowledge he had only an eleventh-grade education and signed his sons' July 1968 contracts "without reading them or having their meaning explained to them." By industry standards, Motown's royalty rates were obviously low, and the company had an ironclad rule against stars writing or producing their own material, Stevie Wonder and Marvin Gaye notwithstanding. Writing and producing was where the real money was, Motown's executives well knew. Motown even owned the name "Jackson 5," and wasn't about to give it up.

"Dancing Machine" temporarily reinvigorated the Jacksons' career, but many in the record business believed they were done. The kids had, tragically, grown up.

Joe didn't buy it. He convened his sons. It was time to leave Motown, he said to everybody but Jermaine, who was married to Hazel, daughter of Berry. Jermaine came home one day from fishing with R&B singer Barry White. His father called. "Come over without Hazel," he said. Jermaine dutifully went to Joe's room at Hayvenhurst and found new contracts on the bed. Everybody else had signed, including Michael.

"Sign it," Joe told his son.

"No," Jermaine said.

Joe's voice rose. He said something about his blood, not Berry Gordy's, flowing through Jermaine's veins. Katherine heard the commotion and demanded to know what was wrong. Jermaine's brothers were angry, too. For six months, the family was gloomy and tense. "I was open to talk to them," Jermaine said. "But I have my pride. They didn't want to talk to me. Why should I keep calling them if they didn't want to talk to me?"

The new record contract had come from CBS, at the time one of the world's biggest labels, home of Barbra Streisand, Simon and Garfunkel, Neil Diamond, Bob Dylan, and distribution deals with important indie soul labels Stax and Philadelphia International. Joe Jackson had been looking for $1 million. At first, the label's top executives said no, but a fast-talking, schmoozing, veteran record-promotions man from Long Island, New York, talked them into it.

CHAPTER 3

On a June evening, Ron Alexenburg left work at the CBS building in midtown Manhattan and walked to his car at the garage next door. Alexenburg was one of those larger-than-life record men, a ten-year veteran of Epic Records. He resembled a mutton-chopped, crazy-haired, wider-faced Wolfman Jack and, like many promo guys, was well-known for his slap-on-the-back handshake. Alexenburg drove past the Warwick Hotel a few blocks away from the garage and noticed kids swarming everywhere. CBS put up guests at the Warwick all the time. Alexenburg spotted a familiar doorman and pulled over.

"What's going on here?" he asked.

"Oh, the Jackson 5 are here," the man told him.

In addition to being a record man, Alexenburg was an R&B man. Growing up in Chicago, he'd drive to see Stevie Wonder, the Four Tops, and the Temptations on the same bill for four dollars, then return home in the morning to get ready for high school. He had even caught the Jackson 5 in their early days on the South Side. At Epic, he had been patiently turning the label around—sales had increased 62 percent in four years—thanks in part to soul-music superstars from Sly and the Family Stone to Harold Melvin and the Blue Notes. He remembered seeing the Jacksons' name on the Radio City Music Hall marquee earlier that year. He knew the Jackson 5 were no longer the smash band it had been in the days of "I Want You Back" and "The Love You Save."

Alexenburg stowed his car, walked into the hotel, picked up a house phone, and asked to be connected to Michael Jackson's room. Miraculously—or maybe just because it was 1975—Michael picked up the phone. "I'm Ron Alexenburg, I'd like to meet you. And just talk, actually."

The Jacksons were off that night, resting up for a show the next day at the Nanuet Star Theatre in Nanuet, New York. Michael, Joseph, and the Jacksons' longtime attorney, Richard Arons, took the elevator to the lobby and shook hands with Alexenburg. The Epic executive knew the group was unhappy with its contract at Motown. Everybody in the industry did. Ron knew Joe was trying to shop his sons to a label deal for more money and more control over their production and songwriting. But he avoided talking business. After Michael left, Joe and his attorney mentioned the smart job Epic had done in working with the R&B stars at Philadelphia International Records.

Ron ventured a key question about Motown: "How long do you have on your agreement?" He didn't get a direct answer, but he secured an invitation to see the group in New Jersey.

The show Alexenburg caught the next night at the Nanuet was not the kiddie Jackson 5 of the early 1970s. MJ was seventeen. Movie producer Rob Cohen would say of him during this period: "He was in a state of such innocence and purity, it was almost hard to fathom."

The group had spent the previous two years expanding its act from teen pop and bubblegum soul to a more grown-up, supper-club style. It's a transition just about every child pop star has tried to navigate— Stevie Wonder and Justin Timberlake succeeded, David Cassidy and Leif Garrett not so much. In retrospect, it's easy to recognize Michael Jackson's talent as so transcendent that he was never at risk of falling into this trap. But at the time, Joe Jackson was worried. He had booked the Jackson 5 at the MGM Grand in Las Vegas, beginning in April 1974, and was desperately rebuilding the band into a family variety act.

It was still the Jackson 5, but no longer were they singing and dancing to roaring crowds of obsessed teenage girls. "It was a Vegas crowd—the man, the wife, the martini set," remembers Ronnie Rancifer, who was still playing keyboards and fleshing out the group's sound onstage. Janet, eight, and Randy, thirteen, had joined the group as a tiny satirical duo, mimicking supper-club favorites Sonny and Cher and Jeanette MacDonald and Nelson Eddy. The Jacksons compacted their early Motown hits into a medley of "I Want You Back," "ABC," and "The Love You Save" (as they'd done frequently on tour) and added what Jackie called "a little of everything," including Vegas-friendly permutations of the Mills Brothers, the Andrews Sisters, "Danny Boy," and the Supremes. No recordings exist of these performances, but judging from the group's TV variety show a couple of years later, their between-song shtick was not quite as evolved as their singing and dancing. "Hi!" Tito would say, faux-annoying his brothers, "I'm Gladys Knight and these are my Pips!" Tiny Janet, wearing elaborate pink outfits of feathers and fur, slayed the crowd every time by imitating Mae West and demanding, "Why don't you come up and see me some time?" Rebbie, who always had a decent singing voice despite her lack of show-business ambition, performed "Fever" with Michael and Marlon as her background dancers. The whole family, particularly La Toya, took up tap dancing—something Michael mastered immediately.

Friends stopped by frequently—old ones like Sammy Davis Jr. and new ones such as comedians Slappy White and Redd Foxx. At first, the Jacksons signed up for two weeks of shows, but they went over so well they added more, then returned in November.

In addition to Vegas, the other event that heralded the Jackson 5's transition from boy band to grown-up pop act was Michael's appropriation of the Robot, the perfect dance step for his long adolescent body. Motown may have influenced him in the way it created "Dancing Machine," but Michael picked up the dance, in part, from *Soul Train*, the syndicated variety show in which regulars such as Damita Jo Freeman and Pat Davis evolved into stars as they danced with James Brown, Joe Tex, and many others. Freeman's extraordinary performances in hot pants and an Afro, kicking her leg to a fully horizontal position and holding it there as she hopped to the beat on the other leg, were mesmerizing not only to viewers but to the guests, including Brown, who once kept an eye on her throughout his set. The Jacksons first appeared on *Soul Train* in October 1972. "The brothers were older, and they liked girls," Freeman says. "But Michael wasn't looking at you as a *girl*. He was looking at the *moves*."

The Robot was just as its title implies—dancers mechanically bending their elbows and knees in perfect right angles as they glide across the floor, as if on invisible treadmills, moving backward and forward, sometimes seemingly both at once. The man who often gets credit for developing this move was "Robot" Charles Washington, an early *Train* dancer who started in a frozen position, then theatrically broke out of an implied block of ice. But when pinpointing the beginning of things, whether it's the Robot or the first rock 'n' roll or disco song, there is always more to the story. In 1968, mime expert Robert Shields did a variation of the Robot in front of the Hollywood Wax Museum in LA. Shields didn't learn it from Washington or *Soul Train*. He studied it, reaching back to a 1920s craze in which dancers suspended their bodies like mannequins. The move became Shields's signature and landed him a scholarship to study with the great mime Marcel Marceau in Paris. By the early 1970s, Shields teamed with Lorene Yarnell, and Shields and Yarnell adapted the movement in their Clinkers routine. Eventually the duo became big enough to perform on TV variety shows, where they would occasionally encounter the Jackson 5 in person. Michael latched on to Shields the way he did with other famous mentors, including James Brown, Joe Simon, Jackie Wilson and the *Soul Train* dancers. "I trained him on the Robot," says Shields, whom Michael befriended in part due to the famous mime's large toy collection at his LA home. "Michael first saw the Robot from me, period. He took it and made it his own."

The truth is Michael absorbed the Robot from several sources at once. After the Jacksons' first *Soul Train* appearance, regulars Patricia Davis and Gary Keys taught the brothers important neck twists as well as acrobatic moves known as locking steps. The Jacksons summoned some of the show's top dancers to their Hayvenhurst home for further lessons, as well as casual video recording sessions, so Michael could study the moves. "It was a playtime for Michael," Freeman recalls. "He always had cameras in his den."

For the Jackson 5's second *Soul Train* appearance, in October 1973, the group performs "Dancing Machine." During the horn break at the center of the song, fifteen-year-old Michael glides through the mechanical arm movements and invisible walking steps with grace and poise, finishing with a broad, proud smile. He's easily as good as the *Soul Train* crew, and afterward dancer Freddie Maxie found Michael and teased him. "Michael, you don't need me to teach you to do the Robot," she said. Michael would tinker with the Robot for years, adding moves he developed from *Soul Train*–style locker movements and augmenting them with Bob Fosse poses and hand gestures, James Brown one-legged hops, Jackie Wilson twirls, variations on Shields and Yarnell rope-pulling, and hip-hop break-dancing. The Robot became his bridge to more exciting dance ideas.

This version of Michael, and the Jackson 5, was roughly what Epic Records' Ron Alexenburg took in that June night in 1975. Alexenburg and his boss Walter Yetnikoff arranged to catch another show the following weekend at the Westbury Music Fair in Long Island. Yetnikoff, who had taken over as CBS's president that year, saw music's past, not its future. "Less than spectacular," he called it. "Their baby sister, Janet, who did a Mae West impression, looked silly. Their dance steps looked tired." He called Michael a "bright spot," but questioned whether signing the seventeen-year-old whose solo showcase was "Ben," a song about a dead rat, could transcend the family group.

In the end, it was Alexenburg's right-hand man, Epic promotions executive Steve Popovich, who talked Yetnikoff into the signing. Yes, Michael had sung a hit about a dead rat. But, he said: " 'Ben' was a smash. We'll make money on this group, believe me."

The Jacksons were demanding a high price, but in addition to their recent lack of hits, they had a couple of blemishes that dented their leverage. Motown owned the name "Jackson 5" as well as the Jacksons' contract through March 1976, which meant CBS couldn't release a Jackson album until then. And there was the matter of the absent Jermaine, who had remained behind with his father-in-law Gordy. Alexenburg didn't care about any of that. He steered the band into a deal including a $750,000 advance, $500,000 for a "recording fund" from which the band could make its albums, a guarantee of $350,000 per album, and a high royalty rate (compared to other recording stars) of 27 percent: 94.5 cents per album in the United States and 84 cents abroad. Sam Lederman, an executive in A&R and administration for CBS at the time, is dubious of some of those widely reported deal points: "One thing I'll tell you for sure: It was not a $500,000 recording fund." But the terms were generous, if not egregiously so for a superstar group at the time. Yetnikoff refused to yield on Joe Jackson's request to let the boys fully write and produce their own material, but verbally, he allowed them three songs per album.

After signing the deal, CBS execs met with the Jacksons at Hayvenhurst. The idea was to kick around concepts for future albums. They met for a few hours, but nothing came out of it except a promise that CBS would try a few producers and see what happened. Michael sat silently on a stool the whole time. Lederman finally turned to him: "Michael, you haven't said anything. What is it you want to do?"

"I want to write and produce my own records," he responded.

The Jacksons may not have been willing to make immediate creative decisions, but Alexenburg had to. "Ron basically had a lot on the line," Lederman says. "Financially or otherwise, Ron put his reputation at stake." Nobody wanted the Jacksons to be known as "Alexenburg's folly." Alexenburg called for reinforcements.

Kenny Gamble and Leon Huff signed the best talent in Philadelphia throughout the 1970s. They created a system. Huff, a flashy dresser, gruffly competitive, played piano and wrote the music. Gamble, who was more outgoing—a communicator—wrote the lyrics. And they had hits—pop-and-soul mini-masterpieces such as the Survivors' "Expressway to Your Heart," Archie Bell and the Drells' "I Can't Stop Dancing," Harold Melvin and the Blue Notes' "If You Don't Know Me By Now."

Where Motown's hits were known for a persistent, jazzed-up siren call, Philly soul was more laid-back and lush, with string arrangements baked into the foundation, and rhythms so warm it seemed like the drummer and bassist were on the next bar stool. Motown had a hit with the Temptations' "My Girl." Philly International tacked on a few years to its audience, putting out the O'Jays' "Use Ta Be My Girl." These songs weren't bubblegum soul; they were sophisticated. "Gamble and Huff were really adult oriented, especially during those times," says label drummer Charles Collins.

Before the Jacksons left Motown, Gamble and Huff had tried to sign them. They had discussions with Joe. Recalled Gamble: "CBS offered them movies. They offered them a TV show, cartoons, and everything. And, of course, Gamble and Huff, we couldn't offer them all those things, so they decided to go with CBS." But the duo wound up working with the Jacksons anyhow. CBS' Alexenburg agreed to pay them 8 to 10 percent of the Jacksons' wholesale record sales.

The Jacksons, who had been touring nonstop since the late sixties, moved to the Hyatt Cherry Hill, in nearby New Jersey, to record their first album at Gamble and Huff's Philadelphia studio. The Philly International stars prized their anonymity back then, and Teddy Pendergrass and Lou Rawls often hung around the downtown studio without much external fuss between sessions. The Jacksons were something different. "It was *the Jacksons*," drummer Collins says. "There were some girls outside, for sure."

The group arrived with an entourage of ten people—the boys, Joe, occasionally Katherine, tutor Rose Fine, security man Bill Bray, and "associated people," as Joe Tarsia, longtime engineer for Philly International's Sigma Sound Studios, recalls. With the Jacksons officially signed to the label, Gamble and Huff immersed them in the system, preparing twenty songs for the group to pare them down to a twelve-song album.

Gamble called Tito a "great guitar player," soothing words after Motown had never let him play a note. Tito had told reporters of his desire to be a producer, and Gamble and Huff were ready to be mentors. But while experienced studio hands gave Tito advice and suggestions, it was Michael who stayed after hours, hanging around the boards, asking questions. "Lemme try . . ." Michael often asked engineers like Tarsia. It was becoming obvious to Tarsia that Michael was a driven, attentive perfectionist. "Just watching Huff play the piano while Gamble sang taught me more about the anatomy of a song than anything else," Michael said. "Kenny Gamble is a master melody man. He made me pay closer attention to the melody. . . . I'd sit there like a hawk, observing every decision, listening to every note."

When Tarsia recognized the boys were lonely, he invited them to his home, where his wife cooked a big family dinner. "They were like lost children," Tarsia says. One time, the Jacksons realized they'd inadvertently crashed Tarsia's daughter's sixteenth birthday party, so they sent their driver to buy a cake. Tarsia also accompanied the group to an all-day tour of Muhammad Ali's training camp, where the engineer snapped photos of Michael fake-punching the Champ. (This would not be the last Jackson encounter with Ali; Jermaine Jackson once walked into his family's kitchen in Hayvenhurst to find Ali with Michael and his mother. Michael spent hours at Ali's house, too, and Jermaine credits the legendary fighter, known for his lighter-than-air moves, for teaching Michael "what it took to be a showman.")

The group's first CBS album, 1976's *The Jacksons*, is so pristinely produced that the music appears to shine. Gamble and Huff provided funky touches like the electric guitars slipping between the choruses in "Think Happy," the slippery synth bass that opens "Keep On Dancing" and the vibe of the laid-back "Good Times." Michael sporadically breaks out the whoops and "oh yeahs" that would become his signature. But the album isn't really about anything other than dancing and having a real good time. "Enjoy Yourself" is the mission statement.

Throughout the recording, Michael's preternatural talent was obvious to everybody, and the Jacksons were experienced professionals in the studio. But not everything was easy for the Philly International hands. "[Michael] had that breathy voice," recalls Tarsia, the engineer. "I recorded a couple albums with Lou Rawls—when he got on the mike, he devoured it with his heavy tone. And Michael was like recording a cloud. You could put your fingers through it."

The follow-up album, *Goin' Places*, a year later, shows a glimpse of a more self-assured MJ. From the first track, "Music's Takin' Over," he's grunting like James Brown, ad-libbing melodies at the ends of verses, hollering and scat-singing, trying on new musical clothes and personalities. Part of his inspiration, while recording the album in Philly, may have been an encounter with "Lonely Teardrops" soul man Jackie Wilson, who lay dying at Hahnemann University Hospital down the street. The entire family, including Joe and Bill Bray, made a pilgrimage there, although it's unclear whether Michael and Jackie spoke to each other, as Wilson was in and out of comas at the time.

Goin' Places, though, had even less to say than *The Jacksons* had—lyrically and musically. Two years into the Jacksons experiment, Alexenburg's folly began to spread like a fungus throughout CBS Records.

"My staff was less than enthusiastic about the Jacksons' commercial prospects," Yetnikoff, his boss, sniffed.

It's hard to say why Gamble and Huff couldn't connect with a group that had had so much success at a like-minded indie label, Motown, and a singer whose superstar potential was obvious to everybody. Maybe it was that Philly International had picked the wrong single: Pete Humphreys and other studio engineers were enamored of the title track, a breezy song about the feeling you get when riding in a jet, and lobbied Gamble to release it first. He did. "It didn't sell real well," Humphreys says. "And it was thrown in our faces. Who knows why? Maybe it didn't get the right connections, the right timing." Or maybe Gamble and Huff didn't feel they owned the project, as they had with Philly bands they'd discovered and created. "I didn't see Gamble and Huff as emotionally involved in that project as they have been in others," says a source close to the label.

One of the first things Joe Jackson did after signing the boys to CBS was take advantage of the synergy with CBS-TV and work out a deal for a variety show. That was too much Vegas supper club for Ronnie Rancifer, keyboardist and crucial tie between the Jacksons and their home region of northwest Indiana. He decided to split: "I just told Joseph, 'Man, I'm tired, I gotta go.' I was pretty much just tired of *him*." Johnny Jackson, whose name had appeared on the Jackson 5 drum kit in the early days, followed soon afterward.

Michael made it explicitly clear he wanted no part of the TV show. "I hated every minute," he said. He told his father it was a big mistake. "On the show our sets were sloppy, the lighting was often poor and our choreography was *rushed*," he said. Watching episodes of the yearlong half-hour hit show from 1976 and 1977, it's hard to comprehend that Michael felt so negatively about the experience. His evident joy seems impossible to fake in his dancing. In a segment with a deliberately clumsy Dom DeLuise, Michael and his brothers reprise a popping-and-locking bit from *Soul Train*, complete with obnoxiously loud patterned outfits, flat caps, and striped knickers. Michael pulls off one extraordinary sequence in which he does the Robot, spins, mimes rope pulling, kicks his leg Damita Jo Freeman style, and splays out his knees. Marlon follows with the splits, and his moves are smooth, but, as ever, he's no match for his brother. One of the most humorous recurring themes of the show is during a segment called "On the Wall," when guests attempt to dance with an inviting MJ. They seem to realize on the spot, in front of cameras, that it's harder than it looks. Young, beautiful Lynda "Wonder Woman" Carter tries, but comes off square in the process. Comic Redd Foxx takes the more effective approach—he gamely half steps with MJ for a second, then wordlessly concludes, "Ah, to hell with it," as he gives up and watches Michael instead.

"Aw, he loved it. He had his own quick spins and his own special moves," says Bill Davis, the show's director and producer, retired and in his eighties. "But there's something about his body style, too—he was so slender, and he seemed to do it effortlessly. That went back to his constant study of Fred Astaire. He just endlessly practiced."

In his whispery voice, Michael delivered commands to Davis on the set. For one dance sequence, he demanded a Western-style saloon so he could dress as a cowboy (not like John Wayne, exactly—he wore a blue-and-white fringed shirt, yellow chaps, and a white scarf, with a Stetson atop his Afro). Davis's designers built a stylized TV background, but Michael hated it. "That isn't a Western saloon!" he blubbered. Davis tried to calm him down: "What's a Western saloon to you?" Michael declared, "Like the one in *Gunsmoke!*"—with solid walls and a solid bar to dance on. In a funk, the singer retreated to his dressing room. Davis had to coax him out.

The moves Michael picked up and worked out during the *Jacksons* series were pivotal to his dance development. But Michael declaimed the show to the end. "Michael hasn't wanted that series to surface in any way," Davis says. "Because it was the old Michael. It was his old face—before he had any adjustments made. He didn't want that comparison. Any retrospectives of the Jacksons definitely avoid that particular series."

But *The Jacksons* had a profound impact. "Huge influence," rapper-turned-actress Queen Latifah would tell late-night star David Letterman, who had himself appeared on the Jacksons' show as a satirical sportscaster. "This is where you realize, like, 'Wow, you can make it onto television. . . . Black people, young like me, little girls, boys: we can do this.'"

The Wiz came along at a perfect time for Berry Gordy and Motown Records. To finish *Lady Sings the Blues*, Gordy had to sink in $2 million of his own money because Paramount's top executive, Frank Yablans, had told him the maximum a studio could spend on a black film at the time was $500,000. "This is not a *black film*," Gordy corrected him. "This is a *film* with *black stars*." There were clashes on the set, as star Diana Ross made her transition from music diva to Hollywood diva, demanding an upgrade of her period-piece wardrobe. But the 1972 drama was a success in the end, drawing five Oscar nominations, although Ross lost Best Actress to Liza Minnelli of *Cabaret*.

Motown's follow-up, *Mahogany*, was more problematic—shooting began with Gordy firing British director Tony Richardson and ended with Ross slapping Gordy in the face and walking off the set. The film, a hastily edited, soap-opera mess, received savage reviews and flopped.

In 1977, Motown bought the rights to *The Wiz*, a script based on a Broadway hit with African-American stars putting their own spin on *The Wizard of Oz*. Gordy and producer Rob Cohen cast Ross, then thirty-three, as Dorothy. The director who signed on, after a number of false starts, was Sidney Lumet, who had collaborated with a young Al Pacino on *Dog Day Afternoon* and *Serpico*. At fifty-three, Lumet was an old Hollywood hand with fast-talking charisma, ending sentences with "darling sweetheart." To give *The Wiz* an orchestral punch, Lumet sought out an old friend to request a favor.

He called Quincy Jones.

Q didn't want to do it. Jones liked only three songs from the Broadway show—"Home," "Brand New Day," and a funky ensemble number called "Ease On Down the Road." But he felt indebted to Lumet, who'd hired him for many film scores in the past. "I felt I owed him more than one," Jones said of Lumet. "I owed him a lot."

The musical production of *The Wiz* was more daunting than anything Jones had ever done. It involved nine singing stars, 120 dancers, six sound technicians, three conductors, four contractors, 300 musicians, 105 backup singers, nine orchestrators, six copyists, and five music editors. Jones hunkered down at his office in Bel Air, frantically scribbling notes and music on a huge bulletin board containing the beginning sections of each of the movie's fifteen numbers. "It's like a war zone," he explained.

Lumet stocked *The Wiz* with top-tier African-American talent— Ross, Richard Pryor, Lena Horne. Rob Cohen, head of Motown Productions, thought Michael Jackson would be perfect for the role of the Scarecrow, and he approached Gordy with the idea. To his surprise, Gordy agreed. "Aw, Michael's great," said the Motown chief not far removed from years of litigation with the Jacksons over contracts. "Michael's a star."

Lumet was harder to convince. He wanted Jimmie "J. J." Walker, star of TV's *Good Times*. "Michael Jackson's a Vegas act. The Jackson 5's a Vegas act," the director told Cohen. Quincy Jones was skeptical of Jackson, too, but Cohen arranged a meeting, flying nineteen-year-old MJ to New York. Finally, Lumet and Jones saw the qualities that Cohen saw. "That boy is so sweet! He's so pure!" Lumet exulted. "I want him as the Scarecrow."

The final barrier was Joe Jackson, who wasn't thrilled about Michael doing a project that separated himself financially from the rest of his siblings. Cohen mollified Joe by offering roughly $100,000 for Michael to play the Scarecrow. When *The Wiz* began filming in New York, the twenty-seven-year-old producer moved Michael and La Toya into a Manhattan apartment, and Michael was on his own for the first time. He lived a normal life, except for a strange habit Cohen happened to discover—taking baths in Perrier water.

The shoots were long and grueling, lasting all day underneath the World Trade Center towers. At night, the young cast went out to play in New York City. Cohen took Michael, along with other members of the cast, to Studio 54, the disco hot spot known for both its crazy sexual escapades and celebrity regulars like Andy Warhol, Mick Jagger, Cary Grant, and Brooke Shields. Jackson danced there, insulated from the public within his broad movie entourage, including extras Iman and Pat Cleveland, both supermodels. One of Cleveland's girlfriends had the hots for Michael. The rest of the club took notice whenever Michael Jackson danced. "The gay side of the dance floor would stop," Cohen says, "and the hetero side would stop."

At Studio 54, Michael wore red pants and a lot of colorful leather, and when he danced, five movie friends gathered around him in a circle. "He danced more like a tap dancer, like a jazz dancer—he'd get down really low and snap his fingers," Cleveland recalls. "That's the only time he seemed rowdy to me, when he was dancing." Jackson didn't stay out late—he had to be on set early in the morning—and he resolutely didn't respond to Cleveland's hot friend or the other impossibly sexy disco chicks who paid attention to him. During lunch on *The Wiz* set, Lumet, the director, told an oblivious Michael that women around him were "like ricocheting bullets all over the place."

On the set, Michael took extremely seriously his choreography sessions with Louis Johnson, who'd been a pioneering African-American ballet dancer over years of punishing Hollywood racism. In the film, Michael's most impressive steps are with Diana Ross, as he clumsily learns to walk after being imprisoned by crows on his scarecrow pole. In giant clown shoes, he stumbles, rolls on the ground, and knocks out his knees. "He had seen Charlie Chaplin. He was a great fan of Fred

Astaire and Gene Kelly," says Johnson, who is in his early eighties, by phone from his New York home. "So I let him use it. . . . He asked me, 'Could I do this?'—and then enhanced it." But Michael also improvised his own simple steps, sometimes just "feelings," as supermodel extra Cleveland recalls, and taught them to the choreographers and dancers on the spot. When he snapped, he threw out his left hand like a windmill, leading the dancers as a soft-spoken drill sergeant: "Did you get that?"

Jackson's Scarecrow costume was hot and cumbersome, with a huge curly wig, a hat and vest stuffed with scraps of newspaper, not to mention a painted-on nose. Tony Walton, the film's production and costume designer, didn't know Michael was tormented by his brothers' constant teasing—they called him "Ugly" and "Big Nose." "He was thrilled to have his nose covered," Walton says. His costume, stuffed with newspaper and bits of trash bags, was more cumbersome, but Jackson made it work. "He would be suffering in the heat, trying to stand still and keep it calm," Cleveland says.

Quincy Jones was always present. (In the film, Jones appears dressed in gold, playing a giant piano in Times Square.) He, too, began to pay attention to Jackson. He frequently approached Tom Bähler, on hand as choir director, and told the veteran songwriter he'd never seen anything like Michael Jackson. Bähler agreed: "He's our generation's Fred Astaire—but better." The two found themselves talking frequently about MJ—how he danced, how he sang, how his discipline didn't come across as drudgery. When they were laying down vocals for the soundtrack at A&R Recording Studios in New York, Ross showed up to do her part on "Ease On Down." As she was singing, Jackson sat quietly in the corner, waiting his turn. She finished, and Jones turned to Jackson: "Okay, Michael, let's just see what you're thinking." Jones and engineer Bruce Swedien played back Ross's vocal. When it came time for the Scarecrow part, Michael stepped to the microphone and began to sing, not the bright-sounding Michael Jackson of "I Want You Back" but the eighteen-year-old MJ whose voice had evolved into something as smooth and powerful as the Concorde. Cohen, the producer, noticed Jones gaping. "He looked at Michael the way a jaguar looks at a goat," Cohen says. "It was like, 'I want *him.*'"

Jones made his move on the set. At one point, he took Michael aside to explain a Scarecrow bit in the script—that the Greek philosopher's name is pronounced "*Sock*-ra-tees" and not "*Sow*-*cray*-tees." As Jones would tell the story, he asked Michael right then if he could "take a shot" at producing his next solo album. That stuck with Michael. During *The Wiz* post-production, he called Quincy unexpectedly during a rare home hiatus from touring. They were on the line for forty-five minutes, the experienced producer doing most of the talking, about studio equipment, *Star Wars*, the newest synthesizer models, and unfinished *Wiz* clips he'd seen. Michael mostly listened, with "mmm-*hmms*" and an occasional "whoo!" When Quincy enthusiastically mentioned he'd seen the Rolling Stones perform, Michael sniffed, "You know it's not talent, though." The key moment in this nascent partnership came when Michael said he'd been writing songs: "I hear something in my head. I make the sounds with my mouth—I can do that." Quincy became excited. "There's an instrument that can make the sounds you want. I can write anything down on paper," the veteran arranger said. "If you can hear it, I can write it down." The exchange, which MJ recorded, ends with Quincy requesting his number.*

The Wiz cost $22 million and did not perform well at the box office. It was a spectacular, flawed experiment. Michael and Diana have terrific chemistry, but Ross is mismatched for the part. Not because she's too old (although she is), but because she plays Dorothy the same way she played Billie Holiday, with an emaciated world-weariness, when the part, as Judy Garland had shown the world forty years earlier, called for a wide-eyed, childish wonder. A less obvious problem was that during

———————————
*593-3527.

filming, Lumet's wife at the time, Gail Jones, daughter of *Wiz* star Lena Horne, had approached the director on set and asked for a divorce. The usually exuberant Lumet became despondent—a quality that came out distinctively in the film, recalls production designer Tony Walton. "Everybody has a crying jag—the Lion cries, and Diana Ross and the Tin Man," he says. "None of which was really in the script."

With Lumet in a dark mood, it fell to teenage Michael Jackson to keep the filmmakers upbeat. "Michael was the most high-spirited and vivacious of everybody on the movie," Walton says. "As anxious as all of us were, Michael was a free spirit."

The Wiz has its timeless qualities, especially the lovingly rendered scenes to Lumet's home city, prominently showing landmarks such as Coney Island, Shea Stadium, and the Brooklyn Bridge. But its reception was marred by racist backlash. Theater chains in white neighborhoods wouldn't schedule *The Wiz* for fear of scaring off white regulars, producer Cohen recalls glumly. "As big and as spectacular and as musical as it was," he says, "we never got a real solid distribution." Black films, aside from *Shaft*, were for black audiences. White films were for white audiences. Just as black music, despite brief exceptions such as Motown and disco, had been for black radio stations and white music for white radio stations.

Somebody needed to fix this problem.

First, though, Michael Jackson had to make another album with his brothers. After *The Jacksons* and *Goin' Places* had essentially tanked, CBS executives were ready to abandon Jacksons Inc. One of Epic's newest executives, Bobby Colomby, felt compelled to step in. His underling, an inexperienced A&R man named Mike Atkinson, called Colomby one day and said, "Hey, boss, I got a song!" They listened to "Blame It on the Boogie," by a white, bearded British singer named, of all things, Michael Jackson.

This led to a surreal *Top of the Pops* competition in which two

Michael Jacksons had the same hit on the British charts at the same time. "There was wonderful confusion everywhere," says the UK Michael Jackson, popularly known as Mick. "The press came out with this title: 'The Battle of the Boogie.'"

The lyrics to "Blame It on the Boogie" were happy and strange— "Sunshine! Moonlight! Good times! Boogie!" went the chorus, oblivious to the fact that those four things were not quite related—but the song had enough lighthearted funk to reintroduce the Jacksons to disco dancers.

Colomby liked Randy Jackson, who had replaced Jermaine after joining the group onstage in Vegas just before they'd signed with CBS Records. He had a useful low voice and was, Colomby felt, an underrated songwriter and keyboard player. He thought Marlon could sing. He took in Tito's bizarre habit of licking a guitar pick and sticking it on his forehead. He considered Jackie a fun-loving womanizer.

Joe dropped by from time to time, and Colomby didn't like his interrupting the band's generally happy vibe: "The plants would wilt," he says. One day, the door to the studio was locked, and Joe made such a commotion outside that the police showed up. Colomby went outside to talk to them. "Tell him I'm the father!" Joe shouted to the police. "I never saw him before," Colomby declared, deadpan.

What Colomby noticed most at the *Destiny* sessions was the blossoming leadership of Michael Jackson. It was hard to miss. Rick Marotta, a session drummer called in to play on "Push Me Away," remembers listening to playback while the Jacksons discussed what they thought of the early mix. Michael was still in the vocal booth in another part of the studio. Finally, one of the brothers hollered, "Wait, wait, wait— 'Hey, Mike, can you dance to it?'"

"Yeah!" Michael shouted from the distance. "It feels really good!"

"If Michael can dance to it, it's good," the brother said.

In the middle of recording "Blame It on the Boogie," Michael abruptly flung off his headphones and rushed out of the studio.

Colomby feared a blast of volume had come through his phones. When he found him in the hallway, Michael was dancing frenetically. "I have to get this out of my system," he said. "I can't hold still and sing."

For the distinctive "Sunshine! Moonlight!" bits in the "Boogie" chorus, Colomby decided to try a vocal technique he'd learned from Queen producer Roy Thomas Baker—instead of asking the musicians to sing their parts individually, more than once if necessary to "stack" the vocals onto the track, he set the boys up to sing them as a choir. They'd do one syllable at a time—"sun! shine! moon! light!"—to create a thick, layered effect that sounded energetic and bright on the record. One of the brothers, possibly Marlon or Tito, according to Colomby's memory, didn't sign on: "That's not the way we've done it." Michael won. "Guys, let's just try it," he said. "What's your problem?"

One day, Colomby showed up at the studio to find Michael directing keyboardist Greg Phillinganes and drummer Ed Green on the same repetitive funky groove, with no variations, for twenty minutes. This wasn't how Colomby did things. It didn't sound like a song, just a groove, over and over. ("It was a very strong, memorable melody," recalls Phillinganes, who had come up with the original beat while dabbling on drums. "It wasn't just a groove that rambled on and didn't have anything to connect with.") But Colomby went with it. After the musicians had cut the track, the producer called in Tom Washington, a well-known horn arranger who went by Tom Tom 84, and asked him to create a horn part for a staccato, Earth, Wind & Fire–type contemporary-soul feel. Over that, Michael sang the first line. Colomby considered it okay. Then he sang the second one—a tense, dissonant, subtle countermelody that fit perfectly. Colomby thought that was genius. The song became an eight-minute jam called "Shake Your Body (Down to the Ground)," a shorter remix of which turned into a huge hit.

"I would have said, 'It's too long,'" Colomby recalls, "but they were building something."

Destiny, which came out in December 1978, was another one of those Jacksons albums with lyrics dealing exclusively with dance. The difference between it and *The Jacksons* and *Goin' Places* was the dynamism of those dance songs—"Blame It on the Boogie" is a post–*Saturday Night Fever* nursery rhyme, sunny and goofy. But Michael's enthusiasm adds rock 'n' roll anarchy to what might have been a disco cliché. "I just can't control my feet," he sings repeatedly. In "Things I Do for You," a midtempo song typical of lighthearted R&B of 1978, Michael delivers the first line like this: "*Ah*-people all over the world-*ah!* Are the same everywhere I go—*ah! ah!* I give in to THIS-*uh*. I give in to THAT-*eh*. Every day it bothers me so—*cha!*" These percussive verbal tics, which become an improvisational instrument for the first time on any Jacksons album, are derived from James Brown, but they are more than that. They are evolving into a crucial part of Michael Jackson's musical identity. Of course the album's centerpiece is "Shake Your Body (Down to the Ground)," which opens with that incredible Phillinganes-Green groove, then one of those Michael whoops. It became a dance-floor smash, hitting No. 7 and selling more than two million copies at the time.

"If I could go back in time," says Mike Sembello, a guitarist for the *Destiny* sessions who studied MJ closely, "I would take Michael Jackson out of the limelight and put him on an island. With all the instruments."

Quincy Jones was so poor that he ate fried rats. His grandmother, who'd raised him briefly in Kentucky, cooked them after she'd caught them in traps. He had spent most of his youth on the South Side of Chicago, during the Depression, a family of four with his father, mother, and younger brother, Lloyd.

People called the brothers' part of town the Bucket of Blood (not to be confused with the nearby Bucket of Blood in Gary, Indiana). The Jones boys fought, robbed, and joined gangs, wielding switchblades and slingshots made of clothespins and inner tubes. Later, after Jones's father had moved his family to Sinclair Heights, Washington, Quincy broke into a local rec center's soda-fountain area with his friends and discovered an upright piano on a tiny stage. He played it and, he recalls, "Each note seemed to fill up another empty space I felt inside."

Jones was destined to be a musician. He finagled lessons out of Clark Terry, the great trumpeter in Count Basie's band, and played with Billie Holiday in 1948. He joined a barnstorming band run by Bumps Blackwell and befriended a young Ray Charles, who, Quincy says, "never acted blind unless there was a pretty girl around, then he'd get all helpless and sightless, bumping into walls and doors, trying to get laid." Quincy wrote scores and carried them under his shirt, with his trumpet under his arm. "I had no control over where I lived, no control over my sick mother, no control over my hard-hearted stepmother and my overwrought father. I couldn't change the attic where I slept, or stop the anguished tears of my little brother Lloyd, who sometimes cried himself to sleep at night; I couldn't control the angry whites who still called me nigger when they caught me alone on the street," he wrote. "But nobody could tell me how many substitute chord changes I could stick into the bridge of 'Cherokee.'" Jones and his contemporaries bonded over racial indignities on the road, especially in the South, where jazz lions Ella Fitzgerald and Dizzy Gillespie had to send white drivers out to pick up their food.

By the time Jones met Michael Jackson on the set of *The Wiz*, he had built up one of the great résumés in American-music history—he had written charts for Count Basie, Cannonball Adderley, and Dinah Washington, played in bands with Lionel Hampton and Dizzy Gillespie, arranged for Sarah Vaughan, Frank Sinatra, and Billy Eckstine, scored more than thirty movies—from *In Cold Blood* to *Bob & Carol & Ted & Alice*—and had numerous pop hits with singer Lesley Gore. He was forty-four, with a warm smile, an avuncular salt-and-pepper mustache, and half-open eyes that concealed the complex musical thoughts whooshing inside his brain. Q was colloquial and fun—he gave everyone excellent nicknames, like "Lily," for white session musician Michael Boddicker—but at work he turned serious and pushed everyone around him to higher standards. Those few musicians who earned a spot in his inner circle were loyal forever.

Michael saw in Quincy's calm-jazz-cat personality a father figure. The one he'd been born with wasn't working out. Quincy was eight years younger than Joe Jackson. Both had struggled under the weight of segregation and racism. But Quincy had no patience for revenge. "It's about recycling energy," he said. "It's a bitch converting hate into love, but if you can do it, it's your only salvation." Also, in Quincy, Michael saw a producer capable of handling any kind of music according to his rainbow-coalition standards. "Quincy does jazz, he does movie scores, rock 'n' roll, funk, pop—he's all colors, and that's the kind of people I like to work with," Jackson said.

Michael had been yearning for a solo career since his Motown days. Two barriers stood in his way: Joe and CBS Records. Joe's agenda was to keep his family band together. His sons were easier to control that way. Joe had hired two new managers, Ron Weisner and Freddy DeMann, and told them, "I've got my boys. We don't really get what we need out of the record company, so I need some white guys to help me out." Overcoming their distaste for Joe's approach to civil rights, Weisner and DeMann agreed to sign on. It became obvious to them, over time, that Michael was the star of the group, and they began to take MJ's side in meetings with both Joe and Epic executives. "There were a lot of problems, a lot of issues," Weisner remembers. "A lot of it would start with Joe, because Joe wanted control of everything. What Michael wanted most was to not be under his thumb and to not have to deal with him." The first battle for MJ's independence involved Quincy Jones.

"It was very nasty and very divisive," Weisner recalls. "You've got to remember, there was no Michael solo career. [CBS executives] figured, 'If we give one of the brothers a solo album, we're going to have to give it to all the brothers,' which they didn't want to do."

Epic's executives considered Quincy "too jazzy," given his background (which was most likely code for "too old"). "I don't care what you think," Michael responded, marching into the Epic offices one day with Weisner and DeMann, "Quincy is doing my record." CBS capitulated.

By the time Jones and Jackson went to the Allen Zentz Recording studio in Los Angeles to record *Off the Wall* in December 1978, disco was beginning to decline, creatively if not quite yet commercially. Quincy Jones and Michael Jackson knew it. They were listening to artists whose albums were informed by disco but were pushing it into different directions: the Brothers Johnson's Quincy-produced *Right on Time*, Heatwave's *Central Heating*, Chaka Khan and Rufus's single "Ain't Nobody," and, of course, Stevie Wonder's sprawling masterpiece *Songs in the Key of Life*.

"Our underlying plan was to take disco out. That was the bottom line," Jones said. "I admired disco, don't get me wrong. I just thought it had gone far enough. We needed to go someplace else." Ron Weisner, Michael's comanager at the time, recalls broader discussions within Team MJ about making hits with broad appeal: "Part of the marketing was all about crossover potential and not limiting yourself to black-music departments."

Michael had talent and seasoning. Quincy provided an experienced comrade willing to give him space, as well as a killer studio team, including engineer Bruce Swedien and British songwriter Rod Temperton. "We tried all kinds of things I'd learned over the years to help him with the artistic growth," Jones says. "Dropping keys just a minor third to give him flexibility and a more mature range in the upper and lower registers, and more than a few tempo changes." Seth Riggs, Jackson's vocal coach, helped expand his top and bottom range. Riggs recognized that as Michael matured, he was still singing, and even speaking, in his jarringly high Peter Pan voice. Riggs encouraged Michael to speak more deeply (which he barely ever did) and added half an octave to his upper register and a whole octave to his lower one. At Quincy's instruction, Riggs worked with Michael two hours a day. One time, the teacher was sitting at the piano as Michael held a high C, then looked up to find Michael doing an endless pirouette. "You don't have to do that," Riggs told him. "Yeah," Michael said, "but maybe somebody will ask me to do that—and I want to be ready."

For Jones, Michael was a blank canvass—someone who fit his idea of R&B so cutting-edge it could become not just black music but pop music. Jones called Michael "Smelly Jelly," a reference to MJ's preferred word for funky. "Quincy and Rod were like, 'Wow, we got this guy who could execute everything we hear in our heads,'" says Ed Eckstine, then an executive for Jones's production company. "And Michael was like, 'I got these two guys who hear everything in their heads—and I can add something on my own.'" Quincy had a way of staving off Michael's prolific ideas without undercutting his enthusiasm. "Michael would come in every day with a new idea: 'This is great!'—and he'd spew fifteen ideas," Eckstine adds. "And Quincy might not respond to any of them: 'Yeah, that's cool.' 'So, Bruce, what are we working on today?'"

Jones and Swedien devised a system to capture moments of inspiration as they happened in the studio. To record Temperton's "Rock with You," Swedien decided he needed the best possible rhythmic setting for the drums, so he asked studio carpenters to build an eight-foot-square, ten-inch-tall platform made of natural wood, "braced and counterbraced." Drummer John Robinson set up his kit on the platform. Then Swedien asked Michael to sing on the same platform, and he wound up with the perfect acoustic spot to capture MJ's habit of snapping and tapping as he recorded his vocals. "I absolutely love those little sounds as a part of Michael's sonic character," he says. To record hand claps, Swedien recruited Robinson, keyboardist Greg Phillinganes (a holdover from *Destiny*), and bassist Louis Johnson of the Brothers Johnson to stand around a microphone. He then played the tape back at faster speed, so the recording sounded like the Chipmunks clapping, and reconvened the trio to clap again in real time.

Thus the hand claps throughout *Off the Wall* have a full sound, treble and bass at the same time.

Quincy Jones, at one point, thought the clapping looked like fun and joined in. Then he hit his wrist wrong and his Rolex crashed to the floor. "You're out," Robinson joked to the superstar producer who'd failed hand claps. "You gotta go."

Jones and Swedien recorded in fragments, then reassembled the songs like a puzzle made of magnetic tape. This inspiration-in-pieces approach extended into the parking lot. After one long day with Michael and Quincy, Louis Johnson was sitting in his car, listening to an unmarked cassette on the $5,000 stereo system he'd rigged for LA commutes. It was a bass-and-drum Brothers Johnson demo he'd recorded in his garage twenty-four-track studio. Michael walked by, hearing the music. "Man, what is that?" he asked Johnson, in the driver's seat. "Oh, something I'm working on. Something separate." "That's *bad*," Michael said. "Can I listen to it?" MJ climbed into the passenger seat as Johnson rewound the tape and they listened. The next day, they returned to the studio; Michael had refashioned the track into "Get on the Floor." The songwriting credit on the record is to Jackson and Johnson, which means, in worldwide publishing royalties, Johnson has made, conservatively speaking, almost $1 million from *Off the Wall* sales alone.

"She's Out of My Life," the ballad that famously made Michael Jackson tear up at the end, came from Tom Bähler, an arranger and songwriter who'd worked with Quincy and Michael numerous times. It was based on a woman Bähler dated after his divorce. Bähler planned to give the song to Frank Sinatra, but Jones called and talked him into holding it for *Off the Wall*. When Michael heard "She's Out of My Life," he called it "the Single." It was the first song they recorded during the *Off the Wall* sessions. Michael changed one line, the last one— from "instead of begging my wife / she's out of my life" to "And it cuts like a knife / she's out of my life."

Off the Wall, which came out in August 1979, opens with one of the most extraordinary expressions of frustration and catharsis ever captured on a pop record. "Don't Stop 'til You Get Enough" was the first song Michael Jackson ever wrote by himself, at his Hayvenhurst studio, with help from session men such as keyboardist Greg Phillinganes. The heart of the composition was a groove, similar to the way he cowrote "Shake Your Body (Down to the Ground)." Quincy knew how to tease a bona fide song from the groove, adding strings, horns, a middle section written by Phillinganes, and what MJ called "guitars chopping like kalimbas, the African thumb pianos," during the fade-out. In the studio, later, drummer John Robinson mirrored the robotic, steady beat on his kick drum; Phillinganes and Louis Johnson later added Fender Rhodes and electric bass, respectively, giving the track a thick and full feeling. "Don't Stop" begins with Michael's subdued voice, at first teary and desperate: "You know, I was . . . I was wondering . . . eh . . . because the force has got a lot of power." The listener wonders whether this is a *Star Wars* reference, or something more mysterious, unhinged. "It makes me feel like . . . ," he continues, dramatically trailing off. Then again: "It make me feel like-*uh* . . . ." There's a pause, followed by a falsetto orgasmic scream so intense that Michael would later have to convince his mother, Katherine, the devout Jehovah's Witness, that his new song was not about sex: "OOOOHHWWWOOOAAAAH!"

The groove on "Don't Stop 'til You Get Enough," *Off the Wall*'s first single, which came out on July 28, borrows a central concept from disco—man vs. machine, relentless, mechanical rhythms matched with a sensual voice. But no disco star, not even Donna Summer or the Bee Gees, had more charisma and humanity than Michael Jackson. Quincy Jones had correctly identified the decline of disco, and *Off the Wall*, when it came out in late 1979, threw the many itinerant disco fans a life preserver, giving them a place to go: "Burn This Disco Out," "Workin' Day and Night," and, of course, "Don't Stop" would become staples at underground dance-party warehouses and post-disco radio stations. It's a short album, ten songs in forty-one minutes, with no ostentatious solos to obscure the impact of Michael's voice. *Off the Wall* contained everything that was fun about disco. Every song has persistent percussive noises, hand claps, cowbells, bongos, and Michael's own vocal tricks, running into and around the central rhythm, like multiple heartbeats competing for space in the same body. "Workin' Day and Night" alone contains melodies and countermelodies, fast and intricate horn arrangements, bursts of wah-wah guitar, Michael oohing, sighing, and *oh no*–ing and call-and-response choruses of *Got me, got me workin' day and night*. The whole work is so damn joyful that when "She's Out of My Life" finally appears, the clear-eyed ballad of love, loss, and desperation is even more devastating.

The cover photo, of a big-haired Michael Jackson smiling against a brick wall in a black tuxedo and bow tie, was a throwaway, an idea from a designer that wouldn't cost much or require any travel. Jackson wanted to shoot the cover at the Hollywood Observatory, but photographer Mike Salisbury wound up capturing him in an alley against the redbrick wall. Salisbury gave Michael the tuxedo. The white socks were Michael's idea—a Fred Astaire move, to focus attention on his dancing feet. "Put a little attitude into it," Salisbury said. Michael moved his hands around and smiled.

It was 1979. There was a gas crisis, an economic malaise. In July, disco crashed, thanks to a massive record-smashing party at Chicago's Comiskey Park led by Steve Dahl, a young radio DJ. White rock fans rioted for the right to never hear disco on the radio again. They almost took down the entire record industry with them, as sales of disco albums abruptly stopped.

Through his cousin, Mike Sembello, who worked on the *Destiny* album, Bud Rizzo landed an informal audition to play guitar on the Jacksons' world tour. He showed up at Hayvenhurst and jammed with the boys for two days. The next day, Tito called back and said, "Why don't you come to rehearsal?" The Jacksons' management negotiated a decent salary, and Rizzo boarded a plane to London in early 1979. By this point, the *Off the Wall* album release was still several months away.

Although Rizzo was in his mid-twenties at the time, he had played with Brazilian-jazz bandleader Sérgio Mendes and became a sort of wizened mentor figure to some of the Jacksons while they rode on a tour bus through Europe. He was a vegetarian at the time and scoured London for Indian restaurants. Michael, also a vegetarian, began to bond with Rizzo over food, music, and spirituality. "Kind of these way-out talks," Rizzo says. Michael and Bud sat together on the bus, and the singer played the guitarist a prerelease demo of "Don't Stop 'til You Get Enough," with Randy Jackson on Coke-bottle percussion, and a version of "She's Out of My Life" with just Michael's voice and piano. Rizzo turned Michael on to Little Feat, the Neville Brothers, the Rolling Stones, and jazz-fusion guitarist Allan Holdsworth.

During breaks before shows, they'd go to the movies together, sometimes with Randy or Tito. Michael had his own cache of Fred Astaire tapes that he'd watch on a VCR on the bus, allowing Bud to draw his own connections between the Michael he saw dancing every night and Astaire's famous elegance. The European tour was a success, although Michael at one point developed a throat infection and had to cancel several shows. The Jacksons began to play arenas once they returned to the US. By the middle of the tour, they needed a horn section, especially to play the more complex dance numbers Michael was about to release for *Off the Wall*. Alan "Funt" Prater, a trumpeter and trombonist, had been in R&B singer Millie Jackson's band and heard about the Jacksons' auditions through a friend. He showed up at Hayvenhurst with his unknown horn section from Montreal, audaciously padding its résumé in advance, and falsely, as a renowned session group called the Memphis Horns. Katherine Jackson answered the door and the young men blew their horns for her; she liked them and introduced them to the Jackson brothers, who invited them to rehearsal at an MGM

Studios soundstage in Culver City, outside LA. When Michael first walked in, he was wearing shorts and unmatched white gym socks and sat on the floor, taking in the music, moving his body and grooving and bopping silently. "Wow," Prater thought, "this guy is kinda nerdy-like." Then Michael stood up, grabbed the microphone, and sang, while doing his astounding twirls and kicks. "I couldn't believe what I just witnessed," Prater recalls. "This guy just flipped a switch—he was this entity. He was *Michael Jackson*."

When the tour started again, Prater noticed what Rizzo had seen earlier that year. The Jacksons were accessible. They'd hang out with the backup musicians in their hotel rooms. Michael and Marlon were the pranksters, setting buckets of water on the top edges of the doors between rooms, then laughing uproariously when a victim took a splash to the head. Jackie was always the one trying to calm them down: "Hey, hey, hey, let's get it right." Joe was always around, as stern as ever. At one point, Prater drew up his courage and scheduled a meeting with him to discuss a raise. "*Raise?*" Joseph responded. "Nah, nah, nah, nah—ain't gonna be no *raise*. I can't do that. You want to be here or *not?*" Groupies were everywhere. Prater returned to his hotel room occasionally to find a young woman in his closet or under the bed. He could never figure out how it happened, given the Jacksons' strong security team, but he developed a habit of searching any given hotel room to weed out unwanted guests before retiring for the night.

The Jacksons took the stage every night underneath a giant sparkly peacock. This, Michael would explain, was "a symbol of what we are trying to say through our music, and it is summed up by the fact that the peacock is the only bird that integrates all the colors into one. . . . To bring all races together through love." Their costumes were over-the-top, even by Jackson 5 standards—for one early 1979 show in London, they wore silver-spacemen outfits. Michael did the Robot during "Dancing Machine." Randy played bongos and keyboards, and he and Marlon subbed in the vocals for the absent Jermaine. Bud Rizzo, in his beard, yellow Nudie suit, and large glasses, played a pretty Spanish guitar line between Michael's vocals in "Ben." And while the band squashed chestnuts "I Want You Back," "ABC," and "The Love You Save" into a brief greatest-hits medley, they stretched *Destiny* tracks such as "Things I Do for You" and "Blame It on the Boogie" into long funk workouts that showcased Michael's dance steps. When Michael sang "I just can't control my feet!," his feet seemed to propel the rest of his body, side to side, back and forth, into flawless spins.

After carefully rehearsed twirls throughout "Keep On Dancing," "Enjoy Yourself," and others, the encore was something different. MJ returned to the stage in a black tuxedo, black shoes, white socks, black bow tie, and what seemed like two yards of white cuff. The band (with Marlon and Jackie on percussion) cranked into the groove for "Don't Stop 'til You Get Enough," a song from *Off the Wall* that had yet to come out in stores. Michael held a pose with his right arm outstretched and his left hand in his pocket. He held a beat. Another. A few more. Then he spun, removed his jacket, hiked up his pants, strutted and kicked. His brothers were still performing in their original garish outfits, and for a moment it looked like the past and the future were converging on stage. "It was the same thing over and over," MJ said after the tour. "It was all for one and one for all, but I was starting to think that maybe I should be doing some things on my own. I was getting antsy." Those around him could sense his frustration. At the end of the *Destiny* tour, Bud Rizzo says, "You could feel something was ending. You could feel the change in the room when [Michael] was around. He was separating himself from the rest of the group." Michael Jackson, finally, was beginning to leave his family behind.

CHAPTER 4

Every singer James Ingram knew, including himself, stood carefully in front of the studio microphone, trying not to move too much and clutter the recording with extraneous noise. The first thing Ingram noticed about Michael Jackson, watching him sing "P.Y.T." at Westlake Studios in LA, was Michael didn't care about any of that. Somebody may have had to hold little MJ's head ten years earlier at Motown, but as a liberated, grown-up pop star, Jackson approached the mike as if twenty thousand people were watching him: he slid his feet, bobbed his shoulders, flailed his arms, snapped his fingers, tee-heed, woo-hooed, gulped, and hiccupped. After Michael finished transforming Ingram's song "P.Y.T." from a little love ballad into a booming, sure-hit, funk-rock anthem, he turned and asked: "Am I singing it right?" Sitting in the dark, Ingram's eyes widened. "Man," he said, "you *killing* it."

The "universities of Berry Gordy and Quincy Jones," as James Ingram refers to them, were two different institutes of higher learning. One was an assembly line, where laborers ran every bit of work by the boss for corrections and modifications. The other was warm and accepting, with hugs for everybody, an organized hippie gathering. "The Motown musicians came from this jazz heritage. It was competitive," recalls Anthony Marinelli, one of the *Thriller* synthesizer players. "With Quincy, it was like coming into this loving family." At eleven, trained into submission by his father, Michael Jackson needed Motown's structure, routine, and instruction. At twenty-four, an artist and songwriter, he needed flexibility, patience, and encouragement. He needed somebody who knew when to let him run off a twenty-minute groove and when to gently reel him in. That was Quincy Jones.

Quincy encouraged Michael to be more self-sufficient for *Thriller* than he had been for *Off the Wall*. Michael was leaning that way already. He had been writing steadily since *Destiny*, and while he had no training (or interest) in transcribing musical notes onto a page, he devised his own method. As he'd told Quincy Jones over the phone years earlier, he heard music in his head and used his mouth to make "sounds of how I want the bass or the strings or the drums or each part to go." Michael described his inspirational process throughout his career as a kind of magic, "like standing under a tree and letting a leaf fall and trying to catch it—it's that beautiful." He used a recorder to capture sounds as they occurred to him (". . . and the piano be going 'da da da da,' and I'll figure out the rest of it later") and to psych himself up. Before writing and producing Diana Ross's 1982 single "Muscles," he taped a message to himself: "I want the biggest drum sounds we can get! Fool around with different sounds! Experiment! Bring to the studio things that influence me—like a child, or pictures of children. Tell all my musicians what I'm looking for—the best—and don't settle for less."

On one level, Michael's songwriting evolution was part of Quincy's plan. But some who worked with both men suggest they began to drift apart during the *Thriller* sessions. "Before *Thriller*, Quincy would do everything. Michael was the artist—he'd do his thing and do an amazing job and just go home," recalls a source who contributed to the album. "For *Thriller*, Michael would do a demo, Quincy would redo it. He wouldn't use Michael's guitar player—he used who he wanted to use. And Michael would have the balls to say, 'I don't like that. I want to bring my guy in.' And they would. That's when Michael started coming into his own as an artist, and he'd speak up. He started getting more hands-on."

Michael was able to record his own songs at his sixteen-track home studio, but it wasn't particularly state-of-the-art. "It was kind of an orphaned, packaged studio," says Brent Averill, the engineer Michael hired to rebuild it in fall 1979, the week *Off the Wall* came out. Averill spent the next several years showing Michael how to engineer during one-on-one sessions at Hayvenhurst. Back then, Michael's family had no regular housecleaning, no gardeners, and no employees, other than Nelson Hayes, Michael's assistant, and Bill Bray, the Jacksons' longtime security man. Michael gave Averill a key to the front gate and the studio, and the engineer gave Michael the tools to record professional-sounding demos on his own. The most unusual feature of the studio was Michael's parrot, who squawked at inopportune times—it can be heard in the background of one of the early "Billie Jean" demos. One time, working with La Toya on one of her songs, Averill made the mistake of laughing at the parrot's antics in the background; Michael's sensitive sister thought he was laughing at her and refused to work with him after that.

At his private studio, Michael wrote and recorded demos for "Billie Jean," "Beat It," and "Wanna Be Startin' Somethin'." "We recorded in a hurry," Averill says. "Sloppy, throw it down, don't fix it, just get it on tape while the ideas are coming." MJ began to invite musicians to his home studio, including rhythm guitarist David Williams, keyboardist Bill Wolfer, and bassist Nate Watts. With their help, he updated and strengthened "Billie Jean."

Michael summoned veteran backup singer Oren Waters, who'd laid down vocals for numerous Jackson 5 songs at Motown, as well as Oren's sisters Maxine and Julia. During the "Wanna Be Startin' Somethin'" demo recording at Hayvenhurst, Waters began to see more complexity from Jackson than he expected. "We had known Michael from when he was a little kid," he says. "The lyrics 'You're a vegetable, you're just a buffet, people eat off of you'—I'm going, 'I see the beginning of a little bit of torment.'"

Waters had no idea what else was happening in Michael's life, and how much Michael and his family were struggling to keep it private. On October 16, 1980, Gina Sprague, a pretty nineteen-year-old secretary and publicist at Joe Jackson Productions, was sitting at her desk when Katherine, Randy, and Janet Jackson showed up at her office on Sunset Boulevard. Katherine, the matriarchal Jehovah's Witness, was not known for her violent outbursts, and neither were Randy, eighteen, nor Janet, fourteen. But the three Jacksons allegedly assaulted her. "Bitch, you better leave my husband alone!" Katherine shouted. Katherine Jackson had happened to pick up the phone at Hayvenhurst and heard her husband on the line, talking to Gina, "graphically describing relations," as she would confide to one of Joe Jackson's other employees, Joyce McRae. Sprague denied the affair, but Joe was a known womanizer. That same fall, he was preparing to announce to his family the outcome of an earlier affair, with Cheryl Terrell, which led to the birth of his daughter, Joh'Vonnie Jackson, in 1974.

After the alleged assault, Sprague landed in Hollywood Presbyterian Medical Center with cuts and bruises. Joseph visited the next day and tried to give her an envelope full of money. She refused. Two and a half years later, Sprague sued Joe, Randy, Katherine, and Janet for $21 million. They settled privately. Katherine Jackson filed for divorce from Joe—again—on August 19, 1982.

During this period, even visiting journalists noticed a shift in Michael's mood. Leonard Pitts Jr., a *Soul* reporter who would write a book about the Jackson family, recalled interviewing Michael at Hayvenhurst for his twenty-first birthday: "He didn't seem very happy. Truth is, he seemed tired. Not from fatigue or exertion. It was an existential tired, as if he felt worn down by the simple act of being. I remember Jackson did not walk about the place so much as haunt it, slumping from room to room as [if] a great weight rested upon his sparrow shoulders." When Robert Hilburn of the *Los Angeles Times* asked during the same period why MJ still lived with his parents, unlike his brothers, he said, "Oh, no, I think I'd die on my own. I'd be so lonely. Even at home, I'm lonely. I sit in my room and sometimes cry. It is so hard to make friends, and there are some things you can't talk to your parents or family about. I sometimes walk around the neighborhood at night, just hoping to find someone to talk to. But I just end up coming home." Earlier, he had told the *Times* of his emptiness outside of performing: "It may sound crazy but I'm a stage addict," he said. "When I'm not onstage for a long time I have fits and I get crazy. I start crying and I act . . . I guess you might say weird and freaked out. I've been doing this for so long," he said. "I sometimes feel like I should be seventy by now."

To deal with these feelings, Michael burrowed deeper into his art. He wrote one of his bleakest songs, "Heartbreak Hotel," dealing with a favorite subject: fear of the public. He sings of faces "staring, glaring, tearing through me," then observes: "Someone said, 'Welcome to your room' / then they smiled with eyes that looked as if they knew me / this is scaring me." When he and his brothers recorded the song for the *Triumph* album, they packed its climaxes with all manner of noisy effects (including a La Toya scream) as Michael collapses into frightened panting. Michael was beginning to come out in public—as a depressive.

In 1979, Michael also had his first nose job, or so he said, after he fell onstage trying to execute a complex dance step during the *Destiny* tour. Bassist Mike Mckinney and guitarist Bud Rizzo have no memory of any onstage accident, during a show or rehearsal, or any midtour trip to a doctor's office, but then again, MJ didn't exactly announce it to the universe. Jermaine walked into Hayvenhurst one day to find Michael with bandages on his nose and cheeks. "*What* in the hell happened to *you?*" he asked. Michael wouldn't say. Katherine shot Jermaine a look suggesting his question was "insensitive." He was "told" later that Michael had slipped and fallen near the living-room bar and required rhinoplasty. Later, Michael was referred to a well-known plastic surgeon, Steven Hoefflin, who suggested a second nose job, then performed it himself.

Necessity or not, Michael hadn't been feeling confident about his face. "Offstage, our merciless teasing only made matters worse, but teasing is what brothers do, and we all had to go through it," Jermaine said. "When my acne first kicked in, they—including Michael—called me 'Bumpy Face' or 'Map Face' and Marlon was 'Liver Lips.' . . . So when Michael was called 'Big Nose,' it was just part of the common initiation into manhood—but he struggled with it." Especially painful, for Michael, was Joseph's adoption of the nickname. "Michael said nothing, and cringed each time," Jermaine recalls. When Jermaine became a vegetarian, avoiding greasy food, his skin cleared up. Michael decided to do the same. As he did this while growing out of puberty, his cheeks sank in and he became unnaturally skinny. Friends and writers have theorized Michael was anorexic, although the singer never confirmed this. "Michael was doing plastic surgery to wipe family off his face," suggests Joyce McRae*, who worked at Joseph Jackson's production company. "Michael was at one point extremely miserable. He had really bad skin problems. He had a really, really horrible self-image."

Michael consistently explained his facial reconstruction as just something people in show business did. But even in these early days of Michael Jackson procedures, perplexed friends and family were seeing broader motives. An old colleague from Motown, singer Jimmy Ruffin, was one of many who believe Michael was beginning to shift away from his African-American identity as he began to approach a broader (meaning white) world of pop culture. "Michael felt under pressure where his image was concerned because of who he is. He was a black guy, he was an inner-city guy," he said. "How could he be the darling of

---

*McRae was a companion of soul singer Jackie Wilson during his final days; today she is Joyce Moore, married to Sam Moore, part of the great soul duo Sam and Dave.

white society? He had to change." Others interpreted Michael's facial moves artistically. He was writing his own songs, making his own music, and resculpting his face. As the world was moving toward "hybridiza-tion," wrote critic Jean Baudrillard, with fewer racial and gender defi-nitions, so was Michael: "In short, he has been reconstructed with the greatest attention to detail." As a kid, Michael Jackson had known only boundaries, from his controlling father to his segregated neighbor-hood, but as a singer, songwriter, and star, he could begin to construct an increasingly limitless world for himself, at least for the time being.

Michael was experimenting in more worrisome ways, too. In 1979, he was staying at the Drug and Arrow Hotel in Leeds, England, for a promotional tour with his brothers, when a thirteen-year-old boy named Terry George showed up at his door to request an interview. Michael was sharing a room with Randy and answered the door himself. "Oh, hi!" Michael said to Terry. The British teen requested an inter-view. "Yeah!" responded Michael, who rarely gave interviews. "Come in." (It was still the seventies, and rock 'n' roll security hadn't fully been developed yet.) They chatted for an hour, and Michael asked to exchange phone numbers. This led to months of international phone calls, sometimes late at night for Terry in the UK. Michael's parents weren't paying attention, and Terry's dad would boast to his friends, "I was just speaking to Michael Jackson on the telephone." During one of these phone conversations, Michael asked Terry whether he mas-turbated. Terry had no idea what he was talking about. "Do you ever use cream?" Michael asked. Terry thought he was talking about sweets. "No," Terry said. "I'm doing it now," Michael told him. Terry, by then fourteen, chose to laugh it off: "It was a bit of an awkward conversation, really," he says today. He kept this highly sensitive information about Michael Jackson to himself, at least for the time being.

Michael turned twenty-one in August 1979. He could feel him-self separating from his family, musically and creatively, and just as he needed his own manager, he needed a lawyer of his own, someone to represent his interests and not Joseph's. It had actually been Jermaine who made the first move in this direction, back in 1975, the year he turned twenty-one and removed himself from the family group to stay behind at Motown. Jermaine called a prestigious Century City law firm and told an attorney there that his brothers had made a ton of money over a decade and didn't know where it was. The attorney referred Jermaine to an accountant who had once been an IRS agent. Michael Mesnick conducted an internal audit of the family's expenses. He found nothing unusual. He was straightforward. Even Joe appreciated that. He hired Mesnick to stay on as the Jacksons' accountant.

At the time, Mesnick was also the Beach Boys' accountant, and knew their lawyer, David Braun. As extraordinary as it sounds today, Michael's landmark solo debut *Off the Wall* had come out as part of the Jacksons' group recording contract. As *Off the Wall* began to take off, in early 1980, Mesnick asked Braun if he could take a whack at extracting Michael from the Jacksons' contract—giving him a solo CBS career in addition to the one he had with his brothers. Braun met Michael, and Michael hired him. Braun had leverage for a contract renegotiation. By contrast, Michael's brothers had almost none. When negotiating with Dick Asher, Walter Yetnikoff's deputy at CBS Records, on Michael Jackson's behalf, Braun was almost openly gleeful. "Suppose it sells *this*," he would say. "Okay," responded Asher, a tough former marine, each time, "if it gets to this, I'll get you another half a point." They kept at it—"suppose it sells *that*" . . . "Okay"—until they reached what they considered an outlandish ceiling of twenty-five million sales.

Michael Jackson's royalty deal was north of 25 percent per album, a big contract even for established pop stars. "We kept using arbitrary numbers, never dreaming Michael would hit them," Braun recalls. "It was probably the most expensive agreement ever in the industry, from a royalty point of view." Mesnick, the accountant, says it was Michael's idea to turn down a big advance and opt for royalty payments based on sales. It was a gut feeling, and it was correct. "Michael was making

equal to what CBS was making toward the end," Mesnick says, referring to Michael's royalties per album sold.

Michael's new five-album solo deal gave him financial independence
from his family, although he remained part of the existing Jacksons' contract as well. In 1980, David Braun quit his job as Michael's attorney to
become chief executive of PolyGram, one of the world's biggest record
labels. He didn't last long. "I left to make some money," he recalls. "If
I'd stayed with Michael, I would have made ten times as much." Braun's
departure left an opening for a colleague at his firm, John Branca, a young,
ambitious entertainment attorney in LA, to join Team Michael Jackson.
In 1981, Branca helped MJ try to move out of Hayvenhurst, buying a
three-bedroom condo in Encino. But in the end, Michael couldn't leave
his mother. He remained at his parents' house while maintaining the
condo as a sanctuary, for himself and his brothers, for years.

After *Off the Wall*, the power dynamics changed between Michael
and his brothers. As the oldest, Jackie may have still been the puta-
tive leader of the family band, but he told Mesnick, the accountant:
"Michael puts us to shame." The Jacksons nonetheless began recording
their *Triumph* album in late 1979, at a point when the brothers were
still wearing skintight outfits and dancing through smoke during the
Destiny tour. They bought a mobile eight-track studio, and at night,
after each show was over, they'd record in a hotel room. All the Jacksons began to buy recording equipment. After the tour ended, they
gathered at Tito's house. He had a modern studio. Michael came over.
He brainstormed songs. When they had some ideas sketched out, they
called Mike Mckinney, the tour's bass player: "Mike, what you doing
today? Come on, let's write." Eventually they booked time at a few different professional studios and started hiring musicians to drop by to
work on parts—one was Greg Phillinganes, who'd played keyboards on
Destiny and *Off the Wall* and manned every *Triumph* track.

"There would be a lot of opinions on what it should be," recalls
Jerry Hey, the horn arranger whom Quincy Jones had recruited for *Off*

the Wall and Michael hired for *Triumph*. "It's always difficult when you have that kind of family trying to work together like that."

Wedged between *Off the Wall* and *Thriller*, 1980's *Triumph* suffers by comparison. Although it feels programmed, it showcases Michael's range. It opens with "Can You Feel It," a rock anthem with an elaborate choir and strings that Michael would compare to "Also Sprach Zarathustra," the theme from *2001: A Space Odyssey*; covers the last breaths of disco with "Lovely One" and "Walk Right Now"; and contains a perfunctory ballad, "Time Waits for No One." The centerpiece is Michael's devastating song of fear and loneliness, "Heartbreak Hotel," retitled "This Place Hotel," most likely to avoid Elvis Presley confusion.

After they finished the album, Michael didn't want to tour. He claimed to hate performing live. Whether or not this was true—this was the same man who had just declared he was barely able to live a sane life without being onstage—Michael succumbed to pressure from his family, promoters who stood to make millions of dollars, and Epic Records executives who saw the tour as marketing.

Michael made it to five days a week of rehearsals, all day, in a large space in a Van Nuys office park. The brothers worked well together, but they weren't always united. Bill Wolfer, who had done some synthesizer overdubs for *Triumph*, signed on as the new keyboardist. "The brothers had different ideas about what I should do," he recalls. Jackie took him aside one day and asked him to play a certain part on a song, bringing him a Walkman to demonstrate a quirk in one of the alternate mixes. Wolfer dutifully learned it the new way, but as he started to play it in rehearsal, Michael stopped the band. "Bill, why you playing that?" Michael said. "Well, Jackie wanted me to play it," Bill responded. The five brothers disappeared for a few minutes, convening to a break room to work out their disagreement—"so they could present a unified front," Wolfer recalls.

Wolfer detected a sad aura surrounding Michael. On the Fourth of July, kids came by selling bottle rockets. Michael refused. "Buy some for your friends!" said one enterprising kid. "I don't have any friends," he responded with a weary smile. Another time, Wolfer was sitting at a table in the break room, and Michael appeared in front of a vending machine. He stared at the potato chips and candy bars for the longest time, then reached into his pocket, pulled out some change, and purchased a granola bar. He studied the wrapper before concluding, "I can't eat this." "The granola bar was not pure enough for him to intake," Wolfer recalls. "He was just so obsessed with what came into him and went out of his body." He also talked a *lot* about colonics, which Wolfer took as a worrisome sign.

The Jacksons' name was on the tour, but *Triumph* belonged to Michael. It began in Memphis on July 9, 1981, and concluded five months later with four sold-out Forum shows in Los Angeles. Like the *Destiny* shows, *Triumph* was meticulously programmed, so the set list was almost exactly the same every night. The Jacksons' sparkly outfits from the *Destiny* tour gave way to eighties-style muscle shirts, black leather pants, skinny ties, and collars opened to the rib cage.

"Can You Feel It" was the perfect opening blast of dramatic rock and funk, with a familiar-sounding bass line that recalled the Jefferson Airplane's "White Rabbit." As before, Michael "argued" onstage with his brothers over the merits of new songs versus old songs. "Number one, it's *old*, okay?" he told the crowd before "I'll Be There." "Number two, the choreography's old!" He added (at the expense of his ancient thirty-year-old brother): "Jackie's old!" The brothers continued to close with "Shake Your Body (Down to the Ground)," and Michael indulged himself with just three songs from *Off the Wall*. That was frustrating, for the audience and the band, because the *Off the Wall* songs were clearly superior, and there was not yet a solo MJ tour. During one sound check, absent-mindedly noodling on his keyboard, Bill Wolfer started plucking out "I Can't Help It" from *Off the Wall*. Michael zoomed over— "like a moth attracted to a flame," Wolfer remembers—and instantly began to sing along. Afterward, singer and pianist agreed they loved that song. "We should do it!" Wolfer told Michael. "I wish we could,"

Michael agreed sadly. Then somebody called him away. *We can do it,* Wolfer thought. *Let's get rid of the song about the rat.* He did not speak up, and "Ben" remained number four on the set list.

One omission was "Dancing Machine," which by 1981 was seven years old and symbolic of the old days, when the Jacksons had no control over their music and were languishing as they grew up at Motown. That meant no Robot. During the *Destiny* tour, Michael had begun to fiddle with something new—something that looked eerily like he was moving forward and backward at the same time. He'd practice it in hotel-room mirrors. By *Triumph*, he was doing it onstage during rehearsals and sound checks. Only the band and crew got to see it. "They cleared out the rehearsal space—just a few of us allowed in there," recalls Reed Glick, the lighting man. "He started out doing dance steps, and the next thing I knew, he was floating across the stage."

Also new were the effects. For the *Triumph* tour, celebrity magician Doug Henning's Illusion Team created a breathtaking stunt involving a life-size cylinder covered with flash paper. Michael climbed nightly into the cylinder, which rose into the air, and once the flash paper burned away, he was gone. Then he reappeared on the other side of the stage, surrounded by six-foot flames. It took a few shows for the crew to get the timing right, and early in the tour, the crowd witnessed Michael climbing back on top of the stage from underneath. Michael was furious. "This isn't working!" he despaired. "You guys aren't trying real hard! I don't understand what's happening!" The crew calmed him down, and soon mastered the effects.

Michael's look was changing. His Afro, which had survived through the *Destiny* era, was replaced with a trendy, frizzy mullet, and fans who paid close attention noticed something new about his nose, not to mention his body, which seemed impossibly skinny due to his strict vegetarianism and his nightly dance routines and non-stop rehearsal. His spins throughout "Things I Do for You" and the Motown medley were tighter than ever, more purposeful, beginning with a *Soul Train*–style leg kick, ending with the walking-backward move that Michael was just starting to develop. As always, he came out at the end of every show in his black-and-white *Off the Wall* tuxedo, perfectly tailored to fit his body this time. It was this image that *Rolling Stone* would use years later to illustrate the show in its "Greatest Performances" issue.

Mike Mckinney noticed fans' growing obsession with Michael in subtle ways. The bassist would send his clothes out to be cleaned, and they'd never come back to his room. That was puzzling, until Mckinney realized his first name had been printed on the clothes: "Anytime they saw the name 'Michael,' it gets ripped off." Girls screamed with the first note, launching themselves onto the stage, crawling toward the Jacksons until bodyguards flipped them back into the audience.

Although Michael had canceled two dates on the *Triumph* tour due to exhaustion, he was creatively energized when he returned to Hayvenhurst in late 1981. He threw himself into renovating the family house, sketching out a white-marble lobby floor, emerald-green carpets, central chandelier, sweeping staircase, brick fireplace, and bedroom suites. His personal quarters would contain a hair salon with a barber's swivel chair, large hot tub, barbecue area festooned with tile, a courtyard of cobblestones with a lamppost, a street sign that said HAPPINESS, and a mock toy store with a display window of porcelain dolls, toy soldiers, and teddy bears. Next to the garage he would install a facsimile of Disneyland, including a candy store and a talking Abraham Lincoln robot. His theater played Fred Astaire and Three Stooges movies. His bathroom faucets were brass swans. Workers wouldn't break ground until 1983, so his creative energy soon transferred into songwriting—"like a machine," Quincy Jones said. On Christmas Day 1981, Paul McCartney recalled: "Michael rang me and said he wanted to come over and make some hits." (They had befriended each other years earlier at a party on a ship docked in Long Beach.) They met at McCartney's London office, where they quickly invented the basic structure of "The Girl Is Mine." Michael wrote most of the words later at his hotel.

Quincy Jones began to reassemble the gang from *Off the Wall*— the "A-Team," including engineer Bruce Swedien and songwriter Rod Temperton—with bigger ambitions. They convened at Westlake Studios, a nondescript beige building on Beverly Boulevard in LA. Outside it looked like a plain, unmarked storefront, but inside it was sleek and modern, with large stones festooned on the walls and simulated tree bark lining the doors. It had the feel of the house in *The Brady Bunch*. Everybody liked it dark. If they were staying up all night recording music, the last thing they wanted to see was the sun—it reminded them daylight still existed, and the outside world went on without them.

Michael wanted to top *Off the Wall*, both creatively and commercially. "No matter what you do, you are competing against your previous product, and everybody expects more," he told a reporter at the time. "Just like motion pictures: *Raiders of the Lost Ark, Star Wars, Jedi*. You really try to top yourself all the time, and it's hard." He also felt snubbed by his peers in the recording industry, who had inexplicably given a Grammy Award for Album of the Year to Billy Joel's *52nd Street* rather than *Off the Wall* (which wasn't even nominated). Somehow, "Don't Stop 'til You Get Enough," perhaps MJ's greatest dance song, received only one award, Best R&B Performance, while the Doobie Brothers' "What a Fool Believes" scored Song of the Year. "I felt ignored by my peers and it hurt," he said. "I said to myself, 'Wait until next time.'"

Jones's A-Team felt more deadline pressure. They were behind from the start, because Quincy was working on the storybook album for *E.T.*, with MJ himself reading the story and providing a new ballad called "Someone in the Dark." CBS Records was unsympathetic, demanding an album timed to the week before Thanksgiving, the kickoff for the crucial holiday-shopping season.

"Everybody was working twenty-four hours a day and had five rooms going at the same time," recalls Humberto Gatica, one of the album's engineers.

The musician-recruitment process was rushed and occasionally humorous. Steve Lukather, a member of hit pop band Toto and one of Quincy's favorite guitarists, was introduced to Michael Jackson in an unusual way. The singer called him at 8:30 A.M.—an absurd hour for a twenty-two-year-old Los Angeles musician who worked eighteen hours a day on studio sessions—and introduced himself. "Fuck off," Lukather said, and hung up. Eventually, Quincy Jones's office intervened, and Lukather found himself apologizing to Michael. "Don't worry," MJ assured him, "it happens all the time."

Quincy and the crew began work on what would become *Thriller* in August 1982. "Okay, guys," Quincy told his team, "we're here to get the kids out of the video arcades and back into the record stores." This was a timely mission statement, due to the sad state of the record industry—disco had crashed, and CDs had yet to kick in.

At first, the A-Team had exactly one finished track, a demo of which Michael had created earlier with McCartney: "The Girl Is Mine." Waiting to hear a cassette version of the song, guitarist Lukather and his Toto band mate, drummer Jeff Porcaro, had wishfully envisioned something like "Sgt. Pepper's Lonely Hearts Club Band" meets "Don't Stop 'til You Get Enough." But after Quincy sent it to Porcaro's house, they laughed. "'The doggone girl is mine'—really? *This* is the song?" they said to each other. They showed up for a three-day recording session in Tucson, Arizona, met Beatles producer George Martin and engineer Geoff Emerick, and found themselves playing a long jam of Stevie Wonder's "I Was Made to Love Her" with Paul and Michael trading vocals. "It was funkier than a motherfucker," Lukather recalls. He and Porcaro kept to themselves, ignoring the assembled "odd group of celebrities" on hand to witness the recording, including, inexplicably, child star Kristy McNichol and game-show host Bob Eubanks. When the pianist, Toto's David Paich, started absent-mindedly plunking out the Beatles' "A Day in the Life," Paul and Linda McCartney joined the band in the studio. Although Paich later said he wished "The Girl Is Mine" had been "a better piece of material," the final version of the song would be a crucial opening move in the campaign to break *Thriller* to the widest possible audience—and smash racial barriers in radio, records, and video in the process.

Beyond "The Girl Is Mine," Quincy began to gather six or seven hundred songs for possible use on the album. Some came from Michael. Some came from other songwriters: "When it was known that Quincy was getting ready to go in the studio for the next Michael Jackson album, every songwriter and music publisher wanted to have a track on that record," recalls Matt Forger, the album's technical engineer. Jones and Temperton listened to each potential album track before whittling them down to ten or twelve. Jones had a process he called "Polaroids"—directing Michael and his all-star team to figure out the arrangement, the key, and the tempo. The process was time-consuming. "I've never seen Quincy so into anything. Ever," Swedien recalled.

Jones had made dozens of film scores, and he knew how to use sound to build drama. "It wasn't how most people made records that I was involved with," says synthesizer specialist Anthony Marinelli. "It was so visual. . . . They cast musicians and arrangers. And like a film, they'd throw all this stuff on the cutting-room floor. They were really looking for that big picture." MJ, with his love for Fred Astaire movies, clicked with this approach.

Michael built his songs from the bottom up, scatting melodies over rhythmic ideas on early working versions of "Billie Jean," "Beat It," and "Wanna Be Startin' Somethin'." To help him translate thoughts into sixteen-track demos, he continued to work with the musicians he'd brought to his home studio. Keyboardist Bill Wolfer soon became an expert on distinguishing Temperton songs from MJ songs. "Rod Temperton had that Quincy Jones sound, which was great—Michael was a fit to it," Wolfer says. "A [Jackson] song like 'Don't Stop 'til You Get

Enough,' that's an extension of what he was doing on *Destiny* or *Triumph*—riff-based, the harmony doesn't change, a groove song. Quincy was able to make it all hang together."

Michael had "Wanna Be Startin' Somethin'" left over from *Off the Wall*. It was the perfect successor to "Don't Stop 'til You Get Enough," with a dance groove that seemed to last forever. He had worked on a demo off and on for months, as far back as the 1979 *Destiny* tour, when he confided to band mates his idea for the "mama-say-mama-sa-ma-ma-koo-sa" bit he'd nicked from Cameroonian star Manu Dibango's seven-year-old hit "Soul Makossa." (Dibango sued Jackson for plagiarism immediately after *Thriller* came out for one million French francs, and MJ quickly settled for somewhere between $25,000 and $50,000—a pittance.) Michael had completed a version of "Startin' Somethin'" months earlier, with the Waters singers on backup vocals. By the time it came to Quincy's attention, it was nearly finished.

"Startin' Somethin'," the first track on *Thriller*, is one of Michael's best vocal performances. After three explosive pops of the drums and a Louis Johnson slap-bass that resembles prison bars slamming shut, Michael lays down his vocal foundation for the album: tense, through his front teeth, more like James Brown than the happy kid from much of *Off the Wall*. The lyrics are dark and fierce, building on themes that Michael introduced two years earlier on "This Place Hotel": Women are scary. The world is scary. The pain is like thunder. Somebody's tongue becomes a razor. A baby cries. Toward the end, the Dibango chant matches the strength of Johnson's bass line. Michael flies above them, soaring and whooping. Searching for percussion for the track, Michael had told Quincy, "There's a sound I want." Somewhere at Westlake, he found a piece of plyboard and stood it up against a wall in the bathroom. Swedien set up one of the dozens of microphones from his elaborate collection, and Michael, his assistant Nelson Hayes, and Jones's driver Steven Ray pounded on it with their hands and feet. "We created this unusual kind of a sound that couldn't be duplicated with a keyboard," recalls Ray, who with Jackson and Hayes would be immortalized in the *Thriller* liner notes as playing the "bathroom stomp board."

MJ had been working on another song for months. He and Wolfer had created demos of it at his home studio. Michael kept a huge cockatoo in a wrought-iron cage. During a break, Michael scooped up a handful of birdseed, went to the front door of the studio, and stood entirely still, holding the seed in his outstretched palm. Wolfer watched with his mouth open as a blue jay flew across the yard, landed in Michael's hand, and devoured the seed. "This guy is different," Wolfer thought.

Michael had asked Wolfer to translate what he heard in his head—a bass line and a rough idea of what Wolfer calls "that three-chord vamp." In Jackson's studio, it took Wolfer almost forty-five minutes to find the harmony part in the loose musical idea Jackson was communicating to him. But Michael wasn't satisfied.

"He couldn't play an instrument. He could barely play a few notes on a keyboard," Wolfer recalls. "He'd come up with not only elaborate songs but elaborate arrangements, in his head, and he'd stick to them. You might lose things you hear in your head. He'd keep his vision and be as patient as he could be until finally he'd say, 'Yeah, that's it.'" It took a while, but Wolfer nailed it. "He knew what he wanted," adds Jerry Hey, who worked on string arrangements for "Billie Jean" at Michael's home studio. "He wasn't a technical musician. He didn't say, 'Play this chord here,' but he could definitely sing it and he had unbelievable rhythm and time."

The 1981 demo for "Billie Jean" begins with Michael asking for "more bottom and kick in the phones" and includes fascinatingly amorphous scat-singing in lieu of lyrics. At his home studio, Michael had recorded the drum machine and Greg Phillinganes had laid down the bass line with a mini-Moog keyboard. Wolfer added the keyboard part with a Yamaha CS-80 synthesizer. Later, Louis Johnson re-recorded the bass line so it sounded less like a tinkly keyboard and more like chunks of rubber set on fire and bounced against the studio walls in precise rhythm. The demo had already been recorded by the time it got to Johnson, but the loquacious bass player recalls Michael approaching him, in his high voice, to describe the part as "dit dit dit dit!" "No," Johnson told him, "it's not gonna go like that. That ain't bass." He adds: "I went in there and showed him how it's supposed to. I double-tracked. I had two basses on there." Johnson tried three or four of his many basses before he and Michael agreed on a Yamaha; he overdubbed three different parts to get the thick riff, and Phillinganes later added his synthesizer bass (as he did on most *Thriller* songs). Swedien used sixteen-track tape, a little thicker than for the twenty-four-track equipment he usually used, to get a fuller sound. For the rhythm, he made one track with a drum machine and the other with drummer Ndugu Chancler's nine-piece wooden jacaranda kit. Everybody who heard it immediately knew it was a hit. Quincy didn't want to call it "Billie Jean" at first because he thought people would associate it with tennis star Billie Jean King, but eventually he made the obvious, correct decision.

As the world knows by now, Michael fleshed out his "Billie Jean" scat-singing into a story about a man confronted by a woman who claims to be the mother of his child. Who was the real Billie Jean? Who knows? In public, Michael insisted she didn't exist: "The girl in the song is a composite of people we've been plagued by over the years." In private, he told Chancler he was thinking about a specific girl: "There was a story about Michael getting up to get something out of the refrigerator over at Hayvenhurst, and this girl had jumped the fence and was sitting at the kitchen table waiting for him," the drummer recalls. "We talked about the lack of privacy that existed in his life, with all the girls and people carrying kids in." Theresa Gonsalves, who says she was Michael's girlfriend during his time filming *The Wiz* in New York, is the most vocal of the many women who have taken credit for it.

In the middle of recording "Billie Jean," Michael walked into the studio with a cardboard mailing tube under his arm. Matt Forger, the technical engineer, didn't think anything of it. But Swedien noticed

Michael had written all over it with Magic Marker. He sang through the mailing tube into Swedien's microphone. "He knew how to make that sound character unique," Forger recalls. "He knew the arrangements, he knew the notations, he knew every note the instruments played, all the vocals, all the lines, absolutely cold. He completely had every song memorized."

Jones was filling the nine song slots he'd mapped out for *Thriller* quickly. He had a vision for how this album would sell: "Two records per household." MJ could have made the funkiest James Brown album in the world, with "Wanna Be Startin' Somethin'," "Billie Jean," and "P.Y.T. (Pretty Young Thing)" at its core, but then all he ever would have done was become the newest James Brown. Both Quincy and Michael had broader goals. They needed a song that would appeal not only to hip young kids but their parents as well. They needed the perfect tearjerking ballad.

Quincy called David Paich, one of the two keyboardists for Toto, later famous for middle-of-the-road eighties hits such as "Africa" and "Rosanna." Through Quincy, Toto had emerged as sort of the house band for *Thriller*. Quincy asked Paich for some musical ideas, and Paich obligingly laid them down on a cassette. Quincy sent a messenger to Paich's house, where he was working with Steve Porcaro, to pick it up.

"Hey," Paich shouted to Porcaro from upstairs in his house, "Quincy's guy is coming over here. Put those two things we did yesterday down on cassettes, will you?"

They'd run out of cassettes, so Porcaro used an existing, unmarked one, flipping it over to dub two new grooves Paich had taped on side A. What Porcaro had forgotten was that the cassette contained a song *he* had written on side B. It was something he had noodled out after his daughter, Heather, a first-grader, had cried because a boy pushed her off the slide at school. Porcaro had blurted out the best fatherly advice he could think of: First, the boy probably had a crush on her; second, people can be strange sometimes; third, *it's human nature*. The lyrics weren't exactly polished—"horrible, self-indulgent things about my daughter, whatever," Porcaro recalls—but the chorus stuck in everybody's head in exactly the way a ballad should stick. When Quincy received the cassette, he queued up the wrong side and listened to Porcaro's song. "Human Nature." Quincy loved the title. He loved the chorus. He didn't like the verses. He asked Porcaro if he could get a prominent lyricist, John Bettis, to perform surgery.

"Absolutely," Porcaro said.

Quincy wanted the widest possible audience, and that involved crossing over to rock radio, the domain of white programmers who perceived their audiences would listen almost exclusively to Eric Clapton and Led Zeppelin. He asked his people for a hard-rocking hit; Michael brought him "Beat It." Instantly excited, Quincy instructed Toto's Porcaro and Lukather to lay down the sing-along rhythms, but Michael felt the snares needed more oomph. One day somebody hauled in a new *gran cassa* bass drum and began unwrapping it from its hard-paper packaging. Something fell on it and Michael whirled around. "What's that sound?" he asked. Swedien hauled everything into the studio bathroom, hung a microphone inside an instrument road case, and rolled tape while Michael pounded on the package. So Michael gets credit on "Beat It" as Drum Case Beater and the drums on the song go not *boom-chk* but *boom-CRASH.*

For "Beat It," Quincy and the rest of his A-Team sent for the Synclavier. "In its day, it was far and away the most sophisticated synthesizer available anywhere in the world," recalls Brian Banks, one of the album's synthesizer players. Noises from the Synclavier wound up all over *Thriller,* from the "BONG . . . BONG . . . BONG" tones* that open "Beat It" to the background drum programming throughout "Billie Jean" to the lush noises that stand in for strings on the title track.

---

*Those "BONG" noises had actually come standard with Synclavier models at the time. They had been programmed by a synthesizer pioneer, Denny Jaeger. When *Thriller* came out, Jaeger contacted Jackson's people and eventually received not only an album credit but keyboard-programming work on the follow-up album, *Bad.*

After the A-Team finished "Beat It," Quincy and Michael agreed it still needed something—a guitar solo. They already had two great guitarists on the track, Steve Lukather and Paul Jackson Jr., but neither commanded attention at rock radio. "What [Michael] was good at as a businessman was marketing: 'We're going to get Eddie Van Halen on "Beat It" because I'm going to sell to long-haired teenage males,'" says John Branca, his attorney. "He had a genius when it came to that." Quincy sent the tape to Van Halen, guitarist for his namesake band and one of the world's biggest rock stars. Eddie would claim he asked to move the guitar solo to a different place in the song, and Quincy agreed. Lukather, who also played bass on the track, remembers the story a different way: Eddie moved it on his own. It wasn't until Quincy heard Van Halen's finished solo, in the wrong place on the track, that he realized "Beat It" would need major studio surgery. "Me and [drummer] Jeff Porcaro had to fuckin' Frankenstein that piece of music back together again," Lukather recalls.

Van Halen's whining, high-pitched solo would become one of the song's signature features—it sounded unusual in the context of Michael Jackson, but not so much in hard rock. Considering Van Halen's involvement, Lukather thought "heavy metal." He recorded the track through Marshall amplifiers and sent Quincy a mix that wouldn't have seemed out of place on Van Halen's *Diver Down*. Q called back. "It's too much," he told Lukather. "You've got to get the small amps out. R&B radio won't play it." This was an important point. Quincy wanted rock-radio airplay, but he still wanted urban-radio play. Lukather did as he was told.

The A-Team kept working. They ordered food from Golden Bird, down the street from Westlake on Beverly Boulevard, which had been serving chicken of all kinds in Los Angeles since the early fifties. Everybody indulged but Michael. He preferred the bean patties and spinach at the health-food restaurant on Vine and Fountain. He made fun of the others: "Bawk, bawk!" Quincy teased him back: "You know you want some of this chicken." Not even the spicy tuna dip could entice

Michael. Vegetarians were rare back then, although drummer Chancler was one, too, and empathized. "There were always good meat/carnivore jokes going around," he recalls.

Within a few weeks, the team had successfully come up with nine finished songs. "We thought at one point we were done," keyboardist Greg Phillinganes said. "And Quincy was like, 'No, not so fast. We need certain missing elements.' Michael was pretty disappointed, but then that's how we got 'Lady' and 'Beat It.'" Landing in the dustbin was "Carousel," written by Michael Sembello, the guitarist who'd worked with the Jacksons on *Destiny* and written a huge hit, "Maniac," for the *Flashdance* soundtrack. It was a nice song, inoffensive, halfway between a ballad and a rocker, but as usual, Quincy was right: it didn't have the same dynamic quality of, say, "P.Y.T."

Because Temperton had come up with the title for *Off the Wall*, Quincy asked him to think something up for the new one. "Starlight Love" was the bland working title. Temperton went back to his hotel and thought up between two and three hundred alternate phrases. "Midnight Man" was his favorite. Quincy liked the mystery of it. Temperton kept brainstorming. The next morning, he woke up with the word *Thriller* in his head. "You could visualize it on the top of the *Billboard* charts," he said to himself. "You could see it in the merchandising. This one word jumped off the page at me." He hastily wrote lyrics to a newly retitled song.

"I'd always envisioned this talking section at the end and didn't know what we were going to do with it," Temperton said. "But one thing I'd thought about was to have somebody, a famous voice, in the horror genre, to do this vocal." Jones's wife at the time, actress Peggy Lipton, suggested Vincent Price, whose precise monotone was associated with horror and thrillers more than anybody else's in the world. Temperton wrote an Edgar Allan Poe–style bit in the cab en route to the studio for Price's session. He cut it so close that when his cab approached the studio, a limousine pulled up and the songwriter watched Price step out of it. "Go round the back!" he barked at the driver. He ran inside the back door and literally grabbed the secretary: "Photocopy this real quick," he ordered. He raced in with the new lyrics just as Price walked in and sat down in the booth. "Just hit it," Temperton recalled. "Two takes." "Thriller" became the title track of the album, and Quincy and Michael immediately began to see its monster-movie potential. Bruce Cannon, who had been an assistant editor on *E.T.*, provided sound edits—a creaking door, footsteps on wooden planks, howling dogs and ghost noises.

By the fall of 1982, Jackson and Jones were still messing with the *Thriller* album to the point that Epic Records had to push back the release date. Epic's parent company, CBS, had laid off thousands of people on what the industry called "Black Friday," August 13, 1982. The label desperately needed a hit, and Michael Jackson had proved with *Off the Wall* that he had the ability to move four or five million in sales. So the possibility that *Thriller* would miss its original Thanksgiving release date, and perhaps a 1982 release altogether, was an intimidating thought.

With Swedien's help, MJ and Quincy frantically tied up loose ends, alternating between three studio rooms at Westlake. Swedien went to work with his complicated techniques, recording rhythm tracks on sixteen-track tape, then switching to digital for a thick sound Quincy called "big legs and tight skirts." Michael added another round of vocals to "Billie Jean." Bruce kept splicing things in and out of the mix, just as he'd done on *Off the Wall*, frustrating the musicians yet again because they would have only a vague idea of who played on what.

When they finally finished, Swedien took the tape to Bernie Grundman's mastering studio. Quincy brought MJ to his house, covering him in a blanket, so he could nap from nine A.M. to noon. They had an appointment to hear the final test pressing of the album before they sent it to Larkin Arnold, by then Epic's head of black music, who had been readying champagne bottles in New York. Michael and Quincy showed up, Grundman queued up the album and . . . it was like a cake had fallen. "It was a disaster," Quincy said. "After all the great songs and the great performances and great mixes and a great tune stack, we had twenty-four-karat sonic doo-doo." Arnold had a bad feeling in his chest. "Oh my God," he thought, sadly contemplating the unopened champagne. "We are not going to make the delivery date if we have to remix it. I can't even drink." Jones told him not to worry, but Arnold spent the next two days in a haze.

Among other things, Jones realized, they had recorded too much music, even with just nine songs. "You need big, fat grooves to make it happen on vinyl," Jones said. "We had twenty-four to twenty-seven minutes [per side], which makes the sound smaller. We had to get it down to nineteen to twenty minutes." Arnold told Quincy the album was "unreleasable." Was it? "I'm not exactly sure," Grundman recalls. "They didn't exactly let me know what they were doing. I know they disappeared, and I didn't see them for quite a while." Quincy instructed the exhausted A-Team to take two days off. That was all they could afford. Holiday shopping season wasn't going to take a break, even for the new Michael Jackson album.

They spent the next eight days rebuilding *Thriller*. They mixed one new tune every day. Temperton cut a verse from "The Lady in My Life." "Smelly finally agreed to give up some of the jelly in the long, long, long intro to 'Billie Jean,'" Quincy recalled. Finally, the album was ready for Grundman to perform some of his own magic. He pumped up the kick drum on "Billie Jean" and added a little more "top end" to the ballads. They had their new mix. "There's more depth and more air—so it really wraps around you," Grundman says. "It definitely came at you in a better way. It seemed to flow better. It seemed to connect better emotionally. When you put it on, it was just kind of more alive."

On November 30, 1982, Larkin Arnold could finally drink his champagne.

CHAPTER 5

Two weeks before *Thriller* came out, Jon Badeaux obtained an advance reel-to-reel tape of the album. Badeaux was the music director of an LA R&B-leaning pop radio station, KDAY-AM, and he had been waiting for new Michael Jackson music for three years. *Thriller* was on lockdown. Epic Records was strictly controlling the release schedule, being careful to release singles one at a time, on the same day, so every radio station had equal access. But Badeaux scored a copy of the tape from a friend who knew Quincy Jones. After one listen, he knew every cut was a hit, with the possible exception of "The Lady in My Life." Before Thanksgiving 1982, he waited until five P.M. on a Friday, strategically, because he knew record-label lawyers would have already returned home for the weekend, thus temporarily unavailable to issue legal cease-and-desist notices. His station started playing *Thriller*.

When Badeaux returned home for the evening, his unlisted phone number was ringing. "You've got to take it off!" the Epic executives pleaded with him. One poor record guy, taking the blame for the leak, actually cried. Epic hadn't released the album to stores, yet, so nobody who heard *Thriller* could buy it. Plus, favoring one radio station over another meant all of Badeaux's rivals would be furious. (That part didn't bother him too much.) But KDAY stuck to *Thriller* all weekend. The phone lines lit up. Listeners actually drove to the station's offices in an attempt to buy the album. Eventually, Epic had no choice but to release the album a few days early. "It was so electrifying that you just could not get enough of it," says Elroy Smith, then program director of Boston's WILD.

Every radio station with a black audience, like KDAY and WILD, instantly used *Thriller* to boost its ratings into the stratosphere. White stations needed an extra push. In 1982, the music world was only three years removed from DJ Steve Dahl's disco demolition riot at Comiskey Park in Chicago. The violent backlash had made Top 40 radio programmers skittish about airing almost any type of black music, and the rare urban (meaning *black*) single that crossed over to pop (*white*) boosted sales dramatically. In 1982, only two singles by African-Americans made the top ten, Lionel Richie's "Truly" and Stevie Wonder's "Ebony and Ivory" (a duet with Paul McCartney).

The entire record industry operated along these racial lines—veteran record executive T. C. Thompkins was promoted to vice president of promotions for Epic Records in the early eighties, but he was only allowed to promote black records to black radio stations. While Epic's white promotions departments were crammed with employees—secretaries, assistants, directors—Thompkins found himself with one lone assistant. "It wasn't any less racist there than it was in the street," Thompkins says. "You're a 'black vice president' in name only. You had none of the tools of the facilities that were made available to the pop department. As quiet as it was kept, as progressive as the industry was supposed to be, segregation was alive and well."

Off the Wall had been fortunate enough to come out in disco-crazy 1979, when 40 percent of songs that reached the top three were by African-Americans, and four singles from MJ's disco-sounding album landed in the top ten. But Michael Jackson felt it should have sold far more—he was beginning to develop his vision for *Thriller* as the best-selling album in history—and one executive at Epic Records agreed. In 1981, MJ and Katherine and Joe Jackson met with Epic's Larkin Arnold at a delicatessen on Ventura Boulevard in Los Angeles. Michael complained the label had done too little to promote *Off the Wall*. He saw no billboards. He saw no push to use the "Rock with You" video he'd filmed—this was before MTV—in which he dances in a gray sparkly outfit and moon boots in front of rotating lasers. He felt Epic saw no need to try harder to cross him over. Arnold promised MJ and his parents that the label would get behind *Thriller*.

Arnold sent "The Girl Is Mine" to white Top 40 stations as a strategic early strike, three weeks before the album release. "This was an attempt, by using Paul McCartney, to break that resistance to white radio," Arnold says. "That was the plan." It worked—the duet hit No. 1 on the black singles chart and No. 2 on the pop chart.

In February 1983, Epic followed up "The Girl Is Mine" with "Billie Jean," and just as the single hit No. 1, the label's promotional staff broke tradition. Usually singles came out one at a time, with one making its debut just as the other began to drop off the pop charts. Instead, Epic released a third single even as "Billie Jean" was still a smash. Frank DiLeo, at that time one of Epic's top marketing executives, took credit for that part of the strategy. "I had this idea that I ran by him—when 'Billie Jean' reached No. 1, I was going to release 'Beat It,'" DiLeo* says. "All of a sudden, I had both singles on the top five." Michael liked this. DiLeo was a funny, fast-talking, short, bald, cigar-smoking singles whisperer. Michael would keep him in mind.

The next single, "Beat It," contained the Van Halen guitar solo engineered to break rock radio's racial barriers. Programmers were at first resistant. In Detroit, WRIF had a playlist based on Zeppelin and Hendrix. Fred Jacobs, the station's program director, did not always

---

*It helped that DiLeo spent $100,000 per single on "independent promotion," a shady variation on payola involving middlemen who took money from record labels and gave it to radio programmers, according to Fredric Dannen's *Hit Men*.

share his audience's opinions, and one night, DJing at three A.M. in the days before *Thriller*, he had thrown on a new song by Prince. The phones exploded. "What are you doing?" came the irate calls. "Are you out of your mind? Why are you playing *that shit?*" Lee Abrams, a rock-radio specialist who consulted for 125 stations, adds: "Historically, the Michael Jackson sound was not us, just like the O'Jays wasn't us." But some of Abrams's stations, including Detroit's WLLZ, played "Beat It" anyway. "What's that song?" listeners asked when they called stations en masse. "Can you play it again?"

CBS had commissioned Steve Barron for a $50,000 video for "Billie Jean," and the British director saw firsthand what the public was about to learn about Michael Jackson. In the video, holding his black leather sports coat over his shoulder, Sinatra-style, MJ spins, makes sharp, knee-bending movements, then lands on his toes and holds the pose for a solid two seconds. Barron held a camera on his shoulder, moving backward and forward as the music played, straining to catch everything. "He burst into this incredible movement. The heat and the energy coming off me as I was tracking him made the whole thing just steam up," Barron recalls. But MTV did not play Barron's video for "Billie Jean" at first, and the reason is convoluted. In its early days, following the example of Top 40 and rock stations in the post-disco era, the network had a reputation for refusing to play artists from Rick James to James Brown. Frustrated with the lack of broadcast time for his funky classic "Super Freak," James said the channel was "taking black people back four hundred years." Miles Davis approached J. J. Jackson, the channel's only African-American VJ, at a party and grilled him; David Bowie did the same to VJ Mark Goodman after an on-air interview.

"Billie Jean" was No. 1 and had been out for two months by the time it landed on MTV in April 1983. It was impossible to ignore. Yet CBS Records executives swear the channel refused to play it until Walter Yetnikoff, the label's fiery president, delivered an ultimatum.

"He called up top MTV executive Bob Pittman and in so many words basically said, 'You know all those Bruce Springsteen and Cheap Trick and Charlie Daniels videos that you guys are playing over there? Pack 'em all up, put 'em in a box, and send 'em back. We are no longer in business together,'" recalls Ron McCarrell, an executive at Epic Records. Responds Les Garland, a top MTV executive at the time: "People ask me if Sony threatened to pull their videos off MTV. It never happened. Folklore, man, folklore. The whole Michael Jackson story about MTV and the racism and all that is such a bunch of bullshit."

Who's right? It's impossible to say for sure. "If key CBS executives are lying, it's to exaggerate their power and importance," write Rob Tannenbaum and Craig Marks in *I Want My MTV*. "If MTV executives are lying, it's to disguise the fact that they had to be forced to play a singer who more or less saved their network."

Either way, MJ integrated radio and MTV. In the three and a half years after white rock fans stamped out disco, and before *Thriller*, black stars such as Lionel Richie had to make middle-of-the-road pop music and behave in a certain inoffensive way in public in order to cross over to broader stardom. Barack Obama would run into this same issue twenty-five years later during a similar kind of time in politics and navigate it with as much grace as Michael Jackson did during the *Thriller* days. "He broke the boundaries," the Black Eyed Peas' will.i.am says of MJ. "There wouldn't be an Obama if it wasn't for the Jackson 5. There wouldn't be an Obama if there wasn't a Motown."

For "Beat It," the follow-up to "Billie Jean," Michael's heart was already set on a *West Side Story* dance concept involving gangs. By this time, MTV's power had kicked in, and director Bob Giraldi's budget was quadruple that of "Billie Jean." It was Jackson's idea to use real gang members. Ron Weisner, his manager, helped with the logistics. He went to downtown LA with a couple of Jackson's security guys and some police officers and met with Crips and Bloods. "Look, here's what we're looking to do," Weisner told them. "If you'd like to participate, we'd love to have you. But we can't afford any problems."

"We're in," they said.

The actors and crew had been rehearsing in a downtown LA warehouse when two busloads of Crips and Bloods pulled up and walked in, girlfriends on their arms, eyeing the dancers in tights. They put on menacing faces and scared the crap out of just about everyone. They temporarily calmed down upon discovering the free cigarettes available on the set, then nearly pushed Giraldi into walking off the set, "smacking each other around." When Michael Jackson finally strode in, the tough-guy gangbangers turned into sniveling fanboys. "These people switched to the nicest people ever," Popin Pete, one of the dancers, recalls. "He did something probably their parents couldn't even do, which is to make them smile."

One might think an openly gay choreographer of Broadway shows would not have the ideal skill set for soothing Crips and Bloods, but Michael Peters was the right dancer for the job. He had grown up living in a housing project in Williamsburg, Brooklyn, son of a white mother and a black father. Although his parents strived to live in integrated neighborhoods, Peters had been beaten up by classmates of both races. Just as piano became a solace for Quincy Jones, dance represented a more accepting world for Peters. He joined the prestigious Alvin Ailey dance company, did choreography for Donna Summer and Debbie Reynolds, and worked on the Tony-winning *Dreamgirls*. He represented an amalgamation of Fred Astaire and the Electric Boogaloos, old and new, white and black—just what Michael was looking for.

Until "Beat It," Peters had essentially turned clumsy music stars such as Pat Benatar and Lionel Richie into competent video dancers. Michael Jackson was different. The star showed his broad physical ideas to the choreographer, who solidified them into routines and explained them to other dancers. "I worked with him totally on a rhythmic basis. He's not a trained dancer, so he has none of the vocabulary," Peters said. "He'd say to me, 'I want a cool step here,' or 'I want a step that's hot and angry.' He'd describe it in emotional terms or even in terms of color." Peters was heavily influenced by *West Side Story*, which made him ideal for the back-and-forth "Beat It" gang fantasy and to solve this new, real-life problem between the Crips and Bloods on the video set.

Peters, dressed in white and wearing sunglasses, and Vince Paterson, a dancer who portrayed the other gang leader in the video, attacked each other with rubber knives. They had been lovers at the time, so the impromptu performance contained real emotional chemistry. They didn't know Giraldi had pulled off a sneaky, dangerous trick. For the second take, he called his assistant director and told him to secretly substitute a *real* switchblade for the rubber knife. "That's illegal," the AD warned, but Giraldi felt the real blades had the effect of frightening Michael Jackson and Michael Peters and impressing the Crips and Bloods. (Popin Pete remembers the scene differently: "Most of the gangbangers [said], 'Using a switchblade, that's like so 1950s.' For them it was funny. 'Where's the gun? Who's going to bring a switchblade to a fight?'")

"Weird Al" Yankovic would memorably mock the poofy hair and ridiculous eighties fashion statements in "Beat It." The tough guy in Al's "Eat It" diner opens the video with a spit take; the guy emerging from his manhole is so fat he can't squeeze onto the street; his dance in the shadowy hallway includes an exaggerated bite of a sandwich. "Back when MTV was in its music-video heyday, the popular clips were played so often that they were seared into everyone's brains," Yankovic says today. "So I knew I would only have to tweak the slightest detail and people would get the joke immediately."

"Beat It" transcends its parody. By then, Michael Jackson was putting everything together—Astaire's grace, the spins and twirls he'd learned from Brown and Wilson, the sophisticated tap dancing he'd inherited from variety-show guest stars such as the Nicholas Brothers, the high leg kicks and Robot moves from *Soul Train*, the miming from Marcel Marceau, Shields and Yarnell, and Charlie Chaplin, and the popping-and-locking energy from underheralded TV dancers of the time such as Pop N Taco and Boogaloo Sam. For "Beat It," Peters added the Worm. Vince Paterson described it this way: "As you back up, the body makes a wormlike movement, like a wave," Paterson says. "You just send this energy wave from your pelvis to the tip of your head." MJ would use the move for years.

In 1983, Suzanne de Passe, still Berry Gordy's loyal number two, had an idea to revitalize the famous but fading Motown Records. She pitched Gordy a twenty-fifth-anniversary reunion show. Profits would go to charity. Gordy liked the idea and thought he could talk most of his former stars into it. He was wrong, at least at first. Diana Ross was living a new kind of life—without Gordy. She spent her days hobnobbing with fashion designers like Halston and Calvin Klein, dining at the Four Seasons, hanging out at Studio 54, and vacationing at her new manor in Fairfield, Connecticut. Her first RCA album, *Why Do Fools Fall in Love*, hit the top ten, and the follow-up, *Silk Electric*, had gone gold, thanks in part to Michael Jackson's heavy-breathing, finger-snapping contribution on the song "Muscles" (which Michael produced, wrote, and named after his boa constrictor). When de Passe called about *Motown 25*, Ross declined. But de Passe knew Ross. She went to the press, predicting Ross would show up as a "special guest star." Ross fans became excited, and the singer realized she couldn't back out without looking bad. So she accepted the invitation.

Stevie Wonder said okay, if he could make it back in time from a tour of Africa. Marvin Gaye was in, if Gordy asked him personally. Ross's *Lady Sings the Blues* costar Richard Pryor, still the world's hottest comedian despite his growing drug problems, agreed to emcee. And Michael Jackson . . . he agreed, too, but how he came to do so depends on who tells the story. According to Berry, Jackson felt overexposed on television and was inclined to sit in the audience and silently show his support. So a cowed Gordy begged him.

Motown's Suzee Ikeda, who worked as a liaison between the Jackson 5 and their record label in the old days, tells it differently. It was ten days before the taping when Jermaine Jackson, still a Motown recording artist, began to call her repeatedly.

"Nobody's asked my brothers to do the show!" Jermaine complained.

"You're kidding," Ikeda said.

"Suzanne hasn't asked them," he responded.

Ikeda called Gordy and asked permission to go over de Passe's head, to call Michael directly for a commitment. He agreed. When Ikeda and Jackson talked, old Motown friends catching up, she was careful to bring up other subjects before *Motown 25*. Finally, she said: "Everybody's coming back to do this show. You've got to do this show," she said. "If the Jackson 5, one of the biggest acts in the company, don't come back to do it, it's not going to be the same."

"Okay," Michael said.*

In both Jermaine's recollection and in MJ's autobiography *Moonwalk*, Michael asked for a solo performance on the spot. Ikeda says it was Gordy who suggested Michael do the song, only privately to Ikeda, without even discussing it with Michael. "I don't think that's a good idea," Ikeda told Gordy. Later, serendipitously, Michael called Ikeda and said, "Berry's going to get mad, but I want to do something—'Billie Jean.'" Delighted, Ikeda strongly advised Michael not to let the regular live *Motown 25* band perform the music—"because they'll never get the groove." Michael and Ikeda thus agreed he would lip-synch his performance to the original track. Ikeda communicated the news to Gordy, who was thrilled.

The dancing itself required no negotiation. Michael would handle everything about that himself. "Nobody else worked with him on it,"

---

*In still another version of the story, Jermaine writes in his autobiography that his mother talked Michael into it, as she'd often done on behalf of Michael's brothers. The account ends the same way, with Michael saying, "Okay." But Ikeda doesn't buy it.

Ikeda says. "He told the director, he told everybody, how he wanted that stage, what type of lighting he wanted. He told them where to put the spotlight. 'When I put my finger like this . . .' He directed them."

Michael often claimed he invented the routine to "Billie Jean" spontaneously, because he had spent so much time rehearsing with his brothers for the show's Motown medley that he neglected everything else. What he did not say was how long he had been thinking about this performance.

The dance Michael chose, the backslide, was hardly new. Bill Bailey, an African-American tap-dancing star, pulled it off as early as the 1950s. Rocker David Bowie does a bit of the move in an early video for "Aladdin Sane." Mimes used it all the time—Marcel Marceau's famous routine "Walking in the Wind" was essentially the backslide by another name, and Robert Shields of Shields and Yarnell learned it from Marceau* himself. James Brown and Bill "Mr. Bojangles" Robinson, both influences on Michael, were among the greats who'd pulled it off. Many dancers would take credit for bestowing the backslide upon Michael Jackson—Damita Jo Freeman of *Soul Train* makes a credible claim, recalling that her lesson came backstage in Vegas in the late seventies. But it was two young dancers, Casper Candidate and Cooley Jaxson, who taught it to him directly.

In 1979, Casper and Cooley had appeared on *Soul Train*. They performed a dance called the Boogaloo, named after a street-dancing group, the Electric Boogaloos. For four minutes, dressed in black, they ignored the laws of gravity and physics, pulling off hip thrusts and acrobatic leaps set to MJ's "Workin' Day and Night."

Casper and Cooley aren't sure how their dance clip came to Michael Jackson's attention, but they suspect he watched the show as it aired—it was his song, after all. Some of those moves, particularly the pelvic thrusts and sideways motions that make dancers' legs look like rubber bands, had already landed in the "Beat It" video. As he was preparing for

---

*When Marceau died in 2007, MJ told *Jet* the moonwalk inspiration came not from the mime but from "watching the great, rhythmic, wonderful black children dance around the world."

his *Motown 25* performance, Michael asked one of his managers to track down the duo. Jaxson, auditioning for *Sesame Street Live* in San Francisco, flew to Los Angeles, where he met Candidate at a large rehearsal space. A boom box sat on the floor. Michael introduced himself. They talked for five hours. All he wanted to talk about was the backslide. "Where did it come from?" he kept asking. "Where did it start?"

They taught him the move. Unsurprisingly, MJ picked it up quickly. But he didn't think he did. "I can't feel it!" he kept saying.

"I understood that at the time," Cooley recalls. "It's more of a mime type of feel. Like you're making a box, but you're not making a box. If you're doing it, it looks like you're gliding."

Cooley has spent much of his career giving credit to others for the backslide—Bill Bailey, James Brown, Shields and Yarnell. What frustrates him, years later, is that Jackson wasn't similarly aggressive about giving credit to his forebears. In *Moonwalk*, Michael refers to the move as "a break-dance step, a 'popping' type of thing that black kids had created dancing on street corners in the ghetto." "We kind of ended up being invisible," says Cooley, now in his early fifties. "But we never said anything about it."

The night before the taping of *Motown 25: Yesterday, Today, Forever*, MJ rehearsed at Hayvenhurst. Katherine and La Toya were accustomed to Michael practicing every Saturday and Sunday in a room above the garage. "I'm sure he was doing the moonwalk up there, but we never knew it," Katherine said. In the kitchen, he played "Billie Jean." "I pretty much stood there and let the song tell me what to do," he recalled. "I kind of let the dance create itself. I really let it *talk* to me; I heard the beat come in, and I took this spy's hat and started to pose and step, letting the 'Billie Jean' rhythm create the movements. I felt almost compelled to let it create itself. I couldn't help it." Michael obviously had been thinking about 1974's *The Little Prince*, in which a grown man befriends a magical young boy in a double-breasted peacoat. The great choreographer Bob Fosse shows up as a snake, modeling a half-dozen poses, gestures, and struts MJ would use for years, in the moonwalk and beyond.

Having secured the talent, de Passe and Gordy were able to make a *Motown 25* deal with NBC. They booked the Pasadena Civic Auditorium on March 25, 1983. During rehearsals, thirty-eight-year-old Diana Ross showed up in a long, white mink coat, Courvoisier in hand, worrying Gordy and de Passe by declaring she had the stomach flu. But the night of the show, she emerged from her limo glamorous as ever, mugging for photographers. Because the producers wanted young, new talent in the show, they hired British MTV star Adam Ant to perform "Where Did Our Love Go?" in awkward new-wave makeup and what appeared to be a Revolutionary War costume. "Now what *Adams Ant* had to do with Motown, you tell me. I have no idea," says veteran Motown singer and songwriter Valerie Simpson, upset to this day that a songwriter segment she'd hosted was cut from the program. Ant, though, was intertwined with Motown history. Gordy had once tried to sign him, which led to his spending the day with Michael Jackson and his family at their house on Hayvenhurst. Later, Michael called about the distinctive brocade jacket Ant had worn in the "Kings of the Wild Frontier" video. Ant put MJ in touch with his supplier, and the next thing he knew, Michael was wearing military jackets everywhere. Watching Michael on *Motown 25*, Ant's concern was simply, "How the fuck do you follow that?" Says Ant: "It was like the Beatles on *Ed Sullivan*, that's what it was."

Michael Jackson and his brothers had taken the stage for the *Motown 25* taping in a conquering mood. Jackie wore a bright-green glittery open-collar shirt and black leather pants. Marlon was in a *Sgt. Pepper*–style topcoat; as a dancer, he had always fed off Michael, but this time he and Jackie came out as dueling dervishes. Jermaine returned to the band and provided an emotional boost. Michael, in particular, seemed moved to have him back. (None of the Jacksons had live microphones except Michael, so when Jermaine sang his bit in "I'll Be There," Michael walked over to share his mike with his brother, and they embraced; it was a beautiful moment of both reclaimed family unity and practiced showbiz.) It was the first time since Vegas that all the Jackson brothers were onstage together, a fact not lost on Michael, who couldn't contain himself when his younger brother, the newest member of the family group, came bounding onstage. "Randy!" he shouted.

Michael ran through "I Want You Back," "Never Can Say Goodbye," and "I'll Be There" exactly as he'd done for fourteen straight years. The Jackson 5 had always exuded an element of contained chaos—Michael had to keep his talent from spilling onto the stage in order to preserve his role within the group. He strutted and stepped in unison with his brothers, sporadically popping in front of them, spinning and crooning. The audience, both that night at the auditorium and a month later, when the show aired on NBC, had every reason to believe this performance would be the show's emotional peak.

Neither the viewers nor the Jackson brothers knew his costume throughout the reunion medley—black jacket covered in sequins (borrowed from his mother), silver lamé shirt, black trousers with high cuffs, white socks, Fred Astaire–style loafers, a white glove on his left hand containing 1,200 rhinestones sewn by hand, and a curly-mullet hairstyle matching the cover of *Thriller*—was designed not for sentimentality but action. After finishing their Motown medley, the brothers bounded offstage, proud, hugging each other, sipping generously, as always, from the crowd's adoration. Then Michael delivered a speech by *Motown 25* scriptwriter Buz Kohan. "Yeah," Michael said, as the applause died down. "Aw. You're beautiful."

The moment begins to resemble the color seeping into *The Wizard of Oz*—out of the past, into the present. "Yeah," Michael says again. "I have to say, those were the good old days." He speaks in short, declaratory sentences, breathing hard. "I love those songs," he says. "Those were magic moments. All my brothers. Including Jermaine. Those were good songs. I like those songs a lot." Then his tone changes, and Michael looks directly into the camera—he's Elvis Presley, aware of his power. "But especially, I like . . ." Somebody in the audience, a kid or a woman, audibly spoils the suspense: "*Billie Jean!*" Michael doesn't care. He raises his right eyebrow. He's star-

ing straight ahead but not at anything, looking beyond the crowd—
". . . the *new* songs."

Music history remembers this speech the way it remembers the
throwaway lines Presley, in the studio with his band, delivered in
1954. After halting the bluegrass ballad "Milkcow Blues Boogie," Elvis
declared, "Hold it, fellas. That don't *move* me. Let's get real, *real* gone
for a change." The resulting fast-paced version of "Milkcow" wasn't
technically the birth of rock 'n' roll, but listening today, it feels like it.
The moment echoed Benny Goodman, onstage in 1935 at Hollywood's
Palomar ballroom, initially leading his orchestra in super-slow dinner-
party music. When nobody paid attention, he reversed course with
Fletcher Henderson's jumping arrangement for "King Porter Stomp."
A dance-floor riot ensued and the big-band swing era was born.

Michael reaches down for his black fedora, which resembles the
bowler Bob Fosse wore in *The Little Prince*. His longtime assistant, Nelson P. Hayes, had placed it there while the camera had been focused elsewhere. "He must have made me rehearse that spot twenty times just to
make sure that hat was going to be there, where it was supposed to be,"
Hayes recalls. It's dawning on the old Motown pros gathered at the auditorium just how meticulously Michael had choreographed this moment.
Drums: Bum-*bap*, bum-*bap*, bum-*bap*. Michael twirls to the left.
He's posing, hat upside-down in his right hand. He plops the hat on his
head. *Bass*. Michael thrusts his crotch forward, again and again, then
kicks his right leg so it's almost horizontal. For the next six seconds, his
movements are so quick and fluid and connected that it's almost impossible to deconstruct and identify them. Michael splays his legs. He does
more kicks. He holds a pose, then another in the reverse direction. He
waves his hat to the right, but it's a basketball head fake, and instead
he tosses it offstage to the left. He claps. He tap-dances, glides a little.
Synths. Two more thrusts of the crotch, then a hair-combing motion—
the suggestion of a rockabilly greaser. At this time, Fred Astaire and
Gene Kelly are old men, and "The Band Wagon" and "Singin' in the

Rain" seem hopelessly out of fashion in the rock era. Michael is bringing them back—the elegance, the dance tricks that seem like magic. Michael concentrates their moves into tantalizing bursts.

As Michael mouths the first line of "Billie Jean"—"She was more like a beauty queen"—his feet are unable to stop, bouncing left and right. Finally he settles down, eyes closed, concentrating into the microphone, tapping his left foot to the beat. He punctuates certain lines—"she caused a SCENE"—with high kicks, nearly parallel to the floor. Every moment is more intriguing than the next—he plants his foot to spin in a tight circle like he did with the Jackson 5, then holds his fists to his face, as if pleading, like James Brown, before hiking up his pants to display his white socks. For a moment, the camera catches a glimpse of the audience, unusually racially diverse for a concert hall in 1983, blacks and whites clapping together in tuxedos and gowns. The "Billie Jean" guitar solo arrives and recedes.

Finally, as Michael executes the moonwalk, formerly known as the backslide, formerly a dance belonging to the Electric Boogaloos, Cab Calloway, James Brown, Damita Jo Freeman, Casper and Cooley, Jeffrey Daniel, Mr. Bojangles, Bob Fosse, Marcel Marceau, and Shields and Yarnell, a sort of screech erupts from the crowd. "During rehearsals, he never did *that*. Only when he did the show," recalls Russ Terrana, who as Motown's veteran chief recording engineer was outside in the sound truck, taping *Motown 25* for posterity. "My crew just went, 'What the hell was that?' You could hear the audience going, 'Awwww-awwwww!'"

Another leg kick, another whoop, another pose on the toes, two more spins, another brief glimpse of the moonwalk, and Michael is done. Is something different about his nose? It looks sculpted, precise, fussy, with thin little nostrils, not big and bold like it used to be. If anybody lingers over this detail, it is lost, for now, in the bigger story about the moonwalk. He bows and he is off. His brothers, mouths open in the wings throughout the performance, recover enough to slap Michael on the back when he returns. Before long, all the Motown stars are huddled around him. "When everybody ran up to congratulate him, it was like he wasn't there. He had an out-of-body experience or something," Valerie Simpson recalls. "He couldn't respond to anybody. He wasn't back to himself yet. He couldn't come down to where he had gone to deal with us. It was just very, very eerie." Afterward, MJ would say he was preoccupied—he had meant to stay on his toes a few ticks longer during the performance, and he felt like he'd failed. Nobody else noticed.

The day after the show aired, on May 16, 1983, Michael Jackson received a call from Fred Astaire. ("Oh, come on," was Michael's first reaction.) Astaire was eighty-four. He had filmed his final movie, *Ghost Story*, two years earlier. "You're a hell of a mover. Man, you really put them on their asses last night," Fred Astaire told Michael Jackson. "You're an angry dancer. I'm the same way. I used to do the same thing with my cane." It remains a mystery exactly where the anger appears in Astaire's elegant ballroom dancing—his persona in movies is bemused and easygoing—but "Billie Jean" was, in fact, an angry song, reflecting Michael's feelings of fear and distrust for those around him. Michael was also angry at his father, who was still tomcatting around on Katherine and milking the family for cash.

"It was the greatest compliment I had ever received in my life," Jackson would say of Astaire's call, "and the only one I had ever wanted to believe."

After Michael spoke with Fred on the phone, he went into the bathroom and threw up.

Another thing happened the day after NBC aired *Motown 25*. "Our sales just exploded," recalls Ron McCarrell, then Epic Records' vice president of marketing. "It just kind of turned the turbo chargers on for that whole project. We shipped one million units a month for eighteen months. We were shipping 'em one way, and they weren't bringing them back." By the end of 1983, *Thriller* had sold twenty-two million copies.

"The *Thriller* phenomenon was so overwhelming, probably more than Beatlemania, more than Elvis," says John Branca, Michael's lawyer. "Studio heads, kings, queens—everybody wanted to get with Michael." It would change the life of everybody who worked on it.

The ascent of *Thriller* brought out the ugliness in Joe Jackson. Michael's managers, Weisner and DeMann, had been signed to one deal, and Joe had continued to manage him under a separate deal. In March 1983, two months before *Motown 25* aired, both deals expired. It was Michael who swung the ax. He remembered Weisner and DeMann predicting *Thriller* sales of a minuscule two million, when, after *Motown 25*, it was selling that amount every two weeks. Weisner received a letter one day from a lawyer saying the Weisner-DeMann management deal was over.

Publicly, Michael's split with Weisner-DeMann played out in the worst possible way. In the pages of *Billboard*, Joe Jackson declared the duo's contract expired, adding, "There are a lot of leeches trying to break up the group. A lot of people are whispering in Michael's ear. But we know who they are. They're only in it for the money. I was there before it started and I'll be there after it ends." *After it ends?* Joe said he hired Weisner and DeMann in the first place "because there was a time when I felt I needed white help in dealing with the corporate structure at CBS and thought they'd be able to help. But they never gave me the respect you expect from a business partner." *White help?*

Michael responded to his father's limited perspective by declaring himself a citizen of the world. "I don't know what would make him say something like that. To hear him talk like that turns my stomach. I don't know where he gets that from. I happen to be color-blind. I don't hire color; I hire competence. The individual can be of any race or creed as long as I get the best," Michael said in a statement. "I am president of my organization and I have the final word on every decision. Racism is not my motto. One day I strongly expect every color to love as one family."

Without Weisner and DeMann, Michael was rudderless at the

moment of his ascendance. He couldn't possibly revert to his father. John Branca had become a trusted adviser, but he was an attorney, not an experienced music manager.

Frank DiLeo, Michael's promotion man at Epic Records, had been bonding with the singer for months. Round-faced and heavy, with a look so *Godfather* that Martin Scorsese later cast him in *Goodfellas*, DiLeo had grown up an old-school soul fan. He was tone-deaf, but he spent his career working in music. And he had a playful side that appealed to Michael; he'd drive him nuts by singing "Born to Run" off-key. In August 1983, in the middle of lunch in a cabana at the Beverly Hills Hotel, Michael asked DiLeo to be his manager. "Gee, Michael, that's nice, let me think about it," Frank responded. He accepted within two days. He became the ultimate gatekeeper—Jim Murray, a public-relations man on the Victory tour, called him Michael Jackson's "blocking back."

Before he became Michael's manager, DiLeo had been instrumental in picking the video to follow up "Beat It." Actually, Michael hadn't wanted to do another one, but Epic's promotional staff, having witnessed MTV's effect on *Thriller* sales, desperately did. In early 1983, DiLeo, then head of Epic promotion, had visited Michael at Hayvenhurst to give him a simple pitch: "I think it should be 'Thriller,'" he said. And the video should be scary. Michael agreed. He'd been thinking along the same lines.

Michael invited John Landis, director of *An American Werewolf in London*, *The Blues Brothers*, and *Animal House*, to Encino along with Landis's producing partner, George Folsey Jr. Together they brainstormed for four hours. Michael, still just twenty-four, charmed them. "He lived in a room upstairs. It was kind of odd—mostly boxes," Landis recalls. "He had a life-size Shirley Temple figure. He was very isolated from his family." Michael didn't have a specific concept for the film, but he knew he wanted to transform into a monster.

Landis wrote a fourteen-page outline, with dialogue, and he and Folsey began working on finances. The production team had estimated the video's budget between $600,000 and $700,000—it wound up hitting $1.1 million, roughly twenty times the most expensive video ever made at that point. It wasn't easy to find the cash. CBS's Yetnikoff agreed to put in a meager $100,000. His phone call to Landis involved plenty of cursing. "Who wants a single about monsters?" Yetnikoff said.

The team approached MTV. "Michael Jackson wanted to do 'Thriller,'" MTV's cofounder Bob Pittman recalls, "and he came to us and said, 'CBS won't pay for it. Will you pay for it?' Now, we have a problem, because MTV did not want to set a precedent for paying for videos, because God knows where that would end." Michael offered to make up the difference, but Folsey came up with an alternate idea. In addition to the big-budget "Thriller" video, they'd film a forty-five-minute *The Making of "Thriller"* documentary for $50,000. For this kind of exclusive behind-the-scenes content, Pittman agreed to kick in $250,000. A new movie channel called Showtime and prominent home-video company Vestron added another $300,000. *Making* cost $29.95 on VHS and Betamax and made $1 million in sales and rentals within a year.

Landis said he and Michael were totally compatible on the "Thriller" set, and the documentary footage in *The Making of "Thriller"* bears this out—Landis seems to know how to talk to Michael, teasing him, hugging him, even physically lifting him. Landis's wife, Deborah, who had handled the costuming for his movies in the past, was in charge of dressing Michael. She picked red to stand out from the sober nighttime set. "The socks and the shoes were his own," she said. "He took that directly from Fred Astaire, who always wore soft leather loafers to dance in, and socks."

At the same time, Michael was obsessed with his face. He watched Ola Ray, his costar, get made up on the set every day. Then he asked her for tips. "I have a shine on my nose that I can't get off," he told her. Ray recalled: "So I'm seriously talking to his makeup artist, trying to explain what to do, and she looked at me and said, 'Girl, don't you know that no matter how much powder I put on his nose it's going to shine?' Then Michael started laughing, because I didn't know he had had nose jobs!"

Unlike Ray, most of Michael's colleagues who noticed the changes in his nose had a hard time broaching the subject. "It was within what I would call reason, I guess, for somebody that was in Hollywood that was caring about their looks," says Anthony Marinelli, one of the *Thriller* synthesizer specialists. "For *Thriller*, it seemed like what an actor would do. I don't know the Michael Jackson after that, which is when, I consider, it went to unreasonable. And of concern." The singer was always secretive about the details, and the gradual, mysterious changes disturbed those around him. "When you're a foot away from his face, I couldn't help but notice—he had on really big makeup—but you could still see some scars around his nose and his lips," says Steve Jander, who would work with Michael on special effects for the Victory tour. Michael went through his second facial surgery in 1981, two years after the first one. For four weeks at the time, he stayed with his old friend from high school, David Gest, by then a music journalist for *Soul* magazine. "I always felt he looked so good after that second one, he never needed to do more," said Gest, no stranger himself to facial surgery.

For Landis and Ray, the "Thriller" video set would take on a surreal quality as Michael's friends—including Jacqueline Onassis (whose Doubleday Books would publish his *Moonwalk* memoir), President Reagan and his wife, Nancy, Lillian Disney, Fred Astaire, Gene Kelly, Marlon Brando, and Rock Hudson—stopped by. One day, Folsey accepted an invitation to Michael's trailer, and when he arrived, MJ said, "George, I'd like to introduce you to Mrs. Onassis." Another day, Michael brought a portly, older gentleman in a polyester suit to see Landis: "John, do you know Spanky McFarland?" Of all the people Landis expected to meet on the set of a music video, the former child star of *Our Gang* was not among them. Michael's parents showed up one night at the set, and Michael instructed Landis to tell Joe to leave.

"What's the matter?" Landis asked. "He just makes me uncomfortable," Michael said. Landis did as he was instructed, and Joe Jackson did not take the news well. "Do you know who I am?" came the response.

Michael Peters, choreographer for "Beat It," returned for "Thriller." On the first day, Peters told his dancers, "This is not a glamour gig. It's going to be uncomfortable makeup and dentures in your mouth and twelve hours of being really weird looking." Adding to that discomfort was the routine, a counterintuitive repeating pattern. The hip-thrusting, shoulder-twisting, arm-raising zombie steps turned out to be hard to learn. "It always makes me sore the next day," says Kim Blank, one of the dancers, who still teaches the moves in classes. "There's a way you catch the move and contract your muscles."

After Landis and Folsey finished filming and prepared for the editing, Michael freaked out. He called his attorney, Branca, and instructed him to destroy the video. The Jehovah's Witnesses had found out about the werewolves and other demons and threatened to excommunicate him. Branca, Folsey, and Landis secured the canisters containing the "Thriller" negatives and locked them in Branca's offices. Later, Michael's security chief, Bill Bray, called Landis to say the singer had been in his room for three days. Landis drove to Hayvenhurst and helped Bray kick in the door. They found Michael, lying in his room, saying, "I feel so bad." Michael hadn't been eating. Landis pushed him to see a doctor, and the next day he was more conciliatory. He apologized to Landis and both agreed the video was fantastic. Michael was still worried about the Jehovah's Witnesses, and Landis suggested he attach a disclaimer at the beginning. "Due to my strong personal convictions," the "Thriller" video begins, in white-on-black print, forevermore, "I wish to stress that this film in no way endorses a belief in the occult." "No matter how wacky something was, it always had some amazing benefit," Landis says. "That disclaimer caused a lot of talk, and it generated a lot of interest."

The premiere at the Crest Theatre, in Westwood, drew stars such as

Diana Ross, Warren Beatty, Prince, and Eddie Murphy, who was moved to shout at the end: "Show the goddamn thing again!"

MTV had already paid for the "Thriller" exclusive, even though Showtime, then a tiny pay-cable network, ran it four times first. "We saw the ratings spike every single play," MTV's Les Garland recalls. "The ratings would jump ten times what they were." MTV's premiere was on December 2, 1983, and by the end of the following year, the *Thriller* album had sold thirty-three million copies.

By fall 1983, it was obvious to everyone that Michael Jackson needed to do something he'd never done: tour as a solo artist. He was growing apart from his brothers. He didn't want to continue collaborating with them. Creatively, the brothers were stagnating. "After *Thriller* came out, we saw him less and less," Marlon said.

Michael had centered his business team on manager DiLeo, attorney Branca, and accountant Marshall Gelfand, but Joe Jackson was desperate for a way back in. He was in financial trouble, and so were Michael's brothers. They'd spent the years since the *Triumph* tour making little money—they weren't exactly dominating MTV—yet continuing to spend like pop stars. They had sports cars and large LA homes. So, unbeknownst to Michael, in April 1983, Joseph began meeting with promoters for a Jacksons tour.

"The best offers coming in were for $200,000," Joe said. "That was too little. I just couldn't let it happen for that amount." The last Jacksons tour had netted each Jackson brother "only a fairly small sum," Joseph complained. He was determined to give the rest of the Jackson brothers, whom he still managed, a chance to make some cash, too.

Joe put out inquiries and wound up with an invitation to a press party for a boxing match in Las Vegas. When he showed up, he could hear Don King's voice in the distance. The promoter wore his usual black tuxedo and frilly white shirt, holding a cigar between two fingers adorned with diamond rings. "I found him extremely impressive," Joe said. The public side of Don King was the fast-talking boxing promoter, the man with the pointy Troll-doll, salt-and-pepper hairdo. But King once served four and a half years in prison on manslaughter charges. He attributed his behavior to "the frustration of the ghetto expressing itself." Years later, the governor of Ohio pardoned him.

After Joe and King met in Vegas, the boxing promoter met with the Jackson brothers and their attorneys at their Encino home. King made his pitch. "You know why you're not as big as Elvis? Because Elvis was white," he said, addressing Michael. After King left, the brothers moved to make their decision. They kicked their attorneys out of the room. Peter Paterno—attorney for Jackie, Tito, Marlon, and Randy— went to the kitchen and ate chicken with seventeen-year-old Janet. Randy assured him they'd never pick the boorish King. But when the brothers invited Paterno back in, Randy had his head down. He muttered, "Don's going to be the promoter. Go negotiate a deal with him."

King offered a guaranteed $3 million to the family, including $500,000 to each brother, plus a cut to Joe and Katherine. Jermaine was impressed, but Michael didn't like King. In family meetings, Michael had repeated the same thing: "No. I'm not going." Joe and the brothers were desperate. They tried guilt, anger, stomping out of the room, and reverse psychology. "Would you get on a plane with a pilot that never flew before?" Michael kept asking them. "Why are we thinking of having him promote our tour?" Responded Joe: "A salesman is a salesman. He can sell anything." Finally, Joe and the rest of the Jacksons tried the nuclear option, which always worked: they called Katherine. She met with Michael, quietly, privately, and the next thing anybody knew, he was on board. Reluctantly. "Michael didn't want to do the tour," Marlon said. "He wasn't happy about it. Not from the word go. Even after rehearsals started, Michael was still making demands and arguing about various details, threatening not to participate at all unless he got his way."

True to character, King asserted himself immediately. "It was constant fights with Don, who was always trying to get a leg up," Paterno remembers. He and King made sport of hollering at each other. The brothers began to court sponsors, and the one that interested Michael most was Quaker Oats. "Had the Jacksons tour sponsorship been shopped, we probably could have had multiple sponsors and perhaps collected twenty million dollars," recalls a source close to the tour. But King was doing his own sponsor-shopping. He met with PepsiCo's chief executive officer, Roger Enrico, and after talking mostly about himself, casually mentioned he'd spoken to Pepsi's archrival, Coca-Cola. He said Coke was interested. That turned out to be untrue. "Nonetheless, we ended up doing a deal with him," Enrico recalls.

Michael, Enrico had heard, was reluctant. His celebrity friends, including Elizabeth Taylor, Paul McCartney, and Jane Fonda, advised him against overexposure: "You shouldn't do commercials until you're on the downside of your career." The other Jacksons were no more enthusiastic. A source recalls King's attorney chasing Jackie Jackson around the house, waving the contract, demanding that he sign. But King was vehement. It wasn't until the Pepsi people showed up at Hayvenhurst with storyboards for TV commercials that the brothers became intrigued.

Enrico spent weeks sparring with King over a deal. That year, Coke had spent $4 million sponsoring the Olympics. That gave King leverage. Pepsi offered the Jacksons $5 million, the most any celebrity had ever received for a tour sponsorship deal. Enrico and his right-hand advertising man, Alan M. Pottasch, told King the only way Pepsi would consider such a gigantic deal was if Michael agreed to film two TV commercials. King and Joe Jackson accepted quickly. But Michael had conditions. He refused to touch a can of Pepsi—wouldn't hold one, wouldn't take a sip from one. "You can shoot my feet," Michael said. "You can shoot my shadow. You can shoot my elbows. You can shoot anything but my face—I don't want it in for more than two seconds."

As Pepsi made plans to start filming the Jackson commercial, King tried to take over the tour. On November 30, 1983, King called a press conference at Tavern on the Green, the New York City restaurant that had long symbolized affluence or, at least, high-end date nights. The Jacksons strolled in, wearing matching aviator sunglasses, and Michael made one of his first appearances in the decorated, military-style uniform that had vague echoes of George Washington. Michael didn't say much, except to introduce his sisters and mother. Marlon managed to squeeze in the name of the tour: Victory, which was a victory unto itself, because Michael had wanted to call it "the Final Curtain." "Before the Victory tour, which was a great tour, got underway," Marlon would say, "it was already the most painful tour we'd ever done."

Michael began to call Roger Enrico regularly about the Pepsi commercial. He was polite, always. "Just very quiet but very determined," Enrico says. One time, he called back twenty minutes after a long conversation and said, "This is Michael Jackson—the person you spoke to earlier?" *That Michael Jackson?* Enrico thought to himself. When the Pepsi people went to the Jacksons' house to show them the storyboards, Michael decided he didn't like the music the in-house writers had come up with. "What do you suggest?" Enrico asked, worried this would be yet another potential deal-killing snag. "Why don't you use 'Billie Jean'?" Jackson said, "and I'll change the words?" *I dunno,* Enrico said to himself, silently thrilled. *I have to think about that.*

To record a new version of "Billie Jean" for the Pepsi commercial, Michael showed up to the Shrine Auditorium in Los Angeles on the evening of January 27, 1984. His brothers had been rehearsing since nine A.M., with Tito standing in for Michael. At 6:30 P.M., they were ready to film. (Before that, there was a moment of panic when Michael dropped his famous white glove in the toilet and shrieked for help; Bob Giraldi, the commercial's director, asked the crew to fetch a hanger, but Michael said, "Oh, forget it," and fished it out himself.) Michael was wearing his *Motown 25* outfit—black sequined jacket, white shirt, short black slacks, black shoes. Giraldi called for the first take. Three thousand fans were in the auditorium, and they'd spent the day chanting, "Jacksons! Jacksons!" Michael strode down the steps onstage and sang the soft-drink lyrics he'd modified to go with the *boom-bap* of "Billie Jean": "You're a whole new generation / you're loving what you do / put a Pepsi into motion / that's all you've gotta do." The lighting guys pulled open the light pods, on cue, for five takes in a row, and the pyro exploded on schedule. "I want more!" Giraldi kept saying. "Why?" the lighting men wondered to themselves. Giraldi sought a three-dimensional effect, with explosions circulating around the stage. Michael stood at the epicenter of this pyrotechnical power.

On the sixth take, as Michael went down the stairs, his hair seemed to spontaneously combust. "Because of the stuff he had in his hair, it just ignited," recalls Reed Glick, who was on the lighting crew. "He was literally standing in a ball of flames." Michael somehow continued his routine. But then he shouted, "Tito! Tito!" Whether he was unaware, trying to put it out with the force of his movements, acting on instinct, or in shock, Michael began to spin around. Finally, several crew members caught up to him, security man Miko Brando first, knocking him to the floor as they snuffed out the flame. When Michael finally came up again, he had a red-orange bald spot on top of his head.

Afterward, as the paramedics arrived to take Michael to the hospital, he motioned to his assistant, Nelson P. Hayes, who had been on the set. "Get my glove, Nelson," Michael said. Hayes glimpsed the bubbly burn on MJ's scalp, even though Michael's head was covered in tape and bandages, and he was strapped to an ambulance stretcher outside the Shrine. Nelson gave the glove to Michael, who put it on. He waved weakly, a gesture dutifully captured by cameras. The image demonstrated Michael's show-must-go-on perseverance. But it didn't take long for the tough part to set in. "When they started skin grafts and stuff, that had to be painful," Hayes recalls. "He had to go through burn reconstruction."

The ambulance took Michael to the emergency room at Cedars-Sinai Hospital, where his plastic surgeon, Steven Hoefflin, noted he was "quite shaken up" with a "palmed-sized area" of second- and third-degree burns and "surrounding burned and singed hair." Joe, Katherine, and Randy accompanied him later as he was switched to the Brotman Burn Center and given warm blankets. He took a sleeping pill but refused a painkiller. (Six years later, MJ's friend Buz Kohan and a TV producer, George Schlatter, visited one of his studios to convince him to appear on a televised sixtieth-anniversary tribute to Sammy Davis Jr. Michael led Schlatter and Kohan to a men's room and placed their hands on top of his head. "You feel that?" he asked. "Those are balloons under my scalp. When my head was burned, in order to save my scalp, they had to cut away the dead tissue, put these balloons in there, and stitch it together. I am in such pain, you can't imagine.") By all accounts, MJ had never consumed drugs of any kind, even when he was hanging out at Studio 54 in the seventies or working at LA recording studios in the coke-fueled eighties. But sometime after he left the hospital, he began to take painkillers.

John Branca called Pepsi's Enrico and told him of Jackson's intention to sue. Enrico reminded him that it was director Bob Giraldi's company that caused the problem, not Pepsi. Branca said he'd sue for pain, suffering, and loss of income. Enrico responded that loss of income would never hold up in court—Walter Yetnikoff of CBS Records had told him the publicity boost from the incident doubled *Thriller* album sales. The story had been in newspapers and tabloids for weeks. Even President Reagan had sent a letter expressing sympathy. "You don't understand," Branca said. "He doesn't want the money for himself. He's going to donate the money." Enrico proposed a deal to join Jackson in a donation, and Branca accepted. Pepsi wound up paying $1.5 million, used to establish the Michael Jackson Burn Center in Los Angeles.

Michael Jackson watched the *Entertainment Tonight* footage from the Victory tour press conference at Tavern on the Green in his bedroom. He'd cringed through Don King's grandstanding at the time, but he didn't realize until viewing it later how bad it was. Exasperated, he called a meeting with Randy, Jackie, Tito, and Marlon (but not Jermaine, Katherine, or Joe, who were King's allies), as well as attorneys Paterno and Branca and accountant Fred Moultrie. Michael repeated the *Entertainment Tonight* footage. "I'm done," he said when the lights came up. "I'm not touring with Don King. If you guys want to go on tour, that's fine. But I'm not going." He left the room. Everybody was silent. The brothers looked at the floor. Two minutes later, Michael flew back into the room. "I came back," he said, "because I want you to know that I'm *serious*." He left again and slammed the door.

King didn't leave without a fight: "If you want to take this tour away from me, you'll have to pay me," he said. They did, and he received 3 percent of tour profits.

The Jacksons replaced King with Chuck Sullivan, an associate at a Wall Street law firm. At forty-one, Chuck was white and balding, with thick eyebrows and a stiff chin. He was the son of Billy Sullivan, founder of the NFL's New England Patriots. An executive for the team, he'd booked David Bowie and the Police at Sullivan Stadium and saw concerts as an important revenue source after the 1982 players' strike.

Sullivan signed a deal to give the Jacksons $41 million—roughly $12 million up front, the rest promised within two weeks of the first show. He had to borrow the money, and he put up 61,000-seat Sullivan Stadium as collateral, for which he took out another mortgage. Sullivan gave the Jacksons roughly 83 percent of the ticket revenue and took about 17 percent for himself. If Victory tickets sold $55 million, which would have amounted to roughly thirty-five sold-out stadiums at $31 per ticket, Sullivan would have walked away with $10 million. But conditions on the Victory tour were far from perfect. The traveling personnel, in addition to the Jacksons and their families, numbered 250, from the riggers who hung a kitchen sink* in the rafters to an ambiance

---

* "We're hanging everything, including the kitchen sink!" they joked to each other.

supervisor, Douglas Lyon, who provided what the *Los Angeles Times* called "ice sculptures, fuchsias, potted palms and other homey touches in the three-room backstage parlor where the brothers begin and finish their concert evenings." The parlor furnishings cost $40,000. The Jacksons' attorneys, led by Branca, drew up a forty-five-page contract for Sullivan, plus twenty pages of attachments. The contract itself cost $196,500. Insurance premiums cost $500,000.

Michael Jackson may not have wanted this tour, but the stagecraft would be his personal canvas. At one early meeting at designer Bob Gurr's facility in Ventura, California, Michael and security man Bill Bray arrived in a Rolls-Royce. Michael sketched his visions on a whiteboard. He wanted a spiderlike apparatus with a giant light source in the middle. Trying to put together MJ's wish list under a deadline, designers had to assemble huge pieces of stage on the fly. Not all of Michael's ideas were good. "Michael came up with the idea of having a tiger onstage," says a source close to the tour. Production people procured the tiger at great expense, but when it showed up and urinated on the set during rehearsal, the tour's production and financial people were able to talk Michael out of it.

Michael's vision was complicated, but he'd hired the best stage designers. They loaded the set with a complex set of hydraulic elevators, which used fluid to push portions of the stage up and down throughout the show. It fell to Nick Luysterborghs, the head carpenter, who had some experience with hydraulics, to make sure all the pressurizing fluid was filled to capacity and the backup systems were ready to prevent even the minutest technical failure. "We did fifty-five shows," recalls Luysterborghs, who worked under the stage during every show with a small crew known as the Mole Patrol. "And I made fifty-five deals with God."

Michael wanted so many lights throughout the set, walls of them stacked on the rear and sides, including super-bright shopping-mall searchlights, or "sky-trackers," that the crew had to design a traveling power source—common with concerts today but unprecedented in 1984. "There was a whole system of engineering and logistical firsts," recalls Robert A. Roth, one of Victory's lighting designers. The crew had to hang fifty-six thousand pounds of lights on the roof above the stage and stack the giant amplifiers on scaffolding structures on either side—draped with hand-painted designs because Michael didn't want to see the actual amplifiers. "He struck me as sort of a kid with an unlimited allowance that could buy anything he wanted. And these were all like big, expensive toys," says Steve Jander, whose company Showlasers handled some of the most spectacular effects, including the one where Randy Jackson vanquishes a group of evil, Muppet-like "Kreetons" (one played by Michael's assistant Nelson Hayes) with a green laser sword during the opening sequence. The set was so big, and so complex, that its crew members published their own newspaper: the *Jacksonville Picayune*, full of inside jokes and intelligence about where the best shows and bars were in a given city.

Rehearsals began June 26, 1984. Michael asserted himself with his typical attention to detail. During an early take of "Wanna Be Startin' Somethin'," Michael abruptly stopped the band and explained that he needed a certain kind of sound so he could get the dance steps exactly right. He restarted the band. "That's not it," he said. "It's got to be big, really big, right there." They worked on that note over and over, so all nine musicians could hit it with what one writer later called "the power of a fifty-piece orchestra." All the Jacksons had their say—Tito tinkered with a guitar harmony and Jackie wanted more punch in the drums—and it sometimes took them hours to get everything right. Even after that, Michael insisted they repeat the song to perfection. Often they'd rehearse till one A.M., then return to the studio at seven A.M. the next day.

After three months of grueling rehearsals, the Jacksons and band moved their rigs to a huge soundstage in Birmingham, Alabama, where they convened with the rest of the crew. "It was like NFL training camp. It was serious business. You had to be prepared," says Gregg Wright, one of the tour's lead guitarists. "All the crew people—rigging, light, laser people, mechanical people, guitar techs—ran through this whole show. We did that seven days a week, fifteen-hour days, for a month. Just labor-intensive." On the van rides between Birmingham's downtown Hyatt Regency and the soundstage, eleven-year-old kids who knew Michael Jackson was in town put on flawless, impromptu moonwalking displays as the entourage drove by.

Few details escaped Michael's attention. At one point during rehearsals, head carpenter Nick Luysterborghs banged his head while lifting something, and he heard a high-pitched voice from the stage: "Oh, sir! Oh, sir! You know you're bleeding?" It was Michael Jackson. And Michael was being watched carefully as well. When laser expert Steve Jander blew up a smoke-bomb device, Jermaine sternly warned his brother. "Michael—Pepsi," he said. "Michael—*Pepsi*." Michael backed away.

The Victory tour lumbered to its opening date, at Kansas City's Arrowhead Stadium, on July 6, 1984. Before the show, Michael, still wearing a hairpiece to cover small bald spots in his scalp, snuck quietly into the Brotman Medical Center to deal with the scar tissue on his head. Not even his family knew he was there for the eighty-minute procedure conducted by his doctor, Steven Hoefflin. Michael arrived in a back entrance, checked in, ate his vegetarian meal, talked to burn-unit patients, then submitted to the surgery, which went without a snag, other than a bit of lingering pain. When he finally arrived at rehearsals in Birmingham, his weight had dropped from 125 to 105—disturbingly low for a five-foot nine-inch male. He asked that his cook, Mani Singh Khalsa, stick to nuts and herbs.

Meanwhile, promoter Chuck Sullivan was beginning to panic. Everything was going wrong. At the top of the list was the stage itself, which was so massive that it was cutting into the number of seats fans could buy on a given football field. Because of this, the Victory tour was selling far fewer tickets than Sullivan had anticipated, just as expenses were piling up. Losses were hitting $1 million a week.

The Jacksons hired Irving Azoff, the longtime Eagles manager and MCA Records mogul, as a tour consultant for $500,000; he in turn hired production manager Ken Graham to solve the staging problem. Graham suggested creating a temporary structural "front porch" on which to build the set, a complicated procedure that allowed the stage to be moved farther back into the stadium, restoring crucial seats. The move cost extra labor, but it wound up making Sullivan more money in the end.

The three opening dates in Kansas City sold out, racking up an impressive total of 135,000 tickets. But the shows also cost $160,000 for 375 security guards, 170 local police officers, and 70 Pocket Redee metal detectors. The roadway that led to Arrowhead was too low for a tractor trailer, forcing stadium officials to bulldoze the roadbed. Later, at Giants Stadium in New Jersey, a concrete beam built into the stadium was also too low to accommodate the big rigs, so stadium officials hired engineers to physically cut the beam. The expenses were high, but no stadium wanted to lose out on the Victory tour.

At the time, most concert special effects built slowly into a spectacular finale, Fourth of July–fireworks style. Michael felt differently. "It was like, turn it all on right now, at the top of this show," light man Robert A. Roth remembers. After Randy Jackson battled the Kreetons with his laser sword, the colored Victory lights thundered on, in banks of silver brackets framing the stage. Then came a blinding burst of green and yellow, after which the silhouettes of the five Jacksons (with Jermaine but minus Jackie, who'd injured his knee and could not participate) rose from a platform at center stage. They descended with thundering footsteps, amid more light and smoke, and dramatically removed their sunglasses. The first song was "Wanna Be Startin' Somethin'," and the brothers roamed the stage, as they did in the Jackson 5 days, only in tighter, more manly (some would say Village People–style beefcake) costumes. At the Dallas show, Tito dressed like Marlon Brando in *The Wild One*, in a tight black leather jacket with a sailor cap; Randy wore bright-red pants with tall white boots, a puffy shirt, and numerous scarves; Jermaine kept it simple with black leather pants and a low-cut white T-shirt; and Michael arrived onstage with a white sparkly jacket, which he stripped off by the second song. During pretour rehearsals, Tony Villanueva, who handled Michael's wardrobe and was in charge of sewing missing crystal rhinestones back onto the $5,000 glove, couldn't find the glove anywhere. Mercifully, Michael did not fire him, but the star kept asking: "Really? What do you think happened to it?" Villanueva commissioned several backups and devised a system of dots, which he marked inside each glove with a Sharpie. Once the tour began, nobody stole MJ's glove again.

The Jacksons' set lists rarely changed. The brothers whirled behind Michael in movements they'd perfected over years of Jackson 5 touring, and Michael occasionally fell in with them, doing the familiar kicks and arm rolls throughout the Motown medley of "I Want You Back" and "The Love You Save." After years of dutifully crooning "Ben," Michael went into his usual spiel about how it's one of his favorite songs, and how it had earned him an Academy Award nomination, but he abruptly cut himself off: "Listen, we've been doing this song for years and years. I'll tell you what, for a change, give me something . . . *new*." He swapped in "Human Nature," the ballad from *Thriller*. Sweaty and glistening, Jackson perfected his rock-star pose, sweeping his arms in broad gestures. MJ's most spectacular dancing didn't come in until "Billie Jean," when he more or less reprised his routine from the *Motown 25* special—holding the pose on his toes for a second or two longer than he'd managed the previous year on television.

One interesting omission from the Victory tour was any song from *Victory*, the album the Jacksons had spent much of late 1983 and early 1984 putting together as a follow-up to *Destiny* and *Triumph*.

Victory was loosely organized, conceptually thin, and not so much a cohesive album as a collection of singles by different people. Michael himself recorded only two tracks, including "State of Shock," his duet with Mick Jagger. The Jacksons receive credit for writing and producing the songs, but the Toto musicians, having worked with Michael on *Thriller*, were heavily involved as well. "Pretty much each brother had their own session with their own guys," remembers Jack Wargo, who played the guitar solo on "Torture." "It really wasn't like a whole gang of people hanging out."

The video for Jackie's song "Torture" was "aptly named," recalls producer John Diaz. CBS Records budgeted $300,000. "Anytime a question came up to [Michael], Jackie would answer it, because Michael wasn't talking about it: 'Michael's really shy,'" Diaz says. "You got the feeling he was being pushed by his brothers." In the end, Michael didn't show, and Diaz had to fly in a Ripley's Believe It or Not wax dummy of the pop star from Nashville. Then Teamsters picketed the video because Diaz had employed nonunion workers. The shoot ballooned from three days to nine, all stretching to twenty-four-hour work days. The budget expanded to $1 million—mostly paid by Diaz's company. Originally, Perri Lister, a veteran actress and director of Billy Idol videos, was supposed to be the choreographer. But on the last day of rehearsals, Jackie showed up with his girlfriend and they began whispering on the other side of a glass partition. The director turned to Lister and said, "I'm sorry, Perri, Jackie Jackson's girlfriend has decided she wants to choreograph the video." His girlfriend happened to be Paula Abdul. She was a Laker Girl whom the Jacksons had met while attending a game. To complicate matters, Jackie was still married. "It was the *Heaven's Gate* of music video," Diaz says.

Within the Jacksons' compound on the tour, life was calm. Michael, the star, flew on his own private plane. His brothers flew on a separate one. Jermaine had been collaborating with actress-turned-singer Pia

Zadora, and she convinced her receptive husband, millionaire Meshulam Riklis, to loan his fleet of seven private jets to the Jackson brothers so they didn't have to cram into flights with members of the band.
The brothers took separate limousines from the shows to the hotels,
and, being family men, for the most part they stayed in different rooms.
Tito invited Mike Merkow, the brothers' old high school friend, to
travel with the band, and MJ was available for babysitting so Merkow
and his wife could go out with Tito's wife, Dee Dee. (The Jacksons
couldn't go out in public during the Victory tour, or they'd be mobbed.)
Michael helped wean Merkow's son off his pacifier by throwing it off a
hotel roof in Chicago. Merkow recalls a placid family existence, with
the brothers enjoying their families and coming together socially in the
privacy of their hotel rooms. But Howard Bloom, the tour's publicist,
describes more ominous relationships. "If there was jealousy, it was only
coming from one brother—that was Jermaine," he said. "He wasn't part
of the family. He had set himself apart totally."

More than 2.7 million people bought tickets for fifty-five performances in twenty cities. Barbara Walters, Yoko Ono, Cyndi Lauper,
Elizabeth Taylor, Sugar Ray Leonard, Robin Williams, and Dustin
Hoffman made their way backstage at various parts of the tour. But
most of the Jacksons' fans were regular folks—*People* called the audience "a Whitman's sampler of Middle America." The mayor of Jacksonville, Florida, told the City Council that Victory would amount to
$70 million in hotels, food, gas, and other fan expenditures during the
Jacksons' three-day stay. Michael was the pop star just about everybody
could agree on. When Victory went to Buffalo, the local *News* ran a
front-page headline: HOLD YOUR BREATH—V-DAY IS HERE. A firefighters' convention was in the same hotel that weekend, and the fire truck
parked at the hotel entrance prompted lobby murmurs that Michael
himself was using it as a personal limousine. The Jacksons finally
emerged at 6:05 P.M., with fans and firefighters jockeying for position
to catch them, and the brothers ran as fast as they could to a van with

black-tinted windows. Michael covered his face with a towel, but once he emerged safely in the van, he could be seen, barely, waving through the window. When Victory didn't stop in Pittsburgh, the local *Post-Gazette* printed a story lamenting the $250,000 that wouldn't go to tax revenues and the 225 local college athletes who wouldn't be pressed into service as security guards.

The Jacksons themselves continued to adhere to their father's unwavering policy from early in their careers: no drugs. Michael's personal assistant, Nelson Hayes, who served as Victory's road manager, was dispatched to communicate that law to every band and crew member. "Michael said it was going to be a drug-free tour, and it was far from that," tour consultant Ken Graham recalls. "Because of the stresses and schedule, all of your usual stimulants were being applied." While Michael may not have indulged in groupies—he was too busy rehearsing his dance steps well into the night, using a portable wooden platform, as guitarist Wright, who occasionally had the room beneath him, remembered all too well—the crew certainly did. "They'd swarm the hotel," recalls head carpenter Luysterborghs: "It didn't take anything to get laid. Head out to a bar with a laminate on. I used to joke about trawling with the laminates—putting 'em on a line and just drawing them through a crowd."

Even today, at age seventy, Chuck Sullivan adopts a tone of "it wasn't that bad." Reports over the years have pegged his Victory losses at $20 million. Sullivan claims $8 million. But the tour stress affected him deeply at the time. By the end, as the Jacksons were playing six shows at Dodger Stadium, Sullivan turned to Jim Murray, his friend and Victory PR man, and said, "Jimmy, I'm gonna fly back to New England. My heart hurts." Murray persuaded him to not get on a plane—and to see a doctor immediately. Sullivan took an EKG, and sure enough, he'd suffered a mild heart attack.

Sullivan eventually lost so much money off the Victory tour that his corporation went bankrupt and he was forced to sell his family's beloved Patriots, paving the way for a paper-products magnate, Robert Kraft, to take over the team. One night, a reporter showed up unexpectedly at a Sullivan Stadium box to discover Chuck Sullivan had apparently spent the night there. Chuck became a sort of Boston urban legend, the millionaire who lost so much money off Michael Jackson that he became homeless. "I was not homeless," Sullivan responds. "I had three homes at the time. I had an apartment in the Ritz Tower hotel in New York, which was one of the most beautiful apartments in the world, and I had views of both rivers. And we have a family estate on Nantucket Sound with five acres of land and three homes and sixteen bedrooms and gardens designed by Frederick Law Olmsted."

In any event, the Victory tour worked out well for its musicians. Many of the band and crew would use their Victory experience to graduate to greater heights—bandleader Patrick Leonard moved on to touring with Madonna, and lighting man Robert A. Roth's company, Christie Lites, works today with the biggest brands in the music business, from Lollapalooza to MTV's Movie Awards. Michael's brothers received their money, of course, although Victory would clearly be the peak of each of their careers. And MJ emerged from the whole thing unscathed, bigger than ever, a pop star for the entire world. At the end of the tour, onstage at Dodger Stadium in Los Angeles, he told the crowd to listen up. "I'd like to say this is our last and final tour," he said. "I think this is our farewell tour. You've all been wonderful. It's been a long twenty years, and we love you all." Jermaine, beside him onstage, kept smiling. But you could tell one of those words registered—not a *great* twenty years, not a *triumphant* twenty years, but a *long* twenty years. This was the diplomatic phrasing of somebody ready to move on.

CHAPTER 6

Of all Michael Jackson's pets—Mr. Tibbs the ram, Spanky the dog, Jabbar the giraffe, Muscles the snake, Louie the llama—Bubbles the chimpanzee was by far the most famous. Michael had to beg to get him. His mother had told her animal-loving family: "You can have whatever animal you want, but you can never have a monkey." Technically, Bubbles was an ape, not a monkey, and after he was born in a Texas biomedical lab in 1983, Michael's mother couldn't resist. At Hayvenhurst, Michael dressed baby Bubbles in OshKosh B'gosh overalls, red designer shirts that matched MJ's own outfits, and pajamas, which Bubbles adorably learned how to haul out of his own dresser drawer every night. He retrieved Häagen-Dazs ice cream from the freezer, dropped to his knees to say his nightly prayers, and appeared happily with MJ in endless photo ops. Dick Clark interviewed him. He sipped green tea during a meeting with the mayor of Osaka, Japan. He drove Queen's Freddie Mercury crazy by sitting primly between the superstar singers when they were supposed to be collaborating. A driver chauffeured Bubbles around Michael's music-video sets in the Bubblesmobile, a van filled with stuffed toys and monkey bars. "Bubbles became a human," La Toya said. "He became one of us." Then he grew up.

As a tween, like most chimpanzees, Bubbles became aggressive, even competitive. His style of play was no longer cute, and he was too big to boss around. "If there was a box of Kleenex in the room, when you came back, that box of Kleenex would be empty. Kleenex everywhere," says Matt Forger, an engineer who worked at Michael's Hayvenhurst home studio. "If you left headphones in the room, he'd play a game of swinging them and throwing them everywhere."

One day, Forger was working in the control room, mixing with analog tape machines. A mechanical pinch roller was spinning rapidly, with the intensity of a table saw, and Bubbles became curious. He cocked his finger as if to stick it into the roller, which might have destroyed the machine, and possibly the chimp's finger as well. Forger, usually unflappable, turned to Michael with a startled look. Michael caught it. "BUBBLES, NO!" the world's biggest pop star screamed, whacking his ape with a rolled-up newspaper. Humiliated by Forger's betrayal to his master, Bubbles flashed Forger a devastating ape scowl—"like he would jump over his skin and be all over you," Forger remembers. The engineer spotted keyboardist John Barnes doubled over with laughter.

"I saw Mike hit Bubbles with his shoe," adds Chris Currell, who manned the Synclavier at the Hayvenhurst studio. "Mike told me that he does not like to hit Bubbles in public because the people would not understand." MJ's coworkers say he did what he had to do, according to chimp-training wisdom of the time, but it wasn't easy. "He hit that monkey so hard, it hurt to watch. He didn't want to," recalls Brian Malouf, another studio engineer. "It was just what his trainer told him he had to do. It was terrible."*

Even with Bubbles in the room, over four years, Michael and his "B-Team" of home-studio producers, including Forger, Barnes, Malouf, Currell, and songwriter Bill Bottrell, managed to build "Dirty

---

*A source close to Bubbles denied Michael ever hit his beloved pet.

Diana," "Smooth Criminal," "Speed Demon," "Liberian Girl," and "Man in the Mirror"—the backbone of what would become the *Bad* album.

"We Are the World" happened because Harry Belafonte was watching television. It was December 1984, just before Christmas, and a news show informed the veteran singer and social activist about Ethiopian famine. A drought had spread through sub-Saharan Africa, causing the soil to dry up and farmland to recede. One hundred and fifty million people were left with little food, water, or health care. The footage of malnourished children with ribs protruding through their skin was impossible to take. Moved by the report, Belafonte called his friend Ken Kragen, who managed country star Kenny Rogers, to say he was inspired to put on a concert for Ethiopian famine relief. This concert would star Michael Jackson, Lionel Richie, and Stevie Wonder. Kragen talked Belafonte down from a concert to a song.

Kragen called Richie, who agreed to write it. Kragen convinced Quincy Jones to produce. Richie called Wonder—who agreed, but only after Lionel's wife, Brenda, ran into Stevie while Christmas shopping and demanded he call her husband at that moment. Lionel, at a doctor's appointment at the time, took the call.

Quincy asked Michael to contribute to the songwriting. It was Michael's kind of project. He was becoming known for his charitable acts, especially those involving children. In the years after *Thriller*, he'd paid for a nineteen-bed unit at Mount Sinai Hospital in New York, for leukemia and cancer research, and he'd set up a $1.5 million scholarship for the United Negro College Fund. Before every show on the Victory tour, he insisted on meeting groups of disabled children near the stage, just before he went on. "He always gave to kids on their death beds. Kids in wheelchairs," recalls Hugo Huizar, a dancer who would work with MJ in the *Captain EO* film. When Michael agreed to

Quincy's request, Kragen and Belafonte had a formidable celebrity five-man squad—Jackson, Wonder, Richie, Jones, and Rogers.

While Kragen set up a nonprofit corporation, soliciting donations, finding a recording studio, and rounding up his roster of celebrity singers—from Bruce Springsteen to Ray Charles to Tina Turner—Jackson and Richie set to work on the song. They fiddled for weeks, as Quincy called to gently prod them—at least write the hook, he said. During one ninety-minute songwriting session, which MJ captured on tape, they brainstormed and coaxed each other. They clapped along to their choruses and paused to scribble notes onto paper. "We didn't mention 'truth' yet," Michael fretted at one point. "No, no, 'truth' we have mentioned," Lionel corrected him, "We didn't mention 'love' yet." Finally, after Richie's baritone and MJ's soprano come together on the newly shaped chorus, Richie exulted, "My brother, we have done it!" On the night of January 21, Jackson and Richie spent two and a half hours buffing the clunkiness out of Michael's demo. In its final form, though, "We Are the World" was less a song than a structure, a sort of musical coatrack on which the world's biggest music stars could hang their voices and personalities. Trading verses on the bridge, Michael and Huey Lewis fail to bring out the same fierceness MJ displayed in his "Billie Jean" voice on the demo.

Jones dubbed a secret cassette and FedExed it to the celebrity musicians he'd lined up: Ray Charles, Springsteen, Turner, Bob Dylan, Cyndi Lauper, on and on. Almost all of them accepted. The plan was to gather the stars after the American Music Awards on January 28 at A&M Studios in LA. Jones posted a sign outside the studio door that would become famous: CHECK YOUR EGOS AT THE DOOR. It turned out to be both necessary and effective. "Everybody came in there with their character," Louis Johnson, the session bassist who'd worked on *Off the Wall* and *Thriller*, recalls. "Cyndi Lauper came with all these chains. [Engineer] Bruce Swedien had to say, 'You have to take those off. You're bleeding into the mike.'"

The CHECK YOUR EGOS sign apparently didn't apply to Michael Jackson, who showed up in military regalia and aviator sunglasses, hair perfectly coiffed. Michael had a little compact and kept pulling it out, flipping the mirror open, pulling his glasses off, touching a small spot on his nose and replacing his glasses.

John Oates of Hall & Oates remembers Michael "as his typical quiet self, but commanding." Stevie Wonder had an idea to get the group to sing a line in Swahili, which didn't quite work out. The entire group debated this point for several minutes. Bob Geldof, the leader of the Boomtown Rats who would organize Live Aid just six months later, had to declare: "Ethiopians do not speak Swahili." It was Michael who solved the problem by rewriting the lyrics to include a nonsensical line, "Sha-lum, sha-lingay." The only star who had trouble singing his verse was Bob Dylan, who had by this point spent more than a decade trying to run away from his archetypal sixties voice. He struggled to find his phrasing on a line he would have never written: "It's true we make a better day / just you and me." Quincy had to teach him how to sing it. Diana Ross bounced around the session hugging people, sitting in Dylan's lap and snapping photos, and lite-jazz singer Al Jarreau was overwhelmed with emotion, crying constantly. Michael, though, "would go off by himself, instead of starting conversations with the other artists there, which most people did," says "Bette Davis Eyes" singer Kim Carnes, who stood next to Michael, by chance, in the chorus. "That's where the shyness came out."

When "We Are the World" hit the airwaves in March 1985, it went into heavy rotation everywhere. The song sold twenty million copies, the first single ever to go multi-platinum, and raised millions of dollars. But it had a cloying, self-aggrandizing quality, as if the stars were singing more about themselves than the starving Ethiopian children. It smashed through the overkill barrier. Radio playlists dumped it permanently. Even MJ rarely sang it live.

One night, Michael and his friend Paul McCartney were eating dinner at the ex-Beatle's Tudor-style house about an hour away from downtown London, after cooking with his wife, Linda, and their kids. McCartney showed Jackson a thick notebook full of song titles he had purchased over the years, including the entire Buddy Holly oeuvre. Jackson barraged him with questions: "How do you buy them? What do you do with them after you have them?"* McCartney responded, "You are now earning a lot of money. You are really hot. First of all, get someone watching the money that you trust. . . . It can all go out of the window and you won't ever know about it. That's an old show-business story." He concluded: "Think about getting into music publishing." It was great advice, even if McCartney himself hadn't followed it.

The saga of the Beatles song catalog, which would become a life-saving asset for Michael Jackson, actually began years earlier with a conversation between John Lennon, McCartney, and a British song publisher named Dick James. He suggested the Beatle songwriters park their valuable copyrights for early songs such as "From Me to You" and "Thank You Girl" into a company called Northern Songs in 1963. (Through a series of convoluted business deals, Lennon and McCartney would, over time, sign away the rest of their catalog, too.) James took 50 percent, and Lennon, McCartney, and their manager Brian Epstein took the other 50. The company changed hands several times, and by 1982, Australian businessman Robert Holmes à Court had taken it over and wound up controlling the entire Beatles publishing catalog. Sir Paul tried to buy it back, but, he would complain later, it was "too much money."

Not long after Jackson's hallway conversation with McCartney, the pop superstars ran into each other again. "I'm going to buy your songs," Jackson told him. "Pfffffff!" was McCartney's reaction. "Elder brother, get outta here! Good joke, though!"

One of attorney John Branca's colleagues had a nickname for

---

*McCartney's recollection of this meeting departs slightly from Michael's account: He and Linda were on their way to lunch at British actor Adam Faith's home. "Can I bring a friend along?" McCartney asked. Faith agreed, then was shocked to encounter Michael Jackson walking through his door.

Michael Jackson's negotiations to buy ATV from Holmes à Court: the Long and Winding Road. It began when Michael, flush with *Thriller* cash and fresh from his conversation with McCartney, called Branca to say he wasn't interested in tax shelters or real estate. He wanted music copyrights. On MJ's behalf, Branca bought the Sly and the Family Stone catalog and a few of his own favorite songs, including Dion's early-sixties classics "Runaround Sue" and "The Wanderer." One day, Branca called Jackson. "I think we hit the mother lode," he said. "ATV is for sale."

Branca and Michael's accountant, Marshall Gelfand, estimated the value of the catalog at $46 million—and delivered Holmes à Court an offer to that effect. Michael was so excited about acquiring the catalog that he'd accumulated a small library of Beatles books and spent his spare time reading about the songs. (He later told the *Los Angeles Times* his favorites were "Yesterday," "Here, There and Everywhere," "Fool on the Hill," "Let It Be," "Hey Jude," "Eleanor Rigby," "Penny Lane," and "Strawberry Fields Forever.") He eventually bought the catalog for $47.5 million.

To run ATV, MJ and Branca hired Dale Kawashima, a music journalist who'd written for the *Los Angeles Times* and *Cash Box* before working with Prince and others to "plug" their songs for potentially lucrative cover versions by other stars. Michael and Branca had decided never, under any circumstances, to license 60 or 70 of the most beloved Beatles songs in the catalog for commercials or TV shows— among them "Let It Be" and "Yesterday," though Carly Simon's version of "Good Day Sunshine" landed in a Sun Chips commercial in the early nineties. Kawashima worked for Michael for more than four years, but by the end of that time, the calls and meetings with MJ began to tail off. "It became harder to get hold of Michael directly," he says.

In 1985, Michael Eisner had just taken over as chief executive officer of the Walt Disney Company. One of his first ideas, in his grand plan to transform Disney from a stale theme-park-and-cartoon company into a media empire, was to make a new film to beef up the parks. "They hadn't made classics since Walter died," Eisner says. The CEO spoke with George Lucas, creator of *Star Wars*, about collaborating. Lucas signed on, as did renowned director Francis Ford Coppola. Michael Jackson, who frequented Disneylands all over the world, sometimes after hours, agreed to star. "It was Michael Jackson doing something at Disneyland that said to the world, basically, 'Disneyland is back,'" Eisner recalls.

Eisner contacted Disney's theme-park construction company, Imagineering, and asked for story concepts to pitch to Lucas and Jackson. Michael picked one with himself as a commander of a *Star Wars*–type vessel who fights intergalactic bad guys. Using disguises (he sat in a rocking chair in old-lady makeup) and subterfuge (he'd pull into a backstage area after everything closed) to throw off fans and media, Michael met regularly with Imagineering's Rick Rothschild at Disneyland outside LA. "He knew his way around the park pretty well," Rothschild says. Disney spent $30 million on the seventeen-minute 3-D film, hiring top actors (like Anjelica Huston as the evil queen) and commissioning more special effects than Lucas used in *Star Wars*. In contrast to his role in *The Wiz*, the Jackson who commands the spacecraft in *Captain EO* is stiff and heroic. His face seems frozen, his body a statue, as he barks out orders to the robots and puppets in his crew. Jackson wrote two songs for the production, "Another Part of Me" and "We Are Here to Change the World." Both hinted at Michael's new musical style, heavy on electronics.

For the dancers on the set, hired through laborious auditions in LA, Michael himself seemed almost as mythical as his *Captain EO* character. Eric Henderson, one of the dancers, was frequently shocked to turn around and spot Sophia Loren, Barbra Streisand, or Steven Spielberg. He once saw Elizabeth Taylor striding around, shouting in a "Yoo-hoo!" tone of voice, "Where's Michael? It's Elizabeth!" Eventually Henderson realized Taylor couldn't find Jackson because he was in his trailer with a friend who couldn't have been older than eleven or twelve. Henderson never learned the boy's name, but he may have been Jonathan Spence, whom *Jet* described at the time as "a family friend" who accompanied MJ to Brotman Memorial Hospital when he sprained his hand on the set. Kevin Bender, another dancer, recalls a boy holding Michael's cape and delivering him refreshments.

During the week of the *Captain EO* premiere, in September 1986, Michael Jackson appeared in a strange photo in the *National Enquirer*, sleeping in a hyperbaric chamber. The story turned out to be a plant, by publicist Michael Levine and Frank DiLeo, with Michael's knowledge. But he underestimated just how damaging the story would be to his long-term reputation—it became one of those undead details in his biography, along with his purchasing the Elephant Man's bones and his secret marriage to Elizabeth Taylor. Michael had been living in seclusion since the Victory tour in 1984, and the press had an interest in perpetuating rumors of his odd behavior. "He was tabloid gold. Everybody around the world was interested in him," says Tony Brenna, a veteran British reporter who covered Jackson for the *Enquirer* and others. "For a really good Jackson story, you could make fifteen to twenty thousand dollars." MJ had fun tinkering with his persona, P. T. Barnum style, but the media experiment would grow far beyond his control. By the time *Captain EO* came out, he was not the funky Han Solo commander depicted in the film but a celebrity who was weird.

For his follow-up to *Thriller*, Michael hired synthesizer expert Chris Currell for Synclavier lessons. Michael wanted to continue working with Quincy and Bruce—everybody wanted that, after the success of *Thriller*—but he didn't wish to be dependent on them. Currell understood. He arrived at Hayvenhurst to give his first lesson, using Michael's own Synclavier.

"First," Currell told the star, "you take this floppy disk, and put it in here."

"Time out!" Michael interrupted. "I don't know what a 'floppy disk' is."

Currell had worked up a three-hour lesson in advance, but, realizing Michael's underwhelming technical capacity, abruptly ditched it. Over three hours, he taught Michael how to turn on the device and noodle around with his own ideas. He went to Hayvenhurst regularly from ten A.M. to seven P.M., making a double-union-scale salary from CBS Records. Along with keyboardist John Barnes, engineer Matt Forger, and others, Currell became a part of Michael's home B-Team, which by 1985 had recorded fully formed demos of "Smooth Criminal," "Speed Demon," "I Can't Stop Loving You," "Liberian Girl," "The Way You Make Me Feel," and "Leave Me Alone"—all of which Quincy and Bruce later transformed into an extravagantly produced pop album. "He walked down twelve or thirteen stairs from his bedroom to the studio," recalls Bill Bottrell, a songwriter, guitarist, and engineer who'd worked with MJ on the "State of Shock" duet, "and started humming stuff to me and John."

After the team worked up a song, Michael added his vocals, and the process of building an idea into a finished track could be laborious. Currell recorded the results of his daily Synclavier experiments on a cassette tape and slid it under Michael's bedroom door before he left for the night. Michael often called back at two A.M.: "Wow, this is really cool. Did you do this?" The two processes—song demos and experimental sounds—began to come together.

"He was very prolific," Forger says. "We recorded a lot of material. Some were just very simple ideas—sketches. Others were completely, fully produced."

Michael had already given "Another Part of Me" to *Captain EO*, but he also had the swaggering love song "Streetwalker," the tranquil ballad "Fly Away," and a snappy piano number called "Cheater." "He'd do it all himself, like a Bobby McFerrin thing. He'd sing all the parts—

keyboards, drums, bass—he'd demo these songs with his voice," Currell says. "He was really specific about clap. Because of groove. The right sound and feeling, so it would really push the tracks." At one point, Michael asked Currell to try out every drum machine on the market. MJ listened to every hand-clap sound, sometimes layering them together, before ditching the electronics and recording claps with his own hands in the bathroom. "Michael would go to the ends of the earth if he had an idea," Currell says. "Money was never an issue with him." During one of Michael's Synclavier sessions with Currell, he began to scat-sing a bass line and the two fiddled with it. Currell provided simple drums; Michael added keyboard bits. That became the heart of the song "Bad."

Everybody agreed "Bad" should be the title track. Michael and Quincy conceived it as a duet with Prince, a sort of head-cutting contest like the great blues guitarists used to have on the West Side of Chicago—which explains the provocative opening line "Your butt is mine." Michael had been listening to a lot of Prince. During the *Thriller* sessions, several people had caught him at Westlake spinning Prince songs on a record player. Also, his sister Janet, after putting out two albums of trendy pop music, had shifted into a more exciting, pointedly Prince-like direction with 1986's *Control*. "We wanted a tough album," Jones said. "We wanted to get a tough image—it's important that you keep trying to change up." Finally, Prince himself met with Michael and Quincy at Westlake. The meeting was contentious and awkwardly quiet. "They're so competitive with each other that neither would give anything up," an observer told *Spin*. "They kind of sat there, checking each other out, but said very little. It was a fascinating stalemate between two very powerful dudes." In the end, Prince withdrew: "You don't need me to be on this," he told Michael's team. "It'll be a hit record." Maybe he agreed with what *Bad* engineer Russ Ragsdale concluded: "It would have been disastrous for Prince to have Michael beat him in a duel."

Michael and Prince had "dueled" exactly once—on August 20,

1983, at the Beverly Theatre in Hollywood. James Brown was onstage and both pop superstars were in the audience. (B. B. King had played the first set.) Michael, his brothers, and their friends took up the third row. Between sets, the Jackson entourage left the theater and waited in their limousines outside. Brown summoned Michael first. MJ feigned surprise, but he was obviously prepared, his Jheri curl perfectly coiffed and his costume immaculate, including aviator shades and a powder-blue military jacket. He pulled off a few easy spins and a brief moonwalk before hugging Brown. Michael then whispered in Brown's ear, and the Godfather of Soul peered into the audience and called for Prince. Soon came a commotion down the aisle—Prince, in black leather, was piggybacking on his beefy, bearded bodyguard, Charles "Big Chick" Huntsberry. Prince then proceeded to blow Michael away, borrowing an electric guitar, stripping to his bare torso and screeching into the microphone. But Michael was gone.

This bizarrely passive-aggressive, too-cool-to-acknowledge-each-other rivalry continued through Michael Jackson's death. Nearly twenty years later, when Michael was living in Las Vegas, his friend will.i.am of the Black Eyed Peas received a call to rap onstage with Prince during his residency at Club Rio, which the singer had renamed 3121. Will invited MJ to the late show, arranging for a private taxi through Prince's people. Prince didn't acknowledge Michael's presence, but he pointedly stepped into the audience to play an especially aggressive slap-bass line in the private section where Michael and Will were sitting.

The next morning, Michael invited will.i.am to his Vegas home for breakfast. Will barely walked through the door and Michael said, "Why was Prince playing the bass in my face?"* Will stumbled out an answer: "I don't think he meant it as disrespect, Mike." But Jack-

---

*Prince did not respond to a direct e-mail asking why he played bass in Michael Jackson's face.

son seemed sad and obsessed. "I don't think you understand," he said. "Prince—he's always been a *meanie*. They always say we're competing, and I'm not competing with Prince. They always say *he's* the song-writer and *I'm* the performer. I wrote 'We Are the World'! I wrote all these songs!" Will tried to soothe him, but MJ kept calling Prince a meanie.

Michael had a point. He'd written great songs, from "Billie Jean" to "Don't Stop 'til You Get Enough," and with *Bad*, his songwriting was about to dominate an album for the first time. In early 1987, as Quincy's A-Team began to take over the project from Michael's home B-Team, Jones and Bruce Swedien realized they needed a bigger studio. Coming off *Thriller*, they had more money to play with. They worked with Westlake Audio's Glenn Phoenix to design a state-of-the-art facility on Santa Monica Boulevard, not far from the smaller *Thriller* studio on Beverly. Studio D cost $500,000 to $600,000 to build, an astronomical amount in those days, and Phoenix was careful to include plenty of rooms (seven), including a kitchen. "We were certainly hoping to create a facility that would keep the number-one client happy," Phoenix recalls. Studio D was bigger than many single-family homes, with a 625-square-foot control room and a 1,120-square-foot tracking room. The studio's covered windows were important. They meant Jackson, at a time when photos of him were invaluable, could work without interruption.

"Michael's Room" was upstairs, a lounge with a skylight and a TV where he'd take meetings with lawyers and entertain visitors, from Emmanuel Lewis to Robert DeNiro to Jones's children, Rashida, the future actress, and Kidada. It contained a king-size bed, an unusual feature for a recording studio, but, as Phoenix recalls, "It was also unusual to have a chimpanzee in the studio." Adds Jolie Levine, MJ's assistant at the time: "He would be in that room a lot. He kept it very, very warm. I mean, really sweltering." Jackson could watch the musicians and producers downstairs from a window and listen to the control room through his headphones. "He was able to hear and see what was going on and monitor things," recalls Cornelius Mims, who programmed drums on several tracks. "Periodically, you might hear on an intercom: 'Quincy!' Quincy would say, 'Okay, guys, give me a second. Gotta talk to Michael.' He'd go upstairs. Then he'd come back: 'Okay, guys, let's get back to it.'" Michael spent anywhere from three to six hours a day in the studio, while others were there much longer. "I grew up watching him on TV," recalls Eric Persing, who played synthesizer. "The first time I saw him, it was really bizarre. His whole body was just shining, bright orange. Because he had been on some sort of carrot [diet] thing. And he already had a lot of the plastic surgery, so he was starting to get that unusual look that he had. Seeing that with shiny, orange skin, it was like meeting E.T. or something."

For the first time, Michael and Quincy began to divide into recording factions. Nobody recalls overt arguments, but it was clear the A-Team and the B-Team had separate agendas. "Michael was growing and wanted to experiment free of the restrictions of the Westlake scene," Bottrell told Joseph Vogel. "We would program, twiddle and build the tracks for much of that album, send the results on two-inch down to Westlake and they would, at their discretion, re-record and add things like strings and brass. This is how MJ started to express his creative independence, like a teenager leaving the nest." Meanwhile, Quincy was having personal problems—his wife, actress Peggy Lipton, had divorced him after fourteen years of marriage, a process Jones likened to "having my arteries ripped out." When Michael began to meet with him about *Bad*, Quincy was distracted. Creative tension set in. Michael took his B-Team tapes to Quincy and Bruce and insisted they integrate Bottrell and Barnes into the A-Team at Westlake. That didn't go over well. "There started to become a real problem between the two factions," recalls Currell, the Synclavier expert, who worked with both teams and tried to stay out of conflicts. "Michael started to feel that in the studio something was happening to the tracks that he didn't understand. They were losing their punch and their aggressiveness." In early 1987, about three quarters of the way through the album, Currell says, "It hit the fan." Quincy and Bruce issued an ultimatum: if Bottrell and Barnes continued to work on the album, the heads of the *Thriller* superteam would quit. Michael huddled with the A-Team and a decision was reached. Bottrell and Barnes could not come to Westlake. "Either he goes or I go," Swedien told Michael. Bottrell understood. "I just got fired," he said. As a dejected Bottrell packed up to leave the studio, Michael's manager Frank DiLeo intercepted him. "Don't worry," he said, "Michael wants you to produce on the next album."

To those on Quincy's team, Michael's demos were obviously unfinished. "Michael had fantastic ideas, particularly starts of songs, and needed a lot of help," says saxophonist Larry Williams, a Quincy loyalist. "Michael got a little more insular—a little bigger ego, obviously, after *Thriller*, and really set up to do *Bad* by himself." But others who worked on the album felt the opposite. Eric Persing, who played keyboard at Westlake on several *Bad* tracks, believed Jones and Swedien were so determined to put their own stamp on Michael's demos that they made the album sound busy and flat. "They had every studio guitar player play every song, and the same thing with drums—the hi-hat from one guy, the snare from another guy, the kick drum from another guy," he says. "That was ultra overkill. It was the ultimate eighties session. Everybody called it the gravy train." Engineers made more than eight hundred multitrack tapes for *Bad*, and Jackson recorded vocal after vocal, leaving Jones and Swedien to tinker with the sounds until, sometimes, 3:30 A.M.

Michael dressed casually for work—as casually as Michael Jackson could. A typical uniform was a red shirt and black pants, a golden eagle on his belt, shades, a brown fedora, and, in his customary touch, white socks and black espadrilles. Bubbles, wearing overalls, climbed all over his body. Quincy and Bruce, often snacking on fried chicken or fast food of some kind, manned the boards as always. The meals, provided by the "Slam Dunk Sisters," Catherine Ballard and Laura Raynor, at precisely noon and six P.M. every day, were gourmet and worth waiting for. "When's Catherine coming?" Swedien would shout in his booming voice just before meals. Everybody ate meat except Michael, who had separate prepared meals, although he did indulge in the banana pudding. Many of the musicians recall the *Bad* sessions as a great time. "They're all happy because everyone's making money," says Douglas Cooper Getschal, a drum programmer. "The studio itself, when it wasn't full of musicians, was full of great food." Michael was alternately gregarious and approachable and shy and sequestered. "Depending on the setting and surroundings, he could be a completely different person and a completely different personality," says Cornelius Mims, who did drum programming on the album. At one point Mims walked through a doorway near the back of the studio and noticed Michael, alone, stooped behind a wall. When Mims spotted him, Michael hastily retreated upstairs. "It's like he really didn't want to be seen," Mims says. "He never did come back down that day."

Musicians came in and out according to the meticulous work schedules Quincy's team had prepared for them. The great organist Jimmy Smith showed up for a fantastic solo on *Bad*, repeating frequent takes without complaint, giving the song's electro beats a bit of old-school jazz soul over nineteen seconds. Michael asked for a take in which Smith's spontaneous vocal grunts are preserved, and he obliged. Run-D.M.C. showed up wearing standard-uniform black hats, white Adidas, and gold braided necklaces. But Michael's reserved manner didn't fit with the rap trio's noisy kibitzing, and the band couldn't come up with anything for the antidrug rap he suggested, so they left without a single contribution.

Even without hip-hop, Michael wanted an album that reflected its title—an aggressive, macho-sounding album centering on the angry

"Dirty Diana," the spastic "Speed Demon," and "Bad." There were softer moments—every Michael Jackson album had to contain at least one ballad like "She's Out of My Life" or "Human Nature," and this time it was "I Just Can't Stop Loving You." But the production of the album was frequently rushed, convoluted, and filled with cool synthesizers replacing the warm congas, bass lines, and disco hi-hats of *Thriller* and *Off the Wall*. Some of that fast, cluttered ambience arrived after Michael had finished the album.

If the central songs on *Bad* had been "Speed Demon," "Dirty Diana," and the title track, it might have seemed cold, the pendulum shifting too far in the direction of metallic synths and buzzing electronic rhythms. Having found success with "Beat It," Quincy Jones requested another crossover song, an "anthem that had a good feel to it, just like some sunshine on the world." He put out the call to one of his top singers, Siedah Garrett. Working one night with her writing partner, Glen Ballard, Garrett flipped through her lyric book while Ballard picked out bits on the piano. She came across the phrase "man in the mirror." After fifteen minutes, they had written the first verse and chorus. Quincy loved it. Where he heard sunshine, Michael heard religion. "Make it sound like church," Michael instructed Andrae and Sandra Crouch, the brother-and-sister gospel team that led the choir on the song. The Crouches picked up on the line "make that change"—Sandra, today an assistant pastor at the late Andrae's church, related to the narrator taking responsibility for changing his own life. The call-and-response between unhinged Michael rambling non sequiturs like "Shamone! Stand up! Stand up and live!" and the precise, structured Crouch choir is one of the highlights of Michael's recording career. (Mavis Staples, who delivered an inspired mispronunciation of "Come on!" in the Staples Singers' 1972 classic "I'll Take You There," took credit for his use of the made-up word *shamone*.)

100 MILLION, Michael had written on his bathroom mirror as he began to contemplate the follow-up to *Thriller*. Michael's ambition

bordered on megalomania, but his record label was ready to help. So was MTV, by now firmly on his side. "He still had great momentum on *Bad*," says John Sykes, one of MTV's founders and an executive at the time. The plan was to duplicate the video roll-out pattern of *Thriller*, which meant a big-name Hollywood director for the title track in the John Landis slot. After the Westlake crew finished "Bad," one of the first songs recorded for the album, Quincy phoned Martin Scorsese, who was at a studio in LA editing *The Color of Money*. Scorsese accepted Jones's invitation,* and they shot with Michael in New York City subways in a rush of four days.

Michael had a new, tougher image in mind for the *Bad* album, something Scorsese captured in the video. They filmed at the Hoyt-Schermerhorn Streets subway station in Brooklyn, where the trains whooshed by underneath the performers' feet. "Wow, this is great! This looks real!" Michael enthused at one point. "There's even some pee stains there!" Michael plays a young private-school student in a hooded sweatshirt who takes the subway to a hardscrabble neighborhood where the homies call him "College" and "Dobie Gillis." A jealous rival, played by young, unknown Wesley Snipes, tries to shame MJ into robbing an old man on the subway. Instead, Michael shows his inner toughness, not with violence but with dancing. Hoyt-Schermerhorn turns into *West Side Story* by way of "Beat It." The story line might have seemed corny, but it crescendoed into an extraordinary face-off finale between MJ and Snipes.

Michael's personal photographer, Sam Emerson, captured this new image on the set, shooting Michael for the album's cover photo. Whereas Michael on the cover of *Off the Wall* is all youthful exuberance, and his world-takeover image on *Thriller* is hungry and elegant, the *Bad* cover is detached and sculpted. Michael wears a tight black

---

*Larry Stessel, the Epic Records executive who worked closely with Michael, remembered DiLeo as the connection to Scorsese.

punk-rock-style leather jacket covered with a motorcycle-gang menagerie of buckles and zippers, and his face seems different still—lighter skin, thicker eyebrows, a thinner and more pointed nose, dark eyeliner, more pronounced sideburns, and a mullet creeping past his shoulders. Perhaps unintentionally, Michael's look drew from Prince's *Purple Rain* movie of 1984—his hair was exactly the same, although Prince favored a vibrant purple Revolutionary War jacket, a hairy chest, and a come-hither look. "They were obviously trying to give Michael kind of a rougher edge," says bassist Nathan East, the longtime Jacksons collaborator. "I always thought it was a little bit forced. It's like trying to change a guy's fingerprints. He's a beautiful guy. He's not that brutal-looking character."

The salespeople at CBS Records weren't immediately enthusiastic. Their first reaction to the "Bad" video was: Great record. Great video. Their second reaction was: what the hell happened to MJ's face? "When that video stopped, everybody was silent," remembers Larry B. Davis, an Epic promotions executive at the time. "We had all seen how much he had lightened his skin and how much surgery he had done. There was delayed applause when that video finished."

A month before the "Bad" video was to premiere on MTV, Epic released what executives regarded as a "throwaway single," as Davis recalls—the lighthearted Siedah Garrett duet "I Just Can't Stop Loving You." Released without a video, the ballad initially stalled at No. 2 and did not receive the all-important bullet from *Billboard* magazine, denoting upward movement on the charts. Frank DiLeo called his former colleagues at Epic Records to say, "This just can't happen." As Davis was walking out of the Epic offices at the end of a long day, a top label executive stopped him. "I don't think you fucking *understand. The fucking record* lost its *bullet.*" Davis returned to his desk and arranged a lengthy phone conversation with *Billboard* about how to turn the single's luck around. "We did our thing," Davis says. "Everybody on the promotions staff, from vice presidents to regional staff, got a bonus every time one of those singles went to number one." The fortunes of the new MJ album soon turned around—the album didn't meet Michael's bathroom-mirror goal of one hundred million sales, but "I Just Can't Stop Loving You" was the first of five straight *Bad* singles to hit No. 1, setting a *Billboard* record. Davis himself went overboard a few times in his promotional zeal. When a major radio programmer pulled one of the *Bad* singles from its playlist, Davis accompanied him to a Jackson concert at Madison Square Garden and pulled a box cutter on him in the backseat. "If you ever drop another of my fuckin' records," Davis told the man, "I'll cut your throat."*

Epic's Larry Stessel was just as aggressive, if not quite as violent, in commissioning Jackson's *Bad* videos. Epic followed "Bad" with "The Way You Make Me Feel," in which Michael somehow gets away with stalking a beautiful woman, model Tatiana Thumbtzen, on the streets after dark, with a posse of young men hooting and gesturing in the background. Naturally, Michael wins over the victimized woman with his charming dance moves—and the main thing viewers came away wondering is why Michael does not kiss Tatiana. "I felt the kiss was too corny," director Joe Pytka said. After "The Way You Make Me Feel," Michael decided he didn't have time to appear in his own videos, at least for the moment. During a meeting at DiLeo's house in Encino, he instructed Stessel to produce the video for "Man in the Mirror." "I don't want to be in it," Michael told him. "I don't want to have anything to do with it." Stessel and a friend, veteran video director Don Wilson, agreed to track down current-events clips taken from stock footage and news channels, from Martin Luther King to Ethiopian famine to the space-shuttle explosion, and patch them together in a way that would seem meaningful to the "I'm asking him to change his ways" lyric. Wilson planted himself for days at a time in dusty video archives to find "the worst things that ever happened." When Michael saw the unfin-

---

*The programmer in question, who shall remain nameless, denies this ever happened.

ished cut, he was moved to tears. He didn't see the final version until the 1988 Grammy Awards, long after the video had been out. He asked Stessel to stage it during his performance—to give him an "emotional burst." The trick apparently worked. During the performance, Jackson abruptly fell down on his knees, prompting backup singer Andrae Crouch to put a hand on his shoulder and guide him back to his feet.

Jackson was under-available for "Dirty Diana" as well. On the first day of shooting, Jackson ran across the stage, dropped to his knees, and slid into guitarist Steve Stevens. He hurt his knee. "I can't film anymore," he told Pytka, the director, "and I have to leave for Europe in two days, anyway. So good luck." He instructed Epic's Stessel, who had minimal filmmaking experience, to edit the clip with the veteran director. The two clashed—Stessel insisted Pytka watch Bon Jovi's "Livin' on a Prayer" video and soup up "Dirty Diana" with the same kind of over-the-top rock drama. Stessel and Pytka battled over tone until Pytka backed down. He put in every conceivable cliché, with MJ singing into Stevens's crotch, MJ's shirt flying open, and fans blowing his shirt and hair every which way as he sings directly into the camera. It was a hit, of course.

The climactic video for the *Bad* cycle was to be "Smooth Criminal." Michael had been preoccupied with it while recording the album. He gave an early version of the song to one of his dance collaborators, Vincent Paterson, who'd battled Michael Peters in the "Beat It" knife fight. Michael was thinking something in tuxedos—ten guys, maybe— and a swanky club with a strong Astaire vibe. He instructed Paterson to listen to the music for a few days, "Let it talk to you, come back and tell me what your idea is." Paterson added "gangster club in Chicago during the thirties" to Jackson's rough idea. Michael approved. By this point, he'd finished the lyrics. Like everyone else, Paterson was mystified by the line "Annie, are you okay?" (Michael had taken a CPR class, and all test dummies are named Annie.) Michael began to work with director Jerry Kramer about making "Smooth Criminal" the anchor for a broader home-video release called *Moonwalker*. At first, *Saturday Night Live* founder Lorne Michaels was supposed to be the executive director, and comedian Phil Hartman had written a script about Michael waking up from a dream and being chased by hundreds of storm troopers. The plan was for a major theatrical release, like any Hollywood film, but the deal fell apart and Michaels and Hartman disappeared from the project. Instead, *Moonwalker* became a series of videos connected with a sparse plot involving Michael and a few little kids being chased by a spacey mobster played by menacing Joe Pesci of *Goodfellas*. The budget for *Moonwalker* expanded to $22 million, which gave "Smooth Criminal" director Vincent Paterson the ability to go crazy with the shooting.

The theme for "Smooth Criminal," originally to be called "Chicago Nights," was hardly a departure from previous Michael Jackson videos: Michael fighting with gangsters, with dangerous dance moves in lieu of weapons. But unlike "Beat It" or "Bad," there is no cornball contemporary story line. Instead, Michael enters the world of Fred Astaire's 1953 movie *The Band Wagon*, in which the characters wear colorful zoot suits and battle each other in a dramatic dance scene. "Smooth Criminal" is Michael's most overt homage to Astaire—he wears a beige suit and fedora, and he does his first real dance with a partner on video, spinning femme fatales in brightly colored dresses in approximations of the Charleston and the Lindy Hop. In a cartoon world where people don't walk, they moonwalk, and they don't trot down stairs, they glide over them, Michael seems more at home than he does in Scorsese's gritty New York.

The *Bad* world tour was set to kick off in September 1987 in Tokyo. It was to be Michael's first solo tour ever, and he worried over the tiniest of details. Musical director Greg Phillinganes took on the laborious task of meeting with Michael, studying his dance moves, then translating them to the rest of the band.

Jennifer Batten, who'd been teaching at LA's Musicians Institute, competed against one hundred guitarists for the job. She had played "Beat It" regularly in a cover band, and during auditions, she nailed it. Batten was hardly a glam-rock queen and wore her hair conservatively. "She's unbelievable!" was Michael's reaction upon taking in the audition. "But we've got to do something with her look." Tour costumers gave Batten a makeover, and she emerged with bigger, spikier hair than any member of Mötley Crüe or Poison, plus a leather jacket festooned with patches and buttons. Once selected, the band rehearsed for a month before meeting MJ in person. "He was just gorgeous to look at," Batten says. "Very radiant and happy."

Sheryl Crow, a singer from Kennett, Missouri, had moved to LA to make it in the music business and was working as a waitress at a combination French restaurant and jazz club. She showed up to the closed auditions uninvited. "I guess they assumed that I had been recommended by Bruce Swedien or Quincy Jones and I sat in front of the cameras and said, 'Hi, I'm Sheryl Crow and I would love to go on the road with you,'" she told Larry King years later. "And he called me back and I sang with three other singers and a few days later I was getting a passport to go to Japan and a month later I was onstage in front of seventy-five thousand people." But some on the *Bad* tour remember her being more ambitious. "She was really dedicated to working. When the musicians would take a break, she might be in the corner jumping rope or something," says John Lobel, the tour's lighting supplier. Crow was integrated into a quartet of backup singers Michael hoped to fashion into an update of Elvis Presley's Jordanaires. At rehearsal, the quartet was going over "Billie Jean" when Michael cut it off. "I want this," he said, demonstrating his trademark pants and hiccups: "Billie *Jean* is not my lover *ah-ah-ah*." Darryl Phinnessee, a backup singer, realized MJ had Bobby McFerrin in him in addition to everything else. "Not just the breaths, but the articulation of where to breathe, was part of his phrasing," he recalls.

Michael was hands-on to the point of irritating his employees. After spending twenty minutes with his backup singers, Michael told them, "When you sing the first 'Ooh!' think of a nice, cool breeze ruffling the tree leaves.'" Allen Branton, one of the tour's lighting designers, recalls: "We'd rehearse and rehearse and rehearse, and as we got closer to the end, we'd run the show two to three times a day, full-speed, costumes, pyro, the works."

The first part of the *Bad* tour, in Japan, began with "Wanna Be Startin' Somethin'." The set list included Jackson brothers retreads like "Things I Do for You" and "This Place Hotel." MJ spent all two hours of every show in constant motion. He moved what seemed like every part of his body, pointing, thrusting, posing, tap-dancing, moonwalking backward, forward, and side to side, and, of course, holding the famous pose in which he grabbed his crotch and thrust his shoulders upward. And everything happened fast. "The vicious challenge was trying to get him to slow stuff down," Phillinganes says. "He wanted to do everything at eight hundred miles per hour, because of his dancing. But he didn't care. The crazy thing was, we did everything that fast without losing that groove."

The Japanese tour set the tone for a new phase of Michaelmania—tickets cost $40, which grew to $700 on the resale market. The tour would sell 4.4 million tickets and gross $125 million over sixteen months, the most ever for a concert tour at that time. Even better for Michael, while he received credit in the media for controlling every detail of the show, DiLeo and tour manager Sal Bonafede, singer Neil Diamond's right-hand man for years, tightly managed the budget. This was in sharp contrast to the Victory tour, where expenses only seemed to go in one unfortunate direction. Each show had a payroll of $500,000, and MJ's money people hewed closely to that number.

During the *Bad* tour, Michael's inner traveling circle shrank to what he called the "B-Crew"—photographer Sam Emerson, DiLeo, makeup artist Karen Faye, and costume designer Michael Bush. It was a close-knit group and Michael seemed liberated from his family. "There wasn't the tension there of him not speaking to the brothers," Emerson recalls. "It was just us." But he began to sequester himself from the rest of the *Bad* musicians and dancers. "During rehearsals, we all had access to him and there were plenty of breaks," Batten says. "Once we were on the road, it was very separated." The one hundred people in Michael's entourage separated into three hotels, one for Michael and security, a second for performers, and a third for roadies. Occasionally, Michael invited the full group to dinner for American holidays or field trips at Tokyo Disneyland, after the park had closed to the public. When dancer Eddie Garcia went on Space Mountain three times in a row and began to get sick, Michael laughed at him.

After Japan, Michael and company decamped to Pensacola, Florida, to overhaul the show with more *Bad* material, and, as a result, more of his solo identity. In the place of chestnuts such as "Lovely One" were "Man in the Mirror," "Smooth Criminal," and "Dirty Diana." That meant more responsibility for Currell, the Synclavier expert, who wore a Spaceman costume onstage decorated with keyboards and electronics. Currell looked goofy, but nobody in the audience knew his machines contained much of the DNA of Michael's new songs, to the point that the musicians didn't have to play on much of them. When Michael asked drummer Ricky Lawson to play a particular kind of hand clap, he dutifully responded, "Oh, yeah, I can do something like this." Currell had to explain Michael wanted the exact hand-clap sound from *Bad*. Michael sometimes wanted his own backup vocals, as they had been recorded on *Bad*, and Currell had to explain to the backup singers that they would not be needed for the job. Few realized just how important Currell's $1.5 million worth of onstage equipment was to the continuing health of the tour. Worried about being accused of fakery, Currell wouldn't discuss the gear—which looked like giant refrigerators toward the back of the stage—with anyone other than MJ. Before a show in Italy, one of Currell's engineers informed him that a roadie had dropped his $500,000 Synclavier, containing all the necessary sounds of the show, off a truck. It took some deadline-pressure joint-soldering, but Currell's technician fixed the device half an hour before showtime.

Michael brought in Vincent Paterson to rearrange the choreography to "Smooth Criminal," "Beat It," "The Way You Make Me Feel," and "Thriller" in a way that resembled their classic videos. As the tour went along, Paterson and others on the crew realized they really didn't need to add much—Michael was the star, and the rest of the show could be minimalistic. "The beauty of watching that thing was, you see Michael Jackson without any of that shit around him," Paterson says. "He doesn't need the sets and the thirty-million-dollar rocket ship coming out of the sky." Tom McPhillips, the set designer, had a similar epiphany after the Japanese shows. No longer did he believe the stage should look like the aftermath of an apocalypse. "I just understood that I was designing a ballet," he says. "It's just really about the floor and perhaps a background. But there is nothing on the stage to distract you from the dance." Not all Michael's ideas worked. He had asked his lighting people to build a tower for him to climb up and point into the audience. Every time he waved, he decided, light would emerge from his fingers. Lobel, the lighting supplier, dutifully visited a naval surplus store in Long Beach, California, to buy a searchlight from a World War II ship. But once the tour started, Michael apparently forgot—he didn't climb the tower at all. It became an inside joke among the crew. Finally, a tour carpenter replaced the light with a mop bucket. "Michael didn't like it when he finally did climb up and found a mop bucket up there," Lobel says.

The *Bad* tour, for the first time, was Michael Jackson's vision—he pressed his handpicked dancers into his own choreography rather than negotiating moves with his brothers. He'd never had a stronger set list, beginning with "Startin' Somethin'" and reeling off one theatrically staged megahit after another, from the colorful zoot-suit ensemble of "Smooth Criminal" to the werewolf and zombie masks of "Thriller." To his meticulously designed costumes of sparkling red-and-white military-style jackets and all-white jumpsuits, he added idiosyncratic fashion touches like tape on his fingers. He scrunched his face into an Elvis-style sneer, which matched his fierce new look, a long, curly mullet and a thinner and more angular nose. He was in constant motion, twirling, moonwalking, kicking, and strutting, but he'd learned a new trick, pointing and posing for seconds at a time to buy himself crucial moments of rest. He seemed determined to show off his singing voice, too, finishing the Motown medley with elaborate "I'll Be There" moaning, scat-singing, and gospel-style speaking in tongues: "Don't go now! Oh me! My gal! Don't know me! Oh my! My gal! Eee-hee! Whoo!" He seemed to sing himself into exhaustion, barely able to pick himself off the floor— very James Brown. Then he leapt up—"I think I'm gonna rock!"—and strode into "Rock with You." Batten and her gigantic platinum-blond hair, which took two and a half hours to tease into a massive Mohawk every night, became his most memorable foil, particularly on the solo for "Beat It" and the heavy-metal histrionics throughout "Dirty Diana." The two chased each other around the stage, Michael kneeling at her feet and mimicking her improvisations with air guitar. "I would use the tremolo bar to do these wild bends. The more dramatic and the more wild, the more he liked it," Batten says. "We played off each other, really. I would feel his energy and it would make me want to take it certain places." Sheryl Crow provided a different female energy, teasing her blond hair into an ultra-mullet and squeezing herself into tiny black skirts. Crow's big duet with Michael, "I Just Can't Stop Loving You," displayed an off-beat sexual chemistry; they stood face-to-face, Michael thrusting into her and miming some kind of crotch massage as she touched his stomach.

On the *Bad* tour, Michael frequently entertained celebrity guests. "Elizabeth Taylor, Princess Diana, Prince Charles, Sophia Loren, Gregory Peck, Marlon Brando, Diana Ross, Eric Clapton, Peter Gabriel, Phil Collins, U2, Jeff Bridges, Dustin Hoffman, Donna Summer," lists Rory Kaplan, the tour's keyboardist. "It was like an event, every night." Prince bought a hundred front-row seats for his entourage, including stars of his own band such as percussionist Sheila E., and was spot-ted backstage, striding stoically, without a friendly word for anyone. The Victory tour had been a pain in the butt, what with the attorneys, managers, NFL owners, Don King, and the Jackson brothers. The *Bad* tour was fun. "It was Michael's absolute, complete, controlled vision," Kaplan says. "What he wanted. Everyone he picked. How he wanted it presented."

The flip side to this freedom was Michael's personal judgment and decision-making skills, which were starting to become questionable as he began to feel the power of conducting one hundred employees in stadiums that held from seventy to a hundred thousand screaming, worshiping fans. Michael had been begging Jolie Levine, who had been a production coordinator for the *Bad* album, to join him on tour as a personal assistant. During the *Bad* recording process, Levine's son, Yoshi, eight or nine at the time, had become one of the singer's play-mates for water-balloon fights and video games—"the popular kid with Michael" at the time, as Levine remembers. Michael wanted Levine to be his assistant for the *Bad* tour, and called frequently to beg her to take the job. Finally, she agreed, hiring a live-in nanny to take care of Yoshi while she was gone. But once she made it to the road, Michael made it clear that she should not invite Yoshi to visit the tour at any point. MJ had another kid with him—Jimmy Safechuck*, another young com-panion Michael had been hanging out with at the time. "He didn't want [Safechuck] to have to feel like he had to compete for Michael's attention," she says.

"I don't think that's a good way for kids to grow up. Traveling with Michael Jackson, it's a whole different thing," Levine continues. "It's private planes and the gold treatment everywhere you go. Nobody says no to you. I didn't think that was very good for him."

---

*Safechuck argued for Michael's innocence while he was alive, but changed his story in a 2014 lawsuit against the Jackson estate, saying Michael sexually abused him and they shared a bed on the *Bad* tour.

Michael's insistence on bringing children with him on the road was beginning to worry the people around him. One day in 1988, during the *Bad* tour in Japan, DiLeo walked into a meeting between Michael and Emerson, his photographer. "I gotta talk to you, Mike," the manager said.

"What about?"

"It's about you having these boys out on tour. I think we have to stop."

"Why?"

"Because one of these days, one of these boys is going to jump up and say something. One of these boys is going to make an allegation."

"It's just watching movies and kid stuff."

"I know that, and you know that, but the public is going to believe the boys."

"That'll never happen."

DiLeo backed down. He had no choice. But Michael's friends and colleagues began to divide into two camps. One group believed MJ's relationships with young boys were innocent fun. Michael had told the public numerous times he considered himself a grown-up Peter Pan who'd been denied a proper childhood. As an adult, he was making up for it. Kids were innocent. They didn't judge. They didn't care about celebrity. They played. Many who knew Michael recall the star walking into some party, mechanically glad-handing the grown-up guests, then cruising to the backyard to play with the children. "When he met adults, they could never seem to get over the fact that he was Michael Jackson," says Levine, his personal assistant. "But when he met kids, they were like, 'Wow, you're Michael Jackson!' for fifteen minutes. Then it was like, 'I'm going to kick your ass at video games.'"

The other camp interpreted these romps in a more sinister way. Tom McPhillips had been the set designer for *Bad*; by the time he reupped for the *Dangerous* tour a few years later, he was becoming uncomfortable. "There were these Australian kids who just seemed to be running wild around the set all the time, and they were part of the entourage. And the question was, 'Where are their parents?' 'Well, they're in Australia,'" recalls McPhillips, a father of two sons. "At that point, I didn't believe anything anybody was saying. Seeing those kids unsupervised for such a long time just seemed to be very wrong." Eric Henderson, the dancer on the *Captain EO* set who had seen Michael spending all his time with an eleven-year-old boy, recalls: "On the back of the set, they were alone, playing this game—you try to smack the other person's hand. This was a private moment that nobody else could see. I saw how innocent it was. But in my mind, I said, 'That is just not good.'"

During the *Bad* tour, DiLeo gave interview after interview, making the case that his longtime client truly wasn't that weird. The press could relate to DiLeo. He was an amiable schlub, overweight and balding, constantly smoking a cigar, charming in his own way, amazed at his own good fortune for having hooked up with Michael Jackson. *People* ran down the laundry list of Jackson eccentricities and DiLeo debunked them.

Did Michael propose to Elizabeth Taylor?

"No, he didn't. And no, there's no shrine to her in his house."

Did Michael take hormone shots to deepen his voice?

"Ridiculous."

Did he have eye surgery?

"He has never had his eyes done."

What about the nose?

"Yes, he did have his nose done, as every person in Hollywood has. Elvis did, Monroe did."

Cheekbones too?

"No."

Did he add a cleft to his chin?

"Yes. He wanted one."

Did he lighten his skin?

"Preposterous."

The hyperbaric chamber?

"He has a chamber. I don't know if he sleeps in it. I'm not for it. But Michael thinks it's something that's probably healthy for him. He's a bit of a health fanatic."

Did he try to buy the Elephant Man's remains?

"Well, everyone has a skeleton in their closet."

DiLeo had a sense of humor, and he kept Michael centered. He kept costs low. "Frank was hard and pretty stern. He just didn't brook any nonsense," says Branton, the *Bad* lighting designer who worked closely with DiLeo. "There was a lot of financial discipline, and everybody kept up with what everything was costing and how long it would take." Along with Branca, DiLeo was one of the few in Michael's circle who could tell him no, sometimes in such a way that Michael would listen.

After the *Bad* tour ended, on January 27, 1989, at Los Angeles Memorial Sports Arena, Michael Jackson fired him.

CHAPTER 7

Nobody forgets a trip to Neverland Ranch. Will Vinton, who directed MJ's "Leave Me Alone" video, accepted an invitation with his wife to view *Star Wars* at the $2 million Neverland Cinema. They stayed for a long weekend at one of the guesthouses. Would anybody mind, Michael Jackson asked him, if his buddy Greg and his girlfriend tagged along for the movie? Not a problem, Vinton said. "Greg" turned out to be *Gregory Peck*.

"I stayed overnight and had Mickey Mouse pancakes," adds Nathan Watts, the veteran bassist who played with Stevie Wonder and MJ. "I had never seen a Mickey Mouse pancake. He had a Disney pancake maker. With the ears and everything."

Aqil "A-Plus" Davidson of hip-hop group Wreckx-n-Effect, who supplied the rap in "She Drives Me Wild," was nineteen when he and his girlfriend secured an invitation in 1991. They arrived early in the morning and left after dark, part of an esteemed group of musicians including *Dangerous* producer Teddy Riley and two members of the super-hot R&B group En Vogue. They drove around in Michael's golf buggy. They watched *Terminator 2: Judgment Day* before it came out in commercial theaters—with Michael's video for "Liberian Girl" as the opening short. Davidson looked up from the Zipper roller coaster to see Michael Jackson in the cage above him shouting, "Woo! The Zipper!" They saw lions, giraffes, and a llama in the zoo. They ate Hershey bars with Michael's own picture on the wrappers. "Mike was our chaperone for the entire day," Davidson says. "An Indian guy with a turban on, with a Latin-style mustache, made us food outside."

Michael's attorney John Branca had not wanted him to buy the property—at least, not for the asking price of $60 million. Its owner, William Bone, a real estate developer, had sentimental ties to the ranch, perhaps leading him to overinflate its value. (It had once been used in *The Beverly Hillbillies*.) Bone was responsible for the 13,000-square-foot Tudor-style main house, elaborate gardens, and four-acre lake. Branca talked Bone down to $17.5 million. Just as Elvis filled Graceland with personal touches such as the Meditation Garden tribute to his late parents, Michael redesigned Neverland as a sanctuary for children, a homage to Peter Pan. One of his newest friends, *Home Alone* star Macaulay Culkin, spent vacations there, traversing the grounds in a black-and-purple cart matching the colors of the Foot Clan from *Teenage Mutant Ninja Turtles*. Michael had a thirty-four-inch stallion named Cricket, a pot-bellied pig named Paula, and an elephant named Gypsy (a gift from Elizabeth Taylor).

The path to Neverland begins in Los Olivos, California, population 1,132. It's just across the highway from the town square, where the weather is almost always mild and wine-tasting rooms outnumber restaurants. When he was in town, Michael used to drop in to this square every now and then, when he needed supplies for last-minute guests, his driver wedging a black limousine into a parking spot next to the sidewalk. He'd pop in to the R-Country Market early in the morning, seeking to avoid public recognition, then pull the friendly owner into a rear office anytime somebody showed up to shop. Locals who grew up in Los Olivos recall Michael summoning their grade-school classes to watch movies, look at the animals, and bounce on the trampoline.

Visitors in the early nineties rarely questioned Michael's motives for focusing so much of his life on children. In 1993, he told Oprah Winfrey, not long before he put the sentiment in verse on his song "Childhood," "I remember going to the recording studio, and there was a park across the street* and I'd see all the children playing, making noise. And I would cry." When Michael showed Will Vinton his living quarters, Vinton couldn't help but notice the pictures of children—some famous, some the director had never seen before—lining his bedroom. Vinton pushed back, gently. "You know, Michael, a lot of people wouldn't understand this," he said. But Michael didn't budge: "I just love children. I think children are this wonderful thing, and they bring me happiness." Vinton backed off. He bought into the notion that Michael was an eccentric recluse who seized on children as an innocent life raft to help him navigate the world. It was easy to give Michael the benefit of the doubt.

In the early nineties, Michael was dumping father figures at a ferocious pace. He'd long since separated from his actual father. For his upcoming album, he decided not to work with Quincy Jones. And although his avuncular manager, Frank DiLeo, was perhaps more of an older brother than a father, Michael ditched him, too. "Simply put, he wanted to be his own boss," songwriter Brad Buxer said. Without this group of men, however, Michael began to run perilously low on people who could tell him what not to do. When Michael fired DiLeo, he gave no warning. Branca, Michael's longtime lawyer, made the call: "Michael doesn't want to work with you."

"Guy doesn't want to work with me, I don't want to work with him," DiLeo told Branca. "What do you want me to do? Kill myself?"

---

*Michael told this story many times, but he never specified the location. Notably, one of Motown's former studios at 4317 Romaine Street in West Hollywood, where the Jackson 5 recorded, is across the street from a park.

People speculated DiLeo lost his job because he had been unable to put the big-budget *Moonwalker* into theaters. (The film did, however, make a killing in the home-video market, shipping three hundred thousand copies in its first week, at $24.98 apiece, in 1989.) The truth was more complicated. In 1989, David Geffen, the smooth-talking record mogul, insinuated himself into Michael's advisory team. Geffen didn't get along with Branca, and he hated Walter Yetnikoff, president of CBS Records and a longtime Michael adviser. Geffen had recently come out as a gay man, and Yetnikoff, ever the crude needler, spread around a story, as he later wrote in his autobiography, that he wanted Geffen "to show my girlfriend how to give superior blowjobs." Geffen engineered a coup. He teamed up with Yetnikoff's CBS number two, Tommy Mottola, and a top music-business attorney, Allen Grubman. Together they worked to sever Yetnikoff's ties to CBS and its new parent company, Japanese electronics giant Sony Corp. Geffen convinced managers for longtime CBS artists such as Bruce Springsteen and Barbra Streisand to pull away from Yetnikoff. DiLeo had been a loyal Yetnikoff underling when he worked at the CBS affiliate Epic Records. As Michael's manager, he provided a stable line of communication between the record company and his client. To break the link between Michael and Yetnikoff, Geffen convinced MJ to dump DiLeo.

Another reason: Michael's goal at the time was to act in movies—he felt *The Wiz* and *Captain EO* were just the beginning. Geffen convinced Michael that DiLeo knew nothing about Hollywood. Geffen's old friend Sandy Gallin was the man for him. In addition to managing music stars such as Dolly Parton and the Pointer Sisters, Gallin was a well-connected Hollywood hand who'd produced *Father of the Bride* and would later help create *Buffy the Vampire Slayer*. The *Los Angeles Times* declared he had "an instinct for recognizing talent, hard-nosed negotiating skills [and] a bottomless schmooze capacity." Michael hired Gallin to replace DiLeo. Thus, Geffen's plan to cut Yetnikoff's connections in Michael's world succeeded. Sony's executives, weary of Yet-nikoff, installed Mottola in his place at the influential record label.

Michael continued to retool his management team. In 1990, he asked Branca to deliver him a new CBS Records contract that was bigger than any other pop star's deal. Branca came up with a suitably impressive, unprecedented proposal, which would have earned Michael an $18 million advance, a royalty rate of roughly 25 percent of each album sale, and a guaranteed $5 million per album (up to $120 million total if he hit certain sales levels). The deal was to begin with an album that had been Branca's idea—a greatest-hits package, *Decade*, with a few new songs, intended to buy time and ease Michael's pressure to create. Branca met with Michael in spring 1990 and asked for equity in the publishing company he'd helped purchase. Michael said he'd think about it. He called Geffen for advice. Geffen, who liked Branca almost as little as he liked Yetnikoff, convinced Michael to dump Branca, just as he'd dumped Quincy and Frank.

Michael's deal with CBS Records had essentially expired by March 1991. The company, now owned by Sony, wanted to keep its biggest superstar, even though his sales power had been diminishing since *Thriller*. Michael's new attorney, Geffen loyalist Grubman, negotiated a new record deal with Sony Music, including a 25 percent royalty rate and a $50 million advance. The deal was lucrative and imperfect—it added a couple of albums to Michael's existing recording contract. But for Michael, the real enticement to the new contract was movie connections. "He admired Elvis Presley's career greatly, and he felt that his career should be modeled against that," says Rusty Lemorande, who wrote and produced *Captain EO* and worked closely with Michael on movie projects through the early nineties. "He felt Elvis Presley was more remembered because of his films than because of his performances." In addition to signing with Gallin, Michael hired well-known Creative Artists Agency to represent him for film projects. The new connections paid off immediately—Sony Pictures executive

Jon Peters attached him to a project with *Batman* production designer Anton Furst (who committed suicide before he could direct his first movie). Later, Michael was supposed to star in *Angels with Dirty Faces*, an update of the Jimmy Cagney gangster film.

The *Decade* greatest-hits concept aside, Michael had begun to record demos for his next album the day after he finished *Bad*. "He never starts an album," says Bill Bottrell, his songwriting partner and producer at the time. "He always starts two bonus tracks on a greatest-hits." By early 1990, MJ was commandeering rooms at several LA studios, at great expense, and was beginning to communicate the music he heard in his head to his collaborators. Some responded with concern. They worried about Michael's ability to focus without Quincy in charge. Others heard the music he was working on and decided he was following, not leading. "He was desperately searching for something," says Chris Currell, who had manned the Synclavier for *Bad*. "He started going to a whole bunch of different producers, throwing stuff on the wall to see what sticks—famous people's names." Currell told him: "You don't have to do that. Your only competition is yourself. Just do what you do." Michael didn't take his advice, and Currell, a collaborator for nearly seven years, finally quit. But Michael had a vision for what his next record should sound like, and he was okay with losing collaborators who wouldn't follow it. At Westlake studio, where he'd made much of *Thriller* and *Bad*, Michael first hummed the main hook for "Black or White."

Michael fulfilled his promise to rehire Bottrell for his next album. MJ considered Bottrell more than a technical hired hand, or even a creative foil off whom he could bounce ideas. "It was a melding of minds," says Thom Russo, an engineer who worked on the *Dangerous* album and considered Bottrell a mentor. "It was kind of a Lennon-McCartney thing, where they would oppose each other a lot, in a healthy way. I'd hear them on the phone, or working together—a lot of times it was, 'No, dude, I don't like it like this.'" Some interpreted Bottrell's creative confidence as arrogance. He was so convinced his approach to a song or an album was correct that he could rub people the wrong way, and he didn't try to sugarcoat his messages. These qualities made him a rival to the friendly, plainspoken Swedien, whom Michael kept on for both his technical expertise and his ties to the *Off the Wall*, *Thriller*, and *Bad* eras. "I don't want to belittle Bill Bottrell's talent, because he is really terrific," Swedien says. "But a good nickname for Bill would have been 'Grouch.'"

As they worked in the studio, Michael and Bill began to transform Michael's ideas into songs—"Black or White," "Dangerous," "Who Is It," and "Give In to Me," all of which made it to the album, as well as early versions of "Earth Song," "Monkey Business," and "If You Don't Love Me." Bottrell, a former garage-band guitarist, turned "Black or White" into a layered, upbeat rock-and-funk song with bursts of heavy guitar (provided by his friend Tim Pierce) and synthesizers. The song grew one section at a time, beginning with the middle parts. The thick, catchy rhythm guitar gave "Black or White" a sort of Kiss-and-Nirvana hard-rock timelessness. One morning, Bottrell woke up and decided the song needed a rap—so he created one himself. At first he was embarrassed about it, but Michael talked him into leaving it in. Eventually, Bottrell decided a white guy rapping was perfect for a Michael Jackson song about not seeing color. The credits attribute the rap to "L.T.B.," Bottrell's in-joke acronym for "Leave it to Beaver."

Also collaborating closely was Bryan Loren, an R&B singer who'd had minor eighties hits such as "Do You Really Love Me" and "Lollipop Luv" and was signed as a songwriter to Michael's ATV publishing company. While Bottrell and Loren were cranking out songs in their respective rooms, Michael hired a cutting-edge funk production team and set it up in an expensive studio. Kenny "Babyface" Edmonds and Antonio "L.A." Reid, along with Janet Jackson's producers Jimmy Jam and Terry Lewis, were in the process of inventing a new and influential form of heavily rhythmic funk known as new jack swing. They specialized in melodies, and Michael coaxed them away from Atlanta to work at one of his many LA studios, Can-Am Recorders. Babyface and L.A. had come up with seven or eight songs, including one Michael loved— "Slave to the Rhythm"—and they worked endlessly to get it right. "We went out and set up camp, and started writing like we normally write," recalls Daryl Simmons, a producer who worked with Babyface's team. "[Jackson] didn't show up for maybe two days. He must have sang fifty tracks. He sang and sang and sang. And then some days he would disappear." Other days, Michael showed up at Can-Am with Macaulay Culkin, and the two would roar around the studio, playing pranks with electrical-shock pens. In the end, Michael opted not to use "Slave to the Rhythm"—he preferred a more driving track to go with Babyface's melodies.

Heavy D, the late hip-hop pioneer who performed the rap on "Jam," would take credit for introducing Michael to Teddy Riley. A member of hit R&B vocal trio Guy, Riley's specialty was a persistent, electronic, hip-hop-style rhythm, something Michael wished to export wholesale for *Dangerous*. It helped that Guy's material sounded like an offshoot of Prince, a more streamlined, harmonic, and radio-friendly interpretation of "Raspberry Beret." Michael had Prince on his mind. "Quincy's productions have a bit more of a jazz musicality to them, as far as chord changes and arrangements," says Dave Way, an engineer who worked for years with Riley before joining the *Dangerous* team. "Teddy's were a lot more beat oriented and stripped-down—very drum heavy and groove oriented." Babyface and L.A. Reid knew they'd lost out to Riley when MJ began to bring them versions of Riley's tracks, often stripped down so it was just the rhythmic hook. "I remember him saying, 'I want Teddy's beats and your melodies,'" Babyface collaborator Daryl Simmons recalls. "L.A. didn't like that, but that's what Michael was after—the hard-driving, new jack beat, with our melody and lyrics."

"I came in with ten grooves," Riley said. "He liked them all."

Michael rooted out the best qualities of each production team.

Buz Kohan, Michael's old friend from the *Motown 25* days, convinced Michael to revisit his tearjerker "Gone Too Soon" as a tribute to Michael's friend Ryan White, the eighteen-year-old AIDS activist who'd died in April 1990. Although he'd waited more than seven years for Michael to record his song, Kohan was lucky. "You could make a lot of money getting on a Michael Jackson record. You didn't have to be in the business to know that," says John Chamberlin, a *Dangerous* assistant engineer. "It means you could be secure for the rest of your life." Michael didn't talk about it much, but some believed he was borrowing a technique from his former Motown mentor Berry Gordy Jr. "He would set up independent teams," says his longtime engineer, Matt Forger. "He was in a search for what was going to be the very best." Jackson spent an estimated $10 million to make *Dangerous*. He recorded in seven studios, including two years of twenty-four-hour access at Record One, at $4,000 a day. The project eventually shifted to three rooms at Larrabee, about five miles away in Hollywood, which over nine months cost roughly $3,000 to $4,000 per day. "There was no deadline," Swedien said, "we could just work on mixes for weeks on end."

The relationship between Swedien and Bottrell escalated from rivals to nemeses. "I had a sense it was very competitive, and they wanted to know what each other was doing," Chamberlin says. "But [they] did not ask to hear each other's stuff." They brought different skill sets to the album. The experienced, personable, and hyper-confident Swedien was a heroic figure in the studio, especially to young engineers who considered the *Thriller* engineer a mentor. Riley, the big-name producer, worked well with Swedien; they frequently teamed up in the same room at Larrabee. Bottrell was not merely a technical guy but a songwriter and musician, and his contributions to the album were more multifaceted. "Bruce would sit there very comfortable in his skin, not swayed by anything. And he made it sound great," Chamberlin says. "But with Bill, there was a sense that he was going to do more. Bruce Swedien couldn't play guitar or drums or any of those things, but Bill could do all that stuff. He could write a song. He could sing it." As work on the album progressed, Bottrell continued to meticulously polish his own songs for the album, particularly "Dangerous," "Earth Song," and "Monkey Business."

"I was feeling increasingly isolated," Bottrell says. "I was really working alone by then."

Although Bottrell remained excited about his work, he perceived that Michael in the big-money *Dangerous* era was a more distant collaborator than he'd been throughout previous sessions. "On *Bad*, he could call me after dinner and say, 'Come on down, we want to do a vocal,'" Bottrell says. "There was no way to not succumb to the blockbuster-movie mode once we got to *Dangerous*." Rather than working long hours with Bottrell one-on-one, Michael would poke his head in Bottrell's studio room once in a while and say, "Hey, Billy, let's do an intro on 'Earth Song,'" or "I've got this poem, here's the words." Some days, MJ worked eighteen straight hours in the studio; others, he'd be on a video shoot and stay away completely.

The adversarial relationship between Bottrell and Swedien peaked one day at Larrabee studio. At issue were Bottrell's working tapes. He had learned his lesson on *Bad*, when Quincy's A-Team would send an engineer, Brad Sundberg, to Michael's Hayvenhurst studio every night to pick up Bottrell's mixes and take them back to the studio. "I had no way of knowing if they used my work, or just re-created it very carefully. During the *Dangerous* album, I kept all my tapes locked—very conspicuously, in the hall," Bottrell recalls. Some interpreted Bottrell's locked tapes as a screw-you to the rest of the studio; by and large, Bottrell did little to dissuade his colleagues from this impression.

At one point during *Dangerous*, Sundberg, an engineer loyal to Swedien, secretly set up two microphones underneath the racks of DAT machines Bottrell was using at his Larrabee studio room. Chamberlin, one of the album's assistant engineers, was sitting in Bottrell's room waiting for Michael to show up. When Chamberlin noticed an unexpected cable leading to the tape machine, he opened the back of a cabinet and found the recording device. Chamberlin called Bottrell. Next thing he knew, Swedien's assistant was in the room and somebody was telling Chamberlin to leave. Bottrell isn't sure who gave the order for this "bugging," and Sundberg wouldn't comment. But, Chamberlin says, "I thought it could've come from Bruce [Swedien]." Matt Forger, Michael's longtime engineer, believes it was MJ himself—so "he could monitor the process." Either way, it left bad feelings with everybody involved—the competition had become not Berry Gordy–style best-you-can-be but ugly and demoralizing. "It was beyond not cool. It was actually breaking the law," Thom Russo, another *Dangerous* engineer, recalls. "That was an awfully fucking weird thing to go down." Swedien, retired and living in Florida, doesn't remember. "Boy, that's great," he says. "I did a record by that name—'Paranoia.'"

As with *Thriller*, the final two-month push to finish *Dangerous* was highly stressful. Epic executives wanted to release the album by Thanksgiving. "When the deadline came, [Jackson] wanted to do more and more songs," Riley said after the album came out. "And his manager came in there and said, 'Teddy, you and Michael, you're not up to your sneaky stuff. Do not write another song.'" Michael, Riley, and Swedien worked all night, drove back to their hotel for a short night's sleep, then returned in the morning. One day, Swedien caught Michael crying at Record One because he couldn't find the right key for "Keep the Faith." Swedien had to play both drill sergeant and therapist to get the performance. "Pull yourself together, face this now," he told Michael. "We're not going home until you've sung this all the way through. Then we'll go home and be able to sleep and continue." Says Swedien: "That was scary. But he did it."

Dangerous came out on November 26, 1991, a bleak time for pop albums, no matter how contemporary they tried to sound. Nirvana's *Nevermind* had arrived two months earlier, the climax of a percolating punk-rock movement in Seattle and elsewhere, prompting music stars to be sloppy, spontaneous, non-choreographed, full of guitar-smashing passion. Still, *Dangerous* sold seventy thousand copies per day, seven hundred thousand in its first two weeks, and held No. 1 on *Billboard*'s album chart through the end of 1991. It succumbed to pop music's inflection point on January 4, 1992, when the slow-building *Nevermind* took over. Reviewers hadn't been especially kind: the *Los Angeles Times* called the album "a messy grab-bag of ideas and high-tech non sequiturs, with something for everyone from the man who has everything." Privately, Michael's people began to worry he was losing his edge. "*Dangerous* was all Michael. He had no one telling him what to do. He just had a bunch of yes-men around him," says Larry Stessel, Jackson's longtime marketing executive at Epic Records. "You have a strong personality like Quincy Jones, you need someone to say, 'That blows. We're not going to do that.' *Dangerous* was just an average album. He was trying to emulate other artists that were out there." Even Matt Forger, Michael's loyal engineer, felt the album didn't have the same concentrated punch as his previous works. "Several factions" contributed to the album, Forger says, including Bryan Loren and his "Minneapolis kind of funky flavor," Bottrell and his more rock-oriented material, and producer Riley in tandem with engineer Swedien. "There was a lot of sharing the production duties at Michael's request," Forger says. "It's not as cohesive as *Bad* was—ninety percent of the songs [on *Bad*] were Michael's. . . . On *Dangerous*, Teddy did half the album, and then Bruce and other people did the other half. At the very end of the whole process, Bruce came in and did the final mix of several of Teddy's songs to maximize sonic quality."

But the very unfocused quality of *Dangerous* gives it a power unique in MJ's album catalog. The first six songs are more explosively funky than anything MJ has ever done, as heavy and punishing as any Miami bass music of the time. "Jam" had begun with Michael repeating the word *jam* over a drum-machine pattern Swedien had set up, and Riley later beefed it up with elaborate horn lines and other sound effects. It opens with shattering glass; a blast of heavy-metal guitar fades into the robotic drums at the beginning of "Why You Wanna Trip on Me"; car horns blare as if activated by rioting in "She Drives Me Wild." Michael's emotions arrive in a jumble, angry and lustful, worried about the world, all in a more specific and pointed way than he'd been in "Wanna Be Startin' Somethin'." "You got world hunger / not enough to eat," he sings, "so there's really no time / to be trippin' on me." Writes critic Susan Fast: "Michael as quirky crossover *wunderkind*, fabulous; inhabiting adulthood as the sexy guy he was, with those looks, his love of kids and kid-like things, his failure to partner up, making blacker-sounding music and talking seriously about race, sex and spiritual life: good God. We were kidding, we don't want him to grow up. Please give us our little boy back."

After that, the booming intensity abruptly drops, as if the lustful, glass-smashing Michael Jackson has rushed off the stage, only to be replaced with Harry Belafonte: "Heal the World" is orchestral and sappy, another pass at "We Are the World," positioning MJ as soothing philanthropist. The second half of *Dangerous* whiplashes from "Black or White" (which contains the best guitar riff ever on an MJ song) to the power ballad "Give In to Me" to a lushly arranged version of Buz Kohan's calculated weeper "Gone Too Soon." Yet this portion of the album includes "Will You Be There," MJ's prayer-poem that taps into the power of gospel music even more intensely than "Man in the Mirror"—its first lines are "Hold me / like the River Jordan," and his teary poetry reading at the end is as poignant as his famous breakdown at the end of "She's Out of My Life." The album closes with the upbeat "Dangerous," about addicted lovers who can never come together, leaving the frustrated, murmuring narrator with, to paraphrase an old blues song, stones in his passway: "I cannot sleep alone tonight / my baby left me here tonight / I cannot cope till it's all right." It's a fantastic album, perhaps the only time Michael ever found the perfect balance between revving up the dance floor and working out his issues.

The MJ of *Dangerous* had grander aspirations than just an album. "Heal

the World" became a foundation, from which Michael intended to actually heal the world. (Its goal, he announced, was to raise $100 million for
children suffering from war and disease, although the foundation wound
up with $4 million before being suspended in 2002 for neglecting yearly
accounting statements.) Around this time, he instructed Epic's Stessel to
give him a title. "Elvis is the King and Bruce is the Boss," Michael said.
"I want to have a name." Capitulating to the star's request, in November
1991 Matt Farber of MTV wrote a memo to his staff, signed by the channel's founder and boss, Bob Pittman: "We need to refer to Michael Jackson
as 'The King of Pop' on-air." MTV complied, awkwardly at first, but over
time, it turned into a formal title. "It was laughed at," Stessel says, "and
then it became part of the vernacular." Executives at Epic's parent company, Sony Entertainment, reluctantly endured MJ's extravagant behavior.
"You just had to deal with unrealistic requests when one of his managers
would come in and ask for millions more for short films," said Tommy
Mottola, the company's president. "More, more, more, more, more."

Joni Sighvatsson, who ran Propaganda Films, should have known when
he signed on to make the "Black or White" video that Michael Jackson
was not going to cooperate. His first meeting with MJ, at a studio where he
was recording the *Dangerous* album, was supposed to begin at six P.M., but
Michael didn't show until eight, bringing Bubbles with him. Then, at 8:30,
Michael insisted on halting the meeting to watch *The Simpsons*. Unsurprisingly, when Sighvatsson came around to shooting the video, Michael was
not particularly reliable about showing up, and the crews found themselves
with little usable footage. So Sighvatsson contacted John Landis, who'd
directed the "Thriller" video. "You have a good relationship with Michael
Jackson, right?" Sighvatsson said. "I think he'll show up for you. Would
you come in and do a video?" Recalls Landis: "They'd blown through
what the budgets were, and produced nothing." The director asked for big
money—and received it—and a paycheck every Monday.

Jackson greeted his old friend warmly. Landis saw that while he pursued his own vision of "Thriller" out of Michael's desire to become a monster, "Black or White" would be more collaborative—"trying to make something out of all of Michael's ideas." Like the *Dangerous* album, the "Black or White" video is unfocused but powerful, beginning with a vignette involving a rebellious Macaulay Culkin, an electric guitar, gigantic speakers, and George Wendt of *Cheers* as the repressive dad blasted into space in his easy chair. Michael dances in a white dress shirt and black pants with African dancers in a desert, with Egyptian dancers in a small room, with Native American dancers on a platform surrounded by guns and horses, with Russian dancers in the snow. Then he walks through fire with a burning cross in the background. The video ends with a new technology, in which actors and dancers, including model Tyra Banks, morph from Rastafarian man to Asian woman to poofy-haired white guy. "There were things I'd always wanted to do, so we took advantage of the budget to do it," Landis says. "'Black or White' is a mess. It was just a bunch of stuff, and I was making it coherent."

The original final four minutes of the "Black or White" video begins with an animated panther walking down a set of stairs, then transforming into Michael Jackson. From there, MJ performs one of the most extraordinary dance sequences of his career. Wearing a black fedora, splashing through puddles, screaming "Ho!" like he would later do in concert, Michael furiously tap-dances sideways, thrusting his hands into and out of his pockets, bending his knees and elbows in unnatural ways. "Making shit up," is how Landis describes it. He was bathed in blue light, dressed in black, and wearing an oddly fashionable lace-up brace on his right arm—that came from a production assistant who'd fallen off his bicycle. ("That's so neat," Michael told him on the set. "Can I wear that?")

In the original cut, Michael-as-Black-Panther causes general mayhem, throwing a trash can through a hotel window, a reference to Mookie inducing the riot in Spike Lee's 1989 film *Do the Right Thing*, and hopping on top of an old car to smash its windows with a crowbar. He also grabbed his crotch numerous times, forcefully, then conspicuously zipped up his zipper, suggesting masturbation more blatantly than he ever had with this longtime stage move. Critic Elizabeth Chin called the panther dance "a taking off of the mask, a revelation of the abiding rage and anger that whites both fear and suppress: a truth that cannot be morphed into something palatable either in dreams or in reality." Michael himself later affirmed these motives: "I said, 'I want to do a dance number where I can let out my frustration about injustice and prejudice and racism and bigotry,' and within the dance I became upset and let go," he said, adding that he ran the idea by his sister Janet. "I think at the time people were concerned with the violent content of the piece, but it's, like, easy to look at. It's simple."

Landis struggled on the set to contain MJ's sexual expression. At one point, as Michael reached into his crotch, Landis yelled, "Cut!" and told Michael to knock it off—this was a family production. Michael defied the instruction, instead unzipping his fly and reaching his hand further into his crotch. Landis stopped filming again and said he was uncomfortable with the move. They asked choreographer Vince Paterson for his opinion; he agreed with Landis. But Michael insisted on calling Gallin, his manager. "Sandy was a screaming queen. A very flamboyant homosexual," Landis said. "Sandy Gallin comes to the set, looks at the playback, and he goes, 'Do it, Michael! Do it! Do it!'" During the editing process later, Landis says he cut the most objectionable crotch-grabbing images and "what's in the finished piece, I thought was fine."

But when the video made its debut, during prime time on a Thursday night in November 1991, angry parents declared the video too violent and too sexual. Network spokespeople criticized the clip. Michael capitulated, issuing an apology and releasing a new version of the video minus the last four minutes. Another version soon came out with swastikas and "KKK Rules" graffiti stamped onto the walls and car windows of the city scene—a tidier target for MJ's complex racial feelings. This version suggests that, as Chin writes, "violence like Jackson's can be understood only if it comes as a response to overt racism (rather than, as in the original, a response to structural racism)." The reaction, and MJ's response to it, was a shame. The dance was one of the few times Michael's social activism came across as something other than benignly trying to unify the races. Today, Landis says he appreciates the timing of the video, panther dance and all, just a few months before the Los Angeles race riots. "Very prescient," Landis says. "When it came out, it generated all this controversy. What does that do? It sells records."

During the actual Los Angeles riots, in spring 1992, Michael Jackson was on Chicago's West Side, shooting a video for "Jam" in an old armory building with basketball superstar Michael Jordan. To maintain secrecy, director David Kellogg and his crew had told Chicago officials they would be filming a mayonnaise commercial. Word spread, though, that for half a day, the two MJs were filming together in this part of town. (The video showed Michael Jackson shooting hoops and Michael Jordan dancing, both graceful but struggling to master the other's discipline; filmmakers later dubbed in a voice actor for Jordan's dialogue.) After the Rodney King verdicts, riots had been breaking out in neighborhoods throughout the US, from San Francisco to Pittsburgh, but they were absent in this part of Chicago. "Something about the presence of these two guys in this neigh-borhood in this moment kind of squashed the notions of riot," Kellogg says. On the third day of filming, long after Jordan had returned to his day job with the Chicago Bulls, Michael Jackson called the director to say he wouldn't be showing up due to a lunch meeting. It turned out to be with President George H. W. Bush, in Washington, DC, to receive a humanitarian "Point of Light" award for his work with disadvantaged children.

His Black Panther days were over.

In May 1992, the *Dangerous* album had been out for six months. MJ was driving his Jeep down Wilshire Boulevard in Beverly Hills when his car broke down. Michael's calls to 911 were of no help—for some reason, the operator didn't consider Michael Jackson in traffic an emergency. Then came a stroke of what seemed like good luck. A woman married to Mel Green, a Rent-A-Wreck employee, happened by Michael's car and took in the sight of the helpless King of Pop in a black turban, a scarf, and mirrored shades. Green went out and retrieved Jackson from the side of the road. Then he contacted Dave Schwartz, founder of his company. Stunned, Schwartz called his wife, June, a beautiful former model whose dark hair was the same shade and length as Michael Jackson's. Her son Jordan Chandler, twelve, happened to be a Michael Jackson fanatic. He'd spent much of his childhood imitating Michael, wearing one white glove and a jacket like the one in "Billie Jean" and mastering Michael's dance moves. Jordan had been an MJ fan since he'd encountered him briefly at the Golden Temple, a health-food restaurant on Third Street in LA, when he was roughly five years old. *Vanity Fair*'s Maureen Orth described Jordie as "fine-boned, delicate and dark like his mother, and who looks much younger than he is"; one of the few photos of Chandler to emerge during this period suggests a movie-star charisma, with big, sad, brown eyes.

The Chandlers were not a happy family at the time. June had recently divorced from Evan Chandler, dentist to the stars, and married Schwartz, which was hard on Jordie and his stepsister Lily. "The parents had separate families, so there was a lot of tension between the families," says Larry Feldman, the attorney who would represent Jordan, "and a lot of finger-pointing between the mom and the dad." That day in LA, though, Jordie and June were thrilled. So was Michael. June gave Michael her phone number and he agreed to call.

The Schwartzes received the call at home within a month or two. It was certainly unusual for the Chandler family that *Michael Jackson* would call to say hello, even after a vague promise, but it wasn't for people who knew Michael. From Terry George in England to the late Ryan White to Australian Brett Barnes to Macaulay Culkin, Michael maintained phone friendships with children, frequently boys, around the world. Michael and Jordie shared a love for video games, and Michael invited his new seventh-grade friend to his "hideout" condominium in Century City, where he had an arcade of his own. But June wouldn't let Jordie go—he had tests at school. Anyway, Michael was preparing for his *Dangerous* tour, scheduled to open in Europe that July.

That tour began much like Victory and *Bad*. It was to be the biggest ever, with the most spectacular special effects, the most brilliant costumes, an unprecedented production, and a fleet of trucks and jets to carry it all.

"The feel was different," says Eddie Garcia, a dancer who'd been on the *Bad* tour. "It was on a bigger scale. This was the first time you had the stage split open and rise up."

Michael asked for a thirty-foot wall containing 350 super-high-powered aircraft-landing lights. When Peter Morse, the tour's lighting designer, finally unveiled it to Michael, he smiled and said, "Now can I get that all the way around, on the sides and the top, too?" Management eventually denied the request.

McPhillips, the set designer, and his staff batted around ideas under pressure—initially they wanted to hang a canopy over the stage, so it would resemble the busy, colorful cover of the *Dangerous* album. But, someone said, "We can't have that. The headlines will say, IT'S LIKE A CIRCUS." When McPhillips showed Michael a model for the stage, he left to think about it, then returned half an hour later with yet another impossibly big idea. "I need rocket man," he said. "I need to fly around the stage."

The equipment to fly MJ around the stage cost $20,000 per show to transport. Michael wouldn't wear the spacesuit—action star Chuck Norris's stunt double handled the job. "Michael would step away and this other guy would run in and he'd successfully fly off the stage with the jet pack," recalls Ken Graham, the Victory veteran hired as a *Dangerous* site coordinator. "The logistics of moving this hazardous rocket fuel from city to city, and on jets and trucks—that was a whole movie unto itself."

The tour was absurdly expensive—a company called Rock-It Cargo, which specialized in massive international tours, had to lease three huge Soviet An-124 air freighters to haul the production between Europe, Asia, and South America.

Michael's musicians and crew noticed he was more distracted, less hands-on and perfectionistic, than he had been for Victory or *Bad*. For the *Bad* tour, Michael and his dancers had started the choreography together, working closely through the entire process; for *Dangerous*, the dancers opened rehearsals not with MJ but Kenny Ortega, the tour's director and choreographer. After they put the steps together, Michael showed up, conferred with Ortega, and, Garcia says, "changed stuff according to his liking." Some who'd been involved with both tours noticed a steep drop-off in Michael's enthusiasm. Sam Emerson, the tour photographer, recalls Michael requiring, in his contract for the 1984 Victory tour, a ten-foot-by-ten-foot dance platform to be assembled in each of his hotel rooms. "He'd have cameras, and the crew set up the dance floor. I'd go there and his shirt literally would be soaking wet and there'd be pools of sweat on the dance floor. He worked himself into a frenzy. He was in the best shape ever. On the *Bad* tour, it was pretty much the same thing—he'd do rehearsal after rehearsal," he says. "For the *Dangerous* tour, it wasn't the same. 'Are we going to go to dress rehearsals and run through this?' 'Nah, I'll be fine.'" A new dancer, Jamie King, often stood in for Michael during rehearsals, and Michael showed up a few days before the tour began and learned all the moves in three long days. Still, Michael had reason to be confident. Rehearsal footage from those days shows the King of Pop fully in command, lean and flexible in black slacks and a white dress shirt, leading his *Dangerous* dancers in lockstep and breaking from the pack to stalk the stage.

What Michael's dancers, musicians, and crew didn't know was that, as he prepared for the tour, he was in severe pain—and seeing a platoon of doctors to help him with it.

The Pepsi-commercial fire had done more lasting damage than he'd let on in 1984. Over time, Michael's scarring led to irritating, bumpy keloids, and the balloons installed to repair his scalp were constantly painful. He began to seek comfort from a friend—Debbie Rowe, a nurse who was the assistant to Arnold Klein, Michael's dermatologist. When Debbie and Michael first met, they clicked immediately. "I said, 'You know what? Nobody does what you do better, and nobody does what I do better. Let's get this over with.' And he laughed, and we just became friends," she recalls. "It was just right away." Rowe had first met Klein when he was a dermatology professor at UCLA and Stanford, working closely with AIDS patients. Later, she was with him when he opened up a dermatology office in Beverly Hills, specializing in collagen and Botox treatments for high-priced Hollywood patients.

David Geffen had referred Michael to Klein for acne treatment. It was Debbie who noticed Michael's low pain tolerance. Over the next two years, Debbie and Michael developed a friendship outside the doctor's office, speaking regularly on the phone, then sneaking past security to rent videos together, often fleeing from fans in the process.

In 1983, Klein diagnosed Michael with discoid lupus erythematosus, a skin condition that leads to uncomfortable rashes and scarring. Klein also noticed he had vitiligo, a disease in which a person's skin loses melanin, a pigment that establishes color, and creates off-putting white blotches. Like other African-Americans with the disease, Michael did his best to conceal the problem with makeup, but people who worked closely with him couldn't miss it. Endre Granat, the veteran LA concertmaster hired to work on the *Dangerous* album, suffers from the same condition; he spotted discoloration on Michael's face and asked him about it one day in the studio. "You have a little spot, like a dime, and suddenly that spot becomes an oval, then the next one doesn't connect to it, so you have black spots or white," Granat says. "He told me he was trying to lighten up his entire body." When Granat saw photos of Michael wearing fedoras in public, he assumed this was due to extreme sun sensitivity caused by the disease. "He didn't want to be spotted up," Katherine Jackson added. "His hands and face and neck and chest—that's the part he had bleached out so it wouldn't look so bad."

Until he divulged his vitiligo to Oprah Winfrey and the world in 1993, Michael kept the reasons for his bleached skin mysterious. He freaked out people who came in contact with him, and to some critics, he seemed like some kind of race traitor. "I'd never seen skin that color before. It was, like, parchment colored," recalls Sonya Saul, an MTV Europe correspondent who covered the tour. "It was very strange." Greg Tate of the *Village Voice* declared in a 1987 essay: "Jackson emerges a casualty of America's ongoing race war—another Negro gone mad because his mirror reports that his face does not conform to the Nordic ideal." Some MJ observers have suggested his vitiligo, while painful, gave him an excuse to mess around more than ever with racial boundaries. "We might say that his disease has liberated him from being bound to a black physicality," critic Michael Awkward wrote. Just as he refused to limit himself to one producer or one musical style, he didn't want to be limited to one look imposed by genetics or tradition. He belonged to everybody.

Michael's health issues were distracting him more than ever when he opened the *Dangerous* tour in Munich, Germany, on June 27, 1992. He was still in superb shape, although Rowe worried about Michael's loss of eight or nine pounds of "water" weight every night due to his grueling performances. "All I knew was that he wasn't eating properly," says set designer Tom McPhillips. "He was drinking fruit juice and eating lettuce or something like that. He was so worried about putting on weight that you felt that he wasn't eating even enough to keep up his stamina for that dance." During the Japanese leg of the tour, a doctor pushed Michael to consume more protein. Michael agreed, a security guard was dispatched for Kentucky Fried Chicken, and presto—after following a dietary regimen for twenty years, Michael was no longer a vegetarian. Soon he was going in the opposite direction. "He was eating cheese pizzas, cheese burritos. Can't live on cheese," says Johnny

Ciao, the celebrity chef who later cooked for the highly particular MJ at Neverland, rejiggering his diet to emphasize seafood and protein. "It was making him weak."

Due to what Michael's people termed throat problems, he canceled Park Stadium, in Gelsenkirchen, Germany, and other shows on the *Dangerous* tour. Michael's European promoter, Barry Clayman, called one of Elton John's longtime doctors. "Can you please come and see Mike?" Clayman asked David Forecast, a gastroenterologist in his late thirties. The British doctor wound up traveling with the tour through the end of its European run in October. By that point, Forecast says, Michael was "happy and working."

On tour, Michael brought with him a rotating crew of children— Brett Barnes, an eleven-year-old from Australia; Albert von Thurn und Taxis, nine, a rich prince from Bavaria; and Eddie and Frank Cascio, nine and thirteen, kids from New Jersey whose father had been general manager of the Helmsley Palace in Manhattan and befriended Michael when he stayed there. Sometimes their parents came along, sometimes they didn't. Their presence discomforted some on the tour. "There was always this family around—this mother and father and these kids— that would be on this tour with us," says a source who worked on the *Dangerous* tour. "I asked, 'Who are these people?' 'They're our advance family. We send them in front of the hotel before Jackson gets there.' It was a very, very weird thing, because when you're on these tours, they're very expensive, and everybody costs money, and the promoter is always looking for a way to save money." MTV's Saul, who hosted an interview-and-news segment called "Dangerous Diaries," was doing interviews on the bus and noticed a big-bed-little-bed situation for Michael and his young friends. "It's just uncomfortable," thought Saul, who has since become a London barrister specializing in rape and sexual-assault cases and other crimes. Also, Michael called Jordan Chandler, the kid he'd met at Rent-A-Wreck, several times while on tour, and they talked for hours.

The shows on the *Dangerous* tour opened with "the toaster," a machine that launched Michael from beneath the stage into a two-foot high-jump. He stuck the landing, then stood, silent and immobile, for three solid minutes, fists at his waist, staring into the distance in giant sunglasses. (He had first pulled off this statue move in rehearsal, without warning the crew. "What's he *doing?*" they asked each other.) Nobody—not Jagger, not Springsteen, not Prince—could hold a crowd with a single pose like Michael Jackson. "Some artists, with twenty dancers, you've got to kind of squint and pick out the artist," says Peter Morse, the tour's lighting designer. "With Michael, you could be back one hundred yards in a lighting tower, and there could be fifty-plus people onstage, and every eye would be exactly on Michael. He had that strong of an aura." In Bucharest, Romania, after holding the pose underneath a rainstorm of orange fireworks, Michael finally, dramatically moved his head to the left ("AAAAIIIEEEEE!" went the crowd of seventy thousand people), then raised his arms and slowly removed his sunglasses. Enhancing this effect was Michael's silver shirt, which seemed to change color underneath the lights, above a yellow onesie snugly wrapped around his crotch. "The revelation of his sculpted, made-up face only deepens the mystery," Susan Fast writes. "It is surely one of the most arresting and powerful ways an arena concert has begun in the history of the genre. This glitzy spectacle might be cheesy if it weren't followed by two and a half hours of nonstop, spectacular dancing and singing that somehow justifies his self-deification at the beginning."

HBO had paid $20 million to film the October 1 show in Bucharest. Producers spliced in screaming, crying, sweating, and fainting by young female fans every few seconds. During the performance, Michael shifts from heavily choreographed ensemble numbers like "Smooth Criminal" to his most loose and improvisational performances—he does an extra-long moonwalk in "Billie Jean," then scats gospel noises throughout "Workin' Day and Night" as he and Jennifer Batten chase each other around the stage.

As the *Dangerous* tour lumbered through Europe, musical director Greg Phillinganes was having trouble getting an audience with Michael. He was beginning to worry about three upcoming nights at London's huge Wembley Stadium, where the audience could detect every nuance. He tried to set up meetings. At first, he made repeated requests through tour security. Every time, someone told him, "No problem, we'll do it this time." Every time, it didn't happen. Finally, on July 5, in Dublin, Phillinganes called security again and insisted. "Okay," they said, "just stay in your room. We'll call you." Phillinganes waited, dutifully, until he became so bored that he turned on his TV—only to see a live report about Michael shopping at some local toy store. "I wasted a day in my room," Phillinganes recalls. "Then I realize that actually he must not care, which was greatly disappointing to me." Phillinganes stuck with the tour for a few months, through Istanbul in September 1993, then left Michael for good.

In three years, Michael Jackson had cut ties with Quincy Jones, Frank DiLeo, John Branca, and Phillinganes, four men who'd done more for his solo career than anyone else.

Earlier that year, Michael had returned home from the first leg of the tour. It wasn't exactly R&R. He performed at the American Music Awards. He took his *Dangerous* band and dancers to the Super Bowl halftime show, where he replicated his hold-the-pose move, this time in a dark military jacket with gold tunic and belt, and did a fine performance of "Jam" before transitioning into "Billie Jean," "Black or White," "We Are the World," and (surrounded by 3,500 singing children) "Heal the World." At President Clinton's inaugural gala, Michael sang "Gone Too Soon," the song Buz Kohan gave him as a tribute to the late Ryan White. And he sat down with Oprah Winfrey.

Michael had been avoiding the press for more than a decade, but in 1993, his brand of dance music was slipping out of pop culture as grunge, alternative rock, and hip-hop continued to ascend. He needed a publicity boost, and he agreed to a ninety-minute interview, preparing his responses so they were a mix of tantalizing truths and showmanship. He fleshed out what he'd only vaguely covered in his biography *Moonwalk*, including details about his vitiligo, his father's beatings (which drove him to tears), whether his brothers were jealous of his fame ("*Hmm*, let me think—no"), La Toya's provocative book about the Jackson family (he hadn't read it), the hyperbaric chamber ("Why would I want to sleep in a chamber?"), and the Elephant Man's bones ("Why would I want some bones?"). It wasn't so much a revealing interview as a performance, as Michael showed off his lighter skin, cleft chin, and proudly thin nose, oblivious to how viewers might have felt about his appearance, and delivered his answers in a high, singsong voice. If his purpose was to dispel myths, he succeeded sporadically. But he didn't exactly answer the questions, either. Why did he mess with his nose? Why did he claim he was dating Brooke Shields when, she said later, they were just good friends? Nobody was requiring Michael to answer questions on the witness stand, but viewers could see through his Motown-trained public relations. Had he been more honest and forthcoming in public, he might have made his very public life a little easier.

Two days after the interview with Oprah, which drew ninety million viewers, Michael called June Chandler and invited her family to hang out at Neverland for the weekend. He sent a limo. He stayed in the main house. June, thirteen-year-old Jordie, and seven-year-old Lily shacked up in the guest house. The fifty-six staff members waited on them. They rode on the Ferris wheel. They visited the zoo. Michael and Jordie played video games. Michael arranged an after-hours visit to Toys "R" Us and bought the kids anything they picked out.

The next weekend, on a Saturday night, Michael appeared at June's home in a limousine. He liked Jordie and was determined to make him part of his Neverland entourage. At the ranch, Jordie, June, and Lily encountered other boys, including Macaulay Culkin, Wade Robson, and Brett Barnes—sometimes in Michael's bed. June Chandler was more than happy to be part of it, especially since Michael kept giving her gifts and inviting the family to luxurious places. June would request food from Michael's staff and "sort of act like the place was hers," recalled Robson, a dancer. "Sort of order people around a bit." Nobody considered the bed thing weird. "It's not like you think," Culkin said. "First of all, it's a huge bed. There's always people, staff, servants, advisers, coming in and out of the room. The door is always open and my family was always invited. They were always around. It was like a giant slumber party."

Michael invited June and her family again and again. The Chandlers grew close to him. Sometimes they stayed at Michael's apartment on Wilshire Boulevard in Century City. The first time Jordan shared the same bed with Michael was in Las Vegas, at the Michael Jackson Suite in the Mirage. In late March, Michael had sent a private jet to pick up June, Jordie, and Lily, and they flew out from the Santa Monica airport. That night, Michael (in sweats) and Jordie (in pajamas) watched a movie: *The Exorcist*. Jordan became scared. "Oh, you want to stay here with me?" Michael asked. "Yeah," Jordan told his friend, "I'll stay here." While his mother and sister slept in another bedroom, Jordie fell asleep in Michael's bed.

It began to dawn on Jordie's mother that something wasn't quite right between Michael Jackson and her son. They wanted to sleep together in the bed, again, the next night. June tried to put her foot down. It was Michael, though, who emotionally appealed June's decision. He confronted her. He trembled. He sobbed. He talked with June for half an hour. He told her he considered the Chandlers part of his family. "Jordie is having fun. Why can't he sleep in my bed? There's nothing wrong. There's nothing going on," Michael said. "Don't you trust me?" June relented. The next day, he bought June a $12,000 gold Cartier bracelet. June withdrew her concerns. MJ and Jordan wound up sleeping in the same room numerous times at Neverland. Michael, too, crashed at June's house with her husband David Schwartz, the owner of Rent-A-Wreck; he would spend the night in Jordie's room, which contained only one bed, numerous times over a thirty-day period. When Jordie left for school, Michael left, too.

At first, Evan Chandler had been proud of his son's relationship with Michael Jackson. It was something to talk about with his celebrity clients. "[Chandler] would go on and on about how much his son liked Michael Jackson and, more important, how much Michael Jackson liked his son," actress Carrie Fisher, one of Evan's patients, recalled. Eventually, Fisher had to interrupt: "Hang on," she told her dentist. "They're sleeping in the *same bed?*" As more of his friends and family reacted with the same shock and indignation, Chandler began to feel something might be wrong. Michael, oblivious to Evan's growing suspicion, continued to travel with the dentist's family. They went to Disney World in May 1993, staying at the Grand Floridian—Lily and June in one room, Jordie and Michael in another. Later, the three Chandlers took a trip with Michael to the World Music Awards in Monte Carlo. Jordan and Lily were photographed on Michael's lap, enthusiastically mouthing along to Tina Turner songs. After numerous such trips, Jordie's family noticed a change in his behavior. "He was not wanting to be with Lily and I anymore, and he was just with Michael the whole time," June would say, "and he wasn't too happy. . . . I didn't have any communication with him, really. He started dressing like Michael. He started acting withdrawn, sort of smart-alecky. Not as sweet as he normally was."

The *National Enquirer* published a May 16 story about "Michael's new, adopted family," including photos of Michael and Jordie together at Disney World. It was time for Evan Chandler to meet this guy. The dentist showed up at June's house, and the first thing he noticed was a new look to his son's room. It was full of plastic army men, toys of all kinds, a life-size cardboard *Captain EO*, autographed photos of

Michael, and a cabinet stuffed with movies, CDs, and video games. Evan described his first, not particularly charitable impression of Michael Jackson: "Ruby red lipstick, thick black eyeliner, long strands of dark hair hanging down in front of his pancaked face. But what struck me the most was how lonely he looked, huddled in the corner staring at the floor. I couldn't help feeling sorry for him." Chandler had brought along his other son, five-year-old Nikki, who immediately fell to the floor and began rolling around with the childlike Michael Jackson, playing with action figures. Later, Evan could no longer hold back: "Are you fucking my son up the ass?" Michael's response to this crudity, unbelievably, was to giggle. He did not flinch. "I never use that word," he said. Evan pressed further: "Then exactly what *is* the nature of your relationship?" Said Michael: "I don't understand it myself. It must be cosmic." On Memorial Day weekend 1993, Evan said he showed up to the Schwartz home in Brentwood and found the King of Pop, in bed, spooning with Jordan Chandler, both fully clothed.

Evan kept making concerned phone calls, but Michael was getting tired of soothing the dentist, so he stopped returning them. June was becoming concerned, too, and Michael soothed her in a different way, through more lavish gifts, including earrings, a necklace, and a ring, which he left on her bed at her home in Santa Monica. Evan "began to get jealous of the involvement and felt left out," Michael Freeman, one of June's attorneys, would say. In a phone conversation with Dave Schwartz that June's husband secretly taped, Evan vowed revenge: "I am prepared to move against Michael Jackson. It's already set. There are other people involved that are waiting for my phone call that are in certain positions. I've paid them to do it. . . . Once I make that phone call, this guy is going to destroy everybody in sight in any devious, nasty, cruel way that he can do it."

Once Evan Chandler decided Michael Jackson was molesting his son, he conspicuously did not report the abuse to the California Department of Social Services' Children and Family Services Division.

Instead he picked out an attorney, Barry Rothman, the "nastiest son of a bitch I could find," as he told Schwartz. Rothman, a longtime music attorney in Century City who had negotiated deals for rock stars from the Who to the Rolling Stones, had problems of his own. Thirty creditors had been after him and more than twenty civil suits involving Rothman had been filed in LA Superior Court, and an ex-wife once said Rothman had so many enemies she was surprised one of them hadn't "done him in." Rothman helped Chandler decide on a plan. Part one was to modify June's custody agreement—Evan asked a court to ban Jordie from seeing Michael.

Michael began to get wind of Evan Chandler's aggressive moves. He called his own $500-an-hour attorney, Bert Fields, who'd represented Tom Cruise, Warren Beatty, George Lucas, John Travolta, and Dustin Hoffman over four decades in Hollywood. Michael had yet to spend away most of his fortune—HBO had just paid $20 million for the live Bucharest video. Fields brought in Anthony Pellicano as a private investigator and negotiator. "If you're on the side he's against, the flamboyant Pellicano . . . is a goon and a bully who fights dirty," *Vanity Fair* opined. "If he's on your side, he is an invaluable ally, a trusted adviser, a canny investigator. He is most often called in when there is deep doo-doo all over that needs to be avoided or slung in the opposite direction." Pellicano began to meet with everybody, including June Chandler and Dave Schwartz, who played him the tapes he'd made containing Evan's belligerence. Pellicano also interviewed Jordie at Michael's hideout apartment. He looked the thirteen-year-old in the eye and asked pointed questions for forty-five minutes: *Have you ever seen Michael Jackson naked? Has he ever seen you naked? Have you ever done anything sexual with him?* "No," came the answer, to every question.

Meanwhile, Rothman contacted Dr. Mathis Abrams, a Beverly Hills psychiatrist, and asked hypothetical questions based on Jordie's relationship with Michael. From this conversation, Dr. Abrams wrote a two-page letter declaring "reasonable suspicion would exist that sexual abuse may have occurred." He also said if such a case actually existed, he'd have to report it to Los Angeles County's Department of Children and Family Services.

Two weeks later, Chandler pulled Jordie's final baby tooth at his dentist office. This might have been a routine procedure. But he had Mark Torbiner, his longtime anesthesiologist, administer a drug called sodium amytal for the procedure. The results were dramatic. When Evan asked, "Did Michael ever touch your penis?," Jordie whispered, "Yes." Evan then hugged his son: "I'm sorry, Jordie," he said. "I'm sorry." To many who'd been following the Michael Jackson child-molestation case closely, this is where the Chandlers' story breaks down. "Sodium amytal is a barbiturate that puts people into a hypnotic state," writes Ian Halperin, an investigative journalist who intended to prove the allegations but wound up flipping to Michael's side. "Once believed to be a truth serum effective in the interrogation of prisoners, it has become associated in recent years with something far more sinister—false memory syndrome." If Jordie had merely said MJ had molested him, the charge would be difficult to deny. But Jordie was on sodium amytal when he said MJ had molested him—a totally different thing.

On August 4, Evan, Jordie, Michael, and Pellicano sat down at the Westwood Marquis Hotel. Michael told Jordie he missed him and stroked his hair. "I've missed you too," Jordie told him. Evan greeted Michael cordially, then blurted out, "This doctor thinks you had sex with my kid." He began shouting at him to "just fucking admit it!" Michael called the charge "preposterous." He and Pellicano cut off the meeting and left. "I'm going to ruin you," Evan said, pointing at Michael. "You're going down, Michael. You are going down." Afterward, Michael said: "Oh, my God. Oh, my God. Oh, my God."

Later that night, Pellicano and Rothman met in Rothman's office. Evan Chandler wanted to make a deal: Michael would give Jordie $20 million in a trust fund, and the Chandler family would drop all of its allegations of child molestation. After a few phone discussions and another meeting, on August 13, Pellicano counteroffered: $350,000 for a three-script screenwriting deal, with the promise of review from a major studio. Rothman proposed Chandler's counteroffer a day later: a three-script, $15 million deal. Some of Evan Chandler's friends who believed Jordie were aghast at these negotiations. "Are you *insane?*" asked Hollywood screenwriter J. D. Shapiro, who had given a credit for *Robin Hood: Men in Tights* to the dentist and moonlighting screenwriter. "A *three-picture deal?*"

As the negotiations between Michael's people and Evan's people continued, the Chandlers continued to fight over Jordie's custody. June had signed an agreement that wouldn't allow her son to leave LA County—even to travel on Michael's *Dangerous* tour, which Jordie wanted to do. But she began to feel coerced into signing it, and on August 16, she filed a motion in California Supreme Court demanding that her son be returned to her. Evan Chandler did not appreciate the pressure. He returned to Mathis Abrams, who had evaluated Jordie's molestation charges hypothetically, and asked the doctor to meet his son in person. Abrams listened to Jordie's actual story for three hours on August 17. For the first time, Jordie revealed details about masturbation and oral sex with Jackson, which, he said, had taken place for months. This time, Abrams reported the claims to the Department of Children and Family Services, where a social worker interviewed Jordie further and concluded he was telling the truth. Two days later, Michael left to resume the *Dangerous* tour in Bangkok. For two days after that, LA police officers raided Neverland and Michael's Century City hideout, digging up boxes of photos and files.

On August 23, somebody woke up freelance KNBC reporter Don Ray to tip him off about what was happening at Neverland. Ray's colleague, Conan Nolan, dug further and learned police had brought in a locksmith to gain access to MJ's house. Nolan called locksmiths all over Santa Barbara County before one finally said: "I can't talk to you, but all I can say is, I hope they don't find what they're looking for."

Nolan called the LAPD, which confirmed an investigation into child-molestation accusations of Michael Jackson. KNBC broke its story at four P.M. LA time. From there, MJ became the lead story on seventy-three news broadcasts in the LA area.

The year 1993 was supposed to be triumphant for Michael Jackson—he was putting on the most elaborate concert tour in history, before hundreds of thousands of screaming fans in every city in Europe, and he'd appeared on *Oprah* and the Super Bowl. Instead, it was full of pain. On March 16, Dr. Gordon Sasaki, a plastic surgeon outside LA, did a procedure to reduce the scarring on Michael's scalp. By late June, Michael began to feel "significant" pain, especially since the hairpiece he used to cover the bald spot he'd had since the Pepsi-commercial accident was pressuring his scalp. Sasaki prescribed Percocet, then ceded his pain-medication control to Michael's longtime doctors, Arnold Klein and Steven Hoefflin. For this procedure, as well as Michael's continuing struggles with discoid lupus and acne scarring—plus his continuing experiments with his nose, chin, and cheekbones—Klein and Debbie Rowe administered pain medication. They were careful not to give too much, Rowe recalls. For early injections of the protein collagen, used for "filling" of his acne scars, they offered no painkillers at first. Later, they expanded to a relatively small 100 milligrams of Demerol.

As *Dangerous* tour rehearsals were beginning in Santa Monica, Rowe worked with an internist and rheumatologist named Allan Metzger to reduce Michael's pain medication. Rowe believed Michael's doctors, Klein and Hoefflin, had been competing to give him more and more potent drugs. For example, to help with the collagen and other procedures on his face, Michael received Diprivan injections through his eyelid—this was also known as propofol, a sleep-inducing drug with heavy side effects. Metzger wrote instructions, and Rowe worked with MJ to carry them out. But one day, Debbie showed up at Neverland, bearing soup, and he was gone—musical instruments, clothes, every-thing. Michael had left for the rest of the *Dangerous* tour.

When Michael arrived in Bangkok on August 21, 1993, to begin the third leg of *Dangerous*, he was hurting, emotionally and physically. His condition was so bad that promoters had to summon Stuart Finkelstein, a general physician who had been traveling with the tour to take care of the crew, to treat Michael in his hotel room. When Finkelstein arrived, MJ put him on the phone with his regular doctor, Allan Metzger, who instructed him to administer pain meds. Finkelstein first tried a shot of Demerol, the painkiller, and noticed scarring on Michael's rear end that suggested he'd had numerous versions of these kinds of shots before. The doctor put MJ on an intravenous morphine drip for twenty-four hours—during which they watched *The Three Stooges* in his hotel room—until the King of Pop was well enough to perform his show. The painkillers MJ took to recover from that surgical procedure, says Eve Wagner, one of his attorneys, who attended a portion of the tour, "led him down the path of something horrible. That was the start of it." By the end of the show, Michael was using an oxygen tank to breathe. "He was exhausted," recalls tour photographer Sam Emerson. He had to reschedule, then can-cel, the second Bangkok show. "Dehydration," promoters announced.

"Michael had to go on stage every night knowing that the whole world thought he was a pedophile," Karen Faye, MJ's friend and makeup artist, would say in court. "He had to stand up in front of all these audi-ences with the physical pain that he had and knowing that everybody in that audience is thinking that he was the vilest pedophile on earth. To this day, I don't know how he did that."

Back in Los Angeles, police were trying to figure out how to handle Jordan Chandler's allegations of child molestation. The investigator from the Department of Children and Family Services who had inter-viewed Jordan had apparently sold her story to the media before the police had a chance to follow up. "So we were behind when we got the case," recalls Federico Sicard, the LAPD detective who investigated the charges. Complicating matters, Jackson employees who may have had firsthand knowledge of what really happened between Michael and Jordie had some kind of interest—they were suing Michael for back payments, selling a story to the press, or trying to get attention.

Philippe and Stella LeMarque oversaw Neverland's household staff; Philippe said he saw Michael groping Macaulay Culkin, who stood there playing pinball as if everything was normal. Stella said she saw Michael groping an Australian boy. With the help of Paul Barresi, a fast-talking former porn director and actor who injected himself into the story as a tabloid middleman, they fielded interview offers of $100,000 to $150,000 from the *Globe* and the *National Enquirer*. A group of security guards at the Jacksons' family home who became known as the Hayvenhurst Five said they'd seen Michael bring thirty to forty boys into his private quarters at varying points between 1987 to 1993, sometimes in the night. They sued Jackson, claiming they were fired because of what they knew. They sold their story to *Hard Copy*. Mark Quindoy and his wife, Faye, had been Neverland estate managers from 1987 to 1991; Mark gave a news conference alleging Michael was a "gay pedophile." He said, "Whatever a gay man does to his partner during sex, Michael does to a child. I swear I saw Michael Jackson fondling the little kid, his hands traveling on the kid's thighs, legs, around his body. And during all this, the kid was playing with his toys." The Quindoys had been fighting with Jackson's people over $283,000 they said he owed in "unpaid overtime wages." They tried to get $25,000 for TV interviews. Blanca Francia, a Neverland maid, told *Hard Copy* she'd witnessed Jackson bathing naked in his Jacuzzi and showering with boys. It came out later that the show had paid Francia $20,000 for her participation in an episode titled "The Bedroom Maid's Painful Secret." Under grand-jury questioning, Francia changed her recollection to say everybody had swimsuits on.

"It was frustrating," says the LAPD's Sicard, now retired. "You know, when you go to court, that's going to come up, and it'll be a tainted witness. The credibility is going to go down. That's pretty much what we're thinking—'Oh, my gosh, make it a little more difficult for us.'"

None of the charges by security guards, maids, and staff amounted to anything, although reporters would repeat them for years, particularly Diane Dimond of *Hard Copy*, in her 2005 book *Be Careful Who You Love*. Police aggressively followed every lead. Detective Sicard flew to the Philippines to talk to the Quindoys. "They kept a diary. We saw the diary. That was going to be a good piece of evidence," Sicard says. "When we went to the airport, 10,299 reporters were there. 'Man, how did they find out?' Of course, the Quindoys probably told them we were going to interview them." A team flew to Melbourne to interview Michael's friend Brett Barnes, who had said publicly he had slept in Michael's bed. When the officers arrived, Brett and his family refused to speak with them, so they had to turn around and take the fifteen-hour flight back. They interviewed Michael's other young friends, including Macaulay Culkin, Emmanuel Lewis, Jimmy Safechuck, Jonathan Spence, and Wade Robson, all of whom insisted Michael had done nothing wrong. The police weren't sure whom to believe—"we were just trying to find out if, in fact, the accusations were true, never saying whether he was guilty," Sicard says—but they were struck by how perfectly Jordan Chandler remembered events. After he told them about the Michael Jackson Suite at the Mirage, in Vegas, where he'd allegedly been sexually molested, the LAPD went to investigate, armed with a warrant. Jordie's description perfectly matched the room, down to MJ's name on the door.

Every cable channel, every tabloid, gave the Michael Jackson child-molestation story full-time coverage. The *New York Post*'s most infamous headline on the subject was PETER PAN OR PERVERT? The *National Enquirer* assigned twenty reporters and editors to the story, and a group of them knocked on five hundred doors in the posh Brentwood section of LA to ferret out Evan Chandler. They succeeded, with the help of property records, and ambushed him in his black Mercedes.

Michael's sister La Toya called a press conference to declare: "I just think Michael needs help. This has been going on since 1981, and it's not just one child." She added that she could no longer "be a silent collaborator of his crimes against small, innocent children. If I remain silent, then that means I feel the guilt and humiliation that these children are feeling, and I think it's very wrong." (Later, she said her Svengali-like manager and abusive husband, Jack Gordon, made her write and say evil things during this period.) "A lot of strange things happened," says Larry Feldman, Jordan Chandler's attorney. "There was a bird in a cage, dead on [the Chandlers'] doorstep. There were swastikas painted on my law office's building." The crush of news reports confused even the cops. "Watching Diane Dimond on TV at times became a source of possible investigatory leads," says Lauren Weis Birnstein, who was part of the LAPD's investigative team at the time and is today a Los Angeles Superior Court judge. "Sometimes she had better information and more resources than the police investigators."

After Michael rebounded from Bangkok, the *Dangerous* tour rolled on, to Singapore, Moscow, and Tel Aviv. But there were inexplicable hitches. In Istanbul, fans had been skeptical about American music stars, but as the trucks rolled in and roadies set everything up in the middle of town, they began to get excited. The day before the show at Inonu Stadium, Michael decided he couldn't perform. "Sorry! I can't do it!" he said, sitting in the back of a van en route to the airport. His local concert promoter was in tears. The fans went berserk. "He left us there to fend for ourselves," recalls Greg Phillinganes, who left the tour shortly afterward. "We almost didn't make it out. They almost didn't let him out. It was crazy. It was a borderline revolt."

Michael managed to keep it together through three shows in Mexico

City, in late October 1993, but then, recalls David Forecast, MJ's personal physician, "Things went belly-up and Mike got in a very bad way." Those close to Michael noticed he wasn't quite right. "He was there, but he wasn't there," says Benny Collins, the tour's production manager.

For a week, Forecast spent his days and nights with Michael. Then he heard a knock on his hotel-room door, and when he opened it, before him stood Elizabeth Taylor and her new husband, Larry Fortensky. The tour's "head powers," as Finkelstein, the tour's crew doctor, had called them, had summoned Liz for an intervention. Forecast wasn't particularly happy to see her: "We had a slight professional discussion that maybe the doctor should deal with the medicine and the actors should do the acting." Michael sorted it out by saying he wanted to keep Forecast on hand for medical consultation, and his old friend Liz would do the rest. Michael announced he was canceling his five scheduled shows at the hundred-thousand capacity Estadio Azteca in Mexico City, as well as the rest of the tour. "The pressure resulting from these false allegations, coupled with the incredible energy necessary for me to perform, caused so much distress that it left me physically and emotionally exhausted," he said in a statement. "I became increasingly more dependent on the painkillers." With help from one of Michael's most trusted security men, Wayne Nagin, his small entourage including Taylor, Fortensky, and Forecast managed to escape Mexico City, where promoters had told members of Michael's team they'd land in prison if they weren't able to do the shows. They took a 737 to Reykjavík, Iceland, where one of Liz's dogs relieved himself. Then they flew on to Luton Airport in London.

Taylor had picked out a rehab facility for Michael—Charter Nightingale Clinic in central London. It didn't work out, due to what Forecast calls "medical issues." The doctor wasn't pleased—he was jet-lagged and annoyed he had to leave his wife, a nurse who worked with him on the tour, behind in Mexico City. "We'd been hijacked by Ms. Taylor," he recalls. Forecast steered Michael to Elton John manager John Reid's

$3 million home at Rickmansworth, Hertfordshire. Michael fell asleep on the sofa. Michael did most of his convalescence at Reid's house, then relocated to millionaire investor Jack Dellal's farm seventy miles south of London. At one point, they had dinner with Elton John and his new boyfriend, David Furnish, at Elton's house. The rehab was a success and, amazingly, achieved Michael's goal of eluding paparazzi completely. "No one knew," Forecast says. "When we left the farm, Mike was in a great place psychologically." When they returned home, they went through customs in Billings, Montana. The customs officer couldn't believe Michael Jackson was on the plane. "Listen," Forecast told him, "we will send your kids more memorabilia than you can buy in the store if you just let us get home without letting the world know who this is."*

When the *Dangerous* crew received the call to cancel the remaining shows in Mexico City—"Okay, tour's over, you're done"—Michael's people had no idea what to do. "We didn't even know where to put the gear," recalls Anthony Giordano, the tour's assistant stage manager. Eventually, working with Rock-It Cargo, they scrambled to break down the production, repack everything into the An-124 freighter jets, and fly it all to Las Vegas, the only airport big enough to accommodate them on short notice.

By fall 1993, Jordan Chandler's attorney, Larry Feldman, had taken charge of the case. Barry Rothman, Evan's attack dog of a lawyer, had resigned. "I went to a lot of different experts and was convinced there

---

*Michael's rehab at this time has long been a mystery to reporters: "For the record," Diane Dimond wrote in her book, "I could never independently confirm that Jackson really entered the London clinic touted to have been his rehabilitation program of choice." One of Michael's bodyguards at the time, Steve Tarling, gave a different, more detailed account of this scene to the British tabloid the *Mail*. Tarling described Michael's pre-rehab appearance as "so drugged up he was like a zombie." I opted for Forecast's version, especially after reaching Tarling via Twitter, where he asked if I paid for interviews, and when I said no, he stopped responding to inquiries.

were lots of reasons to believe this boy," Feldman says. "He had a lot to deal with. He had his parents separated, he had Michael Jackson in his life, [he had] the enormity of what he's about to be doing . . . at a very just horrible time for kids, in general, as they're going through puberty." On September 14, the day before Michael was to play Luzhniki Stadium in Moscow, Feldman filed Chandler's lawsuit against Michael Jackson in LA Superior Court. The filing included a four-page affidavit in which Jordan declared Michael Jackson "put his tongue in my mouth," "rubbed up against me in bed," "masturbated me to a climax," and "masturbated me many times both with his hand and with his mouth." In terse, horrifying, declarative sentences, Chandler recalled how Michael kept telling him all these activities were okay and he'd done them with other kids.

For Michael Jackson, the public humiliation of that complaint was nothing compared to his private humiliation on December 20. Jordan Chandler had given police a description of Michael's genitals, including an image he'd drawn by hand—Michael had distinctive "splotches" on his rear end and penis, both of which were "a light color similar to the color of his face," according to an affidavit by Deborah Linden of the Santa Barbara County sheriff's department. Jordan drew a picture of Michael's genital area, declared him to be circumcised, and added, "He has short pubic hair. His testicles are marked with pink and brown marks. Like a cow, not white, but pink color." Police raided the offices of Klein and Hoefflin for Michael's medical records. Finally, they obtained a search warrant to examine Michael Jackson's entire body, from penis to scrotum to buttocks, and take photos. They had to see if the real thing matched the description.

This is where Tom Sneddon, the Santa Barbara district attorney, comes into the story. He was a former boxer who'd attended Notre Dame and UCLA law school. He had been known as "Mad Dog," a prosecutor who was "sharp-tongued and tenacious," as *USA Today* once called him. He was not flashy, didn't care for the spotlight, and had been interviewed sparingly over the years, emerging in news stories only when he sought publicity for his crackdowns on toxic polluters and deadbeat dads. He and his staff had come to believe Jackson was guilty. "We were pretty satisfied that he was molesting Jordan Chandler," says Ron Zonen, Sneddon's number two. "He would come over when Jordie got out of school and would spend the night with him for weeks." Sneddon considered himself a crusader bent on ridding the world of a predator; one of Michael's later attorneys, David LeGrand, would take the opposing view, widely held among MJ fans, saying Sneddon had a "hard-on for Michael."

Sneddon, along with the LAPD's Sicard, was part of the team of investigators who arranged a trip to Neverland, on Sneddon's turf in Santa Barbara County. After long discussions on how to access Neverland without media attention, they decided to hide in plain sight, driving down the narrow dirt road in Los Olivos toward the ranch entrance in a stretch limousine. They drove past the media trucks. They drove past the gates, about a mile down the main driveway, and parked by a pond and a replica of the Main Street in Disneyland. Michael's own security team met them there. His guards had guns, too. The police investigators sat in the car for half an hour. "People are getting ticked off, because that's not usually how police are used to being treated," recalls Richard Strick, a dermatologist working for the Santa Barbara DA's office. "The guys had guns out and they were deciding if they had enough weaponry to take on [Michael's] people."

Finally, a half dozen helicopters flew in and landed on the other side of Michael's house. They contained Michael's dermatologist, Arnold Klein, and a team of his attorneys, including Howard Weitzman and Johnnie Cochran. Nobody bothered to turn off the harp music that had been blaring all this time through the Neverland speakers. When he left the car, Strick made a crack. "I'm glad we're finally getting to do this—that harp music is driving me nuts." Weitzman wheeled around: "I don't appreciate that comment," he snapped at Strick. "I don't find one fucking funny thing about this." Strick returned fire: "Me neither, I don't find one fucking funny thing about this," he told Michael's attorney, "especially with that *fucking harp music*." The two of them approached each other with clenched fists and said, "Oh yeah?" a few times before Cochran, the high-profile celebrity attorney who had been one of Strick's patients and knew both men well, calmed them down.

The police showed Weitzman the search warrant. For the first time, Weitzman realized the DA wanted a close-up examination of what Jordie had described as the "splotches" on his genitalia. Weitzman whispered this into Michael's ear, and he began to melt down: "Get out! Get out!" he hollered. Weitzman called for Cochran, who had been downstairs negotiating with the visitors. The two attorneys huddled with Michael. Both sides agreed the team examining Michael Jackson would include Klein, Strick, Forecast (who was present as Michael's personal physician), and Gary Spiegel, a photographer from the sheriff's office. Two detectives accompanied them. Cochran ushered the group inside, and they met Michael's security chief Bill Bray and his own photographer, Louis Swayne. Bray led them to a small room on the second floor. Michael was sitting on a couch, wearing a tan bathrobe. When Detective Russ Birchim of the Santa Barbara County sheriff's office and Sicard introduced themselves, Michael gave a meek "Thank you." Then he broke into a tantrum. "He was whining and complaining," Strick says. Forecast, Michael's doctor from the *Dangerous* tour, was the one to tell the pop star to calm down. Michael slapped him and told him to "shut the fuck up," as Strick recalls. Forecast insists this slap never happened—he had long been out of the room by then. Detective Sicard says MJ slapped Forecast's leg, not his cheek. Strick is sure it was the cheek.

Strick began his examination. He noticed the vitiligo, and could see Michael had undergone treatments to dye his skin into a more uniform color. It wasn't working. He observed the discoid lupus erythematosus, Michael's painful skin disease that had been diagnosed years earlier; he could see the disease had destroyed nose cartilage, which might have explained some of Michael's plastic surgery. Strick can't say firsthand whether the photos he took of Michael Jackson's genitalia fit Chandler's description, but through conversations he had later with investigators, he concluded, "It sure would appear that some young boy had pretty close views of his genitalia." Did Chandler's drawings match the real thing? This is a matter of historical interpretation, since the public has thankfully been spared photos of Michael Jackson's genitalia. To *Vanity Fair*, Sneddon answered yes. But Reuters quoted an unidentified source in January 1994 who said, "Photos of Michael Jackson's genitalia do not match descriptions given by the boy." Either way, tellingly, as Ian Halperin points out, Sneddon did not indict MJ.

A civil trial between the Chandlers and Michael was scheduled for March 21, 1994. For months, despite the surreal negotiations over screenplay deals, Michael refused to give any money whatsoever to Evan and his family. He and his people considered the celebrity dentist an extortionist. But Elizabeth Taylor counseled Michael to fix the problem quickly: "Get rid of this thing, you've got all the money in the world. Why do you have to fight it?" One of Michael's attorneys, Bert Fields, disagreed. "I felt that paying any substantial amount would be a tragic mistake—that he should fight it," he says. "I was convinced he would win." He wasn't Liz.

At the time, Michael had money to spare. In fall 1993, when Sony offered to buy half of the ATV catalog, containing the Beatles songs, for $75 million, he called his former attorney, John Branca. "Are you crazy, Michael?" Branca asked. Michael rehired him. (Branca believed Bert Fields had made a huge mistake by not offering a comparatively small settlement with the Chandler family much earlier. Branca was the one who advised MJ to bring on Johnnie Cochran as a defense attorney to replace Fields.) Instead of selling out half of Michael's crucial financial engine to Sony, Branca made a $150 million deal with EMI to administer the ATV catalog. It would not be the last time he would use the ATV catalog as a life-saving money machine. The $20 million settlement Michael Jackson made with the Chandler family was something he could afford. Evan and June received $1.5 million apiece. Jordan received $15.3 million. Larry Feldman, the Chandlers' attorney, has been widely reported to have received $3 million in legal fees due to the settlement, but he refuses to talk about it. After the settlement, Jordie Chandler essentially vanished, changing his name and moving to a $2.35 million home in eastern Long Island. Evan Chandler, too, changed his identity. In November 2009, his body was discovered in his sixteenth-floor waterfront home in Jersey City, with the gun he'd used to shoot himself. Tom Mesereau, Michael's future defense attorney, would spend a lot of time overcoming the public assumption that Michael settled with the Chandler family because he was guilty. "He would've been better off just beating them in court," he says. The settlement, he adds, was a "Pandora's box" leading to a wave of lawsuits that would continue through his death. "The word got out you can sue Michael Jackson," he says.

CHAPTER 8

Rupert Wainwright's two-year adventure with Michael Jackson began with a phone call on the Hollywood set of a TV commercial he was filming. The voice on the other line belonged to Sandy Gallin, Michael's manager. "You are Michael Jackson's newest favorite director," he said. Wainwright had only made one film, *Blank Check*, a 1994 flop starring Karen Duffy and Miguel Ferrer. The next thing he knew, a helicopter was picking him up in Santa Monica for a seven P.M. meeting with Michael at Neverland Ranch. Wainwright and his girlfriend had signed "like eight hundred non-disclosure agreements" and weren't sure what to expect, but as they descended into the Santa Barbara–area mist and spotted the lights and rides, they were charmed despite themselves. They were ushered to an antechamber in an all-white house and a woman "who looks like something out of *Downton Abbey*" asked the young couple if they'd like a drink. Wainwright requested a gin and tonic. The woman responded, "I'll see if we have it!" Beneath an eight-foot-by-two-foot painting of MJ as the pied piper, with dozens of children following him over a broad landscape, they dined on tofu and soft-boiled chicken with Michael Jackson before white-knuckling through the pirate-ship ride.

Michael called again, a few weeks later, at 11:45 P.M. on a Sunday. He explained he had an idea for a short film, a "teaser" designed to publicize his upcoming album *HIStory*, and he'd like to discuss it in person. So the British director was whisked to Orlando, where he took an anonymous passenger van, then checked in to a hotel under a pseudonym, for a meeting with Michael. The singer hired Wainwright, and his production company designed storyboards and planned a budget, hewing to Michael's vision, for $4 million. Sony reps tried to secretly advise Wainwright to keep the costs down, but the director could see they had zero control over MJ.

Michael's vision was to be dressed in full military regalia, shiny gold on his chest, with mirrored shades, benevolently waving to roped-off proletarians shouting "Michael!" as he and hundreds of jackbooted troops paraded down the streets. His factory-worker minions were to hold KING OF POP and WE LOVE YOU! signs, waving flags as a banner of Michael's enlarged eye flew overhead.

"It was insane," Wainwright recalls.

The director and his crew traveled to Eastern Europe without Michael, scouting locations before settling on Budapest, a city with the right mix of historic landscapes and modern accommodations. Wainwright's producer hired four hundred real-life local soldiers in boots and jackets, flying in trainers from London, New York, and Los Angeles to school "these very confused Hungarian drill sergeants doing Jacksonesque choreography," Wainwright recalls. The work was laborious and complicated. "Each day was like closing Wilshire Boulevard," he says. Michael shot a few scenes on a green screen in New York, decided he was having a good time, then flew to Budapest to be part of the movie. Once MJ showed up, the director recalls, "You'd look in the skies and there'd be at least eight helicopters buzzing and dodging overhead."

In Budapest, Michael began to slip storyboards underneath the door of Wainwright's hotel room. Wainwright's punishing schedule involved filming all day, then unwinding with a couple of drinks before falling asleep at two A.M. This would have given him six hours of sleep before the next day's shoot. But Michael regularly called at four A.M. from the presidential suite: "Do you have a pencil?" He had a specific vision for a scene involving two young women behind the barriers, one curly-haired, one blonde, and when MJ passed by, they would faint into a policeman's arms. He described exactly how the women's hair would look. "You're writing this down, right?" Michael asked as Wainwright sleepily took dictation.

The Budapest shoot turned into a story more dramatic than the one depicted on film. Wainwright showed up to the set one day and all the troops were gone. They'd been called to defend the Hungarian borders during the Croatian War of Independence. In their place, one of Wainwright's resourceful producers had imported 150 British paratroopers on a chartered 707, at a cost of $500,000, for arrival the following morning. Wainwright's people had to hire 150 Hungarian police cadets to stand in for the marchers. The catch: they were scheduled to take final police-academy exams on the Monday of shooting; the film crew stationed minivans outside the exams to whisk the cadets back to the set. ("You're done, you've got an A, get in the van.")* In the end, the budget for the proposed $4 million video ballooned to $8 million.

Wainwright has fond memories of MJ, and he recounts these events with a mixture of humor and disbelief. "Michael was such a dreamer and such a perfectionist. I don't know if he was ignorant of the finances, or chose to ignore them. But clearly in Michael Jackson Land, the financial consequences of choices in a creative manner—the reality of that was diminished in his mind. He knew it would cost something but he just figured it was affordable, or it just didn't really matter, or it just had to be done right."

---

*Computer-generated graphics, later used to fill out war scenes in movies like 300, were still too expensive and cumbersome, even on Michael Jackson's budget, in 1996.

It was MJ's job to rescue and liberate the world, not remind people of its limitations.

To those who worked with Michael Jackson at the Hit Factory, a one-hundred-thousand-square-foot studio on West Fifty-Fourth Street in New York where stars from Bruce Springsteen to Stevie Wonder to John Lennon had made albums, the King of Pop arrived in a cloak of secrecy. "He never touched New York City's dirt," says Tony Black, one of many assistant engineers who worked on his newest album. "He would go from the indoor garage in the Trump [Towers], where he was living, to his car or truck or van. They would drive him into the building of the Hit Factory, into the freight elevator, and go up from there into the studio."

As with *Dangerous* at its outset, the first vision for *HIStory: Past, Present & Future, Book I* was a greatest-hits collection. The idea came from Sony Music executives, who began talking about it within two weeks of Michael's 1994 settlement with Jordie Chandler over child-molestation charges. They wanted a stopgap, a way of reminding the public of their best-selling star's good qualities until he could make a proper comeback. "It was really a simple formula," says Dan Beck, an Epic Records marketing executive who worked closely with the singer. "But with Michael, it's never simple." What Beck and his colleagues didn't know was that Michael had been recording new music for nearly two years. Word soon came back to the label that he had five songs ready to go. It was difficult for Epic executives to communicate directly with Michael at that point—DiLeo, who was fluent in raspy record-business-ese and could translate Michael's inexplicable behavior, was long gone. Gallin was more of an MJ yes-man, "offering no personal opinion, really doing the bidding of his artist," as Beck recalls. Finally, Beck and Dave Glew, head of Epic Records, dropped in on MJ at the Hit Factory, heard the music, and came back with the idea for a double album.

Beck and Glew perceived darkness in the new material, a willing-
ness on Michael's part to address his personal anger through his songs
more explicitly than he'd done since "Leave Me Alone." Michael had
been working with a few different producers and songwriters, sketching out the songs he heard in his head, as always. These included the
Jimmy Jam–Terry Lewis team, longtime Prince collaborators who'd
engineered smash albums for Michael's sister Janet. On one gorgeous
early-fall day, Michael flew to their Minneapolis studio to work on
vocals for their song "Scream." (It looked like Michael might record
his entire album there, until a frigid December trip involving hoods
and parkas changed his mind.) Michael began to record at his usual
collection of studios in LA, from Westlake to Record One, but the
1994 Northridge earthquake scared him, so he relocated the operation to New York. To maintain Michael's privacy, studio engineers were
told to prepare for a session with a "Mr. Sherman." The discretion was
ineffective—fans and paparazzi were a constant presence on the street
outside the studio.

Michael's primary songwriting partner at the time was Brad Buxer,
who, like Greg Phillinganes and other key Jackson collaborators, had
been a veteran of Stevie Wonder's band. When the two met in 1989,
Buxer said, "a current immediately passed between us." After Phillinganes dropped out of the Dangerous tour, Michael elevated Buxer to succeed him as musical director. For HIStory, Buxer and Michael worked
in a makeshift Neverland writing room. "Brad was his comfort-level
guy," says engineer Tony Black.

Unlike Bill Bottrell, who had a darkness to his personality, Buxer
was upbeat to the point of being irritating. "Brad was one of the most
hyper people I'd ever met," says James "Trip" Khalaf, sound engineer
for the Dangerous and HIStory tours. "He lived and breathed that
music. He knew every little nuance of everything. He tried to make me
put things in the [tour] mix that weren't even on the records because
they were on the original multitrack studio recordings." CJ deVillar,

an engineer who worked with Michael after the *HIStory* sessions, was suspicious of Buxer's role within Michael's organization. "He had his own power, and he sort of wielded it," he says. "Anybody who went up against Brad seemed not to fare well." Beginning on the *Dangerous* tour, where they worked on songs in their hotel rooms, Michael and Brad began to conceive "Stranger in Moscow," "Money," "Childhood," and "Little Susie." It was obvious to everybody that Michael was entering a more explicitly autobiographical portion of his career, inspired by the recent trauma in his life. "Stranger in Moscow" is one of Jackson's bleakest songs, using Iron Curtain imagery as a metaphor for his feelings of oppression—the first line is "I was wandering in the rain / mask of life / feelin' insane." Michael turned the song into a meditation, offsetting the heavy-handed lyrics with a sparse torch-song ambience. As they began to put the album together, Jackson and Buxer viewed "Stranger in Moscow" as the centerpiece.

The Hit Factory producers and engineers settled in for eleven months of solid work, including frequent twenty-three-hour days. "We were regularly handing in 220-hour time sheets," Black says. "There was no Sunday off." Often, Michael was right there with them, camping out at the studio for hours at a time, popping into and out of one of the multiple rooms to check on producers and engineers. He spent most of his time with Buxer, figuring out harmonies for new songs and recording vocals. Occasionally he'd disappear, to Los Angeles or Saudi Arabia, checking in by phone with Buxer, Bruce Swedien, or another engineer, Eddie Delena. He'd ask to hear a song in progress, then say, "I want it a little faster, and one key up." Whichever engineer happened to be talking to him would dutifully remind Michael that the changes he was requesting were expensive: "We're going to need ten or fifteen hours [of paid work] for this." Michael didn't care. "I know," he sharply responded.

The crew was overworked and occasionally beleaguered, but they had plenty of perks. Michael housed much of the staff at the New York

Palace, overlooking St. Patrick's Cathedral in Manhattan. The Hit Factory rooms alone cost roughly $4,000 per day, plus additional staff and food deliveries. "Everything costs and costs and costs," Black recalls. "You just can't go down the street to go get a slice of pizza. There's got to be two security guards and a van, and all of a sudden that slice of pizza costs forty-eight bucks." Swedien called his old colleague Bernie Grundman, the mastering whiz who had worked on most of Michael's solo albums, and invited him to leave his LA studio and join the *HIStory* crew in New York. Jackson's people put up Grundman at a suite in the tony Pierre Hotel and arranged for him to work at the $400-an-hour Sony mastering operation. He told Swedien he'd have to haul in bulky equalizers from his own studio, at great expense. Over two weeks, Grundman worked on exactly one song—"Smile." In the end, since Michael didn't want to stick around for the cold New York autumn, Grundman wound up mastering everything else at his LA studio, as he had suggested to Swedien in the first place. He estimated his personal costs at $200,000. "*HIStory* was probably the most expensive album. I know it was for mastering," he says. "Really extreme."

"The crew, all these second engineers, they'd find the most expensive places in New York City. They were ordering, like, steak and lobster to go," adds a source who worked on the album. "It was like nobody was minding the store. It was crazy. There was no naked women and drug use going on, but it was like there was no budget."

By *HIStory*, Michael had given up on his *Bad*-era goal, written on his bathroom mirror, to outsell *Thriller*. That hubris had morphed into a different one: create sounds the human ear had never heard before. He repeated this mission statement often to collaborators. "Fiery and angry. There's a lot of things to be angry about at the world, and I want a lot of sounds the kids will relate to," Michael told Chuck Wild, former keyboardist for the new-wave band Missing Persons. Through his friend Swedien, Wild signed on to create four or five "soundscapes" every day, then FedEx them from his California home to the Hit Factory.

Gus Garces, one of the engineers, worked with an audio-technology expert for four straight days on a newfangled electronic panning effect, in which a sound passes from one speaker to the other in the recording. It wound up taking exactly ten seconds of the album. To create the effect in "Childhood" of a little girl with a music box opening a door, engineers sampled a variety of music boxes and recordings of doors opening and closing. Swedien sent Wild a Synclavier; using Michael's money, Wild hired people to wander LA, recording sounds downtown, near railroad tracks and such, and he combined them with samples built into the synthesizer. The electronic "whoosh-vroom" toward the beginning of "They Don't Care about Us" came from Wild's lab, but the rest of his sounds appeared briefly and sporadically.

"They Don't Care about Us" embodied Michael's approach to recording during this period. The song is sort of a sound-poem, stringing angry words together in the style of Billy Joel's "We Didn't Start the Fire" or R.E.M.'s "It's the End of the World as We Know It (and I Feel Fine)." Electronic drums move in and out of the song, as do a clapping children's choir and heavy-metal guitar. Unlike "Billie Jean," "Bad," and most of Michael's best-known songs, in which he conceived them fully formed, "They Don't Care about Us" was a studio creation. It began with a metronome and a basic four-count kick drum. "Michael wanted the drums to have a certain attack—he really wanted it to hit you over the head," says Rob Hoffman, a *HIStory* engineer who worked on the track. "It took time to go through millions of samples to build up that groove. Just the percussion element of that was probably twenty tracks or more." Michael repeated the boom-boom-tak-tak groove for hours, over loud studio speakers, as he wrote the rest of the song in his head. Eventually he added the verses. Buxer added other elements and Chuck Wild sounds, and Michael and Brad brought in guest musicians to play briefly. "I've never seen so many people doing a session in my life," recalls Trevor Rabin of veteran rock band Yes, who contributed the distinctive high-speed heavy-metal-guitar bit in the middle. Guns

N' Roses' Slash, who'd played on "Give In to Me" on *Dangerous*, added another bit, and engineer Hoffman's own guitar part survived as well. Michael and engineer Delena "sat for days mixing and matching and compiling all the different layers," Hoffman recalls.

Although Michael had intended "Stranger in Moscow" to be the focal point of *HIStory*, a leftover from the *Dangerous* sessions emerged throughout the recording process that would become not only the album's most distinctive song but what critic Joseph Vogel would call Jackson's "magnum opus." Michael had begun writing "Earth Song" in 1988, during the *Bad* tour, standing outside his hotel in Vienna, looking over the museums and cathedrals on Ringstrasse. "It dropped into my lap," he said. As Michael began to conceive *Dangerous*, he brought up the unfinished song to Bill Bottrell. At the time, Michael was starting to break away from his strict Jehovah's Witness upbringing—he quit the faith in 1987—and develop, according to Vogel, "a much more inclusive, liberating understanding of himself, the world, and the divine." While working with MJ on what would become the *Dangerous* album, Bottrell laid down the intro on a grand piano. Michael played it for Buxer, too, who loved it. Jackson and Bottrell worked for months on the song, trying to capture Michael's vision of a gospel song linked to an elaborate Pink Floyd production, with booming drums and rich electronic bass. "It became quite the obsession for both of us," Bottrell would say.

Michael and Bill tinkered endlessly with the song, but just as Bottrell felt the song was finished, Michael inexplicably left it off *Dangerous*. "I was pretty disappointed," Bottrell says. "I loved the whole thing, but I could tell, in Michael's mind, 'the song's not done.' I never got him in to write the last few lines—he sort of mumbled and sang them."

By the time Michael began recording *HIStory* in 1994, he had essentially cut ties with Bottrell. But he brought up "Earth Song," again, with arranger David Foster, who had become an accomplished producer and film composer since he'd worked with MJ on the *Thriller* album. The song had "gravitas," as arranger William Ross described it, and while Michael had channeled his desire to heal the world or save the children into ballads before, none of them had the presence of "Earth Song." It would become a centerpiece of his concerts.

As usual, celebrities showed up regularly at the Hit Factory, sometimes to work and sometimes to hang out. Magic Johnson dropped by. Shaquille O'Neal and doomed hip-hop star Notorious B.I.G. were brought in to rap. Prince made an appearance, as he'd done for the *Bad* sessions, forcing the engineers to clear out of the studio.

There was another celebrity presence in the studio. The *HIStory* crew didn't think much of it one day when Michael told them, "I'll see you guys tomorrow," and took off. The next thing they knew, he was in South America, marrying Lisa Marie Presley.

It was inconceivable to reporters—and not just in the tabloids—that Lisa Marie could have fallen in love with Michael Jackson. To them, Michael's motives seemed obvious: he needed a "normal" woman to establish that he was not a child-molesting predator. Upon spotting Michael with Lisa Marie at a Temptations show in Las Vegas, an Associated Press reporter called them "an unearthly pairing." The *Daily Oklahoman* opined: "If Elvis really were alive, this would have killed him." The *Washington Post*'s Richard N. Leiby concluded the only conceivable explanation was her creepy connection to the Church of Scientology. "Scientology has been known to tell people to get divorced or married for public-relations purposes," declared one of Leiby's ex-Scientologist sources. The idea that Lisa Marie could have been in love rarely crossed anybody's mind.

But really, why else? She didn't need Michael's money—her mother, Priscilla, had turned Graceland into a tourist attraction, and since the King's death in 1977, the value of his estate had grown from the low millions of dollars to more than $100 million. Lisa, twenty-six in 1994, was to inherit the cash when she turned thirty. She had her own fame, too, and didn't need more of it. "In spite of what some people speculated while I was with him that I wanted a career or was trying to do something, it was absolute B.S.," she said. "[I] loved being next to him and taking care of him. I was on such a high from doing that. It was a very profound time of my life."

Presley, a little girl running around at Graceland when her father died on August 16, 1977, had grown into a troubled young woman. Elvis and her mother divorced in 1973, and Priscilla Presley raised Lisa herself. It wasn't easy—she went through a three-year drug phase and a long-term "destructo mode." Singing became an escape. At age twenty, she needed a six-pack of beer and four takes to cover Aretha Franklin's "Baby I Love You." "I wouldn't change anything on that song. I think I did pretty okay, for the first time ever," she recalls, years later. "But I do not, thankfully, need to drink anymore. People who are drinking think they sound good, but they really sound awful." She began to write music in her early twenties, and used songs and poetry as therapy. This characteristic alone might have made her a good fit for Michael Jackson, who in 1994 was channeling bleak life events into his own lyrics. Lisa Marie was blunt, with a knack for subverting tragedy with disarming humor. "My dad's family's from *Hee-Haw* and my mom's family's from *Falcon Crest*," Presley told Clif Magness, a songwriter who worked on her 2003 debut album *To Whom It May Concern*. In addition, she was developing a talent for nurturing people. In 1988, she had married musician Danny Keough, who was struggling, in and out of bands.

Lisa Marie was still married to Keough when artist Brett Livingston-Stone introduced her to MJ during a private February 1993 dinner at his home in LA. They had terrible fathers and damaged childhoods in common, and bonded over music and creativity. The night they met, Lisa had been trying to figure out how to start a music career. At the end of the night, shy Michael Jackson flirted with her in a bold, confident way: "You and me, we could get into a lot of trouble. Think about that, girl."

Michael called her frequently from the road in Europe and Japan. "He was freaking out," she says. "I believed that he didn't do anything wrong, and that he was being wrongly accused and, yes, I started falling for him. I wanted to save him. I felt that I could do it." But she could tell something was wrong. As someone who'd had her own dependency demons, she picked up on his zoned-out demeanor and encouraged him to go to rehab. Like Elizabeth Taylor, she advised him to settle the child-molestation accusations with the Chandler family, just to excise the stress from his life.

After his stint in rehab, he returned home to relax with Lisa. At Neverland, the couple walked the grounds while a nanny took care of Lisa's two young children. To answer a question the world wanted to know about Michael Jackson, she hinted strongly the two were actually, truthfully having sex. "We're together all the time . . . how can you fake that twenty-four hours a day with somebody?" she told Diane Sawyer in their widely viewed hand-holding ABC interview in 1995. Eventually she would say her sex life with Michael was "very hot," which made Lisa Marie Presley one of the few women to publicly confirm a sexual relationship with Michael Jackson. (Another, for the record, is Theresa Gonsalves, who claims to have been Michael's girlfriend while he was filming *The Wiz* in New York. "There were other girls," says Gonsalves, who has written books about their relationship. "I met a couple of them.")

Eventually, Michael pulled a ten-karat diamond from his pocket, dropped to one knee, and proposed. Presley accepted. (She had divorced Danny Keough twenty days earlier.) The wedding was held in the Dominican Republic. The groom wore black, a pony-tail, and lipstick. Lisa Marie wore a beige dress. The happy couple arrived with an entourage of lawyers and a bodyguard. The ceremony lasted fifteen minutes at the judge's home. Gold bands were exchanged. The couple stayed at Donald Trump's Mar-a-Lago mansion in Palm Beach, Florida. "They spent a full week in the tower and almost never came down," recalls Trump, the perennial GOP presidential candidate. Hundreds of photographers soon rooted them out and stormed the beach.

When they returned to New York to live in a duplex apartment suite at Trump Towers, Michael went back to work on *HIStory* at the Hit Factory. Lisa frequently accompanied him. "The magazines were questioning whether it was a publicity stunt, but from our observance, it was totally real and natural," says Rob Hoffman, a *HIStory* engineer. "They were both pretty quiet people. When the two of them were in the studio, they were into each other. In our small, enclosed studio group, she was just very much the supportive wife." The couple made an impression—on several levels. Rupert Wainwright, who filmed the *HIStory* teaser film in Budapest, recalls Lisa dressed in black chiffon even in August. "Wherever she walks, she's always in slow motion," he says. When Wainwright visited Michael in one of his LA-area mansions to go over video special effects, the house began to shake from an earthquake. MJ and Wainwright ran in a panic to the center of the house, physically collided with Presley, and they collapsed into a group hug as paint chips fell from the ceiling. When the tremors ended, they separated, looked at each other awkwardly, and returned to their business.

Michael pressed Lisa into service for one famous publicity stunt, designed to show the world that he was, in fact, not a renegade child molester. At the 1994 MTV Video Music Awards, MJ walked onstage, hand in hand with Lisa, in aviator shades, a white shirt, a black jacket, and red armband, while she clung to him wearing a black dress and a nervous smile. "Just think," he said, "nobody thought this would last." They embraced, kissed, and walked off as Lisa waved shyly. She looked like the dutiful, doting wife, said absolutely nothing, and allowed her man to guide her in public. But this was not Lisa Marie, and she said as much years later. "His hand was blue afterwards after we got off that stage. He showed me and it was completely blue, I had squeezed it so hard," she told Oprah Winfrey. "I did not want to do that. It's not in my nature to do that sort of thing. But I understood . . . he needed to do things like that." (Of her topless appearance nuzzling Michael in the dreamy and romantic but frustratingly unfocused "You Are Not Alone" video, Lisa would speak in similar, helpless terms: "I don't know why I did it. I was sucked up in the moment. It was kind of cool being in a Michael Jackson video. Come on!")

Although Michael had told Oprah, "I love my family very much," and spoke of frolicking at Tito's or Jermaine's houses on regular family days, his relationships were strained throughout the late eighties and early nineties. Jermaine's 1991 song "Word to the Badd!!" seemed lyrically addressed to Michael: "You only think about you, your throne / be it right or be it wrong," Jermaine sang in his high-pitched, lover-man falsetto. Later, Jermaine clarified: "The bottom line here is that this song was written as a private message to help get my brother to heal our relationship."

La Toya's 1991 autobiography, *Growing Up in the Jackson Family*, divulged that Joe had sexually abused her when she was a child. She had intended to add that Joe had sexually abused Michael, too, but Michael's lawyer John Branca stopped that by threatening a lawsuit. La Toya reportedly received a $500,000 advance from the publisher for the book, and her business manager, Jack Gordon, reportedly tried to extort Joe and Katherine out of $5 million in exchange for withdrawing it. La Toya's literary marketing plan included a nude spread in *Playboy*, complete with strategically arranged boa constrictor. At thirty-three, La Toya had married her Svengali, the fifty-year-old Gordon, who purportedly wielded an unhealthy control over her life and career. La Toya's second book, *Starting Over*, opens with a 1993 scene in which Gordon beat her nearly to death. In the book, and elsewhere, she recanted *Growing Up in the Jackson Family* and blamed everything on the late Gordon.

Since the Victory tour, Janet had been the only Jackson sibling other than Michael to truly succeed with any kind of musical career. La Toya and several of the Jackson brothers had shown signs of questionable judgment. Jermaine divorced Hazel Gordy, Berry's daughter, who then accused Jermaine of refusing to pay child support. Margaret Maldonado, Jermaine's common-law wife and mother of two of his children, wrote a tell-all book declaring, among other things, that Hazel accused Jermaine of raping her. After living with Jermaine and taking in the drama at the family's Hayvenhurst home, Maldonado gave up and fled. "I had been abused and humiliated and my children had been subjected to mental and physical cruelty," wrote Maldonado, who directed 1992's *Jacksons: An American Dream*, then became an agent for stylists and photographers. "We had to leave." Jackie cheated on his wife, Enid, with Lakers cheerleader Paula Abdul; one night in 1984, Enid sought out Jackie and Paula at the Sepulveda Drive-In, grabbed Paula by the hair, then dragged her out of his Range Rover and across the theater lot.*

Janet's career was a sharp contrast to that of Jermaine or La Toya. She began as a child performer, entwined with her brothers in the family shows in Vegas in the seventies. Janet snagged roles on *Good Times*, *Fame*, and, most memorably, *Diff'rent Strokes*. With Joe as her manager, she landed a contract with A&M Records, home of the Carpenters and Peter Frampton, and put out a self-titled kiddie-pop debut that was, at least, more memorable than anything by La Toya.

Janet would arrive at the studio with a driver and her tutor. "She sounded like a young Michael Jackson," says Bobby Watson, who wrote many of the songs and helped produce her debut. "She was really shy. Really, really, extremely shy." Watson and his fellow producers started the project with visions of Motown, but the 1982 album came out

---

*While Jackie was helping Paula, Enid jammed the car into reverse, running over her husband's leg, according to Margaret Maldonado Jackson—which is why he couldn't perform during the Victory tour.

more like mini Chic—wah-wah guitars, synths, and drum programming.

Against her parents' wishes, Janet took a career detour and married James DeBarge, a singer in another family band. They eloped in Grand Rapids, Michigan, DeBarge's hometown, but annulled the marriage a year later. Jackson skated through album number two, *Dream Street*, but by 1985 she was contemplating a new musical direction. That was when an old Jackson family friend, John McClain from Walton High School, resurfaced as the urban music director at A&M Records. In what *Rolling Stone* would call a "masterstroke," McClain paired Little Janet with Jimmy Jam and Terry Lewis, the duo from Prince's on-again-off-again backup band, Morris Day and the Time. Joe Jackson, still managing his daughter, warned them: "I don't want my daughter sounding like Prince." The crew ignored him. In the studio, Jam and Lewis coaxed Janet out of her shell and asked her to play more instruments and feel around for her identity. She found it with *Control*, an aggressive dance-rock album with booming rhythms, Time-style funky synths, and a commanding vocal sound. "If we did something she liked, you could see the excitement in her eyes," recalls Jesse "Jellybean" Johnson, the Minneapolis production team's guitarist. Janet's first album with the team, *Control*, distanced itself from its two light-weight predecessors with a funky mission statement: "This time I'm gonna do it my way." Setting the stage for Miley Cyrus, Janet seized control through a sensuality far removed from her child-star persona: Among the best songs on *Control* are "Nasty" and "The Pleasure Principle." By her second Jam-Lewis album, *Rhythm Nation 1814*, Jellybean Johnson was thinking "Beat It" and bestowed upon Janet the slamming rock-and-funk anthem "Black Cat." "I wanted her to sound like a rock queen," he says.

By 1994, for the first time in three decades, Michael Jackson was not the hottest Jackson in the music business. Janet's *Rhythm Nation* had made her an MTV megastar. She appeared provocatively on the cover of *Rolling Stone* and she was eclipsing Madonna as the top female star in dance and pop music. Michael, by contrast, hadn't put out a new album in three years and his career was plagued by scandal. It made sense for him to borrow some heat from his younger sister in a collaboration.

"Scream" came together because, as Janet said, MJ called during her successful *Rhythm Nation* tour and asked to do a duet. She refused. But by 1994, she was confident "people would see that I'm holding my own," and accepted the invitation. The original plan was to include "Scream" on Janet's upcoming album, but "working on that with Michael kind of pulled us into *HIStory*," recalls Steve Hodge, a recording engineer for the Jam and Lewis production company. Jam and Lewis tested four or five ideas for songs with Janet over a period of two days, and Janet pegged "Scream" immediately as her brother's choice. Sure enough, when the team arrived at the Hit Factory and played all the tracks for Michael, he listened to each for a couple of minutes and asked to return to "Scream." "I told you," Janet told Jam. After Jam and Lewis worked up the track in their Minneapolis studio, Michael and Janet recorded their vocals separately. As usual, Michael put everything into the process, singing, dancing, snapping, clapping. Janet had many talents, but she was far from the most naturally gifted Jackson singer. "She wanted to work really hard to get up to his intensity on the record," Hodge recalls. "So we had to redo it a few times."

"Thriller" had led to a world in which superstar music videos could cost millions of dollars to make—an average video by a Sony artist cost $75,000. "Much of what we were doing was trying to hold things back," says Epic's Dan Beck. "Not to stop things, but just keeping it from being crazy." The $1 million mark was significant—if expenses went over that amount for a project, according to a source with knowledge of Michael's videos, he paid for them, not Sony: "It was like, 'Michael, write a check.'"

The budget for "Scream," thanks to its director, Mark Romanek,

ballooned to more than $7 million—which made it the most expen-
sive video of all time, according to the *Guinness Book of World Records*.
(Romanek later said many other videos were costlier, adding: "I am
annoyed that I am on record as this profligate maniac who spent $7
million." Still, the shoot took fourteen days, when it had been scheduled for six.) Set in what appeared to be a black-and-white spaceship,
with Michael and Janet dancing in black plastic pants, the video had
a sleek, modernist feel, as if viewers were wandering through an art
museum. (Before Michael and Janet slid down the floor on their knees,
choreographers had to spread out a strip of baby powder to avoid fric-
tion between the pants and the floor.) Romanek mostly captured
Janet and Michael dancing individually—which made the video great
in itself, because both were the best dancers in pop music, Madonna
notwithstanding—but he also found tiny moments in which the two
teased each other on a couch while playing video games. It was before
computer-generated graphics, so Richard Berg, the art director, had to
create eleven sets on five different stages. The filmmakers had lofty
artistic ambitions. Romanek was inspired by Stanley Kubrick's *2001:
A Space Odyssey*, and Berg designed the distinctive long hallway after
works by Spanish architect Santiago Calatrava.

Janet had agreed to the project only if her choreographers, Tina
Landon and Sean Cheesman, could create the dance steps. Although
Michael used his own people for choreography, he agreed to Janet's
condition. When he met with Landon and Cheesman, he gave them
one instruction: "Make it magical." The lack of specificity confused
them, but they designed something that involved a lot of jumping up
and down and rolling on the floor, with an element of movie special
effects that would make the Jackson siblings appear to fly into space.
When Michael signed off on the steps after a meeting with Janet and
the choreographers at Neverland, he had Landon and Cheesman teach
the "Scream" routine to his longtime tour dancer, Travis Payne, who in
turn taught it to Michael.

By the time Janet and Michael arrived at the set, in separate trailers, a competitive spirit was in the air. "It wasn't a good vibe at all," Landon recalls. Michael's team stationed people on set with video cameras to shoot behind-the-scenes footage. When Landon, Janet's choreographer, gave directions, the cameramen paid no attention; when Payne, or another MJ dancer, LaVelle Smith, gave directions, the video people snapped into action. Landon felt humiliated. Also, when Michael did his moves, his people draped his dancing area with dark curtains so nobody on set could watch; when Janet danced, everything was open. Cheesman, who had started his career as a seventeen-year-old dancer in Michael's "Bad" video, detected a change in MJ's personality. "When I first met him, I felt him being very open, and he just loved being around dancers, and we could talk freely," he says. "During 'Scream,' he was very guarded, very competitive." Janet was so taken aback by her brother's behavior that she was frequently in tears. "You would see Janet [go] from being Janet Jackson the superstar to Janet Jackson the little sister who adores her big brother," Cheesman recalls. Added Janet herself: "Everything gets worked out in the end. But yeah, the camps were butting heads."

"Scream" would become symbolic of the record industry of the mid-nineties, where pop stars and their labels could blow millions of dollars on art projects with almost no return. But the video remains a classic. Despite the personal politics between Michael and Janet on set, the video captures a genuine sibling camaraderie in the few seconds they're on screen together. "It was a dream," recalls Berg, the art director.

Nick Brandt, who conceived and filmed the "Earth Song" video not long after "Scream" came out, ran into the same MJ complications every director endured—Michael neglected to show up on schedule, or at all, for expensive shoots, and occasionally he'd fall asleep while a makeup artist propped up his chin in the palm of her hand. ("When we subsequently found out about all those painkillers he was on," says Brandt, who also directed "Childhood," "Stranger in Moscow," and

"Cry," "I began to understand why, so often, he would turn up and seem to be a bit out of it.") But the redemptive moments were worth the ordeal. It was Brandt's idea to position Michael as the last line in a defense against loggers and foresters, hanging on to burned-out tree stumps in what appeared to be a raging hurricane. Brandt had received orders to capture MJ in his black-and-red outfit in exactly one take. (He successfully begged for a second one.) And Michael Jackson nailed the performance. "It was absolutely electrifying in a way I'd never seen before," Brandt recalls. "I had these wind machines in his face, with all the shit flying in his face, and his eyes were streaming. People were just hypnotized and transfixed. That was glorious to see in a New Jersey field at four in the morning."

As with every Michael Jackson album since *Thriller*, the final touches on *HIStory* were rushed. Although the album would contain fifteen tracks, the Hit Factory team worked on at least forty. For some songs, the recording crew labored on them for months—after recording "Little Susie" with a full orchestra, Michael changed his mind and asked Toto keyboardist Steve Porcaro to rebuild it with a synthesizer orchestra instead, and for "Childhood," Michael changed arrangers and arrangements. "On another budget, where every orchestra session is fifty thousand dollars, that's a panic moment," says Rob Hoffman, one of the engineers. "But with Michael, that's more a speed bump: 'We'll do it right, and that's the way I want it.'" The only truly spontaneous song was a sparse version of Charlie Chaplin's ballad "Smile," which Michael and arranger David Foster knocked out after a fruitless writing session. "[Songs] would come in and out of favor at any point over the course of the record," Hoffman says. "We might think a song was hot, in the running, and literally completely disappear, never to be heard from again." One of the orphans was "Much Too Soon," a teary ballad about people who've died.

The *HIStory* crew labored for sixteen to eighteen hours a day until the last month of work. "I'm sorry," Michael told engineers Hoffman and Eddie Delena, "but I don't think any of us are going to sleep this weekend." Work hours expanded to twenty per day. Sony wanted to put out the album in winter 1994, in time for holiday shopping season. "Michael was like, saunter, saunter, saunter, saunter, and then: emergency finish!" says CJ deVillar, an engineer who worked with him later.

After Michael was satisfied that LA earthquakes were no longer a threat, he moved the team back to more familiar terrain. Chuck Wild, the effects man, arrived at Record One just about every night at midnight to personally show Michael the four or five sounds he'd come up with that day. Michael was always asleep when Wild arrived, so Wild would wait around. When Michael woke up, Wild played his sounds and they talked about Thomas Edison. It seems the famed inventor deliberately deprived himself of sleep, a creative method that fascinated Michael Jackson. "It was a conscious decision," Wild says. "He chose not to sleep continuously . . . just to go on this odd schedule." One night at three A.M., after five hours of last-minute work on one song, they finished the album, and Grundman speedily mastered it— this time, fully, in his own Los Angeles studio.

The *HIStory* album cost $10 million to make, and in spots it sounded like it. The songs MJ had labored over for months on *Thriller* and *Bad* were restrained and minimalist compared to the title track of the all-new second disc. It opens with a huge-sounding classical orchestra, with ringing bells and tympani rolls—actually a sample from the Classical Kids album *Beethoven Lives Upstairs*. Then it mashes up bits of historic radio broadcasts about Hank Aaron, Lou Gehrig, and Charles Lindbergh, and splices in a few Chuck Wild electro effects before getting to the pretty-sounding motivational speech ("Don't let no one get you down / keep movin' on higher ground") that serves as the chorus. The title track represents the grandiosity of Michael's ambitions—the cover of the two-disc album is an MJ statue, fists clenched, with dark clouds breaking into a pink sunrise in the background. In fifty-one pages of liner notes, Elizabeth Taylor, Jackie O, and Steven Spielberg celebrate Michael in lofty prose—Liz says he's "filled with deep emotions that create an unearthly, special, innocent, childlike, wise man." Given the greatest hits on disc one, the album serves not just to sum up MJ's career but to deify him.

The new songs on *HIStory* have a punk-rock quality of personal rebellion. "Stop pressuring me!" MJ and Janet plead throughout "Scream." He aims the Broadway-style ballad "Childhood" at his parents and the machine-gun drums of the Jam and Lewis "Tabloid Junkie" at the media. Michael's most tortured lyric is "Stranger in Moscow," which uses Kremlin imagery to draw a parallel between oppressed Soviet citizens and Michael himself.

"They Don't Care about Us" takes the concept over the top—the children's playground chorus quickly gives way to Michael's pleading *Beat me, hate me / Will me, thrill me*. But then comes *Jew me, sue me / Everybody do me / Kick me, kike me*. The lyrics incensed Jewish activists. Reporters demanded an explanation. Michael never quite came around to one, although many critics would interpret the song as MJ empathizing with victims everywhere, responding to the very invectives he lists in the lyrics. Although he apologized, he said it was for the pain he'd caused rather than for the words he spoke. Given Michael's background as a humanitarian who claimed to transcend segregation and prejudice, many Jewish leaders were inclined to give him the benefit of the doubt. Abraham Foxman, director of the Anti-Defamation League, said Jackson "never intentionally meant to be offensive, yet the anti-Semitic words cut deeply," and his Jewish manager, Sandy Gallin, would say he felt the same way. But Michael's Jewish friends in showbiz, including Geffen and Spielberg, did not rush to defend him. (Spielberg's silence was particularly notable, given his soliloquy on MJ's greatness in the *HIStory* liner notes.) "He tried to convince me to do it," Gallin said, years after refusing to justify MJ's behavior in public. "I knew it was the wrong thing to do, I wouldn't do it. He was very upset about all of this, and he thought that maybe I thought he was anti-Semitic. And he fired me." Jackson severed ties with Gallin, Geffen, and Spielberg. Epic's Dan Beck had to promise reporters that Michael would change the lyrics for a new version of the song. After meticulously working on *HIStory* with dozens of people on both coasts for nearly three years, Michael walked into Sony Music's New York studio one day with Beck, his comanager Jim Morey, an engineer, and a video cameraman and laid down replacement lyrics in half an hour.

For all its weird megalomania and confusing lyrical bursts, *HIStory* was an effective Michael Jackson album—it's pointed and personal, melodic and funky, persistent in some places ("Money") and soothing in others (a version of the Beatles' "Come Together"). It aspires to sound big, and frequently succeeds—notably "Earth Song," his most effective save-the-world ballad, trumping "Heal the World" and "We Are the World" with stronger lyrics, better melodies, and "Man in the Mirror"–style ad-libs at the end. Had *HIStory* ended after eight songs, it might have been a masterpiece of angry self-righteousness. But the last several songs are among the least electrifying in Michael's catalog—"Childhood" is unconvincing self-justification in the form of a treacly ballad; "2 Bad," "Little Susie," and "Tabloid Junkie" are retreads of *Dangerous*-style new jack swing; the title track is a mishmash of jumbled-up sounds and fractious lyrics; and while the closing "Smile" shows a more personal MJ, it relies not on intimacy but a Broadway-style distance between the singer and the audience.

To promote the album, Michael had a $30 million Sony budget. "I wanted everybody's attention," he told Diane Sawyer, and he got it with thirty-two-foot statues of himself, which Sony officials installed on top of a MICHAEL JACKSON HISTORY vessel and sent down the River Thames, as well as Cape Town, South Africa, and elsewhere.

He was still at his peak creatively. Many dance aficionados believe Michael's watershed moment as a dancer was not the classic *Motown*

25 performance but his fifteen-minute appearance at the 1995 MTV Video Music Awards—the one where he drops to his knees as Slash plays a guitar solo, jamming in a cloud of smoke even after a roadie tries to stop him. The tour de force is "Dangerous," in which he leads an ensemble of gangsters in black suits and skinny ties through a series of impossible body-bending moves. Janet, caught on camera in the audience, shakes her head in stunned disbelief.

After viewing this performance, Sony executives were excited about a two-hour HBO special Michael had agreed to do in December 1995, three months after the MTV awards. The plan was for the new MJ to be like the old MJ, doing his best-known dance routines at the Beacon, an art deco theater on New York's Upper West Side. "It was going to be the man and his music, as opposed to lightning, flash pots, or gags," said his comanager, Jim Morey.

To produce the show, Jackson picked Jeff Margolis, with whom he'd worked on TV tributes to Sammy Davis Jr. and Elizabeth Taylor. Jackson and Margolis spent nearly four months sketching out the show in all-night sessions in MJ's hotel suite before moving to a Sony Studios soundstage big enough to accommodate the cast of one hundred rotating dancers. The show would have an orchestra and one special guest—Marcel Marceau, who was to appear on a dark stage, improvising mimes in a spotlight as a motionless Michael sang "Childhood" in a smaller spotlight. "It would have been one of those moments on TV that everybody would talk about forever," Margolis says.

While MJ's longtime collaborator Brad Buxer worked on the music, coordinating the orchestra away from the Sony stage, Margolis hired *Dangerous* tour veteran Kenny Ortega to supervise six choreographers, including Debbie Allen, the dance great who'd appeared in *Roots* and *Fame*, as they designed new routines for signature songs such as "Thriller," "Smooth Criminal," and "The Way You Make Me Feel." Some were old MJ hands, such as longtime dance partners Travis Payne and LaVelle Smith Jr., who designed a new, stripped-down look for

The Jackson 5 in Gary, Indiana, before the Motown years (Tito, Jackie, and Jermaine, *top*; Marlon, *middle*; Michael, *bottom*). "Their voices blended together like—I don't know how to explain it, but it was beautiful," says Earl Gault, one of the group's early drummers. "They had it." (*Rudy Calvo Collection/Cache Agency*)

In the early days of the Jackson 5, shown here in the '70s, MJ "copied a lot of things from a lot of people," Carl Fisher of the Vibrations recalls. "He was a natural at what he did anyways—a born, natural talent." *(Soul Legacy Collection/Cache Agency)*

Michael Jackson on the basketball court. The Jackson 5 later appeared in a surreal 1971 TV special, "Goin' Back to Indiana," playing hoops against a team of athletes including Bill "Skyscraper Jones" Russell, Elvin Hayes, Elgin Baylor, and Rosey Grier. Jackie led them to victory. Bill Cosby and Tom Smothers were on hand for comic relief. *(George Rodriguez/Cache Agency)*

They may not have always liked it, but the Jacksons were MJ's most sympathetic backup band—Jermaine's Four Tops–like yearning played the perfect vocal foil, Jackie's falsetto covered the gaps, Tito was an economical funk and blues guitarist, and Marlon was an accomplished dancer. *(Cache Agency)*

"People responded viscerally to Michael Jackson's beauty": The Jackson 5 (Jackie, Jermaine, Tito, Marlon, and Michael), early '70s. (*Cache Agency*)

Michael Jackson in the
Thriller era. The year
after this backstage shot,
at LA's Pantages Theatre
for Lena Horne's "The
Lady and Her Music"
in 1982, MJ unveiled
the moonwalk during
Motown's twenty-fifth-
anniversary special.
(*Rudy Calvo Collection/
Cache Agency*)

"He's all colors": Michael Jackson and Quincy Jones at the 1984 Grammy Awards,
celebrating *Thriller*. (*Cache Agency*)

Although Pepsi was MJ's most famous sponsor, sources say the singer preferred to work with Quaker Oats—until Don King made the cola deal. (*Chuck Pulin Estate/Cache Agency*)

Quincy Jones, Dionne Warwick, Michael Jackson, Stevie Wonder, and Lionel Richie *(from left)* celebrate their Grammy Awards for "We Are the World" at LA's Shrine Auditorium on February 25, 1986. *(Cache Agency)*

Randy Waldman, who played synthesizer during the *Bad* sessions, summed up MJ's creative method: "He would hum different melodies, and I'd plunk around on the piano and he'd go, 'Yeah, that's what I want to do.'" *(Courtesy of Randy Waldman)*

Keyboardist Rory Kaplan calls the *Bad* tour "Michael's absolute, complete, controlled vision—what he wanted, how he wanted it presented, everything from choreography to handpicking dancers to singers and all the band members." (*Greg Allen/Cache Agency*)

MJ on the final date of the *Bad* tour, LA Sports Arena, January 27, 1989. (*Cache Agency*)

Wearing a $250,000 necklace Michael rented for her for the occasion, Elizabeth Taylor appeared at the Jacksons' Madison Square Garden reunion show in September 2001. Onstage, she called MJ "the most successful recording artist in the history of popular music and, most importantly, to me, my closest friend." (*Cache Agency*)

"Dangerous" based on A Clockwork Orange, with bowler hats, jock-straps, and combat boots. Another was Barry Lather, who'd danced in Captain EO and took over the HBO-show redesign for "Thriller"—"a futuristic, gritty, industrial feel" involving trench coats and high-powered flashlights, he says. MJ's schedule was absurdly complex, as he dropped in to learn new steps from all the choreographers in different studios. After twelve days, Michael showed up at Sony to watch Lather and the dancers perform the new "Thriller" routine, twice in a row. He and Lather then worked together, one-on-one, and Michael mastered the moves after six separate days of three-hour sessions.

Finally, Michael and his various choreographers and dance com-panies were ready for full rehearsals on the Beacon stage. A few days before the show, although Marceau believed MJ to be in fine health, choreographer Lather could see Michael wasn't feeling well. To Epic's Dan Beck and manager Jim Morey, too, he seemed on the brink of ill-ness. They met with the singer over dinner at Sony's studios, where he sipped some kind of broth. The two music-business veterans moth-ered their star client as best they could—"You need to eat! Don't worry so much about the show!" They figured he was anxious. For rehears-als, they strategically placed heaters between the Beacon's door and Michael's trailer, a preemptive measure to prevent the star from catch-ing a full-blown cold.

Five months earlier, Michael had seen one of his doctors, Allan Metzger, for a physical exam. "He is exercising regularly and taking only vitamins. He does not drink or smoke and takes no recreational drugs," the doctor wrote in his notes. But his severe pain from his scalp burns and skin conditions persisted. He regularly visited at least two doctors at the time, including Metzger and his plastic surgeon Steven Hoefflin. Metzger prescribed Vistaril, an anti-anxiety drug, and Ultram, a pain-killer. Neither was serious or addictive, but MJ was growing frailer and more sensitive to pain.

Five days before the broadcast, only three songs were properly choreographed. Yet HBO and Sony had arranged tickets for international journalists, and Michael's band had already rehearsed at the theater. On December 6, while dancing during a dress rehearsal for "Black or White," Michael Jackson collapsed. "He fell super-duper hard on a metal grating," recalls Lather, who today handles choreography for Usher. "Me and my assistant were watching: 'Oh my God, did you just see that?'" George Duke, the prolific jazz keyboardist who had contributed to *Thriller*, had arranged strings for the orchestra and was in the Beacon at the time. "My manager and I looked at each other: 'This is over,'" Duke recalls in an interview shortly before his death. "I got paid anyway."

Bodyguards surrounded Michael Jackson, picked him up, and carried him away. Morey called 911. Paramedics put MJ on a gurney and sped him to Beth Israel Medical Center North on New York's Upper East Side. Michael's stated reason for the cancelation was exhaustion—EMTs gauged his blood pressure at an "abnormally low" 70/40 and said doctors gave him oxygen and water mixed with salt and other minerals. Trip Khalaf, MJ's longtime sound engineer, is dubious whether the singer wanted to do the show in the first place. "Michael got himself into this shit and he didn't know how to get out of it," he says. HBO canceled the show and took the insurance money. Although he adapted some of Lather's choreography for his "Ghosts" video, Michael Jackson would never dance the newly created HBO routines in public.

On the *HIStory* tour, which began in fall 1996, whatever was left of Michael's budgetary restraint appeared to evaporate. On Michael's first day of rehearsal, at an airline hangar in San Bernardino, California, he walked into a room full of people, looked around, and called over his production manager, Benny Collins.

"Who are all these people?" he asked.

"Those are the lighting guys."

"Okay, they can stay."

"Who are those guys?"

"Those are the sound guys."

"Okay, they can stay."

"Who are *those* guys?"

"They're the accountants."

"Send them away."

The *HIStory* tour came together much like the *Dangerous* and *Bad* tours. "Billie Jean," "Smooth Criminal," "Beat It," and "Thriller" were to proceed more or less the same as always. To introduce "Billie Jean," he laid a suitcase on a stool in a spotlight, silently removing his white glove, black fedora, and sequined jacket as if unpacking in a hotel room. Those on the tour took in the massiveness of it all. "There were people screaming and crying everywhere we went," says Stacy Walker, one of the dancers.

In previous tours, Michael had developed a bond with his dancers and band, and even much of the crew. This time, not long after his child-molestation settlement, things were different. "It was just a general feeling that there was a lot more going on, and it wasn't the kind of happy-go-lucky feeling it used to be," says sound man Trip Khalaf. "He became a lot more withdrawn from all of us. He used to be around a lot, then all of a sudden he wasn't."

The *HIStory* tour had Michael's most elaborate effects and skits. It began with a roller-coaster video, from the point of view of the rider. Then a large, white *2001: A Space Odyssey*–style space pod appeared onstage and Michael emerged in a spacesuit and large white robot helmet, anticipating Daft Punk by half a decade. Then he fell in with his dancers for "Scream" (which he sang by himself, sans Janet), jiggling his shoulders and moonwalking sideways in a gold robot suit and boots.

In previous tours, Michael was in constant motion, to the extent that his doctors worried about him losing too much weight. For *HIStory*, he was perceptibly picking his spots. By this point, Michael had fully mastered the art of the pose, spreading out his arms in a variety of Christ-like contortions, holding up his fists one at a time or lifting his arm like a conductor. At thirty-eight, he was still unusually limber. He pulled off the usual well-known moves in "Billie Jean" and "Smooth Criminal," but he clearly was more limited. In bursts, he moonwalked forward and sideways, thrusted his crotch, bobbed his shoulders. The high point was "Stranger in Moscow," for which he stood in a spotlight and appeared to improvise, flowing with the wind that blew up his shirt and jacket.

At some point on the tour, which lasted for a little more than a year, Michael's insomnia intensified. In July 1996, he became so desperate for sleep that he enlisted two German anesthesiologists who showed up at his hotel suite, Debbie Rowe reported, with "enough equipment where it looked like a surgical suite." They administered Diprivan, also known as propofol, the potent sleep-inducing drug he'd received in his eyelids during procedures before the *Dangerous* tour a few years earlier. Debbie, with her medical knowledge and familiarity with Michael's pharmacological history, tried to talk him out of taking it: "What happens if you die?" she asked him. But Michael wasn't worried about the medication; he'd had plenty of experience taking painkillers and sleep aids. He told Rowe he was at the end of his rope—he desperately needed sleep to restore his energy for the shows—and didn't know what else to do. Michael took Diprivan twice, before each of his scheduled shows in Munich. He performed flawlessly.*

Rowe had become more than a nurse, friend, and traveling companion, especially after Michael's relationship with Lisa Marie had ended with a disagreement over having children. Lisa Marie had three from her previous marriage and worried about future custody battles. "Debbie Rowe says she'll do it," Michael told Lisa Marie. "Okay,"

---

*MJ fans often say *HIStory* was the first tour in which he lip-synched, at least in spots, to give himself a break. True? "That is a controversial question," backup singer Darryl Phinnessee says coyly. "It's akin to asking about a magic trick on the show."

she snapped, "have Debbie Rowe do it." So Debbie did it. The public wouldn't learn about her "gift" to Michael until years later, but she became pregnant in December 1995. Lisa Marie filed for divorce in January 1996. (In official documents, she noted the separation date as December 10, 1995—when she visited him in the hospital after he canceled the HBO special.) By the time of the *HIStory* tour, Rowe was with Michael constantly, even showing up on the sets of his videos. "He relied on her a lot," recalls Mick Garris, who worked closely with Michael on the screenplay for 1997's *Ghosts*.

On November 12, 1996, Rowe left her golden retriever, Cuervo, and German shepherd, Harley, with neighbors in her apartment complex in Van Nuys, took a fourteen-hour flight to Sydney, Australia, and checked in to the $2,750 presidential suite at the Sheraton on the Park hotel. After Michael Jackson's concert at the Sydney Cricket Ground, with about thirty friends, Debbie and the star of the show married at two A.M. Michael played "Here Comes the Bride" on a grand piano; Debbie wore white; within ten days, she was pregnant. How Rowe became pregnant remains one of the central mysteries in MJ's life. She has refused to answer all questions about the conception. Not long after fending off paparazzi in front of her $840-a-month one-bedroom apartment, she gave birth to Michael Joseph Jackson Jr.—Prince—on February 13, 1997, at Cedars Sinai Hospital in Los Angeles. Debbie had Michael's second child, Paris Katherine Michael Jackson, on April 3, 1998. Then, because the marriage had always been more of an arrangement than a relationship, Debbie requested a divorce. Michael agreed to pay her $10 million as part of the settlement, with installments beginning in October 1999.

When his kids were young, Michael did everything he could with them. Prince was shy, while Paris was bubbly, girly, and doting. Michael traveled with them and took them to his studios. Working with CJ deVillar, an engineer at the Record Plant, Michael abruptly handed Prince to him and strode into the vocal booth. DeVillar wasn't accustomed to wiggling toddlers, especially when he was expected to work the faders and master talkback buttons with two hands. "I can tell on his face, he's enjoying me struggling. So now it's a game," deVillar says of Michael. "I can tell he's trying to mess with me." At one point during the hour-long vocal session, Prince hit the wrong button and ruined the take—MJ didn't mind. He took his kids on outings, often covering them with masks so they wouldn't register in paparazzi images. For this, Michael received a lot of ridicule in the tabloids, but it made sense. When they weren't with Michael, the children could go about their lives anonymously. Michael hired Grace Rwaramba, a Rwandan-born former office assistant, as their nanny. When Michael and his family later traveled the world, Rwaramba scouted for locations, negotiated prices, and assessed security before Michael gave his approval. Randy Jackson insisted Grace enabled Michael's abuse of sleeping pills, while others saw her as a stabilizing force. "Michael trusted her one hundred percent with the kids," says Dieter Wiesner, one of MJ's managers after Sandy Gallin and Jim Morey departed his camp. "But he did not want Grace too close to the kids. Sometimes, when the kids started to see Grace like a mom, then he stopped her for a week."

After the *HIStory* tour ended in October 1997, Michael spent the next few years puttering around high-priced recording studios in LA, vaguely pondering his next album. Beginning in early 1998, he worked on as many as a hundred different tracks. He spent the Grammys the following year at Marvin's Room, a studio named for the late Marvin Gaye in Hollywood, where MJ first invited Sony and Epic executives to hear the new material. The song he emphasized was "Break of Dawn," which he recorded with a young producer named Dr. Freeze, in addition to "A Place with No Name," a reinterpretation of America's seventies hit "A Horse with No Name." (Sony's president, Tommy Mottola, was so excited about the new music that on the return flight from LA to

New York, he asked another executive, Cory Rooney, to write his own song for MJ, "She Was Loving Me.") At LA's Record Plant, during this period, engineer CJ deVillar's routine to prepare for an MJ recording session was to brew tea, turn on the Cartoon Network, mute the TV sound, and twist the studio knobs so Michael could record. Over ten days, Michael and CJ compiled forty vocal tracks.

In the twenty-five to thirty-five sessions deVillar worked with him, Michael canceled numerous times. He often left early. At first, Michael showed up with an entourage that prepared for every eventuality. "I may go *here*," Michael would say offhandedly, prompting a flurry of travel arrangements involving four booked flights to different parts of the world—three of which had to be canceled the second Michael stepped onto one of the planes. "Michael wastes a lot of money," deVillar says.

That was true—in payments big and small. Back in 1993, Michael's Neverland Ranch payroll included salaries for ninety employees— among them, five elephant trainers, eleven gardeners, and three reptile handlers. *Rolling Stone* reported MJ paid $1.54 million for producer David O. Selznick's *Gone with the Wind* Oscar and $5,000 an hour for his own plane, usually packed with high-priced assistants. The work he was doing with deVillar, Dr. Freeze, and others for his upcoming album would eventually cost $20 million in production. Plus, during this time, a California jury ordered him to pay more than $20 million to Marcel Avram, one of his longtime promoters, for canceling two shows in 1999. And there were smaller, persistent expenses. While working on the *Invincible* album, which would come out in 2001, Michael took Harvey Mason Jr., a trusted songwriter, engineer, and coproducer, on spontaneous shopping trips. One day they went to the Virgin Megastore in Times Square; Michael was dressed like a Middle Eastern sheik to avoid recognition. "Get anything you want," Michael told his new friend. Sheepishly, Mason selected a CD. "You're not doing a good job of shopping!" Michael admonished, then swept an entire shelf full of CDs and DVDs into his shopping cart. "Do it like *that*." Mason happened to mention he was a James Bond fan, and the next day, a complete set of Bond DVDs and a new, high-end portable DVD player showed up at the studio.

"Michael would believe somehow that Sony was paying for it all, and they were," says one of his associates and confidants, Marc Schaffel, who wound up suing him. "But they were charging it to him. Anything he did, whether it was hotels or private jets or whatever, they paid, but they charged him for it. So he was using up more and more of his income and going deeper and deeper into debt with Sony."

By 1998, Michael's total debt was $140 million.

He wasn't broke, but he was heading in that direction. His album sales weren't as grand as they used to be, and while the *HIStory* tour had grossed $165 million, due to the expenses, he'd actually lost $11.2 million on it. (*Dangerous* had broken even.) "He was simply addicted to Number One hits and roaring crowds, and he didn't care what he had to pay to get them," wrote Tommy Mottola, chairman of Sony Entertainment. What saved him from bankruptcy, over and over, was his 1984 investment in the Beatles catalog. In 1995, he sold half of his stake in ATV, the publishing company, to Sony for $90 million; the two owners, Michael Jackson and Sony, essentially became partners in running the company. "He said it very explicitly: 'Don't talk to me about the money. I will spend whatever I need to . . . it's my money,'" recalls Michael Schulhof, who as Sony Corp.'s American chief executive oversaw MJ's record label through 1996 and met personally with the star numerous times. "He burned through a lot of money and it's ultimately why we were able to get fifty percent of the ATV catalog. I remember thinking to myself at the time: 'He'll eventually run out of this, too.'" His problem, in addition to the spending, was keeping an eye on the "vampires" and "spiders" in his camp, as Lisa Marie Presley called them. "I was always scolding him and warning him: 'Who are you traveling with? Why don't you have someone who would take good care of you?'" recalls Uri Geller, the Israeli-born celebrity "mystifier" who first befriended MJ when he was a teenager. "There must have been some good people around him, too, but he did whatever he wanted." By 2001, Henry Aubrey, MJ's bodyguard and de facto business manager, noticed employees were paying $3,000 a week on two SUV rentals. Aubrey cut that to $300. "He didn't keep on top of every single dime, because he had people doing that for him," he says. "And the people who were doing that for him weren't doing a very good job."

Although the HIStory tour had officially ended in 1997, Michael flew overseas in 1999 for two shows for children's charities—one in Seoul, South Korea, and one in Munich. They were more or less the same shows he'd done on the tour, only with a few added effects, like a levitating, mechanical bridge during the finale to "Earth Song." In Munich, while singing on the bridge, high above stage center, the pyrotechnics went off as scheduled and the curved structure steadily fell some thirty feet to the bottom of the "hole," a section of the stage where the orchestra pit normally goes. It looked like part of the act—Michael kept singing as he landed—but it wasn't. Wayne Nagin, Michael's bodyguard, and assistant stage manager Anthony Giordano noticed the problem right away and charged off the stage into the hole. "There were a lot of guys going, 'Oh, no, we've killed the pop star!'" recalls Trip Khalaf, the sound engineer. Astoundingly, Michael finished the song, albeit slower and more slumped than usual. But the moment represented his decline as a performer. The spirit he'd shown at the beginning of the song seemed snuffed out. After the show, he collapsed in his dressing room, then went to the hospital. He was never formally diagnosed with anything, but Karen Faye, his makeup artist, would say: "He suffered back pain from that moment on."

Michael reserved expensive studios all over the world so he could pop in and record song ideas from Los Angeles and New York to Norfolk, Virginia, and Montreux, Switzerland. During this period, he worked with his largest collection of producers, engineers, songwriters, and collaborators. As the album-making process dragged on, Michael brought in pop star R. Kelly, DeVante of hit R&B duo Jodeci, Babyface, and his old friends Bruce Swedien and Brad Buxer. Teddy Riley worked in a studio inside a bus, alternately stationed at the Hit Factory studios in New York and Miami. "We would all have our different planets where we would work, and Michael would fly to the different planets and add his own flavor to them," Dr. Freeze says. "He kept everybody on their feet. We had to be in our different worlds to give him a different perspective of the record. If we all sat in the same room every day, every song would be the same."

"Look what Teddy did, Freeze," Michael would say, teasingly.

"Oh, shit," Freeze invariably responded.

"A lot of egos going around, and a lot of competition," Freeze continues. "It's kind of a psychological thing. I had to worry about Rodney Jerkins. Rodney Jerkins had to worry about Dr. Freeze. We had to worry about R. Kelly. . . . 'Oh my God, I got to do it better.' [We were] creating this, like, Frankenstein of an album, with one piece of an arm, a leg, another leg, until the body was formed and it could get up and walk away."

After tinkering for months on several songs, Dr. Freeze finished his work. "Break of Dawn," a smooth, easygoing soul song that recalled the work of nineties rappers PM Dawn, would be Freeze's main contribution to the album.

Rodney Jerkins emerged as the main producer, and he immediately bonded with MJ over melody and workaholism. In his first meeting with Jerkins, Michael gave the producer unconventional instructions: "I want you to go to your studio and I want you to take every instrument, and every sound that you use, and throw it away. And I want you to come up with some new sounds. Even if it means you've got to bang on tables and hit bottles together." Jerkins dutifully found trash cans to slam at a junkyard, recording them via DAT for use on the album. "It was a lot of 'Do it again,' 'Let's try something new, something different,' 'We're not there yet,' 'Let's mix it again,' 'I want to do another vocal,'" Jerkins recalls. "His style of perfection helped cultivate me as a producer and songwriter." *Invincible*'s opening three-song funk punch— "Unbreakable," "Heartbreaker," and "Invincible"—showcases how Jerkins surrounded MJ's layered harmonies with electro snaps, crackles, and pops. Over three years, Michael recorded a total of a hundred songs with Jerkins and his Pleasantville, New Jersey, production crew, including "You Rock My World," the first song Jerkins wrote for MJ; it began with a conventional rhythm, and Jerkins kept adding to it until it was finally ready for producer LaShawn Daniels to come up with the story and write the words. The producers installed beds in the studio so they could work uninterrupted for weeks.

Jerkins and his people internalized Michael's money-is-no-object approach. "It cost a fortune to record that project," says Jerkins's cousin, Robert "Big Bert" Smith, part of the family production crew known as Darkchild. He meant that as a compliment, but others saw it as a deadly inefficiency. "Most of the record could have been done in two months, but went through the Michael Jackson Process," says Brad Gilderman, one of the album's recording engineers. "'Let's see what Dr. Freeze is up to.' 'Let's go back to good old Teddy Riley and see what he comes up with.' It was just going around the horn again to see what other producers, other writers [would] come up with for him." Michael put up his studio staff at "way too expensive hotels," as Gilderman recalls, when they weren't living in the studios. The engineers remade Sony's biggest rehearsal room into an MJ bedroom-and-living-room combo, including a large TV, couches, and beds, some of which were earmarked for tiny Prince and Paris. "If inspiration happens at two in the morning, at least we'll all be here and be ready," Michael would tell his people. But, Gilderman says, "[That] never really happened. It turned into a bunch of people sleeping there, not getting any work done. I wasn't allowed to go back to my hotel room to change and shower. You're paying a lot of money for a hotel room I never see, and you go up to the Gap to buy me clothes."

For Michael's hopeful, midtempo song "On the Line," Babyface commissioned a fifty-voice choir and a fifty-voice orchestra. Michael heard it and loved it, but the next day, he returned to the studio with a new instruction: "Everything should be a key change—we should go up half a step." This was before Pro Tools editing, and changing the tone of live orchestras and choirs involved reconvening singers and string players, an expensive process. Michael still wasn't satisfied. He kept tinkering with the keys, adding new orchestral parts, until the changes cost more than $50,000. "Everything was one hundred percent over-the-top," Gilderman says of the album. "Hundreds of takes."

As Jackson, Jerkins, and their engineers alternated between studios, Sony's Mottola kept showing up to check on the album's progress—and his multimillion-dollar investment. "Where's my record?" engineers heard him say. Finally, Mottola couldn't take it anymore, and toward the end of the recording process, he abruptly cut off production: "We like it the way it is." Michael responded, "No. I'm not finished. We have to keep recording." They were at a tense impasse for a week. Jackson and Mottola worked out some kind of compromise, allowing the engineers to keep recording for about six more months. "We were advancing Michael tens of millions of dollars to rent all this studio space, pay an army of producers and writers and directors to create his short films," Mottola later complained. Jerkins found himself in the middle. He had a recording contract with Sony, but he was emotionally invested in his creative process with Michael. "Tommy was calling Rodney for days, and Michael's like, 'Yo, nobody gets anything—no music or nothing,'" Robert "Big Bert" Smith recalls. "Rodney had a very unique pressure." Smith empathized with Mottola, but Harvey Mason Jr., who coproduced portions of *Invincible*, came away admiring Michael's artistic principles. "He did not succumb to pressure as it pertained to creating art," Mason says. "'I don't care how much time it takes, I don't care how much money it costs, I want a great record.' "

As the album began its final push into Bernie Grundman's ever-reliable mastering process, Michael continued to add songs at the last minute. John McClain, one of his managers at the time, had played Michael some unreleased songs from a new British poetry-and-soul duo called Floetry, particularly a puffy, hypnotic soul jam called "Butterflies." In March 2001, McClain summoned the group's two young women, Marsha Ambrosius and Natalie Stewart, and brought them to the Sony studio. Michael was at a piano when they walked in, warming up with his vocal coach, Seth Riggs, and he flashed the peace sign before introducing them to his children as "Miss Marsha" and "Miss Natalie." Ambrosius, who wrote the song, took over the session, instructing Michael on his vocals from the studio booth, while Stewart sat back and took everything in. "He had a natural harmony within his voice—like three voices harmonizing, a lower, middle, and upper range," Stewart recalls. "He was very precise. He didn't try to sing the whole song down, he focused on areas, the chorus and the verse, then the next verse, then the bridge." Michael wanted to duet with Marsha, something he rarely did with another singer. She pushed Michael to a new place—in the dreamy song, his verses suggest a more reflective MJ, a falsetto middle ground between angry "Billie Jean" and teary "She's Out of My Life."

Invincible, which came out October 20, 2001, was more relaxed than anything Michael had done, even on the three heavy Jerkins funk tracks that set the tone. He seemed to inhabit the songs rather than take them over, as he'd done in the past. In "2000 Watts," Riley steps into his own thumping production, reciting a deep mantra of "bass note, treble, stereo control," before Michael begins to swirl in and out of the empty spaces. Michael commandeered the most personal songs for himself: "Speechless" is a sparse, theatrical love-and-spirituality ballad; "The Lost Children" returns to the old "Heal the World" well, but it's more of a hymn akin to Bob Dylan's "Forever Young." If any Michael album is the anti-*Thriller*, it's *Invincible*—heavily produced, full of elaborate beat-box sounds and layered vocals, but somehow it captures Michael as if he'd sung the whole thing in a room with a piano.

Still, people who worked on the record wondered what might have been. "By the time it came out, it was dated," Robert "Big Bert" Smith recalls. "The music is timeless, but the industry changed. At that particular moment, that's when we really first started feeling the effects of the Internet. Electronic music just started to hit the States. The album was probably five years in the making." Mottola's assessment, after Sony went $40 million into the red for the album, was more blunt: "good, but by no means Michael's best work."

Jerkins outtakes (such as the ominously funky "Can't Get Your Weight Off of Me" and "We've Had Enough," a slowed-down, more topical "Billie Jean" dealing with violent crime), Brad Buxer collaborations (including "Hollywood Tonight," an upbeat noir story that sounds like a sequel to "Smooth Criminal"), and many other gems went straight to the vault. "There were some songs that we loved, loved, loved," recalls engineer Harvey Mason Jr. "We recorded a lot more than were on there." Mottola said Michael wound up with twenty to thirty outtakes from every album: "Every time that he recorded, he over-recorded. Any of them could have been as big a hit as the ones that came out and were hits."

Michael had big marketing plans for *Invincible*, but Mottola thwarted him. It became obvious to Sony executives that MJ was no longer the immortal King of Pop, and *Invincible* was a lower priority than any of his albums had been in the past. Michael didn't do nearly as much as he'd done in the past to draw attention to the album—no big Diane Sawyer or Oprah interviews, and no international tour, although he hinted at the possibility a couple of times. And Michael clearly felt Sony didn't do enough to promote it. He wanted to do a video for

"Butterflies." Mottola didn't, and the two clashed in a Sony conference room. "They just had disagreements," recalls Henry Aubrey, Michael's bodyguard at the time, who witnessed the conversation. "Tommy said things he probably shouldn't have said." Aubrey would not elaborate, other than to call Mottola's comments "very inappropriate."

Sony execs invited Michael to the label's Santa Monica office, buying *Invincible* billboards and bus-stop signs along his travel route to give him an exaggerated impression of the marketing campaign. (This was a common trick among major record labels and Hollywood studios.) Waiting for Michael were longtime Epic executive Polly Anthony and Cory Llewellyn, the label's head of digital-music strategy, who set up web pages and Internet chats. Michael pulled up with a phalanx of vehicles and strode into the hallway with his people. "All you heard were radios: 'Garage is cleared! Second floor is cleared!'" Llewellyn recalls. "You expected light to burst in the room. It was like, 'Wow, this is a serious entourage. He doesn't move freely in a Prius.'" Michael finally arrived, wearing mirrored sunglasses, even during a slide show in the dark. Llewellyn had been given instructions on how to behave when talking to Michael—one of the first items on the list was to refer to a music video as a "short film." Llewellyn nervously botched that instruction within minutes. Through his sunglasses, MJ regarded Llewellyn and said, "Oh no, they're not videos. They're films. Films are thirty minutes long and they have actors." Via video conference from New York, Sony's top executives, including Mottola, patiently waited for Michael to finish his explanation so the meeting could begin.

Llewellyn met Michael Jackson a second time not long afterward. He was organizing a chat room, through Yahoo! and GetMusic, in which MJ answered questions from his fans. When one requested Michael's favorite *Invincible* song, Michael asked if he could pick three. The host, music journalist Anthony DeCurtis, said he could do whatever he wanted. (The answer: "Unbreakable," "Speechless," and "The Lost Children.") During the interview, Michael talked for an hour about the spirituality of his songwriting process, how he pushed Rodney Jerkins aggressively to get the sound he wanted over repeat takes and long hours, how he likes to hear music loud, and how in his show-business career he'd "been through hell and back." A fan asked where the inspiration for "Speechless" came from. Michael gave an unexpected answer. "I spend a lot of time in the forest," he said. "I like to go into the forest and I like to climb trees. My favorite thing is to climb trees. I go all the way up to the top of a tree, and I look down on the branches. Whenever I do that, it inspires me for music."

He continued. "There are these two sweet little kids—a girl and a boy—and they're so innocent. They're the quintessential form of innocence. Just being in their presence, I felt completely speechless. I felt I was looking in the face of God whenever I saw them. They inspired me to write 'Speechless.'" Taking in the exchange at his office in Los Angeles, where Michael had called in from a friend's house in New Jersey, Llewellyn didn't think enough of the answer to remark on it. But Frank DiLeo, Michael's former manager, might have reacted this way: *Uh-oh*.

CHAPTER 9

The he members of the Jackson 5 formed a horizontal line onstage, as they'd done off and on for thirty years. 'NSYNC, including Justin Timberlake in black leather pants and a fedora, fell in next to them. It was the middle of "Dancing Machine," on September 7, 2001, and as the familiar pre-disco rhythm dragged the song to the instrumental break, everybody in the crowd knew what was about to happen. The horns came in, and Michael Jackson stepped to the front of the line, at center stage, lifting his shoulders to start the Robot. It had only been two years since his last public performance, in Munich, which had been energetic and spectacular, and everybody was expecting the same this time around. But forty-three-year-old Michael, perhaps for the first time ever, didn't seem into it. He hopped forward and sideways and bent his skinny body into the usual mechanical shapes, but his dancing had no life. As tens of thousands of fans watched at New York's Madison Square Garden, and millions more on the CBS broadcast, Michael Jackson looked for all the world like he wanted to go back to bed.

The September 7 and September 10 concerts, marking the thirtieth anniversary of MJ's first solo hit, "Got to Be There," had not been his idea. David Gest, the Jacksons' longtime friend, a show-business veteran, and the future husband of Liza Minnelli, wanted to produce it. When Gest had called Michael to suggest a concert with a Jacksons reunion, Michael declined. But Gest knew Michael's financial situation. "He was basically bankrupt, more or less," recalls Ronald Konitzer, one of MJ's business partners of the time. Gest appealed to Michael's wallet. Fans could get nosebleed seats at the Garden for $45, but those who wanted to see the stage would have to pay as much as $2,500—the most expensive ticket in concert-business history. Gest explained that, thanks to a licensing fee for a later CBS special, Michael would receive a guaranteed payment of $7.5 million. The numbers talked Michael into it. He insisted on inviting his famous friends. So when Elizabeth Taylor demanded a $250,000 necklace to wear to the show, he agreed. And when Marlon Brando demanded $1 million merely to sit on a couch and say a few words, as well as appearing in a later video, Michael agreed to that, too. Jermaine had all kinds of "requests and demands," as Michael's associate Frank Cascio recalled. During one secret Hollywood rehearsal, Jermaine called paparazzi in advance and was outside chatting with photographers when MJ's people showed up in a vehicle, took a look at the scene, and abruptly reversed course.

Stars were summoned. In addition to 'NSYNC, Britney Spears, Whitney Houston, and Gladys Knight signed on to perform classic MJ songs. Michael did not rehearse, although he showed up unexpectedly to watch his protégé, Usher, who'd spent much of his young career talking up Michael's influence. "Good," Michael had told him. "Very good." His hero's presence made the young, usually unflappable R&B superstar nervous, which showed during the early seconds of his elaborate "Wanna Be Startin' Somethin'" routine. "It's like LeBron James and Michael Jordan sitting courtside, watching," Usher said.

Gest nailed down a plan for MJ to sit in the front row at eight P.M. By 8:30, he wasn't there. Karen Faye, Michael's makeup artist, went to his hotel room, where a doctor she'd never seen before intercepted her and said he'd given the singer a "sleeping aid." Soon Gest sent Frank Cascio to Jackson's hotel room.

Cascio found him and called back. "He's sleeping."

"What do you mean, he's asleep?" Gest responded.

"I could tell he's out of it and not completely there. I started shouting at him," Cascio would say. "I said, 'What did you take?' He told me he took a shot of Demerol. He said, 'My back was killing me.' I said, 'You're just looking for an excuse to get out of the show. Isn't that right?' He wouldn't answer me. I knew that was what it was."

Jackson managed to rouse himself, climb onstage, and muscle-memory his way through the old routines, from the Motown hits to "Billie Jean" to "The Way You Make Me Feel." It was Marlon Jackson, though, who killed it, in a shiny gold jacket, dropping to his knees and bouncing up again, Godfather of Soul style, in the night's most impressive single move. MJ did a bit better on the second night, but he was clearly not the same King of Pop the world had seen during the *HIStory* tour just five years earlier.

The 1997 *HIStory* tour had sapped Michael's spirit, and the back injury he suffered during his 1999 charity show in Munich continued to plague him. "I usually come to the show not feeling like I really want to do it because of being overworked, but once I get there I feel the spirit of the entire audience before I even get on stage," he told one interviewer. "And then the magic takes place—no matter how you feel, even dead sick and weary—suddenly you just go out and do it. The energy comes out of nowhere. It's like the gods are blessing you." Buried within the usual MJ rhetoric about magic and energy were revealing words—*overworked, dead sick, weary*. During the interview, he pledged to never again do a world tour and to focus instead on records and films. But Hollywood hadn't been enthusiastic about filming a Michael Jackson movie after the Jordan Chandler situation. While his name floated around as a possible star for a role in a film about Edgar Allan Poe, studios remained skeptical, even nasty. "Whenever he wanted to make a movie, it was impossible," says Howard Rosenman, a veteran Hollywood producer. "How could you put that face on a screen, sixty feet high, with that nose he had, and that skin? He looked like Phantom of the Opera."

So no tours. And no movies. Which meant no income, other than the undying engine of the Sony ATV catalog—Beatles songs were still lucrative at a time when MP3s, Napster, and the Internet were ravaging the record industry.* Recording extravagances, Neverland upkeep, and shopping expeditions plunged him deeper into debt. From 1995 to 1999, the Sony catalog paid him between $6.5 million and $14 million a year. The publishing catalog for his own songs, Mijac, added another $2 million to $9 million annually. But his accountants, lawyers, and business partners were resolutely unable to convince Michael to stop hemorrhaging so much cash. "You couldn't just confront him with the reality," says Ronald Konitzer, one of Michael's financial advisers at the time. "The mistake they all made was talking in *their* language—there was a lawyer talking about legal problems, there was an accountant talking about accounting and cash-flow problems. Three minutes into a conversation like that, he would fall asleep."

In the late nineties, Michael had turned to Korean-born and University of Chicago–trained lawyer Myung-Ho Lee, who ran a Seoul company called Union Finance and Investment Corporation. Lee set to ruthlessly overhaul Michael's finances. "Michael gave him all kinds of ability and authority and power, and he exercised it to push John [Branca] out, any way he could, and push me out," says Zia Modabber, one of Michael's longtime lawyers, who had defended him in a number of cases after the Chandler settlement turned Michael into a legal punching bag. Lee became close enough to Michael's business affairs to

---

*Years after MJ's death, Sony executives would at least consider selling the still-lucrative Beatles catalog due to the record industry's uncertain digital future—it had a "rather complex capital and governance structure and is impacted by the market shift to streaming," the electronics giant's chief financial officer, Kenichiro Yoshida, wrote to a colleague in an e-mail leaked in late 2014.

realize the singer was "cash poor." Michael had exhausted a $90 million loan in 1998; through Bank of America, Lee secured new loans for a total of $200 million over the next two years.

Lee had to be constantly vigilant to save Michael from what he would call "erratic behavior"—throwing his money down any number of rabbit holes. At one point, Michael met a woman named "Samia," who claimed to be a personal adviser to a Saudi Arabian prince. While Lee's people were investigating Samia, Michael communicated with her directly, believing promises she would buy him a $40 million villa and a yacht. With Lee's help, Michael paid $7.4 million to MJ Net, a German entertainment-memorabilia company, for use of his likeness on products, including a state-of-the-art audio speaker system with photos of Michael on the front panels. He invested $2 million in a fuel-cell technology company. He was "extremely interested" in a company that had engineered a magnetic motor, for use as a high-efficiency generator, and attempted to invest $10 million before reducing his stake to $2 million. For all these deals, Lee took a 2.5 percent fee. Eventually, Lee sued Michael, divulging juicy details in his complaint: Michael had wired $150,000 to a Mali bank to pay Baba, a voodoo chief who ritually sacrificed forty cows in a ceremony designed to curse Steven Spielberg and David Geffen. By way of response, Jackson's attorneys accused Lee of using Michael's assets to enrich himself in elaborate ways: he paid for his sister's $50,000 Lexus and the rent on two Century City condos, including furnishings, utilities, and cable bills.

Another person Michael brought in to help with his financial affairs was Marc Schaffel, who had been a freelance ABC cameraman and shot footage of the Jacksons during the Victory tour in 1984. An entrepreneur with an unusual past—he'd directed and produced gay pornographic movies such as *Every Last Inch* and *Tomorrow Always Comes*—Schaffel connected with Michael in 2000 at the home of their mutual dermatologist Arnold Klein. In June 2001, Michael authorized Schaffel to form a company, Neverland Valley Entertainment, to work on film and video projects. He was also what he called Michael's "bag man." Bank of America, as Michael's lender, imposed restrictions that, as Schaffel would say, made it "difficult for Jackson to spend and distribute money as he wished." Because Michael didn't maintain a bank account, fearing creditors would try to seize even more of his money, he had Schaffel take out his own cash from the bank and reimbursed him later. Schaffel delivered these cash loans in paper bags, sometimes from an Arby's restaurant—to the point that Michael told Schaffel he liked how his money smelled. "He liked his french fries—which was code for 'bring me cash,'" says Howard King, Schaffel's attorney. "And if he wanted a lot of cash, he'd ask Marc to 'supersize his fries.'" Schaffel's loans to Michael included $380,395 to buy custom cars, such as a Bentley Arnage and a Lincoln Navigator, and $30,000 for unpaid temporary security guards who were threatening to quit.*

"We all had large amounts of cash on us," Schaffel says. "But fifty thousand dollars was petty cash for a day shopping for MJ."

On the morning after the second thirtieth-anniversary show at Madison Square Garden, Michael had slept just an hour or two. His friend, Frank Cascio, was due to return a $2 million diamond watch that Michael had borrowed from Los Angeles jeweler David Orgell to wear for the concerts. Cascio's plan was to wake up early and return it to a Bank of America outlet so Michael could avoid buying it permanently. Cascio slept through the alarm. Aubrey, MJ's bodyguard, woke him up with a phone call: "Hello, sir. I just want to let you know that planes hit the twin towers."

---

*Henry Aubrey, Michael's bodyguard, questions Schaffel's repeated claims in interviews and court documents that he provided cash in this way. "I pretty much doubt it," Aubrey says, adding it was he, not Schaffel, who carried as much as $50,000 at a time for MJ's impromptu spending needs. Schaffel responds that Aubrey was a security guard, "nothing more, nothing less," and Michael dumped him when he "felt Henry was stepping out beyond his duties as bodyguard." Schaffel does, however, credit Aubrey for arranging to get Michael Jackson a driver's license, privately, at a Department of Motor Vehicles office.

Schaffel says Michael, like everybody else in New York, was "completely freaked out." He feared marauding terrorists were out to kidnap his children. He asked for $500,000 in emergency escape money, in case his family had to "go underground." But Aubrey insists Michael never asked for cash, handled the disaster with no panic whatsoever, and spent the morning watching the news in his hotel suite.* Michael left Manhattan for the Cascios' home in Franklin Lakes, New Jersey. The bridges and tunnels were closed, so Michael's entourage of Paris, Prince, Grace, and the four Cascio brothers relied on a retired New York cop who served on Michael's security team for permission to leave the city. "As we crossed the George Washington Bridge, we looked downtown and saw the smoke," Cascio wrote. "The first tower had fallen." Schaffel recalls Michael and his group staying at the Cascios' house for a couple of days; Aubrey says they were there for roughly a month.

After that, in Schaffel's recollection, Michael left New Jersey for White Plains, New York, where Sony provided him with a private jet at an airport hangar. Michael's entourage and actor Mark Wahlberg's entourage then reportedly fought over the use of the jet until Sony awarded it to Michael. (In a TMZ interview after Randall Sullivan published this revelation, Wahlberg strenuously denied it ever happened.) Then Michael decided he didn't want the plane and made plans to return to California by tour bus. "We all flew back on the plane to LA, minus MJ, who took a bus back across the country," Schaffel recalls. Other reports say Michael flew to Santa Barbara.

Through all this, Michael had been thinking about a song he'd written, "What More Can I Give?," inspired in part by his visit with Nelson Mandela in South Africa in 1990. As with many of his compositions, he'd been tinkering with the song for years, under various

---

*Schaffel identifies Michael's hotel on September 11 as the Plaza Athénée of Manhattan; Aubrey can't remember, but believes it was the Plaza, a larger hotel not far away.

titles, at first intending to put it out as a charity single for Kosovar refugees. After 9/11, Jackson talked with Schaffel about retooling the song into a tribute for families who'd died in the attacks, and Schaffel met with McDonald's executives about selling it in restaurants. The fast-food men estimated they could sell five million copies and made a deal for $20 million. With Schaffel as his middleman, Michael signed Beyoncé, Mariah Carey, Tom Petty, and other pop superstars to contribute. Celine Dion teared up in the video. Schaffel kept the rights to the song.

Then McDonald's began to hear complaints from the public: What was this family-friendly chain doing with an alleged child molester? The executives retreated.

Adding to Michael's disappointment, Sony Music was uninterested in "What More Can I Give?" as his record label was focusing on his other 2001 project—the *Invincible* album, expenses for which had ballooned to $51 million. In the video for 2001's "You Rock My World," a $75,000 exploding-building scene starring Chris Tucker had to be deleted in the days after 9/11. "That was a crazy job that should have taken two weeks but took almost two months with all the false starts that we had," producer Rubin Mendoza recalls. "There was a huge sense of deflated relief when it was done." Suffice to say, Sony was not excited when Michael asked for roughly $8 million to fund the video.

Michael became irate. Although Mottola, the Sony Entertainment chief, had been his ally for more than a decade, their relationship was frequently tense. "The problem for Michael Jackson was when Tommy got married," recalls Michael Schulhof, Sony Corp.'s US chief executive in the nineties, referring to the label chief's 1993 wedding with pop star Mariah Carey. "Michael was worried that she would divert the company's resources in favor of her. . . . It was always touchy." As the *Invincible* marketing campaign dragged on, Michael became more and more frustrated. He clumsily attempted to elevate his clash with Mottola into a civil rights issue. He turned to Al Sharpton, but the outspoken reverend was a friend of Mottola's and didn't consider the record mogul a racist.

Alone in his crusade, in June 2002, Michael attended a London fan-club event and called Mottola "a devil." He rallied his fans for support and displayed photos of his boss wearing devil horns and carrying a pitchfork. He called him "very, very devilish." In his 2013 autobiography, *Hitmaker*, Mottola called the attack "sad and pathetic," and responded: "It had nothing to do with race, heaven or hell. It had to do with an artist who was starting to melt down because he couldn't adjust to his shrinking album sales."

Traditionally, pop stars who wanted to promote their albums went on tour, and nobody could generate more worldwide publicity through a tour than Michael Jackson. But he had no interest. One of his many business advisers at this time, James Meiskin, was meeting with Michael in his Neverland office when a fax arrived from a prominent Asian promoter. He was offering $11 million to $15 million for one concert. Michael threw the document into the trash. "No way I'm gonna do that, Meiskin," Michael told him. "I lose eleven pounds per performance. These promoters, they break me. I never make any money from these concerts. They don't know what I have to go through."

In lieu of making money from concerts, Michael told Meiskin, Konitzer, and others, he wanted to buy Marvel Comics, home of Spider-Man and the Incredible Hulk—something for which he'd taken a few meetings with Stan Lee, the company's founder, as early as 1999. The investment idea was savvy. The 2002 *Spider-Man* movie was about to open the door for a flood of smash comic-book hits, from *X-Men* to *Iron Man* to *The Avengers*. The price, though, was $800 million. Far too high.

Rather than lecturing Michael about financial prudence, Konitzer returned to his home in Vancouver and spent two or three months coming up with a new concept—MJ Universe, a multifaceted plan involving investments in technology companies, providing new content for short films and commercials, developments such as theme parks and school programs, and licensing MJ's image. Everything but singing and dancing. Konitzer and his ally, manager Dieter Wiesner, came up with an animated presentation they considered "light and funny." Jackson loved it. He began to call Konitzer with ideas three or four times a day. Wiesner and Konitzer built a team of what they called "new, fresh, motivated people—at least to some degree, non-Hollywood." They secured power-of-attorney documents, enabling them to speak on Michael's behalf when approaching companies.

To deal with expenses, Michael needed a specialist of a different kind—essentially, somebody who would pay for everything. Every ninety days, past-due invoices came in from a variety of sources that billed Michael for a total of roughly $10 million. Some of this was for Four Seasons hotel rooms and shopping. Some of it was . . . unusual. After November 1993, when police searched Katherine and Joe Jackson's home on Hayvenhurst in Encino, looking for evidence that Michael had molested Jordan Chandler, he decided to wipe the physical memory of that unpleasant incident out of his system. Michael leased an eight-thousand-square-foot hangar at the Santa Monica Municipal Airport and hauled everything he had from Hayvenhurst into the space for storage—an inoperable Rolls-Royce, pinball machines, a bureau full of clothes. He also owed a Santa Monica electronics store $80,000 for TVs he purchased for his friend Marlon Brando.

"He owed money to everybody," says David LeGrand, his attorney at the time, who later tried to sort through his finances.

In 2001, Michael developed a close friendship with Miami entrepreneur Al Malnik, whose forty-year-old Miami steakhouse, the Forge, had served Sinatra, Judy Garland, and President Nixon. By this time, Michael had become a father for the third time. Prince Michael II, known as Blanket, was to outsiders the singer's most mysterious child; MJ announced he'd had a surrogate mother, and Debbie Rowe clarified the baby did not belong to her. Blanket was blond-haired and, like his siblings, obviously white, suggesting Michael himself may not have been involved in the conception, either—although friends would say Blanket inherited his father's dance talent, pulling off popping-and-locking moves as he grew up and nailing a perfect version of the "Billie Jean" moonwalk. Michael and Al Malnik, who had a younger wife and children around the ages of Prince, Paris, and Blanket, frequently gathered their children for family get-togethers. They became so close that Al agreed to become Prince's godfather—and "bring up Blanket in the event anything happened to him." Every few months, the press asked Malnik whether he was Blanket's father, scuttlebutt he denied.

Malnik met with Jackson's advisers. He met with Bank of America executives. With the help of Charles Koppelman, a veteran record executive advising Michael at the time, Malnik began to turn things around. Malnik and Koppelman worked with Fortress Investment Group, which had expertise in taking over distressed debts, to buy the Bank of America loans and stave off any kind of Jackson bankruptcy—at sky-high interest rates. Their meeting with Goldman Sachs would have "solidified all of Michael's assets in the music-publishing world," as Koppelman recalls, then pay Michael a stipend to handle his prolific expenses. But, Koppelman adds, "Michael was spending probably double the amount of money he was earning. And he had loans that were coming due that, if he wasn't able to pay them, he was in jeopardy of losing his most valuable assets." Also, Malnik loaned MJ a total of $7 million to $10 million over time. "Al personally wrote checks to pay down a lot of Michael's bills," Marc Schaffel says. "Al almost had Michael's finances to the point of a turnaround. And then it all just blew up."

Back in 1994, Michael Clayton had paid $185,000—$50,000 more than he wanted to—for a small white building in the center of Santa Maria, California. It was worth it, he figured, because he was a lawyer, and the one-story former single-family adobe home was across the street from the Santa Barbara Superior Courts. For ten years, he enjoyed the short walk between the buildings, but one day in January 2004, Clayton left his office and noticed, to his dismay, that the City of Santa Maria had erected chain-link fences on both sides of the street, forcing him to detour two blocks out of his way, cross at a street light, and enter the courthouse through the back door.

Clayton was annoyed, but soon people began to enquire about his roof. Before the forty-something lawyer knew it, roughly two thousand reporters—not to mention fans, gawkers, people promoting random dot-coms, and one woman wearing a promotional bikini top made of lettuce—had descended on his city of eighty thousand to cover Michael Jackson's trial for child molestation. Could the BBC pay to set up cameras on his roof? Could Sky TV, the BBC's New Zealand–based competitor, do the same? What about CNN? "Sure!" Clayton told them. He marked off ten-by-seven-foot spots on the roof, each of which could fit four people, and charged the networks $2,500 apiece for the space.

Clayton took a hiatus from his legal work, becoming a sort of journalistic concierge. After Michael Jackson showed up for the first time to attend a hearing, he famously stopped his black SUV in the street, climbed to the top of the vehicle, and did an impromptu dance. The spectacle happened to be immediately underneath Clayton's roof. Upon seeing this, TV producers who'd been uncertain whether to make a deal with Clayton told him: "We want our spot. We will sign for this spot right now. *We want it*." In the end, he made $300,000. "If I didn't do what I did," he says, "I would've been the worst businessman, at that moment, in the United States."

The end of Michael Jackson begins with a ten-year-old boy who had a sixteen-pound tumor in his abdomen and lesions in his lungs. In the early 2000s, Gavin Arvizo was living with his mother Janet, his father

David, his thirteen-year-old sister Davellin, and his nine-year-old brother Star in an East Los Angeles studio apartment. He underwent chemotherapy for a year, which caused him to lose much of his hair and made him so frail that people gasped when they saw him. Doctors told his family to prepare for his funeral.

The Arvizos had famous and influential friends. Before he got sick, Gavin and his siblings attended a summer camp at the Laugh Factory, a comedy club that opened in 1979 and went on to book just about every major stand-up—Redd Foxx, David Letterman, Jon Stewart, Sarah Silverman. The club's founder, Jamie Masada, was a philanthropist in addition to a businessman, and he held a summer comedy camp for underprivileged kids.

The Arvizos became a sort of personal charity for several comedians. Gavin gave Masada a list of famous people he wanted to meet—comedians Chris Tucker and Adam Sandler and Michael Jackson—and the Laugh Factory founder dutifully spent hours working his contacts, including someone who gave him Quincy Jones's office number. Some of the savvy stars who took these calls perceived the story of this sweet family with the sick child had cracks in its foundation. Jay Leno said he detected something "scripted" about the voicemails Gavin left for him. Others, such as writer-producer Louise Palanker, were touched by their story. She befriended the family, arriving at the Arvizos' apartment one Christmas with a Sony PlayStation and a microwave oven.

Using his famous contacts, Masada landed a phone number to Neverland. Soon MJ was making his first of many calls to Gavin at the hospital. One day in 2000, a limo arrived to pick up the entire Arvizo family to take them to the ranch. The kids spent the night in a guest room; Janet and her husband, David, a grocery warehouse employee, were in a nearby room facing a lake. At first, Gavin's father didn't want him to ride on the rides, because he had just had surgery, but Gavin talked him into it. The kids played in Michael's arcade, drove his go-karts, and toured the zoo and the movie theater on his grounds that seemed to go on forever in the perfect California weather. The kids grew close to Michael Jackson. Michael called Gavin "Doo-Doo Head" and "Apple Head" and nicknamed his brother Star "Blow Hole." The family became a ubiquitous presence at Neverland, indulging in the staff help, high-class meals, and luxurious bedrooms. "The kids genuinely liked Michael, but I also remember people taking care of the mom—spending time with her, giving her money," recalls Christian Robinson, Jackson's videographer at the time.

One day, Michael asked Gavin Arvizo if he still wanted to be an actor. Gavin said he did. Michael told him a British broadcaster, Martin Bashir, was on the way to Neverland and would like to interview Gavin and his siblings. "I'm going to put you in the movies," he told him. "And this is your audition. Okay?" Gavin agreed.

Over his eighteen-year career, Bashir, a British journalist, had interviewed numerous high-profile celebrities, including Princess Diana. He spent five years trying to score an interview with Michael Jackson. "Michael adored Princess Diana . . . and when Bashir knocked on my door to ask me to introduce Michael to him, he showed me a crumpled letter he carried in his wallet—a thank-you letter from Princess Diana," says Michael's friend Uri Geller, who introduced MJ to Bashir and calls it "my devastating mistake."

Michael granted approval to Bashir, who at the time was working for ITV, the UK's biggest network, to visit him at Neverland, as well as at his posh suite in Las Vegas. Filming began in late 2002 and lasted through January 14, 2003. *Living with Michael Jackson* came out in February, almost exactly ten years after Michael's big Oprah interview. For much of the first hour of the episode, which drew fifteen million viewers when it first aired on British television, Michael attempted to seduce the camera and charm the interviewer, as he'd done repeatedly since he was a kid. He told the old stories, like the one about yearning to play with the kids in the park across the street from his Jackson 5 studio, and the one about how his musical inspiration arrived as a gift from God. Early in the episode, Bashir dutifully played the wide-eyed journalist, cowed by Neverland, gleefully racing Michael in a go-kart.

Slowly, almost undetectably, Bashir's tone shifted from bemusement to scolding incredulity. "You never want to grow up?" he asked. "No," Michael said. "I am Peter Pan." Bashir corrected him: "You're Michael Jackson." At this point it was clear, to both Michael and the audience, that this interviewer wasn't empathetic Oprah. "I'm Peter Pan at heart," Michael clarified. Over time, as Bashir's tone continued to change, Michael's people began to piece together what the interviewer was doing. At one point, driving with MJ in Berlin, Dieter Wiesner, his manager, came to believe Bashir was asking "really, really bad questions," and put his hand over the camera to stop the interview.

In some portions of *Living with Michael Jackson*, Michael came across more sympathetically than ever. He seemed prepared, rehearsed, suppressing sobs when detailing the iron cords and belts his father used on him and his brothers. The goodwill he generated from this portion extended through the shopping section of the show. In Vegas, where Michael spent months at a high-end hotel because "it's a fun place to visit," Bashir couldn't comprehend Michael racking up $500,000 on a couple of high-end urns or $89,000 on a chess set. He seemed to say: *Can you believe this guy?* But the viewing audience remained on Michael's side.

Then Michael spent the last half hour dismantling this goodwill. Bashir was confrontational—kind of a jerk, really—but his personality was far overshadowed by the insane language Michael used to describe himself and his lifestyle. He stared straight into the camera and lied about his facial surgery. Cheek implants? "No!" Dimple in chin? "Oh, God!" Reconstructed eyelids? "It's stupid! None of it is true! They made it up!" Bashir asked whether Debbie Rowe had been upset to hand over Paris so quickly after she was born. "She said, 'Go right ahead,'" Michael claimed. He said he swaddled Paris immediately after birth, placenta and all, and rushed her home in a towel. "They told me it was okay!"

Bashir was an eyewitness to one pivotal event in MJ history. In

November 2002, Jackson had flown to Berlin for the annual Bambi Awards. He brought his entourage, including manager Wiesner and nanny Rwaramba, to a fourth-floor hotel room. Fans began to buzz outside, and Michael made one of the worst snap decisions of his career. He seized his infant son, Prince Michael II, underneath the armpits, and displayed him to the fans below. He held Prince tightly—as he would later say repeatedly on camera—but his mistake was in displaying the baby on the outside rather than the inside of the balcony barrier. The incident lasted less than three seconds, but once paparazzi developed their film, the image became damning, iconic, the perfect clip to kick off the nightly news and the front page of the *National Enquirer*. Michael appeared to be the most monstrous celebrity father ever. Bashir said in his TV narration months later: "I was worried. There was a manic quality about him that I had never seen before." Wiesner, who was in the room at the time, didn't catch any of this dark subtext. "For us, it was not something special," he says. "Next day, we realized this disaster."

Finally, Bashir delivered the crescendo. Capturing Michael at home in Neverland, Bashir zoomed in on twelve-year-old cancer survivor Gavin Arvizo, who gazed in a fond, babyish way toward Michael and placidly rested his head on his older friend's shoulder. He seemed as comfortable as a twelve-year-old boy with his head on Michael Jackson's shoulder could be. Gavin was giddy and fast-talking. He started to ramble: "I was, like, 'Michael, you can sleep in the bed,' and he was like, 'No, no, you sleep in the bed,' and I was like, 'No, no, no, you sleep in the bed.' And then he said, 'Look, if you love me, then you'll sleep in the bed.' I was like, 'Oh, man.' So I finally slept in the bed." Michael chose the floor—an important detail that might have allowed him to escape the interview unscathed. But instead of emphasizing this point, he insisted to Bashir that a forty-four-year-old man sleeping in a bed with children who are not in his family was the most natural thing in the world. "I have slept in the bed with many children," he said, citing Macaulay Culkin and his brother, Kieran, from an earlier Neverland era. "We're jammed in there, like a hot-air balloon. It's very right. It's very loving. That's what the world needs now. More love." Then he asked Bashir: "You don't sleep with your kids, or some other kid who needs love, who didn't have a good childhood?" Bashir, outraged, disagreed. "I would!" Michael shouted. "Because you've never been where I've been, mentally!"

It wasn't until after Bashir's final interviews, in Miami, that the enormity of the project began to sink in with MJ and his people. "We got information it was going to be bad news," Wiesner recalls. "[Michael] was sitting on the bed and crying. I said, 'Michael, it's too late now.' He was down. He was on the floor." The Bashir documentary sent Jackson and everyone around him into full damage-control mode. In a statement, he said he felt "devastated" and "utterly betrayed." After the show aired in the US a few days after its British viewing and drew an audience of thirty-eight million, Michael called his ex-wife Lisa Marie Presley. "Dude," she said, "that documentary fucking *sucked*, man. What were you thinking?"

The morning after the show, Schaffel was sitting in his kitchen with MJ videographers Hamid Moslehi and Christian Robinson and publicist Stuart Backerman. They were eating breakfast from McDonald's, wondering what to do about their boss's crumbling career, when Moslehi mentioned to the group he'd been rolling his own tape of the Bashir interviews. He caught the British journalist delivering bromides such as "Michael, I love the way you are with children. It's spectacular the way you treat them." Schaffel and Backerman shouted at him: "Get your ass in gear right now and get your butt out that door and get that footage!" Moslehi did as he was told, and Schaffel was soon conducting a bidding war between ABC (considering a $1 million offer), NBC ($2.5 million, and the promise to kill an upcoming *Dateline* special on Michael's plastic surgery), and Fox ($3.5 million) over the new film.

The bids went up considerably, and Schaffel finally sold the show to be called *Michael Jackson Take Two: The Footage You Were Never Meant to See* to Fox for $7.3 million, and a companion piece called *Michael*

Jackson's Home Movies for $4 million—and negotiated a 20 percent fee for himself. (*Home Movies* bombed in the ratings, discouraging the team from creating part three.)

Thus did two Michael Jacksons emerge on television. The first, as interpreted by Bashir, showed MJ talking directly to the camera, in such a way that emphasized every touched-up portion of his face. In the rebuttal videos, the camera angle was more forgiving. Viewers could see only a portion of Michael's face—set in the best light to avoid his chin cleft and thin nose. Bashir's coverage suggested a trip to a zoo in Germany, in which crowds swarmed Michael and his children and jostled little Prince, was an example of indifferent or even negligent parenting. Michael's version explained how his people contacted the zoo in advance, attempting to arrange a visit when it was closed to the public, but the situation escalated unexpectedly.

The rebuttal video is an extraordinary MJ performance, an hour and a half of public-relations spin disguised as a hard-hitting documentary, hosted gravely by afternoon-TV host Maury Povich. As for Michael's business of sleeping with children, Debbie Rowe says, authoritatively: "Apparently there's some confusion with sleeping in beds. My favorite thing to do is to sit in bed and watch TV. If you're coming over, take your shoes off, get on the bed, we're watching the TV." Those who slept in her bed, most likely, were aware she'd never been accused of molesting children.

The most dramatic moment of the rebuttal, though, was when Schaffel and crew trotted out the Arvizo family to unequivocally clarify their presence in Neverland. Janet Arvizo added an emotional touch: "My children and me know what rejection is, to be neglected, to be spit on, talked about, to be made an outsider—only because of our status in life, or what we were going through," she said. "Gavin was the one who asked him, 'Could I call you Daddy?' and Michael said, 'Of course.' . . . Very innocent and beautiful relationship, but everyone has spun it out of control."

The more than $11 million MJ received for the rebuttal videos gave him, in a small and temporary way, a financial lifeline. Until that point, Wiesner and Konitzer had the unpleasant task of informing Michael he lacked the funds to plant flowers around the trees at Neverland or water certain lawns. MJ wanted to buy his mother something like $20,000 in cosmetic pharmaceuticals—but a budget for it didn't exist.

Rebuttal or no rebuttal, child advocates were growing disturbed by watching a forty-five-year-old man admit on national TV to sleeping with young boys. Dr. Carole Lieberman, a well-known psychologist, filed a formal complaint with California officials: "I felt enough was enough," she told reporters. "I just couldn't believe that the world was standing by and letting these children be potentially harmed." LA's Department of Children and Family Services, as well as the police department, investigated, but concluded the complaints by Lieberman and others were "unfounded." Tom Sneddon, the Santa Barbara County district attorney who'd gone after MJ in 1993, told reporters he couldn't act unless victims came forward.

Despite Michael's cash-flow problems, the Arvizos were "shopping all the time, coming back with drivers and bodyguards and a load of toys," Konitzer recalls. "Dieter [Wiesner] took care of the situation, and from that day on, we were the enemies."

Stung, the Arvizos began to describe a third, more sinister reality beyond the one in Bashir's video and the one in Michael's rebuttal.

Michael would never recover from it.

On June 13, 2003, police in Santa Barbara County received new information. Dr. Stan Katz, an LA child psychiatrist, had sent a report about a meeting he'd had with the Arvizos.

Katz was an experienced soldier in the Michael Jackson child-molestation wars. He had interviewed Jordan Chandler at length in the early nineties to help his family prepare for a civil case before they ended up settling. He had spoken with Janet Arvizo, then conducted a formal interview with Gavin. For the first time, Gavin Arvizo said Michael molested him. His brother Star corroborated the story. Katz believed them—and still does. "Kids who fabricate are usually given a script. They often exaggerate where they can," Katz recalls. "[The Arvizos] didn't exaggerate."

The accusations were enough for Santa Barbara County district attorney Tom Sneddon, Michael's old nemesis from the Jordan Chandler investigation, to make a move. More than seventy sheriff's deputies piled into Neverland on November 18, raiding the property in search of anything to implicate Michael—books, videos, papers, computers. Holed up at the Mirage in Vegas, where he'd been working on the "One More Chance" video, Michael did not take the news well. Upon hearing screaming and breaking glass in MJ's room, hotel security had rushed to his door. "Go away!" the singer told them. When Wiesner finally arrived with a key to open the singer's room, he found the remnants of a rampage—Michael had destroyed a glass table, knocked over breakfast carts, flung food, dishes, lamps, and vases, and tossed chairs at the wall, prompting a hotel bill for $250,000 in damages. His kids gaped fearfully at what publicist Stuart Backerman called "some berserk, out-of-control madman in those monstrous moments of his rage."

For many who'd been working with MJ, the raid represented the end. "Everything fell apart very quickly," recalls Ronald Konitzer, who had been launching the plan to overhaul Michael's finances. "Within two weeks, it was clear we can bury MJ Universe." Santa Barbara authorities arrested Michael and hauled him to jail, where he posed for one of the most disturbing celebrity mug shots ever—sculpted lips and nose, freaked-out eyebrows, and a wide-open fish eye. Michael's new defense attorney, Mark Geragos, had been making arrangements for the star to fly from Vegas back to LA for his booking. While that was happening, Karen Faye flew to Las Vegas to prepare his makeup for the shot, but she was no match for the anxiety on MJ's face. He took a private Gulfstream IV to the Santa Barbara Municipal Airport and surrendered to sheriff's deputies, who hauled him to the station in a black SUV. Despite his preparation, the mug shot, Backerman says, "wasn't even the Michael that I knew. It was some strange, pathetic, pasty-skinned, pink-lipped, doll-like dandy that gazed out wide-eyed and witless at the camera." Michael posted $3 million bail—Malnik supplied the cash. (Through a discounted bond service, it wound up being less than $300,000 up front.) The sum was more than three times as much, the Rev. Jesse Jackson would note, as the bail set for white murder suspect Phil Spector. Rick James, the outspoken funk singer, reminded viewers on CNN that Elvis Presley, who'd slept with his wife Priscilla when she was fourteen or fifteen, was never prosecuted. "As soon as you get famous and black, they go after you," James said.

With these kinds of arguments in mind, Grace Rwaramba and Jermaine Jackson reached out to the Rev. Louis Farrakhan, leader of the Nation of Islam, the black-nationalist group whose members Jermaine had befriended while traveling in Saudi Arabia in the late eighties. Michael met with Nation officials twice—they "called him 'Sir' and gave him respect," providing security, not ideology, Jermaine said. But when Wiesner, his manager, pounded on his door one day, Michael let him in and began to whisper in a strange voice. "Dieter," Michael said, "the devil is listening. The devil's up there; the devil's on the roof. The devil's listening to what we're saying." After that, MJ stopped returning Wiesner's calls. He was shutting out the rest of his advisers as well, including Schaffel and Malnik. "And there was no access anymore," Konitzer recalls. "Nothing you can do."

The most pointed personal attack Michael Jackson ever delivered in his music, buried within the end of the *HIStory* album, was against someone called "Dom Sheldon," or "D.S.," for short. In the recording, it's impossible not to hear the words *Tom Sneddon* repeated throughout the chorus—even the National District Attorneys Association referred to

Sneddon as "the only D.A. in the nation to have an angry song written about him by pop megastar Michael Jackson." Sneddon, the sixty-three-year-old Santa Barbara district attorney, was three years away from retirement when the Arvizos' accusations landed on his desk. MJ supporters believe Sneddon, after the Jordan Chandler investigation devolved into a settlement, had revenge on his mind. "Was he eager to put him in prison? Any prosecutor who recognizes there's a sexual predator among us was eager to take care of that problem," prosecutor Ron Zonen says. "Were we more eager with Michael Jackson than anybody else? No, absolutely not." Still, Zonen calls Sneddon an "aggressive sort of guy."

On January 16, 2004, the day of his first court appearance, Michael showed up in a black coat with a military insignia, black pants with white stripes, huge sunglasses, and a white armband. The courts had prepared barricades along the courthouse entrance so Michael and his entourage, including his parents and Jermaine and Janet, could be funneled into the front double doors without being touched. He pleaded not guilty, as expected, but he showed up twenty-one minutes late to the 8:30 A.M. hearing, earning a rebuke from the judge. After the hearing, when Michael Jackson's black SUV pulled out of the courthouse parking lot and abruptly stopped in the left-turn lane, and Michael climbed onto the roof, performing to his cheering fans, the Associated Press's Linda Deutsch called her editor. "Turn on your TV," she told him, "you're not going to believe this."

This spectacle proved to be a huge public misstep for a defendant accused of a serious crime. The defense attorney who took the fall for it was Mark Geragos, who had represented actress Winona Ryder, after she'd been arrested on shoplifting charges, and accused murderer Scott Peterson—but lost both cases. Michael soon lost confidence in Geragos, who was representing Peterson and other clients while simultaneously building MJ's defense. "He's way over his head," Michael told confidants. "And he can't win." By this point, with the help of Nation of Islam figures such as Leonard Muhammad, Randy Jackson had taken over his brother's business and legal affairs. Seeking an alternative to Geragos, Randy called Johnnie Cochran in April 2004, when the famed defense attorney was in the throes of an inoperable brain tumor. "If it was me, I'd want Tom Mesereau," Cochran said.

Thomas Mesereau Jr., fifty-three, was slick and charismatic, with silvery-white, shoulder-length hair. He met with Michael in an Orlando mansion where the pop star was temporarily living. His first move didn't sit well with several of Michael's advisers: "I don't want the Nation of Islam. I don't want Jesse Jackson or Al Sharpton up there," Mesereau told Michael and his people. "This is going to do nothing but alienate white jurors." As he studied Michael's career, Mesereau learned about the singer's message of racial equality in songs like "Black or White" and the way he integrated MTV. He wanted that MJ. "This message of inclusion, rather than exclusion, was something white people resonate with," says Mesereau, a veteran civil rights attorney who defends a murder case every year in the South using his own funds.

Mesereau's trial strategy was to target Janet Arvizo. His team felt she was unstable and would weaken under direct attack. And they felt prosecutors were overconfident to the point of being "on cloud nine"— they didn't think they would lose. The underdog role suited Mesereau.

Ron Zonen denies this accusation of prosecutorial hubris—he said numerous times throughout the trial that MJ's celebrity and clout put his side at a disadvantage. "I never felt it was in the bag," he says. "I understood the person we were going at was quite possibly the most recognizable face in the world, and quite possibly the most popular person in the world." On the first day of the trial, Zonen walked to the courthouse and noticed three helicopters overhead and two thousand people out front. "Okay," he thought to himself, "my life is about to change rather dramatically."

Santa Maria is eighty-five miles north of Santa Barbara, a college town that looks like a movie backdrop when the sun sets over the

Pacific Ocean. It's also about half an hour north of Los Olivos, the small town encompassing Neverland. Mesereau spent much of his trial preparation roaming Santa Barbara County, riding his motorcycle in jeans and a leather jacket, stopping in bars for a glass of wine or a meal. He learned quickly the southern part of the county, which includes the University of California Santa Barbara campus and Los Angeles refugees and retirees, was the wealthiest and most liberal. The northern portion, full of ranches and farms and blue-collar workers, was more conservative, almost libertarian, respectful of quiet, law-abiding residents—including, as Mesereau discovered, Michael Jackson. Fortunately for Mesereau, MJ's trial would take place in Santa Maria—the north.

Judge Rodney Melville had expected ten thousand fans and three hundred satellite trucks to descend on Santa Maria. The numbers turned out to be one thousand fans on the busiest days, not counting media, and just ten or fifteen trucks. On December 18, 2003, when Sneddon filed his complaint, Melville's court administrator prepared five hundred copies to give to reporters. "They fought for copies," Melville said. "They nearly crushed him. The police literally had to . . . rescue him." The judge allowed half of the courtroom seats to the media, half to the public, and a front row of family members and guests. *Rolling Stone*'s Matt Taibbi called Jackson's trial, from the formal charges on December 18, 2003, to its conclusion on June 13, 2005, "a goddamn zoo, a freak show from sunup to sundown." An average day drew about thirty fans, including, as Taibbi wrote, "a fat white psychopath from Tennessee who thinks Jackson is Jesus and a rotund Latino in a FREE MICHAEL T-shirt who lives in his mother's basement a few miles from the courthouse." The media circus drew partisans on both sides. Sheree Wilkins, an Inglewood, California, preschool teacher in her early thirties, resigned from her job, moved to Santa Maria, and split a $200-something-a-week room at a Best Inn with a fellow MJ fan. She found a night job at a local Jack-in-the-Box and spent her days outside the courthouse. "I believe the connection was pain," says Wilkins, who was crushed when her parents divorced and her brother became involved in drugs and gangs. "[Michael] was in pain, and we were in pain." On the anti-MJ side was Diane Dimond, a Court TV reporter who had covered the Chandler accusations for TV's *Hard Copy*. After interviewing twenty children who claim to have been "possible victims," she says today: "I think Michael Jackson was one of the most prolific pedophiles, publicly and privately, that we've ever seen."

Dimond wasn't the only journalist who arrived in Santa Maria with such biases. "A lot of people came there as Jackson haters," recalls Linda Deutsch, the veteran Associated Press reporter who covered the trial, "people who had made their whole careers on going after Michael Jackson."

The eight-woman, four-man jury included a disabled man in a wheelchair, a *Simpsons* fan, a country-music aficionado, the grandson of a registered sex offender, and a woman related to one of the doomed pilots on September 11. The youngest was twenty-two, the oldest seventy-nine. Mesereau had no complaints—he and his partner Susan Yu had craved women, whom they perceived as more sympathetic—but prosecutor Zonen was less sure. "I like people who are businessmen, responsible for other people, who run operations, who hire and fire people," he says. "I knew we wouldn't be able to get any of them because they'd have to take six months off the job. That means we were left with jurors [who were] unemployed or underemployed, or often retired, or housewives, or very young. That's not my ideal jury."

Those in the media who breezily predicted victory for the prosecution did not count on a few crucial factors. For example, Sneddon, the DA, was not likable. *Rolling Stone*'s Taibbi described him as a "humorless creep whose public persona recalls the potbellied vice principal perched on the gym bleachers watching you slow-dance." Sneddon struggled to find the right tone for his indignation—he believed Jackson to be a child molester, but MJ was also an entertainer beloved by millions, and if Sneddon was too harsh or sarcastic, he risked losing the jury. Earlier, in response to a reporter's question about the timing of the indictment with Jackson's new *Number Ones* album, Sneddon had sniffed, "Like the sheriff and I are really into that kind of music." *That kind of music*—only the most popular of all time—was a false note. He began his opening statement with a clunky cliché: "On February the third of 2003, the defendant Michael Jackson's world was rocked. And it didn't rock in a musical sense. It rocked in a real-life sense."

Sneddon* jumped from topic to topic and was often difficult to follow. He detailed an elaborate Neverland travelogue, mapping out bedrooms, stairways, and alarm systems. He named sexually explicit magazines and DVDs, with titles like *Hustler Barely Legal Hardcore*, containing both Michael's and Gavin's fingerprints. He emphasized Gavin's accusation that Michael humped a mannequin and walked around naked, with an erection, in front of his young guests. Reporters noticed the prosecution gradually deemphasizing Sneddon and playing up Zonen. "Sneddon was much more abrasive. You could see in his style, and hearing in the tone of his voice, he was just more of a blunt character. At the beginning, his microphone wouldn't work properly and he would get increasingly irritated," recalls the BBC's Peter Bowes. "Everyone liked Zonen. Very different personalities."

The prosecution made tactical errors. The state spent a full day and a half going over phone numbers. "The way the state structured their case was just awful. It was so confusing and so convoluted," Diane Dimond says. "The best courtroom performances are the ones that are simple." The prosecution also played up the sexually explicit websites, briefcases full of nudie magazines, and centerfold cutouts investigators had found or learned about in Michael's private Neverland stuff. "He was a drug addict, an alcoholic. He lived in a room filled with por-

---

*Sneddon died November 1, 2014, of complications from cancer. "A man of integrity has died," Diane Dimond wrote on Facebook. "He abused the legal system," Karen Faye countered on Twitter.

nography and booze," Zonen says. But the strategy backfired. It made Michael Jackson seem like a heterosexual American male.

"Ladies and gentlemen," Mesereau said, pointedly, after Sneddon's performance, "I have an *organized* opening statement for you." He zoomed in on Janet Arvizo and how she tried to exploit rich comedians and actors, from Jay Leno to Jim Carrey to George Lopez to an actress on *The Fresh Prince of Bel-Air*. Mesereau emphasized Janet's days on welfare, then the bills she racked up during February 2003, at Michael Jackson's expense: a $50 leg wax at Bare Skin Salon, $448.04 worth of clothing at Anchor Blue, $454.64 worth of Jockey socks, bras, and underwear.

Mesereau then began to pick apart Gavin Arvizo's account of what happened in February 2003, shortly after the release of Bashir's documentary. Reporters, Children's Services, and the police were descending upon Neverland, and Jackson's associates were scrambling to assemble a rebuttal film. "And guess what happens, they say, in the middle of all this?" Mesereau asked. "That's when they say the child molestation begins. . . . Can you imagine a more absurd time?"

The first high-drama day in the courtroom came with the arrival of Davellin Arvizo, an eighteen-year-old college freshman who'd been an eighth-grader when Michael allegedly molested her brother. She mentioned that Gavin's yearlong battle against cancer involved a major surgery, in which doctors removed his spleen, a kidney, lymph nodes, and the tumor in his abdomen. Gavin was always a high-strung kid, but during his time with Michael, her younger brother was "very talkative. Running around. Very, very playful. . . . It was just more than usual. Like more talkative, more jumpy and stuff." She called MJ's manager, Dieter Wiesner, "real aggressive," and said he handed them a script of "nice things" to say about Jackson for the rebuttal film. After a few days, the Arvizos perceived the situation as threatening.

Under Mesereau's cross-examination, Davellin began to wilt. Over two days, she said variations of "I don't remember" more than 160 times and "I don't know" more than 130, leading Mesereau to ask: "Did someone tell you that when the defense lawyer asks you questions in court, if you've got a problem, to say, 'I was very young and I just don't remember'?"

During Mesereau's cross-examination of Davellin, Michael stood up to go to the bathroom. This was not allowed without permission. MJ's unflappable attorney had to chase him down. At the beginning of the trial, Michael had seemed to not understand the gravity of the situation. In February 2005, media helicopters filming his arrival caught his SUV taking an abrupt turn away from the courtroom and toward the hospital. Doctors would later say he had flulike symptoms, for which Judge Melville gave him an excused absence. While listening to these events unfold on the news via car radio, Tony Baxter, Disney's vice president for creative development at the time, received an unexpected call on his cell phone. It was Michael, his friend. "I got dressed for this court date and I was really nervous and my stomach got really upset. I couldn't face getting out of the car in front of all the people I knew would be there, so I told the driver to turn around and take me to the hospital," he told Baxter. Then he abruptly changed the subject to a theme-park project they'd been discussing.

In March, Gavin's younger brother Star, a nervous, fidgeting fourteen-year-old who was growing into a beefy freshman football player, detailed a scene in Jackson's bedroom in which MJ's associate Frank Cascio was surfing the Internet on his computer. Michael's kids, Paris and Prince, were asleep. Cascio allegedly called up five or six porn websites, including one with a woman who "had her shirt up," to which the singer said, crudely, "Got milk?" Then Jackson leaned over a sleeping Prince and said, in his ear: "You're missing some pussy." Michael instructed Gavin and Star not to tell anybody about it. The two brothers slept next to each other that night in Michael's bed, while the King of Pop slept on the floor at the foot of the bed. On the flight from Miami to LA, Star saw Gavin leaning on Michael's chest. He saw Michael lick Gavin's head. He saw Michael intoxicated on "Jesus Juice." Finally, he described a bed containing Michael, himself, and Gavin. "My brother was outside of the covers," Star told the jury. "And I saw Michael's left hand in my brother's underwears and I saw his right hand in his underwears." The King of Pop was, according to Star Arvizo, stroking himself.

In his cross-examination, Mesereau asked Star about the *Barely Legal* porn magazine he'd identified, and noted that the August 2003 date on the cover was long after the Arvizos had stopped visiting Neverland. "I never said it was exactly that one," Star responded. "That's not exactly the one he showed us." Mesereau reminded Star he'd reconstructed the same events three or four different ways, twice to a grand jury, once to psychiatrist Katz. By the time Mesereau was through with Star, the jury didn't know what to think.

The prosecution's star witness, Gavin Arvizo himself, took the stand on March 9, 2005. He was fifteen. On the first day, he talked poignantly about having surgery for cancer. He recalled his first trip to Neverland. "[Michael] was like my best friend ever," Gavin told the jury. Jackson called him "son," and Gavin dubbed MJ "Michael Daddy."

His testimony was apparently too much for Michael. On the second day of Gavin's appearance, Michael was not in the courtroom. The judge asked Mesereau for the whereabouts of his client. He turned out to be at the Marian Medical Center in Santa Maria. Melville had run out of patience with the unexpected disappearance of a criminal defendant. He gave Mesereau an hour to find his client. Otherwise, he'd issue a bench warrant for Jackson's arrest and forfeit his bail if he didn't show up within an hour. Jackson turned out to have slipped in the shower and injured himself; he showed up, dutifully, within the hour, wearing pajama bottoms. After a few weeks, the trial was clearly beginning to wear on Michael. No longer was he the defiant superstar who saluted fans from the top of his SUV. "You could see his health declining," says Peter Bowes of the BBC. "He was painfully thin and very, very white."

MJ had reason to be anxious. On the stand, Gavin said of him: "We were under the covers, and I had his pajamas on. . . . And then that's when he put his hand in my pants and then he started masturbating me." This went on for five minutes, Gavin said, and at the end, he ejaculated. "I kind of felt weird. I was embarrassed about it," he told the jury. "And then he said it was okay, that it was natural." Then they fell asleep. It happened again, on a different day, in just about the same way.

Then Mesereau asked Gavin whether he'd had trouble in school, long before he met Jackson. The boy acknowledged teachers found him "uncooperative and disruptive"—he'd refused to sign detention forms and asked questions without raising his hand. "I would stand up to the teacher," he said. "A lot of the kids would kind of congratulate me." Mesereau caught Gavin in a startling admission. He asked whether Gavin felt "abandoned" after the Arvizos left the ranch for the last time. "Yes!" Gavin responded. It seemed obvious that he loved Michael Jackson and had been sad to leave him.

Michael Jackson's defense was going well. But the prosecution still had one major card to play, and it was Mesereau's biggest worry. Earlier, Judge Melville had allowed the prosecution to bring up previous child-molestation allegations against Michael Jackson, meaning Jordan Chandler could testify. Mesereau sympathized with Michael's desire to "close the book" on those charges, but he also acknowledged "most people thought anybody who would pay that kind of money must be guilty of something." Sneddon and his prosecutors felt the same way. Sneddon called Chandler at least twice at his home in New York to try to persuade him to testify, taking care not to make threats and promising he would not issue a subpoena. "We wanted a cooperative witness," Zonen recalls, "not an angry one." But Chandler declined.* It seems Jordan Chandler's settlement with Michael Jackson stipulated

---

*In June 2004, Zonen and Gordon Auchincloss, a senior DA, had attempted to get the FBI involved in the prosecution, but two agents met with Chandler later that year and found that he had "no interest."

the young accuser would never have to deal with these issues again. "Michael wasn't paying him twenty million dollars so he would go into a criminal proceeding. He was paying him twenty million dollars to essentially go away," Zonen says.

Instead, the prosecution called Chandler's mother, June, to the stand. "Dressed impeccably, Ms. Chandler looked like a vision, like she just stepped off the pages of *Vogue*," Aphrodite Jones wrote in a book defending MJ. "It was obvious that Sneddon was impressed by this exotic-looking woman." Chandler recalled the "Don't you trust me?" argument in which Michael tearfully insisted on sleeping in a bed with Jordie, above her objections. But Chandler also testified about MJ giving her the Cartier watch and a $7,000 gift certificate from a posh LA boutique. During Mesereau's cross-examination, her testimony grew cloudy. "I don't recall," she kept saying. She said she hadn't seen Jordie in eleven years. What came across most clearly from Chandler's testimony is how much she benefited from Jordie's relationship with Michael.

"Gold digger," Aphrodite Jones wrote.

It took only a few minutes of Janet Arvizo's four-hour testimony to finally dismantle the prosecution's case. She didn't mention child molestation even once. Instead, weirdly, she was obsessed with MJ's alleged imprisonment of her family. She insisted he and his coconspirators, including Cascio, Wiesner, and Konitzer, pressured the Arvizos to read scripted remarks about Michael's innocence for the rebuttal video, then refused to let them watch the documentary. She repeated Davellin's story, in a more rambling and confusing way, that MJ's people wouldn't let the Arvizos leave Neverland until an employee snuck them out. But the imprisonment of the Arvizos seemed farfetched, especially when Arvizo became forceful and animated as she talked, snapping her fingers and turning her chair toward the jury, as if ordering them to believe her story. "It was just startling," recalls Linda Deutsch, the AP reporter. "She seemed to think the courtroom was hers."

If she'd been imprisoned, Mesereau asked during his cross-examination, did she ever go to court to get a restraining order against MJ? "I was too scared of him," she said. But she had hired several lawyers by that point, right? Her response: "I don't understand what you're saying." Then Mesereau mentioned a 1999 incident in which the Arvizo family went to JC Penney, left with allegedly stolen merchandise, scuffled with employees and security, then sued the department store for $3 million before settling. Her response was too convoluted to quote succinctly here, but she said, in part: "I would like to make that correct statement because the statements that were there were incorrect."

"Don't judge me," she concluded, which seemed like a bizarre thing to say before a jury.

Mesereau opened his defense with the one-two-three punch of Macaulay Culkin, Brett Barnes, and Wade Robson, who were well-known friends of Michael when they were kids, and all three testified that nothing untoward happened when they were with him. (Robson would change his story after Jackson's death.) The prosecution had done most of Mesereau's work for him, allowing the Arvizos to undercut their own accusations, but nonetheless, he paraded witness after witness onto the stand: Jay Leno, Chris Tucker, George Lopez, Larry King. ("Why not Merv Griffin and Dick Cavett, too?" asked Matt Taibbi in *Rolling Stone*.) The defense rested on May 25, 2005.

On June 14, the court followed prearranged protocol for the jury verdict and gave Michael Jackson ninety minutes' notice, just enough time for him to drive with his city motorcycle escort from Neverland to Santa Maria. The courtroom and overflow room began to fill up with reporters. It took two hours for the courts to get everybody in place and announce the verdict. Peter Shaplen, the media pool producer, had a two-way radio and narrated the action for reporters in other parts of the courthouse as Jackson arrived—"Judge Melville has come in . . . Judge Melville has taken his seat . . . Judge Melville has opened the verdict first and put the envelope on his right side." He kept up the play-by-play as verdicts for each of the fourteen counts were announced: "Not guilty." In the courtroom, upon hearing the first two words, Katherine Jackson wept. Joe Jackson clasped his hands together and stared straight ahead. Michael showed no emotion, then slumped in his chair. Fans cheered and chanted outside.

ABC's producers worked quickly. They convinced six jurors to board a jet to take them to a taping of *Good Morning America*. CNN pried away another couple of jurors. The network was so paranoid about losing its scoop that it dispatched all available staff members to stand arm in arm, locking out other networks from making their own pitches.

MJ fan Sheree Wilkins, the teacher turned fast-food employee, suffered an emotional collapse. Paramedics arrived in the midst of the courthouse chaos to carry her away on a stretcher. She'd been praying for Michael, fasting and not drinking. Her blood pressure had dipped to dangerously low levels. "I had given absolutely everything," she says. While other fans drove to Neverland to celebrate at the gates, Wilkins received IV fluid at the hospital.

"The one thing I really regret," says Michael Clayton, the attorney and MJ trial entrepreneur across the street, "was when the verdict came out, I didn't drop a banner with a ten-by-thirty-foot NOT GUILTY."

Michael wouldn't have noticed. In his mind, he had already moved to his next phase: leaving Neverland forever.

CHAPTER 10

For more than a decade, Formula 1 race cars have whooshed through the desert on a track fifty miles south of Manama, the capital city of Bahrain. On this oil-rich island, affluent Saudi tourists could take a break from their repressive laws and legally drink alcohol, watch movies in theaters, shop and eat in coed establishments and, occasionally, pick from an armada of Thai and Chinese prostitutes. Into this "baby Dubai, with its prenatal skyscrapers and tax shelters, with its rinky-dink wildlife park and the Dolphin Park water show," as GQ called it, flew DJ Whoo Kid of Queens, New York. The sheiks had hired the affable member of hip-hop star 50 Cent's G-Unit posse to provide music for a Formula 1 party in October 2005. His flight from the US to Bahrain was going fine until he lost his passport during a stop in the Dubai airport.

Whoo Kid was in trouble. Dubai officials were threatening to send him back to the US, even though his Formula 1 appearance was scheduled for later that day. In a panic, he texted the man who'd hired him, Sheik Abdullah bin Hamad Al Khalifa, crown prince of Bahrain and second son of the king. Next thing he knew, a member of the sheik's family was outside, on the runway, searching underneath the planes for his lost passport. The Bahrainis found nothing, but they took care of everything—airport officials in Dubai and Bahrain swept him through every security checkpoint even though his only form of ID was a card for an American fitness center. Whoo Kid stayed in the sheik's palace for four days, two waiting for a new passport. He wandered out to a huge pool to get a drink. And that's when he saw Michael Jackson, his bright-white legs exposed in shorts.

The DJ, who had been eleven when *Thriller* came out, spun around. "Do you not *understand?*" he asked. "I'm a *black person.* Why didn't you tell me *Michael Jackson* is here?"

"Oh, he's just my neighbor now," the sheik responded.

As Whoo Kid understood it, Abdullah paid for Jackson and his kids to live at a second complex, next door to his own. The King of Pop would walk or drive over to hang out for hours at a time in blissful privacy.

To Sheik Abdullah bin Hamad Al Khalifa, Jackson was more than a neighbor. He was a kindred spirit, a collaborator. "It's difficult to explain to people without it sounding weird—they were friends," says Guy Holmes, chief executive of 2 Seas, the record company MJ and Abdullah created together. "They would play video games together. They would tell stupid jokes. They loved toy models, scale electric planes, cars and bikes." Abdullah had reportedly written a ballad called "Where Have You Been?," and it received regional airplay, although no trace of it exists on the Internet. It seems the prince had been producing a local artist for his own record label, and had been looking to expand his entertainment empire internationally.

"It was like we'd already spent time together," Abdullah said at the time. "As soon as they met, my daughter and his daughter started chatting like thirty-year-old women, and the boys were playing like boys do. It was great. Michael is now as much my brother as my blood brothers are." During MJ's trial, the sheik had loaned him more than $2 million.

On June 29, 2005, Michael arrived in Bahrain via private jet with his three kids and Grace Rwaramba, their nanny. The courtroom ordeal had ravaged his health and appearance. "Michael was really, really ill and not well," Guy Holmes recalls. But Michael's time in Bahrain was uneventful and relaxing. The most exciting thing he did was take his kids to *Harry Potter and the Goblet of Fire* and *King Kong*. In public, he often wore a woman's black *abaya*, or cloak. Rwaramba acted as his onsite manager, securing assurances from theater and shop owners that nobody would take photos. DJ Whoo Kid was told Bahrain actually had a law that locals could not approach Michael Jackson.

Whoo Kid joined Jackson, Abdullah, R&B star John Legend, actor Tyson Beckford, and others in town for the Formula 1 event at an opulent palace dinner. Hundreds of expensive cars were parked nearby, including a James Bond–style Aston-Martin and a Mercedes with a gold engine, gold steering wheel, and beige leather seats. At dinner, Jackson dressed like a "black superhero," glittering in a suit. He insisted Whoo Kid sit next to him. The DJ mentioned to MJ that he heard Neverland was about to be sold. This moved Jackson to rail about how America had betrayed him. He said he felt like Jesus Christ on the cross. And he shocked the room by cursing. "Fuck that place," he said. In the discombobulating pause that followed, the DJ asked for music. Abdullah arranged for the walls to open, displaying a one-hundred-inch TV set blaring one of MTV's Asian channels.

Abdullah was serious about being part of the international record business, and after a few months, Jackson was more coherent and driven—he wanted to work with certain well-known musicians and make an album and a documentary about his life.

Holmes, a veteran European record executive, signed on to be the CEO, and Jackson sent him boxes of his business documents. After poring over papers for three days, Holmes learned Jackson was no longer under contract to Sony Entertainment and had the right to record for any company he wished. Jackson and Abdullah agreed Michael would keep 76 to 80 percent of all the revenue from his music after costs. Holmes and Abdullah concocted a multifaceted plan to gradually reintroduce Michael Jackson to the world, beginning with music, a biography, and a movie, then building up to live appearances. At that point, more than three dozen lawsuits were pending against Jackson. He was $275 million in debt, overspending by $15 million to $20 million per year. The team hoped to find Jackson's old artwork, some of which had been in storage for decades, to help raise cash. "He knew he wasn't that fit. Our plan was not to do any concerts for quite a long time," Holmes recalls. "Our plans didn't require him physically to do a lot of work."

Holmes set out to improve Michael's physical and emotional health. The sheik brought in Tony Buzan, a British neurology expert whose "mind-mapping" techniques are designed to maximize brainpower. Michael's stay in Bahrain, says Qays Zu'bi, a regional attorney who worked with him, functioned as a post-trial, paparazzi-free tonic, enabling him to "regain his health and overall stability." It helped that the sheik provided for his every need, funding his shopping trips for expensive DVD players and hair dryers, providing the requisite Häagen-Dazs and a Ferrari. In the end, the sheik would say, including the money he sent Jackson during his trial, he gave him $7 million as a loan. He expected his partnership in the Michael Jackson business to make up for it. Michael, however, perceived all this lavish spending as a gift. Or so he'd say.

In 2005, Michael was still spending truckloads of cash on travel, as well as upkeep for the unoccupied Neverland. But that was nothing compared to the interest he paid to borrow other people's money. He was taking in $15 million a year, which would have been more than adequate for any normal human, but he was spending anywhere from $24 million to $45 million—$4.5 million per month in interest alone.

The debt weighed on him. In early 2005, during his trial, MJ had attended the funeral of celebrity attorney Johnnie Cochran at the West Angeles Cathedral in Los Angeles. Ron Burkle, the billionaire investor, came across a crying Jackson and said he didn't know he'd been so close with the late celebrity lawyer. "No," Jackson told him, "I'm in trouble. They're turning off the lights at Neverland." By the end of the year, Michael had to pay off a $270 million Bank of America loan or potentially give up his entire share of the Beatles catalog, which he'd put up as collateral. Jackson asked for Burkle's help. "Sure," Burkle said. "I'll put you on the same plan that I'm on. My office will pay all your bills. But I don't want anything to do with any of your money. You sign all your checks." Burkle lent Jackson a few hundred thousand dollars and studied his finances.

Michael was introduced to a large New York private-equity firm, Fortress Investment Group, which specialized in distressed debt. After haggling in vain to buy portions of the lucrative Beatles catalog jointly owned by Sony and Michael, Fortress changed course and bought the singer's longstanding Bank of America loan outright. This gave Michael a new cash flow of $330 million, but it pushed him even more heavily into debt. Still, the new loan was better than the one from Bank of America, which Donald David, a lawyer who worked on the deal, calls "grossly disproportionate" with interest rates of the time. "It made a lot of sense," says David, who represented Prescient Acquisition, which steered MJ into the deal, then sued him (and settled) for reneging on a finder's fee.

In December 2005, Michael hit another panic point. Fortress, now in charge of his nine-figure loans, began to charge cripplingly high interest rates. Sony executives were afraid that if Michael went bankrupt, his share of the publishing company they owned together would slip into auction, where it'd be sold to the highest bidder—and Sony executives preferred to be in business with Michael and his people rather than some rich unknowns who knew nothing about music. Rob Wiesenthal, chief financial officer of Sony Corp., and another company executive arranged to meet with Michael five days before Christmas in the $9,000 presidential suite at Dubai's mega-luxury Burj Al Arab hotel. In the room with him were Sheik Abdullah bin Hamad Al Khalifa and twelve MJ advisers. Michael did most of the talking. "He went through literally every key title we had in our catalog—he had an incredible memory of all our songs," Wiesenthal recalls. "He was clearly the kind of guy who plays dumb when it's convenient for him, but when he's engaged, it's fantastic."

Wiesenthal offered to help Michael restructure his debt. In return, Michael agreed to give Sony officials day-to-day control over the company—decisions about which Beatles songs to license would be theirs, not his. Wiesenthal asked for an option—at any point, Sony could buy half of Michael's stake, or roughly 25 percent of the catalog, worth a total of roughly $1 billion, at a set price. Michael agreed. His advisers said nothing. Wiesenthal went to Citibank, which, according to a *New York Times* story a few months after the meeting, took on Michael's debt for just 6 percent interest, rather than the exorbitant 20 percent Fortress had been charging. But before Wiesenthal could make the deal with Citibank, Fortress matched the terms. For the time being, Michael's cash-flow problems were over. As part of the loan agreement with Fortress, Michael immediately bought back his former attorney Branca's 5 percent stake in the ATV catalog. As a result of this convoluted deal, Michael was able to keep his stake in the Sony catalog, but his people had to take out a mortgage on Neverland. This deal would lead to his estate losing the ranch years after his death, something MJ said he'd never let happen.

In Bahrain, the sheik came to believe Michael had been free-loading. Their friendship disintegrated. Guy Holmes, the hard-nosed record executive, was on the sheik's side. "Mate," Holmes told MJ, "if you don't do what we're recommending here, you're going to be in big trouble." That sort of logic, delivered in that sort of tone, had never gone far with Michael. Instead of dealing with the issues Holmes was raising, he insisted to Abdullah that the British record man stop with the excessive cursing. Holmes told MJ to fuck off. Michael and his family took a vacation and never returned. Later, Michael sent Holmes a conciliatory letter: "Thank you, and I appreciate your help, and I'm going to have other people look over my stuff."

Michael Jackson was on the run. Tom Mesereau had told Michael he could never live in peace at Neverland after local prosecutors and police had been humiliated during his trial. "There's always going to be someone gunning for you. Some child wandering through a fence. They're never going to stop," the defense attorney said. "You'll never have peace here." So Neverland was out of the question. "America really let him down," recalls one of his European doctors.

For about six months in 2006, the small Jackson entourage traversed the Irish countryside, staying in four opulent residences, beginning with the thirty-thousand-euros-a-week Luggala Castle in Wicklow, where fans swarmed the property during his six-month stay. They spent time at *Riverdance* star Michael Flatley's castle in Cork County, discussing a future collaboration.

Wherever he went, Michael needed doctors. His vitiligo was spreading, whitening his skin as the darker spots receded. He wore wigs to conceal painful scarring in his scalp. And he liked his sleep medication. Still, when he visited a medical clinic in Europe while traveling with his family, a doctor who did not want to divulge his name found MJ in "pretty good health." Recalls the doctor: "He had the body of a dancer and decided to keep it that way. He was very meticulous about his weight." A consultation grew into a friendship. The doctor became close with Jackson's children, carrying the reserved Blanket to bed while Michael stuck close to the more loquacious and outgoing Paris. The doctor treated Michael five or six times for what he called "dermal fillers in his face" (a dermatological treatment to soften wrinkles and lines) and problems in the area surrounding his nose, as well as vitiligo and discoloration of his face, hands, and lower legs. He observed Michael's history of what he estimated to be two or three nose jobs. MJ asked for sedation due to extreme pain sensitivity, so on two occasions, the doctor administered propofol, the sleep-inducing drug that he considered safe under supervision. During both procedures, a trained anesthesiologist was on hand. Jackson never mentioned sleep problems to the doctor, although he did seem familiar with propofol. He called it "milk."

Michael was beginning to think about recording a new album. At the Grouse Lodge studio, he summoned various musicians and producers for collaborations, including Rodney Jerkins, his collaborator on *Invincible*, who stayed for a week. He contacted will.i.am of the Black Eyed Peas, whom he'd been pursuing for months by phone. MJ's manager at the time, Raymone Bain, asked Will how much he wanted to be paid for the collaboration. Nothing, the rapper said. "Because Michael always has leeches around him," he told her, "and I don't want to be that guy." Before embarking for Ireland, Will prepared electronic dance beats in his studio he thought would work for MJ. One work-in-progress track sounded like sixties-style soul music pumped up with hip-hop beats—in the style of Kanye West's "Touch the Sky." The bridge softened into a loungey organ sound. "Nice rhythm," Michael declared.

MJ and will.i.am made a deal—they maintained separate computer hard drives for their works, Michael with his vocals and Will with his music—and neither would take the other's contribution without permission. They worked on five songs together, including "I'm Gonna Miss You," which MJ wrote after James Brown's death in 2006; a song influenced by Estelle's hit at the time, "American Boy"; and an anthem that had the feel of the Jacksons' show-opening "Can You Feel It." "You gotta turn the *snare* up! I need you to get some *ice!*" Michael enthused to Will. "I want you to put the *crunch* on that snare. I want it to be *tasty*. Like people can *bite* it. I want you to feel like you could just *eat* it."

After staying at Grouse, the Jackson family relocated to Blackwater Castle, a twelfth-century fortress on a fifty-acre estate. Michael asked Grace Rwaramba to scout more luxurious and secluded properties. Soon their van pulled up to Ballinacurra, a forty-acre mansion in Kinsale, a sort of heavy-drinking Martha's Vineyard. Rwaramba did most of the talking, then the van door slid open and a shy, polite Michael Jackson stepped out. "You could have pushed me over with a feather," says Des McGahan, the proprietor. They agreed to rent the property. McGahan practiced reverse psychology with the locals, leaving the gate unlocked so he did not appear to have anybody important staying on the grounds.

The small Jackson group took over all twenty-two bedroom suites. When Michael grew restless with the Irish home cooking provided by McGahan's wife, he instructed his driver to pick up McDonald's, KFC, and Chinese food. Paris played with the McGahans' daughter Scarli; when Michael's daughter found a CD of *Thriller* in the library, she told her friend, "Oh, that's my dad." Scarli responded by showing off a homemade mix CD her dad had compiled, which he titled *Ballinacurra Day One Interiors of Sound*, and insisted her dad had an album, too.

When James Brown died on Christmas Eve 2006, Michael flew to Georgia to attend the funeral. The Rev. Al Sharpton, Brown's longtime friend and former employee, helped with arrangements. At three A.M., Sharpton received an unexpected call from Charles Reid, the funeral director who had been preparing Brown's body for one of the public ceremonies. "What's up, Mr. Reid?" Sharpton asked, bleary-eyed. "I need authorization," responded the mortician. "Michael Jackson's in town and he wants to see the body." Sharpton told Reid to have MJ call him back. He didn't.

An hour and a half later, Sharpton called Reid again: "What happened?"

"He told me I did James's hair all wrong and he combed his hair."

"He combed a corpse's hair?"

"He worked on his hair about forty minutes."

Finally, Sharpton received his call from Michael. "I got the hair straight," he told him. Michael Jackson had spent four and a half hours with James Brown's body.

The next day, at the James Brown Arena, Jackson wore a black

leather jacket, a skinny black tie, and sunglasses, and poignantly eulo-
gized his mentor for one minute. Sharpton and the Rev. Jesse Jackson
stood at attention behind him, watching warily as people shuffled onto
and off the stage. "What I'm going to say is brief but to the point: James
Brown was my greatest inspiration," Michael said, with no preachy
flourishes. He said when he was a boy in Gary, his mother had woken
him up whenever JB was on TV. "When I saw him move, I was mesmer-
ized," MJ said. When Michael went to view the body, he reached down
and kissed Brown. One last time, he fixed his hair.

This taste of America inspired Michael to return home. But not to
Neverland. In addition to the bad memories and legal predators, he'd
laid off most of the staff earlier in 2006, and forty-six of the remaining
employees had been working without pay for so long that California
Department of Industrial Relations officials were penalizing Jackson
more than $100,000. Even Michael's beloved animals were under legal
scrutiny—veterinarian Martin Dinnes, who had once helped MJ acquire
his giraffes, elephants, and orangutans, sued him for $91,602 in back
animal-care bills. (When Bubbles grew into an adult, MJ allowed his
trainer to take the chimp to his own facility; in 2005, the four-foot-six,
185-pound Bubbles moved to the Center for Great Apes, an orangutan
sanctuary in Wauchula, Florida, where he lives with other chimps.)
Everything else, from the train to the movie theater, made for a Michael
Jackson Ghost Town.

Michael had an idea: Las Vegas. Celine Dion had been pulling in
more than $500,000 per show at the four-thousand-seat Colosseum
in Caesar's Palace since 2003, and grossed roughly $80 million in a
year. (MJ apparently ignored the fact that she needed 147 shows to
make that kind of money.) Older rock and pop stars from Elton John to
Carlos Santana were beginning to set up similar residencies. Michael
rented a fifteen-thousand-square-foot mansion at 2785 South Monte
Cristo Way, with seven bedrooms, ten bathrooms, a gated entrance,
and what his security would call an "absurdly oversized living room."

It had a private movie theater, a two-thousand-square-foot master bed-room, and a pool house and tennis courts out back.

During Michael's time in Vegas, he couldn't help but encounter his father, Joe, a longtime resident of the city. Joe showed up one day, unannounced, in his PT Cruiser, circling the block four times before stopping near the front gate. When Michael's head security guard, Bill Whitfield, stuck out his hand to greet him, Joe said, "You're probably one of those putting needles in my son's arm." Michael refused to see his father.

At one point, Randy, Jackie, and Rebbie zoomed past the gate in a black Hummer, demanding to see their brother. "We need to talk to him *now*," Randy informed the security guards. Michael refused. After the siblings were escorted off the property, Michael told Whitfield: "Bill, that can never happen again. Never. Do you understand that?" Michael told his security guards his family was trying to extort him, as always, for some kind of Victory–style reunion tour. Later, Randy Jackson actually plowed his gray Mercedes SUV full-speed into Jackson's front gate with a neighborhood-rattling crash. According to Jackson's guards, who pulled a gun on him, Randy kept saying, "Michael owe me money! I want my fuckin' money!" and threatened to call the press.

Michael and his family were locked in a sad cycle of mistrust. He perceived them as financial leeches, even when they were trying to help him. Whenever they did show up, they bothered him about his drug problems. They knew he'd employed associates and security guards to procure opioids since 1993, and they believed his use had escalated.

Dr. Alimorad "Alex" Farshchian, a Miami doctor who specialized in orthopedic regenerative medicine, confused many in Michael's entourage when he first showed up. Michael had approached the doctor to treat a sprained ankle during the Madison Square Garden concerts back in 2001. Once he became comfortable with Dr. Farshchian, Michael confided that he had a problem with Demerol and asked for treatment. In late 2002, the doctor installed a Naltrexone implant into Michael's abdomen, which supposedly inhibited the effect of narcotics. Farsh-chian installed the implant four or five times over the next year or so. MJ's friend Frank Cascio, dubious at first, came around to the doctor's plan of weaning Michael off narcotics. But Henry Aubrey, Michael's bodyguard in the early 2000s, was one of several business associates who mistrusted the doctor. He told his boss: "If certain things continue with this Dr. Farshchian, you'll have to fire me, or I'm going to have to quit." Michael told him, "Things will stop." They didn't. Randy Jackson and various other family members had showed up at Michael's home several times over the years, beginning early in the Santa Maria trial, to stage drug interventions. They continued to do so when he lived in Vegas. In Randy's view, Grace Rwaramba was both the enabler and whistle-blower. Before one intervention attempt, Randy said, she called him three times, begging him to come over and help Michael with his drug problems: "It was ironic because she was the one giving it to him, but at the same time complaining about it. I think she had a hard time saying no to him."

"Michael struggled with substance abuse, to the point where he, numerous times, wanted to get clean and couldn't," adds a source close to him at the time. "He'd be clean for a while and then he would relapse. He was an addict and he struggled with it."

Michael continued to work on his album. Upon arriving in Vegas in December 2007, Michael moved in to one of the sky villas in the Palms hotel, which happened to contain a full-service studio where the Killers, Paris Hilton, and others had recorded. George Maloof, one of the brothers who owned the NBA's Sacramento Kings, arranged for Michael to use the hotel elevators without detection—room service left his food in an alcove outside his suite, so he never had to directly answer his own door. Sometimes Maloof himself would personally escort MJ from his room to the studio. "He was good at hiding," recalls Zoe Thrall, the studio's director. During his time at the Palms, Michael worked with Akon (who said he "clicked instantly" with the star on a song called "Hold My Hand"), will.i.am, and rising R&B singer and songwriter Ne-Yo. MJ also collaborated with SoBe Lifewater on a TV commercial with tiny lizards singing "Thriller" that appeared during the 2008 Super Bowl.

Michael's plan to build a Celine-style Vegas residency wasn't going anywhere. He met several times with his old friend, Steve Wynn, owner of the Wynn resort and casino, but promoters insisted he work the standard five nights per week. Jackson preferred three. "I can't just be like the Osmonds," he said. "I can't just sit on a stool and sing 'Kumbaya' like these old Vegas crooners. People want me to dance from beginning to end." "Billie Jean" couldn't be performed without a moonwalk routine. "Smooth Criminal" couldn't be performed without a Hollywood-level production of gangsters in zoot suits and dancers in garter belts. It never occurred to Michael that he probably could have gotten away with crooning his old songs on a stool—that might have been a refreshing new look. But "perfectionism" may have been code for "fear of change."

What Jackson didn't know was that while he was stalling out with Vegas promoters, Terry Harvey, who'd been managing his brother Tito, was meeting with his semi-retired manager Frank DiLeo. In 2007, Frank began telling people he was back on MJ's team, which had a grain of truth. After DiLeo had regularly attended Michael's child-molestation trial, silently showing support for his old friend and client, the *Thriller* and *Bad* teammates were beginning to talk again for the first time in years. Harvey and a group of promoters, Allgood Entertainment, devised a plan: a one-time reunion concert, starring Michael and all his brothers, Victory tour style, at Texas Stadium in Dallas. They'd sell pay-per-view rights and everybody would get rich.

The Allgood team initially met with Joe Jackson, who said he'd participate on one condition—he wanted an RV with $50,000 in cash packed in the glove compartment. Patrick Allocco, the New Jersey promoter in charge of the Allgood promoters, found that reasonable. Insane, but reasonable. The meeting was contentious—Allocco recalls "a good amount of infighting" between Harvey's group and Joe's group—but they agreed to move forward.

To get Michael on board for a July 9 show in Dallas, Allocco met with Katherine Jackson at a Benihana-type grill. Michael's mother kept saying, "This is a good deal for Michael." Allocco's team estimated $9 million to $12 million in gross ticket sales. And if the promoters added merchandise and concessions, Allocco says, "Michael could have walked away with $24 million pretty effortlessly." That made sense to DiLeo, Joe, Katherine, and Debbie Rowe, whom Allocco had also approached for support.

Due to his debts and spending, Michael had just $668,215 in cash, according to an audit conducted by Thompson, Cobb, Bazilio, and Associates. That may seem like a lot, but dozens of people were suing him. At one point, a man showed up at Jackson's house to serve him with legal papers; the farthest he got was one of Michael's security men, Javon Beard, who wouldn't touch them. "People would come up and drop these things through the gate, onto the driveway, and we wouldn't go near it," Beard wrote. "We'd just go get the water hose, wash it right back out into the street."

Still, in Vegas Michael continued to aspire for bigger and more opulent homes. He became obsessed with an estate containing a thirty-seven-thousand-square-foot house on 99 Spanish Gate Drive that belonged to the Sultan of Brunei. But it was a fixer-upper, and banks wouldn't loan Michael the money. In spring 2007, Jackson's publicist-turned-manager Raymone Bain and his attorney Peter Lopez met with a big-time concert promoter, Randy Phillips, chief executive of AEG Live in Los Angeles, about staging a run of comeback concerts at London's new O2 Arena. MJ rejected the idea. He wasn't ready.

The lease on MJ's family home in Vegas was set to expire at the end of June 2007. Jackson needed a vacation. The family flew to Middleburg, Virginia, to stay for five months at the Goodstone Inn, a former plantation west of DC, which was close to his new attorney, Greg Cross. MJ's former manager, Dieter Wiesner, had sued him for fraud and breach of contract (they later settled for $3.5 million). When Michael showed up at Cross's office for a deposition, he owned up to an important detail. Wiesner's lawyer, Howard King, asked Michael if, in 2003, he was "under the influence of drugs or alcohol that impaired your ability to understand what you were doing." Michael's revealing answer: "It could have been medication, yes." During the same deposition, Michael acknowledged he gave Wiesner and business partner Ron Konitzer power of attorney to make his financial decisions when he was "under the influence of prescription medication."

In August 2007, Michael and his kids took off for New York. They showed up at a birthday party for Frank Cascio's mother. "You're surrounded by idiots again," Frank lectured his old friend. "Get back to what you do best. . . . Start working, start writing, start producing." Michael stayed with the Cascios for four months, working with Frank's brother Eddie in his home studio on several songs, including two schmaltzy ballads called "Best of Joy" and "(I Like) The Way You Love Me." While Frank found Michael to be "alive and excited, getting back into being creative and free," his financial problems were weighing him down. Fortress Investments, which held Neverland's $23 million mortgage, was threatening to auction Michael's beloved but abandoned ranch if he didn't pay the amount he owed by March 19. One of Michael's new attorneys, L. Londell McMillan, bought him a few extra weeks by arranging a confidential deal with Fortress, but later that year came another financial blow—Sheik Abdullah bin Hamad Al Khalifa, crown prince of Bahrain, was suing him in British Royal Court for $7 million. It seems all those luxuries MJ received from the sheik had been loans, not gifts.

Debt had no impact on Michael's expensive ideas—during this period, he and Jermaine, apparently with straight faces, were discussing a plan to create a *Wizard of Oz*–style "leisure kingdom" in the Middle East. Jermaine asked around for well-connected businessmen with ties to the region, and an architect friend gave him a number for Dr. Tohme Tohme. What was Tohme a doctor of? He wouldn't say. He did, however, exercise "his extraordinary gift for facilitation, brokering assorted deals that drew alternately on sources of Middle Eastern or Southeast Asian money, as well as an impressive range of international contacts," wrote Randall Sullivan, one of the few to interview Tohme at length. Jermaine first met with Tohme in March 2008. Not long afterward, Jermaine called again, this time in a panic. Michael was about to lose Neverland. "Is there *anyone* you know who'd be willing to help?" Jermaine asked. Tohme answered the question by pointing to a bald-headed man on the cover of a business magazine. "This guy," Tohme said.

"This guy" turned out to be another Lebanese businessman, Thomas Barrack, founder of Colony Capital, a $35 billion international real estate investment firm. When Tohme first called, Barrack wasn't interested. But Tohme was persistent. While in Vegas for a business meeting, he called Barrack again, put on the hard sell, and Barrack agreed.

Barrack and Tohme met Jackson at his rented home on Palomino Lane in Vegas. Michael was making one of his kids a peanut-butter-and-jelly sandwich. "I don't understand what's happening," MJ told them. "All of a sudden I got to this place where they're saying Neverland will be foreclosed on Friday." Barrack studied the documents and caught up on the MJ story—he hadn't toured in a decade, he hadn't released a new album in seven years, and most of his income came from his song-publishing catalogs. Like many of Michael's previous advisers, Barrack told Michael he'd have to stop spending outrageous amounts of money and work on growing his income. This time, Michael was desperate. He appeared to listen. "Are you willing to start down that line?" Barrack asked. "Yeah," Jackson responded. "I am."

Michael suggested the same types of risky ventures he'd discussed with Ronald Konitzer and Marc Schaffel—3-D films and holograms—

none of which would force him to work very hard. Barrack countered with a more traditional idea: concerts. After years of avoiding the inevitable, Michael finally agreed. Barrack decided to buy the $23 million Neverland note from Fortress, entering a partnership with Michael Jackson that put incredible pressure on the singer to pull himself out of insolvency.

Barrack had done business with Phil Anschutz, the reclusive billionaire who owned concert promoter AEG—short for Anschutz Entertainment Group. Anschutz put Barrack in touch with Randy Phillips, the Live division's chief executive. Phillips had met with MJ about doing concerts the previous year, but this time it was obviously serious. Phillips was old-school music business. He was ambitious and shrewd. He told people he got into it not because of the music but because of the deal. "He's a real nonstop salesman. He gets emotionally excited about things," recalls Arnold Stiefel, who used to manage rock star Rod Stewart jointly with Phillips. "Indefatigable in his efforts for things he believes in." Phillips and Stiefel had met Jackson years earlier, in the early nineties, when they facilitated an unprecedented $20 million endorsement deal between the King of Pop and the LA Gear shoe company.

At the Turnberry Isle luxury condominiums in Vegas, Phillips gave a presentation about AEG Live. Michael made a desperate play to sell the veteran promoters on movies instead of concerts, showing the AEG executives *Ghosts*, his fantastic 1996 short film in which he plays himself as well as an overweight, balding white man. Phillips listened politely, but he wanted the showman, not the filmmaker. He was experienced dealing with artists; he knew when to push and when to hang back. He waited patiently for MJ to come around.

In late 2008, Phillips's meetings with Jackson started again. This time, thanks to Barrack's counsel, Michael didn't mention *Ghosts*. They inched toward a deal. Phillips predicted Michael could net $1 million per show, after all his costs. AEG's lawyers, Kathy Jorrie and Shawn Trell, negotiated a deal with Tohme and attorneys Dennis Hawk and Peter Lopez—a 90–10 split, which meant Michael took home 90 percent of the net ticket sales and the promoters were left with 10. (That wasn't counting AEG's income on beer, popcorn, and parking, plus a share of lucrative ticket service charges, of course.) AEG agreed to give Michael an advance of $5 million, $3 million of which went to settling his case with the Bahraini sheik, as well as a $15 million line of credit that he would pay back out of his salaries for the O2 shows. From that credit, AEG gave Michael $100,000 a month, or a maximum of $1.2 million, to rent a house, which wound up being in Los Angeles's tony Holmby Hills—100 N. Carolwood Drive, a two-story mansion near Sunset Boulevard with plenty of privacy for his children, plus security, a nanny, and a chef. That worked for the Jackson family, even if it loaded Michael up with more debt that he'd have to recoup through the concert revenues. MJ prepared to leave Vegas.

E-mails between the AEG executives suggest a nervous optimism. AEG's Paul Gongaware, another veteran promoter who'd worked with Michael as a *Dangerous* tour manager, sketched out a first-draft look at a worldwide tour, to begin in January 2009 and run through April 2011: thirty shows at London's O2 Arena, then a total of 186 shows (including fourteen private ones, presumably for corporations) in arenas and stadiums throughout Europe, Australia, and the US. At 2.5 concerts per week, $100 per ticket, he predicted a gross of $275 million. MJ would receive $132 million; production costs would be $108 million and AEG's fee as promoter and producer $27 million. "It's a big number, but this is not a number MJ will want to hear," Gongaware e-mailed to his colleagues. "He thinks he is so much bigger than that."

Michael met with AEG officials and Phil Anschutz at the billionaire's personal villa at the Mansions at MGM Grand in Las Vegas in September 2008. Gongaware had warned his colleagues that MJ would want to talk about starring in movies, not performing 186 shows on a massive worldwide tour. Also, he advised: "I do not recommend wearing suits to the meeting as MJ is distrustful of people in suits." (Phillips wore a suit anyhow.) AEG officials liked what they heard, and in November, promoters within the company were making plans to route their other big touring stars, including Britney Spears and Kings of Leon, around what was still a fantasy itinerary for Michael Jackson's comeback. Phillips arranged for a meeting with Jeffrey Katzenberg, the DreamWorks Animation mogul, to discuss what Michael was really interested in: a 3-D film version of *Thriller*, for which Anschutz had committed $1 million toward a script. "For you, for sure," Katzenberg responded to Phillips, "although there is zero chance that it's something we will end up getting involved with." During a relaxed hour-and-a-half meeting at Michael's new rental home in Holmby Hills, Katzenberg methodically talked the singer out of his idea for the film. Phillips was grateful to Katzenberg for changing the subject. "You have a major AEG I.O.U. that can be cashed anytime," he e-mailed the film mogul after the meeting.

AEG's people waited through a long holiday vacation for Michael to make his decision on the shows. "One hopes that MJ will see the light eventually," accountant Timm Woolley wrote to his colleagues on December 10. Two days before Christmas, the staff passed around an e-mail glibly referring to journalist Ian Halperin's widely circulated report that Michael had a potentially fatal condition that required an emergency lung transplant. "He can have my lung later," executive Dan Beckerman wrote, "if he plays the O2 now." Finally, in early January, negotiations picked up again. "MJ is getting very real," Phillips wrote to colleagues. Gongaware outlined a new schedule of thirty-seven initial O2 shows, from July through early October. Many, internally, feared the worst: "Do you think he can pull this off?" Beckerman wrote. Phillips responded, "He has to, or financial disaster awaits"—a reference to Michael's own potential financial disaster. On January 26, 2009, AEG's Phillips, Gongaware, and Shawn Trell, as well as Michael's reps Tohme, Hawk, and Lopez, met with MJ at his house on Carolwood. They signed a tour contract. They drank champagne. Everybody hugged.

AEG then contacted Lloyd's of London about buying a $17.5 million insurance policy in case Jackson, who had a history of canceling shows and was not known to be in perfect health, became unreliable. The insurers insisted Michael take a five-hour physical by their own doctor, in New York. Phillips told every reporter Jackson "passed with flying colors." But Phillips's wry, sunny disposition in the press masked a growing private concern about Michael's health. AEG officials considered it curious that Michael's handpicked doctor, Conrad Murray, immediately demanded $5 million, something the budget-conscious promoters told him was never going to happen. The promoters preferred a licensed doctor in London, but Michael insisted Murray was non-negotiable: "This is the machine," he told them, gesturing to his body. "We have to take care of the machine. This is what I want. I want Dr. Murray." Only when AEG officials were in a car with Michael himself did Murray back down on his extravagant demand. "Offer him one fifty!" Michael instructed AEG's Gongaware. The promoter dutifully called Murray and repeated the $150,000-per-month proposal. "No," Murray responded, "I really couldn't do that." Gongaware snapped back, "That offer comes directly from the artist." Murray abruptly changed his tone: "I'll take it."

Waiting for the AEG advances to come in, Michael was still desperate for capital. He made a deal with Darren Julien, owner of a high-end Beverly Hills auction house that had sold items from the estates of Johnny Cash, Jimi Hendrix, and Elvis Presley. Julien asked Michael what he wanted to sell, and the response was "everything"—two thousand items he'd packed within the 2,700 acres of Neverland Ranch, from statues to trash cans to cars. The Julien's catalog showed a diverse cross-section of Michael Jackson's wealth, erudite artistic tastes, and questionable home-decorating decisions. Glenna Goodacre's bronze statue of a bound, long-haired American man, his feet sunk into concrete, would start between $150,000 and $250,000; the wrought-iron, gilded front gates of Neverland, emblazoned with a crown, Michael

Jackson's name, and horse-covered crests, went for $20,000 to $30,000; the rest of the glitzy catalog included X-Men, Simpsons, and Star Trek pinball games and a 1999 Rolls-Royce limousine equipped with a big-screen TV. Costumes, gloves, MTV awards, childhood books—Michael left nothing out. Jay Ruckel, cofounder of La Crasia Gloves, who would design the "Billie Jean" glove for the This Is It tour, had his eye on a 1945 book called Love of a Glove that MJ had personally annotated. "That was the ultimate glove-wearer in modern history," Ruckel says. "I would do anything to look at that book. It's probably still in a warehouse somewhere."

Everything from the auction is probably still in a warehouse somewhere. Julien sent trucks to Neverland and personally visited the grounds some 125 times. His first impression was that a "creative genius" must have built the place. He also noticed that while the main house was in pristine condition, ripped tarps were spread haphazardly over the bumper cars and grass grew into the bases of the rides. Neverland was in decay. "There was no question in our mind that he would never return to the property," he said.

Julien packed up the items, meticulously inventoried them at his own expense, then stored them at warehouses. Then Michael told Julien he didn't want to part with any of these things after all. Julien responded that he'd spent $2 million in expenses and wanted his commission. Tohme, who'd brokered the auction deal between Jackson and Julien, was in the middle of the dispute. He sent a fixer, James R. Weller, a veteran ad man who'd worked on election campaigns for Ronald Reagan and George H. W. Bush. He was no help. Instead, Julien accused Weller, in court, of threatening his life.* Michael fired Tohme, and the two stopped speaking. That made AEG executive Phillips's life more

---

*I asked Weller for an interview, and he said he'd be available in October, more than three months later, well after my deadline. I asked, "Why October?" and he replied: "Because it is sooner than November, December, or Never. However, you may choose one of the above, if you prefer." When I followed up in October, he declined.

complicated—generally, the only way he could reach MJ was by calling Tohme. This was a problem, because the big This Is It press conference to announce the long-rumored tour was scheduled to take place at the O2 Arena on March 5, 2009.

AEG executives were concerned, to the point of hostility, about Michael's behavior and its potential impact on their high-risk O2 plans. "We cannot be forced into stopping this, which MJ will try to do because he is lazy and constantly changes his mind to fit his immediate wants," Gongaware wrote. By the time the Jackson family was ready to travel to London for the press conference, Tohme* was back on the team, but his relationship with Michael was tenuous. Then, at Michael's hotel suite an hour before the scheduled three P.M. announcement at the O2 Arena, Tohme met with Phillips.

"We have a little issue," he said. "Michael got drunk."

Phillips seethed. Tohme suggested he would return to MJ's room to sober up his star client. Phillips waited in the hall. Bodyguard Alberto Alvarez was stationed outside. Phillips sent an e-mail to his AEG colleagues that would later be leaked to the press: "MJ is locked in his room drunk and despondent. Tohme and I are trying to get him sober and get him to the press conference." His boss at AEG, Tim Leiweke, responded bluntly: "Are you kidding me?"

Phillips approached the beefy Alvarez at Michael's door. "Alberto," he said, "you've got to let me in. This is not good. This is a crisis situation." Alvarez could see in Phillips's face that this would not be a good time to keep him out, so the bodyguard stepped aside. Three thousand fans and 350 news crews were waiting at the O2.

Phillips found Michael sitting on the couch, wearing a robe and pants. He saw a bottle of what he assumed was booze on the floor. Jack-

*In 2012, Tohme sued MJ's estate, demanding a 15 percent commission on his client's revenue and a finder's fee for helping him secure a Neverland loan. The estate fought back, insisting Michael fired him in March 2009 and he manipulated MJ into "unfair financial compensation." The case is pending.

son opened up. He said he worried nobody would want to see him any-more. Phillips did his best to soothe him, speaking of all the fans who'd camped out overnight at the O2 for a chance to glimpse the King of Pop.

Finally, Michael emerged, in black slacks, boots, and a white V-neck T-shirt. Phillips sent another widely quoted e-mail to his colleagues: "I screamed at him so loud the walls were shaking." He described MJ as "an emotionally paralyzed mess riddled with self-loathing and doubt now that it is show time." The ever-spinning Phillips claimed in court that he'd exaggerated in his e-mail, and had yelled at the King of Pop in a motivating, coachlike way.

The crew took a van to the O2 arena. "And when he went through that curtain," Phillips remembered, "there was Michael Jackson." Standing behind a podium marked MICHAEL JACKSON, wearing aviator shades, he blew kisses, flashed fists and peace signs, and began with "I love you so much."

The crowd chanted, "This is it!" and MJ cracked a smile. "These will be my final show performances, in London," he said. "When I say 'This is it,' it really means 'This is it.'" It was the first time many had seen him in years. His nose looked sculpted, his hair dyed, and his chin cleft deeper than ever. Before he turned to leave, he abruptly returned to the podium, as if magnetized there, smiling, preening, gesturing.

To prepare for the This Is It shows, Michael kept telling his people: "Bigger." It was a familiar theme in his life. He'd said it about Dangerous-tour special effects, and he'd said it about the HIStory album. And it was how he felt about his homes—he tried to buy a forty-thousand-square-foot LA mansion for $93 million, until Phillips gently reminded him of his debt. Even the name "This Is It," like Thriller or Bad, suggested a grandiosity to which Michael always aspired. "When I'm on that stage," he told promoters, "this is the place in the world to be." He wanted special effects that had never been done before. "That's what motivated him," Phillips said. His costume people created a silver spacesuit with huge blue shiny diamonds and elaborate square robot shoulder pads, plus mirrored shoes and sunglasses containing three million individual Swarovski crystals. Jay Ruckel, the La Crasia glove designer, was enlisted to stitch together a one-handed "Billie Jean" glove containing 6,600 crystals. Bruce Jones, a visual effects supervisor who'd worked on three *Star Trek* TV series, met with Michael to discuss a series of short 3-D interactive films on a 130-by-30-foot LED-screen backdrop. Michael wanted butterflies coming out of a rainforest during "Earth Song" in such a vivid way that fans could reach out and touch them. "He had these great ideas, but they were all over the map," recalls Jones, who spent sixteen-hour days aspiring to MJ's vision. "I tried to place them into more of a linear format." Michael asked for a live monkey scrambling down a tree, but Jones's staff convinced him the show's $6 million visual-effects budget couldn't accommodate monkey food and training.

Michael picked Kenny Ortega, who'd worked with him on the *Dangerous* and *HIStory* tours, as the producer. (The star paid 95 percent of Ortega's salary.) "MJ and I are already so in sync," Ortega wrote to Gongaware in mid-March. For musical director, Ortega found Michael Bearden, a keyboardist from Chicago's South Side who had worked with Madonna, Sting, and Whitney Houston. (MJ had called his first choice, old Jacksons friend Greg Phillinganes, to ask if he was interested, and the keyboardist responded, "*Of course* I'm interested." But AEG stepped in and "prevented it from happening," Phillinganes says—which annoyed Michael.*) Travis Payne, Michael's longtime choreographer who knew his steps so well that he often performed as a body double, also returned. Other familiar faces were brought in—drummer Jonathan "Sugarfoot" Moffett, Bashiri Johnson, a percussionist who'd played with Michael during the thirtieth-anniversary concerts in 2001, and Stacy Walker, a dancer and choreographer who'd worked on *Dangerous* and *HIStory*. "He was thinner than I remembered seeing him," Walker recalls. "Cer-

---

*A source with knowledge of the discussions denies MJ wanted to hire Phillinganes; an internal AEG memo showed Phillinganes cost $200,000 more than Bearden.

tainly his energy wasn't the same. Maybe his moves weren't quite as sharp or dynamic." This made sense, she figured—Michael Jackson may have been frozen in time as a twenty-five-year-old defying physics, but now he was fifty, a dancer with a new kind of grace.

Michael watched the final backup dancer audition at the Nokia Theatre in Los Angeles. "He just walked in with about five or six body-guards, like the president," recalls Chris Grant, one of the dancers, a longtime MJ fan who got so close he could smell the star's cologne, Black Orchid. "They were wearing all black."

In mid-April, rehearsals began at CenterStaging, a plot of profes-sional studio spaces in Burbank. Dancers practiced in one room and the band in another; the production team worked on special effects in a third. Michael showed up occasionally to give tips. AEG's Gongaware asked his friend Tim Patterson to help document the rehearsals, then use the video for the tour's promotional videos. Every night, he and his colleague, Sandrine Orabona, dumped their footage onto a hard drive, after which Patterson transferred it to his home-office computer.

The musicians and crew convened for about twenty-five rehears-als, beginning May 20. Michael attended about ten of them. When he wasn't there, Travis Payne stood in. Michael showed up to CenterStag-ing in late May to work on the music for "The Way You Make Me Feel." "Michael asked to have the lights turned down," recalls Patterson, who filmed him as he walked in. "He was shy, and it was part of his mys-tique." As the *This Is It* film would show, Michael gently encouraged his sidemen to meet his exacting standards. Bearden, the keyboardist and music director, played a pulsing reggae beat on one of his synthesizers, and the old "Bad" hit sounded funky and crisp. But MJ, wearing a black jacket with cartoonishly high and pointy shoulder pads, instructed the experienced bandleader not to "change so soon." Bearden, momen-tarily confused, kept his eyes fixed on Michael as he held back the beat just a bit. "It should be simpler," Michael said. Bearden suggested he put "a little more booty" on it. "A little more booty—that's funny,"

Michael said. "But you know what I mean, though," Bearden said. "No, no, you gotta let it simmer," Michael told him, repeating the phrase. "Just *bathe* in the *moonlight*. Let it sim-*mer*." Bearden managed to do as he was told, and by the end, the song sounds fantastic, a hybrid of Bob Marley and James Brown—slinkier than "The Way You Make Me Feel" had ever sounded. Later that night, Michael sang "Human Nature" onstage, wearing aviator shades, and the band fired him up so much that he gave a little snarl during the line "I like ah-*lovin'* this way."

"He was very in charge and knew what he wanted. If something wasn't right, it had to be right," Grant recalls. "He was never mean, but was very particular about certain things."

Michael hadn't done a bona fide show in nearly eight years. He was slowly building his strength, working out with conditioning coach Lou "The Incredible Hulk" Ferrigno. He rarely went full-speed during rehearsals, instead running through numbers to "mark" where his musicians, dancers, and effects people had to be. On June 5, Michael and Judith Hill, a young singer in the Sheryl Crow role, dueted for the first time on "I Just Can't Stop Loving You." Ortega, stocky and amiable, wearing a white T-shirt, jeans, and little glasses, barked out instructions. He was always concerned about falling behind the schedule, but rarely let on. "Kenny never shows stress," recalls Erin "Topaz" Lareau, who designed some of the costumes. "That's why he was so great at his job."

In early June, rehearsals shifted from CenterStaging to the Forum, a larger arena in Inglewood where the Lakers and Kings used to play. Michael began to show up every day around six P.M., work on vocal exercises for a couple of hours, join the band onstage around eight or nine P.M., then leave between eleven P.M. and one A.M. Ortega was beginning to combine the rehearsal pieces into a cohesive show. The pyro people set off explosions. Michael Curry, the puppetry and design expert, showed off his huge black widow spider. Michael sailed above the invisible crowd on a cherry picker, just as he'd done on the *HIStory* and *Dangerous* tours. When Michael appeared, people snapped to attention.

"He would just fill the room up, man, with joy," says Tommy Organ, the guitarist. Although still not yet at full speed, Michael was sharp as he ran through "Wanna Be Startin' Somethin'," "Jam," and "The Way You Make Me Feel." To Michael, these works-in-progress were raw, unfinished performances, the kind he was never willing to show to the public. But as he shuffled through his familiar moves with a skinny, casual grace and sang in a light, almost raspy voice, he gave surprising glimpses of his humanity as a performer. Around midnight on June 6, as he began to re-create the steps of "Billie Jean," the dancers and crew began to cheer. Michael soaked up the enthusiasm and pushed himself harder. Wearing a blue *Sgt. Pepper's* jacket, MJ didn't go all the way—no high leg kicks, no climactic moonwalk. But he seemed relaxed. He strutted, snapped his fingers, and futzed with his aviator sunglasses as they snagged in his long, sweaty hair. He tapped his foot, turned and walked, spun, jogged in place, pulled up his belt, bounced his feet around. By the end, MJ was fully engrossed in the performance, grabbing his crotch and improvising air guitar. The camera captured his "crowd" screaming below the stage. Michael shrugged off the adulation. "At least we get a feel of it," he said.

AEG had put the tickets on sale for the first ten O2 shows in March, and instantly sold out seventeen thousand seats for each one. Promoters determined they'd have far more fans who wanted to see the shows than could fit in thirty-one O2 Arenas. So Phillips called Tohme and asked for more shows. Michael himself called back, Phillips would say. He agreed, in exchange for two things. One was a home for his family in London during the entire run, "an English country estate with rolling hills and horses and greenery and stuff like that," Phillips recalled. Second was recognition by his beloved *Guinness Book of World Records* once he beat Prince's record for most consecutive concerts at the same venue.* *Deal,*

---

*After AEG officials boasted of this feat to reporters, Phillips had to do damage control—with Prince. "This booking has nothing to do with breaking your record," he wrote in an e-mail to the Purple One, whose tour AEG had promoted five years earlier, "but keeping the arena booked for as many nights as possible."

the AEG reps quickly responded. They ratcheted the number of shows up to fifty. Some in the concert industry warned Phillips that Michael, given his reputation, would never make fifty shows. John Scher, a veteran New York promoter, essentially spoke for the concert business when he predicted MJ would wind up doing 75 percent of them. "I just believed in him," Phillips told the press.

When Karen Faye, Michael's longtime friend and makeup artist, first heard about the fifty dates, she said to herself, "He can't do this." She was dubious that Michael ever agreed to the additional number of shows. Even during his peak tours, *Bad, Dangerous,* and *HIStory*, he spaced out the dates so he'd have a few days of rest and travel between shows. These were too close together. "He might last a week," she thought. She approached Ortega with her concerns, but he laughed them off. For a while, Ortega's confidence in Michael's stamina seemed justified. "I never noticed frailty in MJ," percussionist Bashiri Johnson recalls. "Whenever I gave him a hug, I was hugging a solid mass of muscle." Michael frequently wore knee pads to rehearsal, and he'd squat while watching the dancers and listening to the band. "He looked like a cheetah getting ready to pounce," Johnson says. "I never heard him complaining about being tired or anything." But not everybody shared AEG's eternal talking point that MJ was in perfect condition. Michael Bearden, the show's musical director, sent a June 16 e-mail to Ortega and Payne declaring Michael "not in shape enough yet to sing this stuff live and dance at the same time." (Bearden added wishfully: "Once he's healthy enough and has more strength I have full confidence he can sing the majority of the show live.") Ron Weisner, Michael's co-manager during the early *Thriller* days, visited his onetime client during rehearsal. "He just looked horrific," Weisner recalls. "It's a shame. He had all these people around him, but nobody was looking out for him." Weisner called Michael's sister La Toya—and she concurred. "I know why you're calling," she told him, "and it's sad." When costume designer Michael Bush told Faye, "Oh my God . . . I can see Michael's heart beating through the skin on his chest,"

Faye anxiously reported this observation to Frank DiLeo. "Get him a bucket of chicken!" MJ's longtime manager responded.

What nobody in the rehearsals knew was that Michael Jackson, under pressure to carry the biggest event in concert history, a production that would have made hundreds of millions of dollars and pull himself out of crippling debt, was spending his nights in devastating sleeplessness. In February, before choosing Murray as his full-time doctor, he'd hired a nurse practitioner, Cherilyn Lee, who specialized in natural sleep products and vitamin C supplements. On April 19, she came to his Carolwood home twice, and each time he asked about Diprivan, or propofol. Michael had used the drug before and seemed familiar with it. "I've got to get a good night's sleep," he kept saying. Lee told him propofol wasn't safe—it was hardly a drug for everyday insomnia. "What if you don't wake up?" she asked. "You don't understand," Michael complained. He insisted doctors (he refused to name them) had told him repeatedly that the medication was safe for home use. One night in April, MJ fell asleep while Lee was monitoring him; after three hours, he woke up at four A.M. and stood upright on the bed. "I told you I cannot sleep all night," he said. He begged again for Diprivan. "I have a very big day today. My day is going to be destroyed," he said. "I need to have sleep." Again, Lee refused. MJ escorted her to security and sent her home. She never saw him after that.

During the June 19 rehearsal, nearly three weeks before the shows were to begin, Michael showed up at the Forum "just lost and a little incoherent," Ortega said. Disturbed, the director brought in a meal of chicken and broccoli, put a tray in Michael's lap, and cut it up for him. "Kenny was getting pulled in five hundred different directions," recalls Abby Franklin, Michael's wardrobe supervisor and backstage coordinator. "I could see the concern." Ortega rubbed Michael's feet, set up a heater next to him, wrapped him in blankets, and called Conrad Murray, who did not respond. Michael asked if he could take a break for the night and let Travis Payne walk through his movements onstage. Ortega agreed. "He just seemed he wasn't there," the director remembered. "There was something wrong." After an hour and fifteen minutes, Michael went home. Ortega panicked. He e-mailed Phillips. "He appeared quite weak and fatigued this evening," Ortega wrote at 2:04 A.M. "He had a terrible case of the chills, was trembling, rambling and obsessing. Everything in me says he should be psychologically evaluated."

Karen Faye was worrying, too. As she spent more time with MJ at the Forum, the makeup artist found him "cold to the touch" and noticed him rambling and repeating things. She begged Ortega, Phillips, DiLeo, and others via e-mail to intervene. They didn't respond. On June 20, Phillips arranged for a meeting at Michael's Carolwood house, summoning Ortega, Murray, Paul Gongaware, and DiLeo. To Ortega's surprise, rather than talking about Michael's physical concerns, Murray turned on him, accusing the director of not allowing Michael to rehearse. "Stop trying to be an amateur doctor and psychologist," Murray sneered at Ortega. Shocked, Ortega appealed to MJ to defend him. "Please," he told Michael, "tell the doctor that is not the way it went down. . . . This was something that we agreed on together." "Yes," Michael agreed, "that's what happened."

Michael took Ortega aside and assured him he was healthy enough to finish the tour. "I am fine, Kenny," MJ said, "I promise you." They hugged. Ortega left.

Rehearsals moved from the Forum to the Los Angeles Lakers' state-of-the-art arena, Staples Center, to accommodate the huge production and special effects. Michael showed up June 23 and June 24, full of life. On the latter day, Michael ran through four songs—"We Are the World," "Thriller," "Dangerous," and "Earth Song." Whereas the CenterStaging and Forum rehearsals had been minimalist and dark, the giant LED screen gave the Staples Center the feel of a show. For "Thriller," the dancers were in costume as stringy-haired zombies and ghost brides, and "all the toys were coming out," as wardrobe supervisor Franklin recalls. Jackson smiled as the spectacle rushed past him. "He was pretty involved and full-out and trying out all the different props and singing," dancer Chris Grant says. Michael had retooled "Earth Song" from a world-peace anthem to a save-the-environment anthem, replacing the ominous onstage tank of the *HIStory* tour with a bulldozer. He instructed Ortega during the performance to "let it rumble!" Afterward, Michael went to the microphone and addressed the performers and crew. "Thank you, everybody, for all your hard work," he said. "Good night, God bless you, and I'll see you tomorrow."

Michael had spent roughly seven hours at the Staples Center that night. After the rehearsal, bodyguard Alvarez took the wheel of Michael's vehicle, which he used to "secure the proper route" for Michael's drive home. Michael Amir Williams, MJ's personal manager, loaded up another SUV for Jackson. Another bodyguard, Faheem Muhammad, drove him in the second SUV 17.5 miles back to his Carolwood home, where his children were sleeping. He encountered a scattering of fans in the driveway. Michael was in good spirits and rolled the window down, as he sometimes did, to exchange a few words. A few gave him small gifts, which Williams, Muhammad, and Alvarez loaded into the car. Williams noticed Dr. Murray's BMW in its parking space in Michael's driveway. He'd been staying with the Jacksons the last several weeks. Williams escorted Michael into the house and left for the night, returning to his home in downtown Los Angeles. Security did its perimeter check and everybody settled down for the night.

CHAPTER 11

Carnival, the annual street celebration in Trinidad, is a sweaty, Technicolor mass of beautiful women in fringed bikinis, hula skirts, and feathered helmets, and drunken men, some in equally colorful and skimpy costumes. In 2005, a two-man energy-drink company called Pit Bull had hired six models to walk through the festival from five P.M. to six A.M. every night for a week. One of Pit Bull's partners, six-foot-four, 220-pound Dr. Conrad Robert Murray, drank a bit and posed shirtless with his young charges, whom he paid $1,200 apiece in addition to expenses. Walking and dancing through one dicey stretch of the parade early in the morning, the models witnessed a fight in which a man stabbed another man. The crowd's momentum pulled Murray away from the scene, but the doctor insisted on going back. He approached the wounded man, frantically motioning for a clump of promotional Pit Bull T-shirts to help staunch the bleeding. "No!" the Pit Bull models begged him. "You can't do it. You have no gloves. Are you crazy?" Finally, Murray found somebody else to help the guy and left with his group. "He is a pleaser," says Karen "Kalucha" Chacon, one of the models.

That is certainly a positive spin on Dr. Conrad Murray, who would be forever marked as the man who killed Michael Jackson. "He knew better.

He shouldn't have done it. He should have walked away," says Detective Orlando Martinez of the LA Police Department, who investigated Murray after MJ's death. But Chacon and other Murray friends make an important point. Murray had no boundaries and found it hard to say no to people who needed help. Sometimes he rushed foolishly into bad situations.

Conrad Murray was hardly the first doctor to enable Michael Jackson and his need for sleep drugs and painkillers, which grew in spurts beginning in the early nineties, when he went to rehab during the *Dangerous* tour. Michael was always scouting for new doctors. He collected them like hotel-room keys. He called them, often unexpectedly, and at strange times. His bodyguards made arrangements for him to show up at their offices after hours. Even in Botox-obsessed Beverly Hills or celebrity-packed Las Vegas, starstruck doctors were thrilled to be making small talk with MJ. He had two main doctor constants over the years. One was Steven Hoefflin, the plastic surgeon who corrected his first, botched nose job in 1979 and stuck with him for numerous procedures. The other was Arnold Klein, the "Father of Botox," as *Vanity Fair* called him, who charmed celebrity patients in Beverly Hills with his regal manner and gruff, fast-talking style. They developed a sort of medical arms race over their care for MJ. Debbie Rowe, Klein's assistant, referred to it as a "pissing contest over who could give the better drug." Significantly, they were never charged with negligence or malpractice at any time.

Michael worked with dozens of doctors over the years, and some became his friends. Scott David Saunders, a UCLA-trained doctor, received a 1998 call from an anonymous woman who asked if he'd make a house call. He said he would, and found himself at a private room on Neverland Ranch, where he encountered the King of Pop lying in bed with an upper respiratory infection. After this first connection, Jackson and Saunders watched *Spider-Man* in the Neverland movie theater. Michael showed up unexpectedly one night at Saunders's house in Solvang, near Santa Maria, and the surprised doctor allowed Michael's kids to play with his kids. Later, Michael gave the doctor a PlayStation 2 and a carnival-style popcorn machine. They'd drive around Neverland in Michael's Navigator and talk until Saunders insisted he had to return home to his family.

Allan Metzger, another longtime personal physician, traveled with MJ throughout the *HIStory* tour and visited him in New York, at Neverland for holiday dinners, and at his Century City apartment on what the doctor called "innumerable occasions." Like many of Michael's doctors, Metzger compiled medical records for his superstar patient under assumed names. (Michael used more than a dozen aliases, including Omar Arnold, Peter Madonie, Josephine Baker, Michael Jefferson, and Paul Farance.) "For confidentiality," Metzger explained.

Once these doctors saw MJ a few times, he felt emboldened to make unusual requests. According to Rowe's testimony, in the early nineties, Rowe discovered Hoefflin had given Michael a bottle of Dilaudid, a narcotic painkiller widely known as "hospital heroin." She confiscated it immediately. Later, according to Rowe, Hoefflin became the first to give him Diprivan, or propofol, used by hospitals under strict medical supervision to put their patients to sleep while they undergo a painful procedure, like breaking an arm for medical reasons. MJ would receive this drug some ten times over twelve years. Metzger insisted he never gave Michael propofol or intravenous drugs of any kind, although he did prescribe anti-anxiety meds such as Xanax and Klonopin. "He had different doctors in different places, and that was one of my concerns," Metzger said.

By 2002, MJ was receiving regular Botox injections, and David Fournier, his nurse anesthetist, was sympathetic to his concerns about pain. "He would be getting hundreds of injections around the eyes and various painful parts of the face, and it was more than the average person would get," said Fournier, one of those medical professionals who had become so friendly with Michael that he received invitations to Neverland Ranch. "So therefore he often needed to be sedated." Fournier administered Versed, a sleep drug, and propofol. "He referred to it as 'the milk,'" Fournier recalled. There was nothing illegal about it—Fournier went by the book, giving Michael a standard lecture about the risks, including death. Over time, Michael began to cut him off. "You've done enough," he said. "I've got it." In 2003, Michael called Dr. Stephen Gordon's office in Las Vegas and asked for lower-eyelid Botox injections for crow's feet and collagen in the sides of his nose "to give a flatter appearance, which is presumed to be more youthful," Gordon recalled. The doctor brought in an anesthesiologist, who knocked out Michael with propofol. Again, Michael called it "milk," which surprised Gordon. "Most people don't really, you know, relate to it like that," the doctor said.

By the early 2000s, Michael's friends, family, associates, and doctors were noticing his erratic behavior. There was the time before the Jacksons' thirtieth-anniversary shows in Madison Square Garden when Cascio couldn't get Michael out of bed for the performance. Another time, a mysterious 911 call came from MJ's hotel room; security called bodyguard Mike LaPerruque, who rushed to the room and found a sobbing Paris and Prince Jackson saying they couldn't "wake up Daddy." LaPerruque gave mouth-to-mouth resuscitation to his boss, who regained consciousness before paramedics arrived. Many around Michael Jackson at that time noticed he slurred his speech. He was unusually tired. He showed up late, or not at all. "I'm not going to lie. I've heard those stories," says Henry Aubrey, an MJ bodyguard during this period. "It was true." By 2009, he'd spent nearly two decades with "profound" trouble sleeping, according to Metzger, who added: "Particularly when performing. He could not come down."

Over the years, some of these doctors pushed back. From 1997 to 2009, Dr. Christine Quinn, a Los Angeles dental anesthesiologist, had put the singer to sleep ten times during a variety of procedures, including a root canal. Early on, Michael left an impromptu message on her answering machine; she called back immediately, and he asked her to meet him at the Beverly Hills Hotel. She brought her sister—"I don't usually go meet people in hotel rooms," Quinn explained—and found herself insisting to Michael Jackson that she couldn't possibly administer propofol to him to help him sleep. "He told me that it's the best sleep that he ever has," she recalled. After Gordon conducted a routine Botox procedure on MJ's face in 2003, the patient asked for a "shot of Demerol for the road." The Las Vegas cosmetic surgeon laughed. "There's no way I'm going to do that, Michael," he said. "You just need to go home and take it easy." Gordon didn't hear from Michael again after that—until May 2007. This time, Michael wanted an injection of Juvéderm, a filler that makes cheeks look thicker and healthier. That request wasn't unusual to Gordon. What was unusual was that Michael had brought a doctor of his own: Conrad Murray. Gordon had never had a patient show up with his own cardiologist before. Murray even spoke for Michael. Afterward, it was Murray who wrote the check. Michael had found his pleaser.

Conrad Murray had eight children with seven different women. While living with his girlfriend, Nicole Alvarez, and their son at a Santa Monica apartment, he met Sade Anding at Sullivan's Steakhouse in Houston, gave her his phone number, and exchanged texts. Later, he introduced Anding to strangers as his girlfriend. He was a "serial womanizer," according to the London tabloid *Daily Mail*, which added: "Had it not been for his voracious sexual appetite he might have achieved great things; for he took up medicine intending to help those who couldn't afford decent healthcare." All those sides to Murray, altruistic and promiscuous, were part of his complex personality.

Murray's parents, Rawle and Milta, met in Grenada, where Murray was born. They split up, and Milta took Conrad back to her hometown, Port of Spain, on the nearby island of Trinidad. The elder Murray was a general doctor, and after he moved to Texas, he sent money to the family. Conrad earned a high school scholarship and planned to become

a doctor so he could return to tend to the poor and sick in his neigh-
borhood. By the time he graduated from his father's medical school,
Meharry, in Nashville, Tennessee, in 1989, he had married pharmacist
Zufan Tesfai, divorced her, then had a child with another woman.

Murray's financial negligence was almost a match for Michael Jackson's. Three years after he graduated from medical school, he filed for
Chapter 7 bankruptcy protection; by the early 2000s, he owed nearly
$45,000 in taxes in Arizona and California. He was running two sepa-
rate cardiology practices, a lucrative one in Las Vegas and a sentimen-
tal one in a section of Houston known as Acres Home. Murray's father
had been treating patients in Acres Home since he opened his clinic
in 1968, and when he died in 2003, he left a vacuum in the neighborhood of predominantly poor, African-American senior citizens. One
of his patients, Dennis Hix, visited Murray for a heart procedure after
another doctor had told him there was nothing he could do to save his
life; Murray installed a total of thirteen stents, and when Hix said his
insurance couldn't possibly cover it, Murray treated him for free. Yet
when Murray came to work for Michael Jackson as his personal physician in spring 2009, he was in what police would term "desperate financial trouble." He owed more than $1.6 million on his home. A college
student-loan company successfully sued him for unpaid bills totaling
$71,332, and various finance companies won judgments against him
for nearly $800,000. "He's not a businessman," says Miranda Sevcik,
a veteran communications professional in Houston who worked with
Murray on crisis public relations. "Look at his financial situation—it
was a mess, a shambles, and yet he would go to Houston every month
for a week to treat people at the clinic his father worked at."

In early 2007, Michael Jackson and his children were living in Las
Vegas when they caught some kind of viral infection—coughing, runny
nose, dehydration. A hospital visit would mean paparazzi. MJ needed discretion. One of his bodyguards tracked down Murray, who, within a few
hours, arrived at MJ's home. Murray wound up treating Michael two or

three times for the infection, and called a podiatrist about painful calluses on his feet. Murray continued to see MJ and his kids from time to time.

In 2009, Murray received a phone call from Michael Amir Williams. MJ was about to play a number of O2 Arena concerts, and he'd "very much like" Murray to accompany him to London. Murray hesitated: "Well, I need more details about that." The next call came from Michael Jackson himself. On May 8, Murray received an e-mail from AEG's Timm Woolley, outlining the $150,000-a-month deal they'd agreed on: the doctor would travel to London on a chartered jet with Michael or, short of that, in commercial first class; he'd live in a guest house on the grounds of whatever property AEG rented for Michael; and he'd wind down his Las Vegas and Houston medical practices over ten days. In negotiating with Brigitte Segal, hired by AEG to secure houses, Murray asked for one big enough for his wife, three daughters ages eight, twelve, and sixteen, and their three-month-old son. "Make sure that the mattresses are in top shape otherwise they will have to be changed to a very suportive [sic] type," Murray wrote in an e-mail to Segal.

Michael invited Murray to spend the night at his house on Carolwood in Los Angeles. The doctor became a fixture. Security took for granted that Murray's 2005 BMW 6 Series convertible would be parked in the driveway every night, and Michael's kids and employees accepted that Murray was the only one allowed upstairs, although household staff occasionally left Michael's meals outside the bedroom door. When Prince and his friends ventured to Michael's room during a game of hide-and-seek, they found the door locked. "I was twelve," Prince would say. "To my understanding, [Dr. Murray] was supposed to make sure my dad stayed healthy."

Murray began to order staggeringly large shipments of propofol—ten 100-milliliter bottles and twenty-five 20-milliliter bottles, which he had shipped to a "clinic" that was actually the Santa Monica apartment of his girlfriend Nicole Alvarez. Bigger shipments followed, of not just propofol but Benoquin cream (to treat MJ's vitiligo) and anti-anxiety drugs such as lorazepam, better known as Ativan. Nobody other than Jackson or Murray knew about any of this. "He liked his privacy," said Michael Amir Williams, MJ's assistant. Michael's family and employees were not privy to a May 9 voice recording he left on Conrad Murray's iPhone. On it, Michael's voice sounded shockingly deep and scratchy, and he slurred his nonsensical words into a jumble. "We have to be phenomenal," Michael declared, referring to his O2 concerts. "When people leave this show, when people leave my show, I want them to say, 'I've never seen nothing like this in my life. Go. Go. I've never seen anything like this. Go. It's amazing. He's the greatest entertainer in the world.'" Two days later, Conrad Murray ordered another shipment of propofol—a total of 45,000 milliliters in sixty-five bottles.

Somebody was suspicious of Dr. Murray. His name was Justin Burns, an underwriter for Cathedral Capital, part of a British company administering the $17.5 million Lloyd's of London insurance policy on Michael Jackson's health for his upcoming O2 concerts. If Michael missed shows, AEG wanted Lloyd's to reimburse at least a portion of the money the promoter would lose. It was standard concert procedure—and Michael, given his history of illness and cancellations, was likely to be expensive to insure. Concerned about press reports suggesting Michael was in ill health and photos of him in a wheelchair, Burns and his colleagues requested medical records and an examination. In a June 24 e-mail, Burns wrote of his concern that nobody had passed along MJ's five-year medical history or a description of his fitness program. He insisted a doctor would have to examine Michael on July 6 with nobody else, not even Murray, in the room. "Anything less," Burns wrote, "would not be considered prudent and arguably negligent on are [sic] part." Burns might have had trouble spelling, but his instincts were correct.

At 12:13 P.M. on Thursday, June 25, 2009, about eleven hours after Michael Jackson's personal manager Michael Amir Williams and bodyguards Faheem Muhammed and Alberto Alvarez dropped him off at Carolwood, Williams received a call. He was in the shower. It went to voicemail. Williams listened to the voicemail, from a 702 number. Vegas. Conrad Murray. The doctor had spent the night at Michael's home as usual. "Call me right away. Call me right away," he said. "Thank you." Within two minutes, Williams called back. "Get here right away," Murray said. "Mr. Jackson had a bad reaction."

Williams lived in downtown Los Angeles. He was too far from Carolwood to reach the house quickly. He called Muhammed, who'd just left the property to go to the bank. "Hurry," Williams told him, "turn around and go back." In a panic, Williams called Alvarez, who was in the security trailer on the property. *Speed up*, Williams told him. With Williams squawking on his cell phone, Alvarez dutifully ran to the front door, where the Jacksons' nanny, Roselyn Muhammed, let him in. (AEG's Gongaware had fired longtime nanny Grace Rwaramba on MJ's behalf in April, paying $20,000 in severance.) Paris was with her. Alvarez saw Murray at the top of the stairs, with his hands on the railing, leaning forward, looking down. On the phone, Williams instructed Alvarez to run up the stairs. He'd been upstairs at the house only twice over the last six months, once to accompany MJ's hairdresser. Murray spotted Alvarez: "Alberto, come. Come quick," he shouted. Alvarez hung up on Williams, leaped up the stairs, and entered Michael Jackson's room. There, he saw his boss, eyes and mouth open, lying on a pillow in his bed, face slightly to the left, reaching out toward the door as if trying to grab something.

Conrad Murray began to give Michael chest compressions. Paris and Prince walked into the room. "Daddy!" Paris screamed. Murray gave orders to Alvarez: "Don't let them see their dad like this." Alvarez soothed the kids—"Everything is going to be okay"—and ushered them toward the door of Michael's suite. Alvarez returned to the room. He scanned Michael's suite, took in a few odd details. A condom catheter—Alvarez would call it "some sort of, you know, medical device"—was protruding from MJ's groin area. Oxygen tubing was attached to his nose.

And, confusingly, Murray was asking Alvarez to help him put some vials from Michael's wooden nightstand into a plastic grocery bag. Alvarez did as he was told. Then Murray asked him to put that bag into another bag. "I thought we were packing," Alvarez would say, "getting ready to go to the hospital." Murray instructed Alvarez to call 911 on his phone. The recording would be etched in history: "He's fifty years old, sir. Yes, he's not breathing, sir. No, he's not conscious, sir. Sir, just, if you can please . . ."

Alvarez helped Murray move MJ from his bed to the floor. Alvarez noticed the tubing from an IV stand connected to Michael's leg. Murray clamped a small device, which Alvarez recognized as a pulse oximeter, to Michael's finger. Faheem Muhammed returned to the room. "It's not looking good," Alvarez told him. Although he was a trained cardiologist, Murray had never given mouth-to-mouth before, but he bent down to touch Michael Jackson's lips with his.

From the nearby Bel Air fire station on Sunset and Beverly Glen, Engine 71 rolled up to the Carolwood mansion at 12:25 P.M. An ambulance followed and pulled into Michael's driveway, where security men opened the large gates into the street and waved the paramedics through. The ambulance parked next to the front door. Richard Senneff, one of the emergency technicians from the ambulance, followed security up the stairs into Michael's bedroom. He saw Murray, Alvarez, and Muhammed moving MJ from the bed to the floor. Michael was wearing pajama pants, an unbuttoned pajama shirt, and some kind of surgical cap. He looked pale and underweight. Senneff could see his ribs. He thought the unconscious patient had been suffering from cancer. Thinking hospice, he asked if the patient had a do-not-resuscitate order. Murray responded, "What?" Someone mentioned Michael Jackson's name. Senneff glanced at his patient's face and recognized it. Senneff asked for MJ's medical history. "Nothing," Murray said. "I'm just treating him for dehydration and exhaustion."

Senneff didn't buy the explanation. Michael had no pulse. His pupils were dilated. His eyes were dry, which meant he hadn't blinked in some time. His skin was cool, his legs were pale, and his hands and feet were tinted blue. Talking to Senneff, Murray allowed that he'd given his patient "a little bit of lorazepam to help him sleep." Senneff injected life-saving drugs atropine and epinephrine into MJ's system to speed up his heart. By this point he was convinced Michael was dead. He believed further rescue efforts would be useless, but the voices at the Ronald Reagan UCLA Medical Center on the other end of his cellphone instructed him to continue. Finally, Senneff and his crew loaded MJ onto a gurney, then hauled him down the stairs and into the ambulance. Murray climbed into the back. Alberto Alvarez had loaded Michael's three children into an SUV and tried to distract them so they wouldn't see their father in this state. The ambulance took off at 1:07 P.M. for the six-minute drive to the hospital, and two Escalades followed, one carrying Alvarez, the other with Muhammed, Williams, and another bodyguard. By this point, the media had gotten wind of the story, and paparazzi were snaking through LA following the emergency vehicles and the official Michael Jackson security tails. The caravan picked up another vehicle. Randy Phillips, chief executive officer of AEG Live, had been at Sterling Cleaners on Westwood Boulevard in LA when Frank DiLeo called from his room at the Beverly Hills Hilton. "There's something wrong," DiLeo said. "Michael's not breathing. I don't know how serious it is. I can't get there fast enough. Can you get there?" Phillips was closer, so he dropped his dry cleaning on the counter, jumped into his car with his business partner, Dave Loeffler, and rushed to Carolwood. The ambulance and fire engine, as well as the two black Escalades carrying Michael's kids and security men, were pulling out of the house. Phillips pulled in behind them. Two paparazzi vehicles almost ran him off the road, but he made it to UCLA before anyone else. He waited in the hallway. Within half an hour, DiLeo joined him. They sat silently.

Paramedics wheeled Michael Jackson into the emergency room. Michael's children waited for their grandmother, Katherine, to show up. "It was madness at the hospital when I got there," Tohme Tohme,

Michael's manager, recalled. "Police, fans, media. The police are keeping everybody back." Alvarez confronted some paparazzi who'd made it into the hospital. "Please," he said, "this is a private moment. Please, just step away." Inside, beginning at 1:13 P.M., doctors continued to administer heart-pumping drugs. A technician did physical chest compressions. At 1:21 P.M., Conrad Murray declared he heard a pulse, encouraging the doctors to continue their work. Nobody else felt one. At 2:26 P.M., Richelle Cooper, a veteran emergency-room physician who had the shift at UCLA that night, pronounced Michael Jackson dead. A nurse came out and asked Phillips and DiLeo, who'd been waiting in the hallway, when Katherine Jackson would be arriving. Michael's mother, giving instructions to her driver somewhere in Santa Monica, was on her way. Phillips wanted to know why the nurse was asking. "Well, I really shouldn't be telling you this," she told them, "but there's really nothing else we can do." The heavyset DiLeo collapsed into Phillips's arms. "I almost fainted," DiLeo would say. By the time Katherine Jackson arrived, Michael was dead. In the hallway, Murray pulled Michael Amir Williams aside. They talked about how horrible everything was. Then Murray confided to Williams that there was some cream in Michael's room, back at Carolwood, "that he wouldn't want the world to know about." Murray asked for a ride back to the house. He'd accompanied the ambulance to the hospital; his BMW remained parked in Michael's driveway. Emotional, and not wanting to deal with the doctor's bizarre request, Williams asked Faheem Muhammed for his opinion. Muhammed said, "I am not giving him the keys." Murray then asked for a ride to get some food. Williams refused, and instructed Muhammed to lock down the Carolwood house and "make sure security doesn't let anyone in or anyone out." By the time police showed up to sequester MJ's body in a secured hospital room, Murray was gone. To avoid traffic and paparazzi, police air-lifted the body to the coroner's office.

Michael Jackson had written a vision of his death, in prose form, back in 1992: "A star can never die. It just turns into a smile and melts back into the cosmic music, the dance of life.

"I like that thought," he added, "the last one I have before my eyes close."

He was fifty years old.

The day Michael Jackson died, June 25, 2009, Travis Payne, his long-time choreographer, had been on his way to the Carolwood house for their two P.M. one-on-one dance rehearsal. Kenny Ortega and the This Is It crew had begun their routines at the Staples Center. Payne's mother called him. She'd seen reports of MJ's death on the news. "I'm sure everything is fine," Payne said. Rumors about Michael Jackson's health were not unusual. Payne called Stacy Walker, an assistant choreographer for the tour, and asked if anything was up. "No," she told him, "we're rehearsing." But before he arrived at Carolwood, Payne received another call—there was an emergency at the house, and Payne should report to Staples instead. Payne rerouted. When he showed up, the dancers were working on choreography for "Smooth Criminal." Nearby, Ortega began to get phone calls—Michael had been rushed to the hospital. Most of the dancers took a break and returned to their dressing room, where they watched the news on Staples Center TVs and refused to believe it. "People say things," they told each other. Then Chris Grant, a dancer, received twenty texts on his phone. In another part of the arena, Abby Franklin, wardrobe coordinator, had been meeting with the tour accountant, who had to interrupt their discussion because he noticed AEG's Paul Gongaware had called him a number of times in a row. The accountant reached Gongaware by phone, and when he turned back to Franklin, he informed her MJ was in the hospital for a heart attack. When TMZ broke the story of Michael Jackson's death, at 2:44 P.M., everybody at Staples seemed to absorb it at once. Payne, Ortega, and choreographers Stacy Walker and Alif Sankey lingered near the stage. Then Ortega received another call, from AEG's Phillips and Gongaware. He paused, then said, "Tell me something that will make me know it's you, and that this is true." Ortega then collapsed, sobbing. Payne hauled him into a seat near the stage. Stunned, Payne went to a desk near the stage and began absent-mindedly typing on his laptop. Elsewhere in the arena, Jonathan "Sugarfoot" Moffett, Michael's drummer since the seventies, was crying so hard friends had to hold him up. Michael Bush, MJ's longtime costume designer, was in a similar state.

Security locked down the building. Nobody could come or go.

Walker went to the dancers' dressing room and broke the news. The dancers split up, one moment a cohesive crew united in "Dirty Diana," the next a disheveled, weeping mass spreading to different corners of the room, trying to figure out what to do with their hands. "It turned so quickly from all of us being happy and joyful, and we were getting ready to go on this tour, to it just being so dark and sad, and you just couldn't believe it," Grant says. "No one knew what to do," Walker adds. "We couldn't leave. We ate dinner there." Crews showed up—nobody knew from where—to tear down the stage, hauling out the pieces that, an hour ago, represented Michael Jackson's triumphant comeback.

"So many deaths, really," Walker says. "It was the end of Michael Jackson. It was the end of a show. It was the end of this family we had created. It was the end of a journey. There was no London. Everybody's plans just shifted immediately. You're done. Good-bye."

The dancers stuck around for a while, and some of the musicians joined them. "The room was dark and candles were lit in the dressing room," recalls Darryl Phinnessee, a longtime MJ backup singer. "It was just quiet." Finally, Ortega led a prayer and the ensemble dispersed. "Is it true?" paparazzi and Michael Jackson fans yelled at the dancers, and others from This Is It, as they finally left the arena. Nobody knew what to say. In coming days, Grant had to turn off his phone, he was getting so many calls.

As news spread that Michael Jackson had died, mourning began small and personal, on plots of land nearest to MJ's body. Hundreds gathered at UCLA Medical Center, some wearing familiar Michael costumes, crying, texting, blasting "Heal the World" on iPods, forcing police and security to block off the entrances; the nearby Sigma Alpha Epsilon fraternity house added to the din by cranking "Human Nature" over its large speakers. Outside Michael's house on Carolwood, so many cars parked along the street that police had to shoo away drivers using a loudspeaker. Fans swarmed the Jackson family home on Hayvenhurst, blasting music and showing off single white gloves. In Gary, Indiana, fans streamed to the house at 2300 Jackson Street to drop off teddy bears and flowers. In Detroit, three hundred people pulled up to the Motown Historical Museum, site of the original Hitsville headquarters, blasting MJ music from cars and trucks. A forty-five-year-old teacher set up a photo of Michael on an easel, surrounded by roses and an American flag, in front of the porch. At the Apollo Theater in Harlem, where the Jackson 5 performed, CNN reported so much dancing and cheering that "it's almost like Michael Jackson's last concert."

Every time an iconic artist dies, fans gravitate to a song, a film scene, or a photo—like Otis Redding's "(Sittin' on) The Dock of the Bay" or Robin Williams's "it wasn't your fault" clip from *Good Will Hunting*. As this process played out via Twitter and Facebook, fans were drawn to "Man in the Mirror," with its cathartic gospel chorus. Mercifully, media coverage finally began to shift from "Michael Jackson is a weird creep" to "Michael Jackson was an entertainment legend." Smokey Robinson went on Larry King to say he was devastated. Kenny Rogers added, "You try to find something to smile about, something to laugh at just to keep you going and get you through this." Berry Gordy said he was numb. Rapper Wyclef Jean called MJ his "musical god." A CNN correspondent called Michael "the Jackie Robinson of MTV." The *Atlanta Examiner* website posted a four-thousand-word list of all the charities to which MJ had contributed. The *Chicago Sun-Times* concluded, "Whatever else you might think, he left us 'Thriller.'"

MJ mourning went international. In Japan, TV stations cut in live from the US. Former South Korean president Kim Dae-jung said: "We lost a hero of the world." Fans gathered in Moscow, Paris, Tokyo, and Nairobi, and officials from South Africa's Nelson Mandela to England's Gordon Brown paid tribute. So many people googled "Michael Jackson" that the massive search engine's computers perceived the requests as some kind of hacker attack. The most common way of mourning involved old-fashioned consumerism. In Grand Prairie, Texas, fans lined up at a record store called Forever Young and bought everything they could find with Michael's name on it—CDs, posters, eight-track tapes. Radio stations, which had been avoiding all but the best-known Jackson singles in recent years, went into all-Michael-all-the-time mode. In New York, WBLS opened the phone lines for listeners, who happened to include MJ producer Teddy Riley, the Rev. Al Sharpton, and Michael Bivins from New Edition. "Although we always had played Michael Jackson, we went back to get many, many more hits that had kind of gotten lost," Skip Dillard, the station's program director, would say. "It was amazing how much people, and all of us, had really missed those." In the week before his death, Michael's top sixty-four tracks, including "Man in the Mirror," "Thriller," "The Way You Make Me Feel," and "Don't Stop 'til You Get Enough," sold thirty thousand copies via iTunes; from June 25 to 28, sales of those same tracks hit 1.8 million; by year's end, he would sell 8.2 million.

The official cause of death was a heart attack, brought on by an overdose of sleep medication. Police wanted to know more. Detectives Orlando Martinez and Scott Smith of the Los Angeles Police Department visited Michael's Carolwood bedroom. "It's just weird," Martinez recalls. "It's not like a room where somebody sleeps. It looks like a room where somebody's being treated." In the clutter of pill bottles, they found one with a hole for a syringe, and that's when they heard the word *propofol* for the first time. They began to treat MJ's death as a homicide investigation.

Finally, Murray's attorney Ed Chernoff provided the doctor's side of the story. At 4:02 P.M. on Saturday, June 27, police met with Murray and Chernoff at the Ritz Carlton in Marina Del Rey. In Murray's retelling, he asked MJ how he was feeling at one A.M. on June 25. "Oh, tired and fatigued, and I'm treated like I'm a machine," the singer told him. He took a quick shower, changed, and returned to his bedroom. Murray administered a dermatological cream onto Michael's back to treat his vitiligo, then connected the needle from an IV drip into the back of Michael's leg. Michael took a 10-milligram Valium pill to help him sleep. Then Murray added 2 milligrams of lorazepam through the IV. But by 4 A.M., Michael was still awake and growing frustrated. "I got to sleep, Dr. Conrad," he said. "I have these rehearsals to perform. . . . I cannot function if I don't get the sleep!" Around 5 A.M., Murray gave MJ 2 more milligrams of lorazepam. At 7:30 A.M., he added another 2 milligrams of Versed. At 10 A.M., after nine straight hours of not sleeping, Michael finally confronted Murray. "I'd like to have some milk," he said. "Please, please give me some milk so that I can sleep, because I know that this is all that really works for me." Dutifully, Murray added 25 milligrams of propofol to the IV drip—an important detail he had neglected to mention to the EMTs and hospital doctors on the day of Michael's death. "I've given it to him before," Murray recalled. "He handled it fine." Actually, the doctor had administered propofol to the pop star every day since he'd begun to work with him two months earlier. Michael, finally, went to sleep.

The doctor did not explain to police that propofol was never intended for home use under any circumstances. "We don't use it for rest or for sleep or psychological reasons," Dr. Alon Steinberg, a cardiologist who reviewed the case, would say in court. "I have never heard of it." Murray also didn't mention he lacked the proper equipment to administer such a dangerous drug—his pulse oximeter did not contain an alarm to alert the doctor in case Michael Jackson's pulse were to abruptly stop, and he had no EKG monitor to check Michael's heart activity. While Murray continues to insist he was trying to "wean" MJ off his propofol dependence, he could not square that with the dozens of bottles he'd had shipped to his girlfriend's apartment.

After administering the drug to Michael Jackson, Murray passed the time speaking to friends and associates on his cell phone. The calls were at 10:14, 11:07, 11:18, 11:42, and 11:51—that last one was to Sade Anding, one of his girlfriends. About five minutes into the call, Anding heard a commotion and realized Murray was no longer on the phone. "I said, 'Hello, hello,' and I didn't hear anything," she would say. "And that's when I pressed the phone against my ear, and I heard mumbling of voices."

It was the sound of Michael Jackson dying.

Memorials, big and small, spilled into every community remotely related to Michael Jackson's life. At the Apollo Theater, July 1 in Harlem, six hundred fans heard the Rev. Al Sharpton pinpoint Michael's role as a sort of ambassador from the African-American community to the white world: "Michael made young men and women all over the world imitate us." In Montego Bay, Jamaica, promoters at the Reggae Sumfest presented Tito Jackson with giant plaques emblazoned with drawings of his late brother.

The biggest memorial, of course, was at the Staples Center, where Jackson had been rehearsing less than two weeks earlier. Twenty thousand people watched as Mariah Carey dueted with Trey Lorenz on "I'll Be There"; Jennifer Hudson sang "Will You Be There"; Usher cried during "Gone Too Soon"; and Berry Gordy Jr., Brooke Shields, the Rev. Al Sharpton, and Lakers greats Magic Johnson and Kobe Bryant sat in the audience. MJ would have appreciated the enormity of the event—big stars, big music, including a full-on Andrae Crouch Choir performance of "Man in the Mirror"—but the most memorable moment was tiny, not like the King of Pop at all. For the first time, eleven-year-old Paris Jackson emerged from the veils she'd been wearing in public most of her life and said, "I just wanted to say, ever since I was born, Daddy has been the best father you could ever imagine." She then collapsed into her aunt Janet's arms. AEG paid most of the $1.5 million for the memorial, and much of the This Is It crew pulled it together in three days. Michael's family wore black. His brothers wore matching black suits and bright-red ties, red roses in their lapels, as they carried his casket.

Once Michael died, Randy Phillips called Tohme Tohme and suggested he lock down the Carolwood home. Tohme hired Ron Williams, who'd worked in the US Secret Service for twenty-two years and was by then chief executive of a private security firm called Talon Executive Services, to zoom to the house and set up security. When the LAPD finished their investigation, Williams's people took over, "with orders that nobody was allowed onto the property," he recalls. (Talon similarly secured the Jackson family's Hayvenhurst house and Michael's Las Vegas property, where he stored valuable items in the basement.) Later that night, though, Ron Boyd, police chief for the Port of Los Angeles, arrived with La Toya Jackson and her boyfriend Jeffre Phillips. In a flurry of phone calls, the security crew discussed shutting out the family, but in the end, they decided to let them be. Katherine Jackson showed up three hours later, and the Jacksons stayed in Michael's home for five or six days. At one point, they brought in a U-Haul truck and, as Williams recalls, "took out whatever they wanted from the residence." It's unclear what the Jacksons removed—*Rolling Stone* and *Vanity Fair* said La Toya carried out bags of cash, but La Toya later sent a cease-and-desist letter to *Vanity Fair*, insisting the allegation was untrue. (She'd said previously that by the time she arrived, all the cash Michael kept around the house was gone.) The *Times* of London quoted Michael's former nanny, Grace Rwaramba, about receiving a call that night from Katherine Jackson in the Carolwood home. "Grace, the children are crying. They are asking about you. They can't believe that their father died," Katherine told Grace. "Grace, you remember Michael used to hide cash at the house. I am here. Where can it be?" Rwaramba suggested Katherine search "the garbage bags and under the carpets." The Jacksons did remove valuable items from the house during this time—Taj Jackson, one of Tito's sons who was in the hit R&B group 3T, recalled Jeffre Phillips giving him two computers, one containing MJ's music. He gave the music computer to Michael's estate and stored the other computer, with a password set by Michael Amir Williams that Taj couldn't crack, in Prince Jackson's bedroom closet. "They backed up trucks, removing everything," Frank DiLeo would say. "They thought Michael owned it all, so they took even the rented furniture."

For several days after Michael's death, his estate was in chaos. Nobody could find a will, so his assets were put in a trust, to be turned over to his three children when they turned eighteen. Nobody else in Michael's family was to receive his half a billion dollars in assets, including 50 percent of the lucrative Sony ATV catalog and the rights to his own songs. (They also wouldn't have been responsible for any of his $400 million in debt.) Katherine applied in court to oversee the estate. She and Joseph filed documents saying they believed there was no valid will.

But the Jacksons received a shock when a voice from Michael's past suddenly resurfaced. Michael had fired his longtime attorney, John Branca, years earlier, but rehired him on June 17, at the request of newly returned manager Frank DiLeo, shortly before his death. When Michael died, Branca and his associates searched their offices and found not one but two wills, the most recent one dated July 7, 2002, bequeathing all of the singer's assets to a family trust, payable to his children when they turn twenty-one, with larger payouts at ages thirty, thirty-five, and forty. (An attorney from a different firm had found a third will, from 1997, suggesting Michael had been crafting new versions with the birth of each of his kids.) As Katherine positioned herself to take over Michael's affairs, Branca submitted documents in probate court June 30. The newly discovered will—conveniently, some in Michael's family would argue—named Branca himself as a coexecutor of the MJ estate along with longtime Jackson family friend and veteran record executive John McClain. Signed by Michael with his usual flourish, his initials scrawled next to every paragraph, this newly discovered will gave Branca and McClain "full power and authority at any time or times to sell, lease, mortgage, pledge, exchange or otherwise dispose of the property," among many other things. Katherine was to serve as guardian for his three children. (Diana Ross was to take her place if something were to happen to his mother, which was an interesting image to contemplate.) He left the rest of his family (and, pointedly, Debbie Rowe) out of the will.

Joseph Jackson and others in Michael's family, particularly Randy, were furious. Michael had fired Branca on February 3, 2003, they said, and instructed him to turn over all legal papers, including wills. Branca had not done so. They also believed Michael had actually been in New York on the date he appeared to have signed the will in LA. (Branca wouldn't comment on the will, but his reps pointed to a 2012 *Forbes* story titled "The Scandalously Boring Truth about Michael Jackson's Will," which noted the three previous versions of the will are "remarkably consistent" and "the will is in no real danger of being overturned.") The Jacksons convened at Janet's condominium in Westwood. Several family lawyers were on hand, including L. Londell McMillan (on the phone). He had initially pushed for his client, Katherine, to take over the MJ estate as executor, but became noncommittal once Branca produced the will. In a presentation to the family at the condo, Jackson family attorney Brian Oxman declared the will a "big fraud," recalls Adam Streisand, another attorney of Katherine's.

On July 7, Mitchell Beckloff, an LA Superior Court judge, backed Branca and McClain to control Michael's estate. Howard Weitzman, a longtime MJ attorney who worked with Branca and the estate, called it "the correct decision" and said the executors would immediately try to "maximize the estate." At first, Katherine's attorneys strenuously objected, but they backed off. Why? Streisand says Katherine confided to him she didn't want to fight with Branca and McClain and was weary of squabbling over the will; Katherine told Randall Sullivan that Streisand aggressively talked her out of going to war with John Branca.

Unlike Katherine, Joe Jackson and his longtime attorney, Brian Oxman, did not back off. In November, they filed a sixty-page document objecting to the appointment of Branca and McClain, listing "violations of fiduciary duties and conflicts of interest" and accusing them of acting "in a fraudulent deceptive manner where their veracity can no longer be trusted." But because Michael had not named Joe as a beneficiary, Beckloff ruled he had no standing in court—and he rejected Joe's request for a monthly estate allowance. On November 10, Streisand told the court his client, Katherine Jackson, withdrew her objections to Branca and McClain, saying it was "high time the fighting end."

That gave Branca an opening to go to work. The first thing the newly formed estate did was ally with AEG. That was controversial among the Jackson family, because Katherine and others in the Jackson family were beginning to form a theory that AEG hired Conrad Murray and encouraged him to prop up Michael Jackson for the shows even when the singer was conspicuously sick. AEG had spent more than $24 million on This Is It costs, including $15 million in advances to MJ. (The promoter filed a claim for its $17.5 million insurance payout after Michael's death, but Lloyd's of London opposed it, suggesting AEG had not adequately disclosed Michael's health and drug issues. The two sides settled out of court in January 2014.) The promoter recouped a portion of its losses by issuing souvenir tickets to those who'd paid for the O2 shows, and Randy Phillips was putting his usual spin on the crushing financial blow: "I don't think we've lost anything," he told a reporter.

The estate had financial problems of its own. In addition to Michael's copious debts, as *Forbes*'s Zack O'Malley Greenburg reported in *Michael Jackson Inc.*, dozens of creditors were after him for a variety of legal claims, from the reasonable (the State of California franchise tax board demanded $1,647.24) to the ridiculous (someone named Erle Bonner filed a $1,109,000,503,600 lawsuit that accused MJ of stealing his cure for herpes). But Branca and AEG's Phillips had an idea. They would make up all the promoter's lost revenue, set the estate on the road out of debt, and permanently restore Michael Jackson's reputation as perhaps the greatest entertainer who ever lived.

When he heard the news Michael Jackson died on June 25, Tim Patterson had just returned home from lunch. The cameraman for the This Is It rehearsals was editing footage at his home office for a promotional clip about the backup singers. He called his boss, AEG's Paul Gongaware, and asked whether he should continue working. "Grab your camera," Gongaware told him, "and come in." After Kenny Ortega composed himself, he invited dancers and crew into his Staples Center dressing room, lit candles and encouraged everybody to recall favorite moments with Michael. Patterson showed up and joined Sandrine Orabona, his colleague, in filming everything until he went home around seven P.M.

The next day, Gongaware called Patterson again. *Load up all your drives*, he said, *and come over Monday.* Patterson had 120 to 140 hours of rehearsal footage, between what he and Orabona had shot. He and a film-editor friend, Brandon Key, reported to AEG headquarters Monday in downtown LA and began to edit the raw footage. AEG posted guards outside the editors' small rooms. Gongaware, Patterson, and Key were the only people allowed inside. To maximize security and avoid leaks, they had no Internet connection. "By the end of that week, Paul and Kenny were blown away with what we had," Patterson says. "So Paul put the word out to the studios."

After a bidding war among Hollywood studios, Sony Pictures bought the footage for $60 million. Soon new guards, this time with pistols on their hips, were sitting outside each of the rooms twenty-four hours a day. Ortega signed on as the film's director and added one of his own film editors, Don Brochu, to the team. For three weeks, Patterson, Key, and Brochu waited for lawyers and courts to hash out the details of MJ's estate and the terms of the contract. After Ortega took a short vacation, the editors put together a two-and-a-half-hour version of the movie. Patterson favored an early version of the opening scene, with the This Is It dancers and musicians reacting emotionally to MJ's death on the evening of June 25. It ended with a poignant quote from a crew member as he watched the stage coming down: "It's like the greatest show that never was." Amy Pascal, cochair of Sony Pictures, loved that cut. In his grief, Ortega killed it. He didn't want MJ's kids watching the movie and reliving the tragedy. He might have made other drastic cuts, too, but Pascal pushed him. "I was traumatized and going through a lot of grief at the time," Ortega said. "Basically, she said, 'You need to step out of your own way. You need to find objectivity or don't do it.'" Still, Ortega insisted on no sad death stuff whatsoever, and Patterson and the rest of the editing team had to use a different opening about the dancers' lives. The editing team worked in secrecy twelve to fourteen hours a day, taking off only MJ's birthday in August.

The deal was to split the proceeds according to AEG's original 90–10 split with Michael for the shows—90 percent for the estate and 10 percent for AEG. *Michael Jackson's This Is It* seemed desperate, like a novelty, when Sony Pictures first announced it. Rehearsal footage of the notorious perfectionist Michael Jackson? But the film turned out to contain a certain magic that served as MJ's swan song, something grieving fans could latch on to the way Kurt Cobain fans binged on Nirvana's *MTV Unplugged* in the early nineties. Some found it ghoulish. "No one can ever watch 'This Is It' again, with any sense of joy," Michael's friend and makeup artist Karen Faye would tweet. "It WAS made with Michael's blood." The film grossed $200 million.

For Michael Jackson's estate, the movie was just the beginning of a path from steep debt to immense profitability. The next step was to sign a deal with Sony Music for ten albums through 2017 in exchange for $250 million in advance payments, plus a high royalty rate for song and album sales. The estate most likely came out ahead, as iTunes-style downloads, then free streaming services such as Spotify and YouTube, began to obliterate old-school record sales and cut into the Sony record label's profits.

Not counting the *This Is It* soundtrack and an *Off the Wall* anniversary compilation, the first estate-approved Sony release was the *Michael* album, which came out in 2010, an attempt to pull together the unreleased album MJ had been working on for a decade. It was a strange hodgepodge of an album, a combination of old, forgotten songs and newer stuff Michael had intended to release during his comeback. *Michael* drew from roughly the period when MJ had lived in exile, in Vegas, LA, and Bahrain. "Hold My Hand," the up-tempo first single, came from Akon, who had recorded dozens of tracks with Jackson in Vegas. "Best of Joy" was a ten-year-old ballad full of happy bromides— "I am forever," "we will always be friends"—that Michael recorded with longtime collaborator Michael Durham Prince at the Bel Air Hotel in 2008. "The Way You Love Me," which had floated around under the unexplained code name "Hanson," contained eleven different vocal lines. "Hollywood Tonight," a fast-paced dance track with a distinctive bass line, was originally conceived for *Invincible*. Sony enlisted longtime MJ producer Teddy Riley to finish most of the tracks; he wound up treating Michael's original vocals with pitch-correction software called Melodyne. But once the album came out, numerous MJ collaborators ripped it as unbefitting of the King of Pop's perfectionism—will.i.am said he refused to release his own unfinished songs and called the album "fucking disrespectful." Quincy Jones added, "It should have all stayed in the vault."

The most mysterious of the new tracks were the "Cascio

recordings"—"Breaking News," "Monster," and "Keep Your Head Up." It was Frank DiLeo who brought the songs to the attention of Sony Entertainment's John Doelp. Michael's longtime manager claimed to have spoken to MJ in 2007, while he was working on new songs with producer Eddie "Angel" Cascio (brother of Michael's friend Frank) at the studio he ran at his parents' home in New Jersey. The Cascio tracks prompted an angry public mystery. Immediately after Sony released "Breaking News" online to tease the upcoming album, Michael's nephew TJ Jackson tweeted the vocals were clearly those of an impersonator. "I'm disgusted, disappointed and saddened," he wrote. Jackson's estate had anticipated this accusation, hiring a forensic musicologist to study the tracks and bringing in six producers and engineers who'd worked extensively with Jackson's vocals over the years for an a cappella listening session. All, including Bruce Swedien, Michael Prince, and Teddy Riley, insisted the vocals belonged to Jackson. But some fans remain obsessively unconvinced. Damien Shields, an Australian MJ fan and self-published author, has conducted numerous interviews to investigate what he considers a conspiracy to hide the truth about these recordings.

Michael was not a blockbuster—it sold 405,000 copies in the US by the end of 2010, making it the year's seventy-fourth-best-selling album, not a detail MJ would have written on his mirror. The next album of posthumous material, 2014's *XScape*, opened with a splash— a *Thriller* throwback called "Love Never Felt So Good," with a newly recorded Justin Timberlake duet vocal. The release seemed poised to dominate the pop charts, especially after the Billboard Music Awards promoted a 3-D performance that brought the King of Pop back to life during a performance of *Dangerous*-era "Slave to the Rhythm." (Almost every report called the trick a "hologram," but it was actually an illusion based on a 150-year-old technique known as Pepper's ghost, in which projectors bounce an image onto a screen tilted at a 45-degree angle.) *XScape* made its debut at No. 2, behind the Black Keys, then quickly dropped off the US charts, although reps for MJ's estate noted it sold more than 2.3 million copies worldwide.

Branca and McClain were making shrewd deals. They trimmed Michael's $75 million loan against the Mijac song-publishing catalog from 17 percent to 6 percent, then paid it in full by the end of 2011. Michael's investment in the Sony ATV catalog continued to provide crucial revenue, and Branca and McClain slashed the loan against that investment, too, from 5.8 percent to 2.9 percent. The catalog began to pay out $25 million per year. By the end of 2010, the estate had racked up $300 million. Not everybody agreed with the way the estate handled its finances. Although Branca and McClain had officially valued the estate at $7 million, the Internal Revenue Service in 2013 set the number at closer to $1.125 billion, demanding $702 million in unpaid taxes and fees. The discrepancies, according to documents filed in US Tax Court, ranged from a 2001 Bentley Arnage (which the estate said was worth $91,600, while the IRS estimated $250,000) to the rights to MJ's image and likeness (estate $2,105, IRS $434,264,000). As of this writing, negotiations are pending. Finally, Branca agreed to take a $500,000 salary in 2014, climbing to $1 million in 2015, as an adviser to the board of Michael's publishing catalog Sony ATV—while he served on the same board. In an e-mail leaked online in 2015, Sony executive Nicole Seligman wondered about a conflict of interest: "The Board is awkward because he is on it, so why pay him to advise it?"

The estate succeeded in helping Michael Jackson to once again became one of the world's biggest music stars—his disembodied voice anchored Cirque du Soleil's Immortal World Tour, which since 2011 has earned more than $325 million, through nearly three million ticket sales. Cirque followed up in spring 2013 with *Michael Jackson ONE*, a residency in Las Vegas's Mandalay Bay casino. Like every Cirque show, it's packed with acrobats bouncing spectacularly on trampolines and tightropes, dancers, tumblers wearing elaborate costumes, and thumping music. The show reinterprets MJ's music in surreal ways, with dancers attacking a central electronic robot system made of wires and flashing lights. The climax is a ghostly, gold-tinted, *Dangerous*-era MJ dancing to "Man in the Mirror," breaking apart into tiny lights and reappearing elsewhere onstage. The show covers Michael's entire career, moving beyond what he had envisioned for This Is It, hauling out obscurities such as MJ's solo Motown hit "Never Can Say Goodbye" and the solemn spoken-word portions of "Will You Be There."

Posthumous MJ has sold fifty million albums as of this writing. He was in $500 million worth of debt when he died; the estate paid it off in 2012. *Michael* and *XScape* had their problems, but tons of vintage Jackson material, including rare tracks Michael had kept locked in the vaults, has come out over the last five years—the *Bad* twenty-fifth-anniversary reissue contained unreleased gems such as "Al Capone" and "Streetwalker," while a 162-song, iTunes-only compilation from 2013 included a fantastic live 1981 version of "Don't Stop 'til You Get Enough," among other things. "His passing—unfortunately—allowed a separation from those things that the tabloids dwelled on endlessly," says Matt Forger, Michael's longtime engineer. "People were able to take a little bit more objective look at what his accomplishments were."

In the early days after his death, as Branca and McClain continued to apply a precise order to Michael's business affairs, his legacy briefly descended into chaos without MJ himself as the center of gravity. No longer could he protect Neverland Ranch: Colony Capital, which took it over when he defaulted on a $24.5 million loan in 2008, stripped out the rides and the zoo, spent millions on upgrades, dialed the name back to Sycamore Valley Ranch, and offered it for $100 million in May 2015. No longer could he protect his children the way he wanted them protected and keep his parents and siblings at the distance he preferred. Tension spilled into the public. Paris, Prince, and Blanket were growing older, and photos of them began to pop up in tabloids and on TV broadcasts without their disguises. At first, it didn't matter—the Jacksons were growing up in public as mature, poised, attractive children. "The most artistic was Paris," says longtime MJ friend Mark Lester, who was Blanket's godfather and spent time with the family until Michael's death. "Prince is more into computer games like any normal sort of kid that age, always playing with his PlayStation and his handheld devices. And [Blanket] used to go off into his own world and had figurines, like Spider-Man, and little cars." After his father's death, Prince has grown into a handsome eighteen-year-old, with a round face, small eyes, and thick eyebrows; family sources say he's the extrovert of the family, easily making friends at school and thinking about college. (Tabloids made a big deal about a photo of him smoking in public.) Blanket is quieter, less chatty with strangers, but every now and then he surprises his family with a dance move that recalls his father during the Robot days. It's Paris, though, with her searing blue eyes, who recalls Michael's complex, tortured beauty. By all accounts, she was a daddy's girl who doted on her father; in the days after his death, every time she heard his name on television, she burst into tears. After being home-schooled her whole life, with specific rules set down by Michael and a succession of nannies and tutors, she was thrust into high school with kids who had no problem mocking her father and family. "She is tough, but she's so emotionally wounded that she just couldn't take it anymore," says a family friend. In July 2013, the fifteen-year-old slit her wrists but survived the suicide attempt; after psychiatric treatment at UCLA Medical Center, the hospital where her father died, she wound up attending the Diamond Ranch Academy in Utah, chosen by Debbie Rowe and Katherine Jackson. She has since left the academy and returned to Katherine's home outside Los Angeles, where she was reported to have been dating a pro soccer player.

Members of the Jackson family are perhaps the only people in the world who insist Michael's three children look exactly like him. And that, as Randall Sullivan suggests in *Untouchable*, may be because everybody in the family realizes the kids are Michael's only true beneficiaries, and the closer they get to the kids, the closer they get to the estate's hundreds of millions. "They are [Michael's] children," Tito told a British tabloid. "Blanket is Michael's, I can tell. Those eyes don't lie. Them eyes are Michael's all over again. . . . Just because they look white doesn't mean they are not his."

After Michael died, Debbie Rowe let slip that Prince and Paris were the products of artificial insemination. That led to a worldwide quest to identify the father: *Vanity Fair* pointed out that Michael's longtime friend and Beverly Hills plastic surgeon, Arnold Klein, looked quite a bit like the two older kids. He denied it, sort of: "Once [I donated] to a sperm bank," he told CNN's Larry King. "To the best of my knowledge, I'm not the father." Other suspects include Al Malnik, Michael's former business partner in Florida, although he has strenuously denied it, and Michael's friend Mark Lester, the British child actor turned chiropractor, who once told a tabloid he saw the resemblance, but has since backed off. "I'm not interested in that," Lester says. "Michael was their father, as far as I'm concerned. It doesn't really matter, biologically, whether he was or not. He brought them up, he raised them as his own. They were his kids."

In death, Michael Jackson cleared up the other great mystery of his life: What had he actually done to his face? Sullivan and *Rolling Stone* declared Michael died without a nose—in a grotesque, final, sensational twist, according to these reports, he had just two holes for nostrils. The official autopsy report, however, contradicts that description. "Absolutely false," says Ed Winter, assistant chief of investigations for the Los Angeles County coroner's department. "He had a nose. He used to put makeup on it and stuff. It was thin. People make it sound like he had this wax nose that he'd take off at night and put on in the morning. No." He did, however, tattoo his lips red and his hairline black and adjust his eyebrows. As for more specifics about what exactly he'd done to his face, his longtime doctors were little help. Steven Hoefflin and Arnold Klein intensified their rivalry after Michael's death. Hoefflin accused Klein of "over-treating him to make money" and addicting his patient to Demerol; Klein sued Hoefflin for libel. Then, in a blunt and lengthy TMZ interview, Klein dredged up old dirt about Hoefflin and his supposed molestation of his own patients, including MJ. "He would put the time of the clocks forward and wake him up and say he did a nose job," the acid-tongued Klein declared, before accusing Hoefflin of supplying MJ with propofol during what he estimated were twenty procedures on his nose. (Hoefflin, who turned down an interview request, has denied the patient-molestation allegations and has never been charged with any wrongdoing.) Perhaps the most accurate posthumous catalog of Michael's facial surgeries appeared in *Allure*, showing Hoefflin's early "two-stage procedure" to narrow Michael's nostrils, shave his excess tip tissue, and round the tip of his nose with shaved ear cartilage. Over the years, Michael also widened his eyes, thinned his nose, tattooed his eyelash lines and eyebrows, added the chin cleft, lightened his skin, sharpened the tip of his nose, sharpened his jaw, reduced thickness in his lips, and thickened the tissue in his face. Throughout his life, he publicly owned up to only two nose procedures and the chin cleft, but that was clearly false. Michael spent much of his life breaking down barriers, of race, gender, and music. Those included the barriers of physiology.

In the years after Michael's death, two court proceedings would reveal the sad details of his final ten or fifteen years. Conrad Murray's 2011 trial for involuntary manslaughter pulled back the P. T. Barnum-style curtain on MJ's life. For the first time, the public learned the secrets of Michael's medical care, as doctors, nurses, and other medical professionals appeared on the witness stand to flesh out his struggles with painkillers, insomnia, scalp pain, and vitiligo. Murray's attorneys did not succeed in persuading jurors he was merely the fall guy for Michael's overwhelming addiction to prescription drugs. On November 20, 2011, jurors found Murray guilty of involuntary manslaughter; he served two years of a four-year sentence. "My entire approach may not have been an orthodox approach, but my intentions were good," Murray told CNN. Conrad Murray's language was eerily similar to that of all the

Dr. Feelgoods who've preyed on pop stars and besmirched the history of music. Elvis Presley's George "Dr. Nick" Nichopoulos and Brian Wilson's Eugene Landy claimed to be helping their celebrity patients, too.

In late 2012, Katherine Jackson filed a multibillion-dollar wrongful-death lawsuit against AEG Live, the promoter of his ill-fated This Is It shows, for hiring Murray and therefore committing negligence with regard to her son's medical care. The case went to trial the next year, and friends, family, and associates spent six months on the witness stand, fleshing out the medical history that Murray's trial had begun to reveal. The public finally heard from much of Michael's long roster of doctors and nurses: David Adams, Scott Saunders, David Fournier, Debbie Rowe, and others divulged thorough medical details. During this trial, e-mails surfaced from Randy Phillips, the promoter's chief executive, suggesting Michael was in far worse shape than promoters had let on as they spun the press while preparing for the shows. AEG won the case, on a 10–2 vote, because, while the jury agreed AEG had hired Conrad Murray, it believed him to be fit and competent to perform the work for which he was hired. An appeals court upheld the decision in January 2015, but as of this writing, Katherine Jackson's attorneys plan to appeal to the California Supreme Court.

Was Michael Jackson a child molester? All evidence points to no—although sleeping in bed with children and boasting of it on international television did not qualify him for the Celebrity Judgment Hall of Fame. The man had a fair trial. Most serious chroniclers of Michael Jackson, with the notable exception of Diane Dimond, come away with some version of the conclusion Ian Halperin prints in *Michael Jackson Unmasked*: "I could not find a single shred of evidence suggesting that Jackson has molested a child. In contrast, I found significant evidence demonstrating that most, if not all, of his accusers lacked any credibility." More evidence may be yet to come, however. In the years after Michael's death, James Safechuck and Wade Robson, who as boys had the water-balloon fights at Neverland and traveled with MJ on tour, accused him in graphic detail of child molestation. Robson testified unequivocally in 2005 that Michael never did anything untoward during the time they spent together—his defense of his longtime friend, along with those of Macaulay Culkin and Brett Barnes, helped attorney Thomas Mesereau win the case. But in 2013 and 2014, Robson, then Safechuck, announced they've only recently, as adults, been able to acknowledge MJ's abuse to themselves. "People can admit it when they can admit it," says Henry Gradstein, an attorney for both men. "That's how victims deal with it—they just compartmentalize it, refuse to believe it, can't believe anything was wrong with it." In May 2015, Judge Beckloff of the Los Angeles Superior Court dismissed Robson's petition to file the claim against Jackson's estate because he filed his probate claim too late. Robson plans to appeal, and two of his other claims are pending. "Wade and James should have the ability to have their claims tried to a jury," says Maryann Marzano, their attorney.

Shortly before Michael died, Jackie, Jermaine, Tito, and Marlon agreed to participate in an A&E series called *The Jacksons: A Family Dynasty*. For a family that had only obliquely referred to its dysfunction in the past, the brothers were unexpectedly open to airing at least some small portion of their conflicts on reality television. They made a record. Jermaine, the domineering prima donna, took charge and recorded his own vocals; he allied with Tito, who was happy to finish quickly and go to lunch. Then Jackie and Marlon returned to the studio, heard Jermaine's track and passive-aggressively erased it. "Jermaine's gonna be upset," Marlon said. "He's gonna go to Momma, probably." Sure enough, Jermaine erupted—it's scripted Hollywood shtick, but it captures the brothers' personalities, too.

Debbie Rowe made a deal to give Katherine permanent custody of Paris and Prince, the two children she had with Michael. One of Rowe's conditions was that Joe, who was already beginning to say creepy and borderline-aggressive things to the press about Blanket's dancing ability and how he was "watching" Paris, could see the kids only during family gatherings. Katherine brought in Michael's longtime nanny Grace Rwaramba to provide a familiar face during a crucial transition period. But Hayvenhurst was not the secluded, one-parent existence MJ's kids had known their whole lives. Suddenly they had to share space in the eleven-thousand-square-foot home with Jermaine's thirteen- and nine-year-old sons Jaafar and Jermajesty, as well as two of Randy's older kids. Also on the premises was Alejandra Oaziaza, who'd married and divorced both Jermaine and his brother Randy. She undercut Rwaramba's strict rules carried over from Michael's parenting. "Anytime Grace would say, 'Do your homework. Don't watch TV. Go to bed,' Alejandra would say, 'Oh, stay up as late as you want. Don't listen to Grace. She's not your family, I am. She's just hired help,'" said former MJ adviser Marc Schaffel, who became engaged to Rowe in spring 2014 and spent time with Michael's family. Rebbie was brought in to help with the kids, but she was too religious for them. Grace eventually fell out of favor, too. "My dad didn't like her, so he tried to, like, keep her away from us. So he sent her on errands a lot," Paris said in a deposition for the AEG trial. "He felt bad because she didn't really have a lot of money. He said she was sneaky and she wasn't an honest person and she lied a lot." It's hard to say whether that's how Michael really felt about Rwaramba, but it certainly reflected how Paris felt about her at the time.

After Jermaine's son Jaafar reportedly shot off a stun gun in the house, Katherine decided to move the kids out of Hayvenhurst. She enrolled them in the posh Buckley School and relocated to a rented, $26,000-per-month, 12,670-square-foot mansion in nearby Calabasas, where she would live with her nephew and right-hand man Trent Jackson. Paris refused to visit until recently. "It's not like it was with her father," said Brian Oxman, the Jacksons' family attorney, "and she's very disturbed by it."

Meanwhile, the Jacksons continued to battle over Michael's will. Katherine was receiving cash from the estate, including a $3,000-per-month stipend and a $115,000 family vacation in 2010, in her role as guardian of Prince, Paris, and Blanket. The rest of the Jackson family, as Michael stipulated in his will, received nothing. That was another source of tension, which blew up in July 2012, after Katherine plotted a trip to follow her sons on their Unity concert tour in a Prevost motor home MJ had bought for her. While she was traveling and out of reach, the media reported on a letter signed by Randy, Janet, Jermaine, Rebbie, and Tito that insisted Branca and McClain resign immediately as executors of MJ's estate. They called Michael's 2002 will "fake, flawed and fraudulent" and accused Branca and McClain of lying to Katherine and making unfounded promises. The siblings also said Mrs. Jackson had suffered a "mini-stroke."

That last reference scared Prince and Paris, who tweeted, "I am going to clarify right now that what has been said about my grandmother is a rumor and nothing has happened, she is completely fine," then added, in a pointed tweet to her uncle Randy, "hello dear FAMILY member I don't appreciate you telling people things that aren't true thank you very much." It turned out Katherine was in fine health, staying at an Arizona resort and spa called Miraval, worrying mostly about her inoperable hotel-room TV. While she sat around playing Scramble with Friends on her iPad, her family frantically searched for her, as did her new attorney, Perry Sanders of Colorado Springs. The last thing Sanders needed was for a court to decide Jackson was somehow unfit as guardian of MJ's children. He booked a last-minute flight to Tucson to meet with Katherine. He didn't find her, although her associates convinced him she was okay.

Later, at the new family house in Calabasas, two SUVs, carrying Randy, Janet, Jermaine, and several of Michael's nieces and nephews, pulled abruptly through the front security gates, breaking a metal barrier in the process. As Jermaine distracted the security guards, Janet went for Paris and Randy approached Prince. Sheriff's deputies eventually pulled up and talked the siblings into leaving. "Gotta love fam," Paris tweeted. When Katherine's hotel power finally returned, she learned on TV she had been abducted and in ill health. Upon her return, she pretended the whole thing hadn't happened.

The Jackson brothers' Unity tour proceeded, ironic name and all, stopping October 20, 2012, at the Beau Rivage casino, a few blocks away from Jackson Street in Biloxi, Mississippi. The concert was small, just a showroom containing a few hundred fans. But the brothers' harmonies still sounded sweet. They acknowledged Michael's absence with a lengthy photo montage. They began with their anthem "Can You Feel It," and rushed through "Shake Your Body (Down to the Ground)," "ABC," and Michael's own "Wanna Be Startin' Somethin'." Jermaine was the focal point, which he seemed to enjoy, his high voice smoother, more romantic, and less straining than it had sounded on "I Want You Back" so many years ago. Tito played the familiar Motown guitar lines in his sparkly costume and bowler hat. Jackie twirled. The show lasted an hour and a half, and nobody attempted to do the moonwalk. Marlon was the only Jackson who really danced. It was a pleasant concert of R&B oldies.

Afterward, in a back hallway adjacent to the casino showroom, the four brothers made brief small talk about the show. Somebody started humming "Hold On, I'm Comin'," the old Sam and Dave hit from Stax Records, Motown's rival label in the sixties, and the rest of the brothers joined in. They sang softly for a few seconds before the elevator arrived to take them up to their rooms at the casino. The Jacksons, for once, were in spontaneous harmony.

Nothing in the entirety of pop music captures the same youthful spirit of the Jackson 5's "I Want You Back." No dance song opens with as much cathartic tension-and-release as "Don't Stop 'til You Get Enough." The

MJ performance of "Billie Jean" during the *Motown 25* broadcast lives forever in a billion YouTube links. All of MJ's short films are viewable for free, and it's easy to kill a day reliving the pointed cartoon playfulness of "Leave Me Alone," the cluttered insanity of "Black or White," the grace and showmanship of "Smooth Criminal," and the white-T-shirt sexiness of "Remember the Time." And while critics have instructed us *Off the Wall* and *Thriller* were the essential MJ albums, *Bad, Dangerous* and even most of *HIStory* and *Invincible* show Michael as a grown-up, airing his fears and ambitions just as Bob Dylan's *Blood on the Tracks*, Bruce Springsteen's *Tunnel of Love*, and Madonna's *Ray of Light* had done for them late in their careers. In her elaborate, eloquent defense of MJ's *Dangerous*, Susan Fast quotes a *New Yorker* critic: "One of the cruelties of stardom is that you never know when you've reached your apogee. For Jackson, decline set in almost as soon as *Thriller* fell out of the No. 1 spot, in April 1984." Fast responds: "Just so we're clear, that would mean tracks like 'Man in the Mirror' are part of a decline. Okay, got it."

Michael spent his early years trapped in a constrictive frame of reference, growing up in segregated Gary, Indiana, surrounded by an abusive father, an enabling mother, and mocking brothers. He would use his talents to expand his boundaries to an almost impossible degree of freedom and creativity—he would swing too far, succumbing at times to megalomania, surrounding himself with sycophants, even persuading a succession of reputable doctors to push their legal and ethical rules to accommodate his whims. The true creative decline of Michael Jackson came around 2001, when he applied this no-limits philosophy to his lifestyle but was no longer using it to pioneer music, dance steps, or shows. He returned to these things too late, when he was in questionable physical condition, pushing himself further than an out-of-shape fifty-year-old could be pushed. For nearly three decades, he was supernaturally graceful, the rare show-business renaissance man who could sing, dance, and write songs. But nobody can sustain such youthful glory forever.

"You got little kids that run around and try to sing, but yo, this boy right here, he was just straight *golden*, man. He was a *genius*," says Ghostface Killah, the Wu-Tang Clan rapper whose solo songs have sampled MJ tracks. "When God gives you a gift like that for the whole world to love you, it's something *special*. He was popular almost like how the *prophets* was popular, because he had the whole world fucking fainting at his feet. But his death was cut at fifty years old. So there's a balance to things. Okay, he fucked around and died at fifty, but he put all this work in, and was the best fucking singer ever on planet Earth. Motherfuckas fainted at him, crying at concerts, all through Europe and Africa and Asia. All that love that God blessed him with, it had to equal out."

ACKNOWLEDGMENTS

It isn't easy for people close to Michael Jackson to publicly discuss their relationships with him—many signed nondisclosures, are writing their own books, have been burned in the press, or don't have the energy to return to the thicket that was MJ's life. But I'm grateful to the 450-some sources who shared memories and insight, and particularly wish to recognize those who have since died, including Deke Richards, David Braun, Bobby Martin, Louis Johnson (the bass player), George Duke, Ricky Lawson, Mike Merkow, and Clarence Burke.

More than twenty potential sources asked to be paid for interviews. I refused all such requests, although I bought Ronnie Rancifer a beer on Halloween 2012 at the American Legion in Hobart, Indiana. (Or maybe he bought me one—can't remember. Crazy night.)

Thanks to my original Scribner editor, Brant Rumble, for his belief in this idea and faith in its implementation. John Glynn shepherded it to publication with equal skill and enthusiasm. (Thanks also to Nan Graham, Colin Harrison, and Brian Belfiglio of Scribner for important support.) My agent, David Dunton, is a great and kind man who understands music and authors. My previous agent, Dan Lazar, circulated an earlier MJ proposal and deserves credit and gratitude for turning me into an author in the first place.

Many insightful people were crucial to the analysis, including dance expert Mark Allan Davis, music-business guru Steve Greenberg (who made important corrections and did a lengthy interview), cultural critic Deena Weinstein, and MJ-fanatic-turned-artist-manager David Russell. Roslyn Raney translated Joe Jackson's book from German to English for a fair price and did a wonderful job. Old friend Larry Mills didn't hesitate to share his connections. *Rolling Stone* colleague David Browne was available any time, day or night, for insight and talking me off the ledge. Also providing advice, contacts, etc.: Rob McGibbon ("cheers!"), Ron Doyle, Jimmy Calinksi, Brian Hiatt, James Bailey, Joel Warner, Larry Solters, Eve Becker, Julie McDonald, Leland Rucker, David Gardner, Glenn Gamboa, Peg Schoon of Indiana University Northwest, and Patrice Cook of the Amite County, Mississippi, Courthouse. My brother Mark joined me on a crucial LA research trip (and funded it!), and Jonathan Boonin arranged an incredible last-minute Las Vegas trip to see Cirque du Soleil's *ONE* show and didn't complain when I rewrote for three days in our hotel room. Thanks to the magazine and newspaper editors who allowed me to continue making a living during this three-year project. And thanks to Mark and Doug for teaching me everything I know.

I aspired to the humor and storytelling of Leigh Montville's *Evel: The High-Flying Life of Evel Knievel: American Showman, Daredevil, and Legend* and the thoroughness and precision of Tim Riley's *Lennon: The Man, the Myth, the Music—the Definitive Life*. It helped that both authors were available for counseling. Robert Hilburn, author of *Johnny Cash: The Life*, who covered MJ for years in the *LA Times*, preached, too, via e-mail.

Finally, I'd like to recognize my father, Morton P. Knopper, who passed away before I could give him a copy of my first book, and my mother, Dorothy Knopper, who was diagnosed with Alzheimer's disease before this one. I know exactly how they would react: "We don't understand any of the material—we like Neil Diamond, Barbra Streisand and *The Sound of Music*!—but we love how you write." I miss them saying that.

NOTES

Unless otherwise noted, all descriptions of performances come from YouTube clips.

PROLOGUE

1 *"Let's get out of here" and Emerson High School strike details*: James B. Lane, *City of the Century: A History of Gary, Indiana* (Bloomington: Indiana University Press, 1978), p. 142; author interview with James Lane.

1 *"Strike!" and "We won't go back"*: "May Settle School Strike Today," *Gary Post-Tribune*, September 28, 1927, p. 15.

1 *Strikers driving in circles and honking horns*: "600 'E' Pupils Go on Strike and Parade," *Gary Post-Tribune*, September 26, 1927, p. 1.

1 *'E' STRIKERS VOTE TO REMAIN 'OUT'*: *Gary Post-Tribune*, September 29, 1927, p. 1.

1 *Wirt miscalculated*: Lane, *City of the Century*, p. 142.

1 *Fifty of three thousand African-American students relocating due to space, Emerson receiving eighteen*: "Mayor Calls School Strike Parley," *Gary Post-Tribune*, September 27, 1927, p. 1.

1 *Screening African-American students for intelligence, manners, light skin*: Lane, *City of the Century*, p. 142.

2 *Wirt insisted segregation had no place in Gary*: *Gary Post-Tribune*, September 27, 1927, p. 1.

2 *"The strikers are firm in their belief"*: *Gary Post-Tribune*, September 29, 1927, p. 15.

2 *Wirt's compromise and demand, including $15,000 temporary school, $600,000 permanent school, and "excused absences"*: "Strike Off; All Happy!," *Gary Post-Tribune*, September 30, 1927, pp. 1–2.

2 *Early Gary history*: Lane, *City of the Century*, pp. 3–4, 11–12, 15, 28–29, 31.

2 *Gary Land Company built 506 houses, 16.7 cents-an-hour laborers*: Raymond A. Mohl and Neil Betten, *Steel City: Urban and Ethnic Patterns in Gary, Indiana, 1906–1950* (Teaneck, NJ: Holmes & Meier, 1986), p. 18.

2 *fourteen dollars per month:* Edward Greer, *Big Steel: Black Politics and Corporate Power in Gary, Indiana* (New York: Monthly Review Press, 1979), p. 69.

2 *Garbage was everywhere:* Mohl and Betten, *Steel City,* p. 23.

2 *Two Garys, including Binzenhof pub, two hundred saloons, Bucket of Blood, Patch, or the Other Gary:* Lane, *City of the Century,* p. 34.

2 *Roosevelt High School:* "New $500,000 Negro School Is Dedicated," *Gary Post-Tribune,* April 20, 1931, p. 1.

3 *Savings, money from wife's stepfather, refrigerator, stove, bed:* Joseph Jackson, *Die Jacksons* (Munich: Random House Germany, 2004), pp. 53–54.

3 *MJ-Rupert Wainwright exchange:* Author interview with Rupert Wainwright.

4 *"With These Words":* Michael Jackson, liner notes, *HIStory: Past, Present and Future, Book 1* (Epic/Sony, 1995).

CHAPTER I

5 *Details of Joe Jackson's job at Inland Steel:* Author interview with Jimmy Calinski (former coworker); Inland Steel photo collection from the same time period at Calumet Regional Archives, Indiana University Northwest.

5 *"It was said":* Jermaine Jackson, *You Are Not Alone: Michael Through a Brother's Eyes* (New York: Touchstone/Simon & Schuster, 2011), p. 23.

5 *Crane operator wasn't especially tough work:* Calinski interview; author interview with Guadalupe Guajardo (former coworker).

5 *Show-business dreams:* Joseph Jackson, *Die Jacksons,* pp. 43–44.

5 *six million in Great Migration:* history.com/topics/black-history/great-migration.

6 *Joe Jackson birthdate:* "Joe Jackson Turns 80," *Chicago Defender,* July 29, 2008, p. 22, refers to Jackson celebrating his eightieth birthday at a "swank" club with young women pressing against him in 2008; other sources, including Katherine Jackson with Richard Wiseman, *The Jacksons: My Family* (New York: St. Martin's Press, 1990), p. 14, say 1929, and Joe in *Die Jacksons* refers to growing up during the Depression, "1929–1935."

6 *Dermott and "light-skinned and tall":* Joseph Jackson, *Die Jacksons,* pp. 9, 22.

6 *Family history, including July, Gina, Nero, and three hundred farm acres:* Ibid., pp. 9–11.

6 *Amite County and "He could probably pass":* Author interview with Thomas Jackson (a descendant of Nero Jackson's girlfriend).

6 *Nero and family leasing land to oilmen for $200 a year:* Record of Oil and Gas Lease, February 27, 1920, Amite County, Mississippi, signed by Nero and Emmaline Jackson, document provided by Thomas Jackson.

6 *Nero and his heirs sold the land during the Depression:* Letter from Centreville, Mississippi, attorney Gene Horne to Thomas Jackson, December 8, 1997.

6 *Nero's death in 1924 and worth $100 million today:* Joseph Jackson, *Die Jacksons,* pp. 12–13.

6 *Nero's youngest son with Emmaline:* Ibid.

6 *Samuel Jackson biography and six children:* Joseph Jackson, *Die Jacksons,* pp. 13–14, 23.

7 *"My mom put the spanking on me":* Author interview with Martin Luther Jackson.

7 *Teacher beatings:* Joseph Jackson, *Die Jacksons,* p. 22, and Jermaine Jackson, *You Are Not Alone,* p. 25.

7   "I was so scared" and Verna Mae: Joseph Jackson, Die Jacksons, pp. 22–24.

7   Joe's age at Verna Mae's death and "As far as my understanding goes": Jermaine Jackson, You Are Not Alone, p. 24.

7   Samuel and Chrystal split: Joseph Jackson, Die Jacksons, p. 31, and Jermaine Jackson, You Are Not Alone, p. 26.

8   "When I stopped crying" and "I constantly traveled back and forth": Joseph Jackson, Die Jacksons, pp. 31, 38–39.

8   Joe courting Katherine: Joseph Jackson, Die Jacksons, pp. 45, 50.

8   Katherine birthdate and family details: Katherine Jackson, The Jacksons, pp. 8, 16.

8   Ernest Tubb and Hank Williams: Katherine Jackson, "How Do You Raise Nine Rockers? Very Carefully," People, November/December 1984, p. 12.

8   Grayson and Stanwyck, saxophone players, and five-man blues band: Katherine Jackson, The Jacksons, pp. 10–13, 16.

9   Prominence of Jimmy Reed and blues in Gary: Martin Luther Jackson interview, and author interviews with Reynaud D. Jones and Wilton Crump (a veteran Gary singer and bandleader).

9   "Tutti Frutti," "Not only did I think": Katherine Jackson, The Jacksons, pp. 14–15, 17.

9   "We have the floor to ourselves" and brown Buick: Jermaine Jackson, You Are Not Alone, pp. 21, 30.

9   Kids' birthdates and Sears: Katherine Jackson, The Jacksons, pp. 15–16, 18–20, 34.

9   Twenty dollars per week and beans and soup: Jermaine Jackson, You Are Not Alone, pp. 19, 23. His parents' combined weekly pay was $75.

10 "we ate so much spaghetti": Ibid.

10 Beds and "It wasn't much bigger than a garage": Katherine Jackson, The Jacksons, p. 29.

10 Joe difficult to really know: Michael Jackson, Moonwalk (New York: Harmony Books, 1988), pp. 15–17; Jermaine Jackson, You Are Not Alone, pp. 25–26.

10 Blast-furnace details and "It was hot as hell": Joseph Jackson, Die Jacksons, pp. 42–43.

10 Jacket with L-shaped rip, passenger van, and tacos: Guajardo interview.

10 "I was strict": Katherine Jackson, The Jacksons, p. 39.

10 "When he arrived home,": Jermaine Jackson, You Are Not Alone, pp. 30–31.

11 Description of Joe's face: Paraphrased from ibid., p. 25, and photos.

11 "Clean the house," and ten "whops": Ibid., pp. 30–31.

11 MJ and mouse: Ibid., p. 32.

11 MJ and candy and throwing objects at Joe: Katherine Jackson, The Jacksons, pp. 24, 26–27.

11 Joe dragging and spanking MJ: Living with Michael Jackson (Granada Television, 2003).

11 "has always been something of a mystery": Michael Jackson, Moonwalk, pp. 17–18.

11 iron cords and "Stop it!": MJ: Living with Michael Jackson.

11 "Joseph" for respect: Jermaine Jackson, You Are Not Alone, p. 18.

11 "I whipped him with a switch": Joe Jackson interview by Louis Theroux in BBC documentary Louis, Martin & Michael (November 2003).

12 Baptist faith, church minister, and Jehovah's Witnesses: Katherine Jackson, The Jacksons, pp. 37–38.

12 Katherine continues knocking on doors: Katherine Jackson interview, The Oprah Winfrey Show (ABC, November 2010).

12 *MJ knocked on doors into adulthood*: Author interview with Ed Eckstine.

12 *Packs of beer*: Jermaine Jackson, *You Are Not Alone*, p. 28.

12 *"The Jacksons didn't come out" and Jackie and Reynaud on baseball team*: Jones interview.

13 *Joe playing Reed and Walker*: Ibid.

13 *Tito broke a string and "WHO'S BEEN MESSING WITH MY GUITAR?"*: Jermaine Jackson, *You Are Not Alone*, pp. 33–34.

13 *"He took care of me for it"*: Steve Knopper, "Tito Talks About Jacksons Getting Back in the Groove: Indiana natives playing shows for first time since '84," *Chicago Tribune*, June 21, 2012, p. 11.

13 *Standard version*: Joseph Jackson, *Die Jacksons*, pp. 65–66.

13 *Evolution of blues into soul and how it played out in Gary and Chicago*: Crump interview; author interview with Casinski; Jones interview; Martin Luther Jackson interview.

13 *Jones's version and "Everywhere you went"*: Jones interview.

14 *Epics, MJ, Marlon joining, "He wouldn't stop," and other early rehearsal details*: Jones interview.

14 *New red guitar*: Katherine Jackson, *The Jacksons*, p. 50.

14 ADULT AND TEEN TALENT WANTED: *Gary Post-Tribune*, August 4, 1965, page unknown, provided by Evelyn LaHaie.

14 *Two hundred performers and description of audition*: Author interview with Evelyn LaHaie.

15 *No. 55, "terrific," "AA++"*: From Evelyn LaHaie's original notes, provided by LaHaie.

15 *"The very minute I saw that little child"*: LaHaie interview.

15 *Name change, Tiny Tots' Back to School Jamboree, and August 14, 1965*: LaHaie interview.

15 *"All I remember"*: Jermaine Jackson, *You Are Not Alone*, p. 56.

15 *Bobbie Rose Jackson suggestion*: Katherine Jackson, *The Jacksons*, pp. 51–52.

15 *Roosevelt High, Masque and Gavel, and front-row balcony seats*: Jones interview.

15 *"My Girl" and "I Got You"*: Jermaine Jackson, *You Are Not Alone*, p. 57.

15 *"Barefootin'" and MJ flinging off shoes*: Katherine Jackson, *The Jacksons*, p. 54.

15 *September 1965*: Roosevelt High School yearbook photos, shared by Crump.

16 *"That was the performance"*: Carl Protho e-mail.

16 *"Jermaine had a few solo parts"*: Author interview with Benny Dorsey.

16 *"Overall, you did good"*: Jermaine Jackson, *You Are Not Alone*, p. 58.

16 *"My dad says you can't come in"*: Jones interview.

16 *"These boys are going to take me" and rehearsal details*: Katherine Jackson with Richard Wiseman, *The Jacksons: My Family* (New York: St. Martin's Press, 1990), pp. 55–56.

17 *"Sometimes we'd want to, you know, slack off"*: Lynn Van Matre, "Michael's maturity, at 13 going on 14," *Chicago Tribune*, July 23, 1972, p. J5.

17 *MJ's leverage and "try to laud him on"*: Katherine Jackson, *The Jacksons*, pp. 56–57.

17 *"His lack of singing ability"*: Ibid.

18 *Milford Hite moved, Leonard Gault, and "Their voices blended together"*: Author interview with Earl Gault.

18 *"All the neighborhood kids"*: Author interview with Keith Jackson.

18 *"They would rehearse"*: Author interview with Johnnie Gault.

18 *Tapping into savings*: Katherine Jackson, *The Jacksons*, pp. 55–56.

18 *"Mom had some doubts"*: Michael Jackson, *Moonwalk* (New York: Harmony Books, 1988), p. 36.

18 *"Gary was called Chocolate City"*: Author interview with Maurice Rodgers.

19 *Club names, Jr. Walker, and Tyrone Davis*: Author interview with Wilton Crump; Bob Kostanczuk, "Breakthrough days," *Gary Post-Tribune*, June 28, 2009, p. A8; Michael Gonzalez, "'The crowd just loved them,'" *Gary Post-Tribune*, June 27, 2009, p. A5.

19 *"Set-up" tray and Elks details*: Crump interview.

19 *One-dollar fried tacos*: Johnnie Gault interview.

19 *Eight dollars per gig*: Katherine Jackson, *The Jacksons*, p. 59.

19 *Five sets per night and "We were playing"*: Michael Jackson, *Moonwalk*, pp. 36–37.

19 *"Skinny Legs and All" and crawling*: Ibid., p. 37; author interviews with Ben Brown and Jessye Williams.

20 *Deals with the cops*: Williams interview.

20 *Summer 1966, Winslow and Old Arcadia Hall*: Jermaine Jackson, *You Are Not Alone*, p. 66.

20 *Fried chicken and pork and beans*: Earl Gault interview.

20 *"Vigorously rubbing his cheeks" and "Just tired"*: Jermaine Jackson, *You Are Not Alone*, p. 66.

20 *red soil, and "Michael used to like nature-type stuff"*: Earl Gault interview.

21 *Johnny Jackson recommendation*: Shirley E. Cartman, *A Teacher Remembers the Jacksons* (Encino, CA: Gabriel Publishing, 1987), p. 31.

21 *"A bubbly, animated little guy" and "the best drummer around"*: Jermaine Jackson, *You Are Not Alone*, p. 66.

21 *Publicity photo*: Michael Jackson, *Moonwalk*, p. 25.

21 *"We were brothers"*: Michael Sangiacomo, *Gary Post-Tribune*, April 21, 1988, p. B5.

21 *Joe dragged Michael to studios for auditions*: Author interview with William (Billy) McGregor; Jake Austen, "The Jackson Find," *Chicago Reader*, September 10, 2009, pp. 17–20, 22.

21 *"Tobacco Road"*: Ibid.

21 *One-derful details, George Leaner's wariness, Jacksons showing up at 5 p.m. daily, "transform a talented teen band," and "Big Boy"*: McGregor interview; author interviews with Ernie Leaner, Larry Blasingaine, and Otis Clay; Austen, "The Jackson Find," pp. 17–20, 22.

22 *Keith called 2300 Jackson Street*: Austen, "The Jackson Find," pp. 17–20, 22.

22 *"It was tough" and Steeltown*: Rodgers interview.

22 *Cartman invited Keith to her house and "The Scrub" and "Lonely Heart"*: Cartman, *Teacher Remembers the Jacksons*, p. 43.

22 *MJ high-jump*: Austen, "The Jackson Find," pp. 17–20, 22.

22 *November 1967*: Ibid.; Steve Walsh, "'King of Tort' faces string of lawsuits," *Gary Post-Tribune*, April 28, 2002, p. A6.

22 *Morrison Sound Studio, "Most sessions were done late" and relocation to black neighborhood*: Author interview with Jerry Mundo.

23 *"Very quiet, well-mannered kids"*: Author interview with Delroy Bridgeman.

23 *Session details and 10 or 11* P.M.: Mundo interview.

23 *Replacement vocals*: Bridgeman interview.

23 *January 31, 1968*: Austen, "The Jackson Find," pp. 17–20, 22.

23 *WVON, one thousand watts, and first station to cater to black listeners*: Barbara Sherlock, "E. Rodney Jones, 75: Legend of Chicago's 'golden era,'" *Chicago Tribune*, January 9, 2004, p. 2C.13.

23 *Jesse Jackson called WVON*: Don Terry, "Raising the Voice," *Chicago Tribune*, March 19, 2006, Magazine Section 10.14.

23 *"If you got a hit on WVON"*: Author interview with Lucky Cordell.

24 *Atlantic Records*: Bob Kostanczuk, "Recordings for sale: Selling a slice of history," *Gary Post-Tribune*, April 30, 2009, p. C1.

24 *"I honestly heard something"*: Cordell interview.

24 *Rancifer and Jacksons*: Author interview with Roderick "Ronnie" Rancifer.

24 *Regal details*: June Sawyers, "When the Regal was something special," *Chicago Tribune*, October 4, 1987, p. H10.

24 *Crystal chandeliers, silk drapes, and Italian marble*: Clovis E. Semmes, *The Regal Theater and Black Culture* (New York: Palgrave MacMillan, 2006), p. 3.

25 *"You'd go in there"*: Rancifer interview.

25 *Five Stairsteps and basketball*: Author interview with Clarence Burke.

25 *"Michael was a very watchful guy"*: Rancifer interview.

25 *Apollo Theater*: Ted Fox, *Showtime at the Apollo* (New York: Holt, Rinehart and Winston, 1983), pp. 286, 288; Jack Schiffman, *Uptown: The Story of Harlem's Apollo Theater* (New York: Cowles Book, 1971), pp. 8–18, 21–22.

26 *"I carefully watched" and dusty curtains*: Michael Jackson, *Moonwalk*, p. 47.

26 *May 1968*: Advertisement and story in *Amsterdam News*, May 18, 1968, n.p. Posted at j5collector.blogspot.com/2010/05/jackson-5-at-apollo-may-24-30-1968.html.

26 *"I don't remember what I told him"*: J. Randy Taraborrelli, *Michael Jackson: The Magic, The Madness, The Whole Story 1958–2009* (New York: Grand Central Publishing, 2009), p. 38.

26 *Vibrations stealing dance steps*: Author interview with Carl Fisher.

27 *"Everybody was ranting and raving" and "Right there, at the Apollo"*: Author interview with Teddy Young.

27 *July 1968 at Regal*: Adrian Grant, *Michael Jackson: A Visual Documentary 1958–2009: The Tribute Edition* (London: Omnibus Press, 1994/2009), p. 9. I confirmed many dates with this source.

28 *Eddie Patterson recollections and "Michael was like a little magic kid"*: Author interview with Eddie Patterson.

CHAPTER 2

29 *Snakepit description*: Nelson George, *Where Did Our Love Go?* (New York: St. Martin's Press, 1985), p. 112.

29 *Worn spot*: From Motown Museum tour, Detroit, Michigan.

29 *"He wouldn't let himself get away," "Michael, this is advanced," and Joe hitting MJ*: Author interview with Ed Wolfrum. Bobby Taylor says the hitting incident

never happened; Motown arranger Paul Riser, who was there, doesn't recall but vouches for Wolfrum; Joe Jackson and all Jackson 5 members refused interview requests.

30 *"If you're going to deal with it"* and *"I certainly morally couldn't leave it alone"*: Ibid.

30 *"I once pulled a gun"*: David Ritz, liner notes, Jackson 5, *Soulsation!: 25th Anniversary Collection* (Motown, 1995), p. 35.

30 *Taylor's first call was to Seltzer*: Declaration of Ralph Seltzer, *Toriano Jackson, et al., vs. Motown Record Corp., et al.*, Superior Court of the State of California, March 5, 1976.

30 *"I had a reluctance"* and *"terrific"*: Author interview with Ralph Seltzer.

31 *"Oh, no you don't,"* Dick Scott, video camera, and eighth floor: Berry Gordy Jr., *To Be Loved: The Music, the Magic, the Memories of Motown* (New York: Warner Books, 1994), p. 279.

31 *"Uh, Mr. Gordy"*: Ibid., p. 281; Jermaine tells a variation in his book.

31 *July 26, 1968, and one and a half or two hours*: *Toriano Jackson vs. Motown*, March 5, 1976.

32 *Joe's argument and Seltzer made a show*: J. Randy Taraborrelli, *Michael Jackson: The Magic, The Madness, The Whole Story 1958–2009* (New York: Grand Central Publishing, 2009), pp. 44–45.

32 *"Most of our artists"* and *"I didn't have gigantic respect"*: Seltzer interview.

32 *Gordy let Taylor take over the Jacksons' career and MJ singing like an adult*: Ritz, Jackson 5, *Soulsation!*, pp. 29–33.

32 *Four-hour drive, mattress and sleeping bags and "projecting"*: Jermaine Jackson, *You Are Not Alone: Michael Through a Brother's Eyes* (New York: Touchstone/Simon & Schuster, 2011), pp. 97–98.

33 *"He got it"*: Ritz, Jackson 5, *Soulsation!*, p. 36.

33 *Steeltown contractual issues*: Seltzer declaration, *Toriano Jackson vs. Motown*, March 5, 1976.

33 *They continued performing and club names*: Jermaine Jackson, *You Are Not Alone*, p. 98.

33 *"How in the world"*: Brenda Holloway interview, *Michael Jackson: The Life of an Icon* (David Gest Productions, 2011).

33 *"DIANA ROSS!"*: Jermaine Jackson, *You Are Not Alone*, p. 95.

33 *"We was quite nervous"*: Tito Jackson interview, *Michael Jackson: The Life of an Icon*.

33 *Gordy and boxing*: Gordy, *To Be Loved*, p. 49.

34 *Supremes, Temptations, Holland-Dozier-Holland, Motown problems, Gordy's first LA home, group Gordy could control*: Gerald Posner, *Motown: Music, Money, Sex, and Power* (New York: Random House, 2002), pp. 182–85, 205–7, 227, 234, 242–43.

35 *"Their music was not the R&B"*: Author interview with Martha Reeves.

35 *"They thought the West Coast"*: Author interview with Clay McMurray.

35 *"Berry was very, very direct"*: Author interview with Paul Riser.

35 *Sound Factory*: Author interview with Deke Richards.

35 *$105 per session*: Author interview with Gene Pello.

35 *Freedom to improvise*: Author interviews with Louie Shelton and David T. Walker.

36 *"The Funk Brothers were all jazz musicians"*: Author interview with Don Peake.

36 *"All we needed was a hit"*: Nelson George, *The Michael Jackson Story* (New York: Dell, 1984), p. 54.

36 *Jacksons moved to LA in August 1969*: Katherine Jackson with Richard Wiseman, *The Jacksons: My Family* (New York: St. Martin's Press, 1990), p. 67; *Toriano Jackson vs. Motown*, March 5, 1976; Michael Sangiacomo, "Reflected Glory: Jacksons' fame, fortune, attract those who knew them when Gary was home," *Gary Post-Tribune*, April 21, 1988, p. B5.

36 *Gladys Knight, "I Wanna Be Free," Joe Sample glissando, and "Don't get on the plane,"*: Author interview with Suzee Ikeda.

36 *"Direct it towards kids"*: Freddie Perren quoted in George, *The Michael Jackson Story*, p. 61.

37 *Make the Jackson 5 sound like themselves*: Nelson George, *Thriller: The Musical Life of Michael Jackson* (New York: Da Capo Press, 2010), p. 33.

37 *"The writers were different"*: Riser interview.

37 *Richards recognized the Jackson 5's versatility, $10,000 session, and "I had to stop it"*: Richards interview.

37 *"More than a tutor"*: Rabbi Shmuley Boteach, *The Michael Jackson Tapes: A Tragic Icon Reveals His Soul in Intimate Conversation* (New York: Vanguard Press, 2009), p. 96.

37 *3:02 P.M.*: Richards interview.

38 CALL PAPA JOE: Deke Richards, liner notes, Jackson 5, *Come and Get It: The Rare Pearls* (Motown/Hip-O Select, 2012), p. 19.

38 *He never called, Jackie's stern hand, Three Stooges hijinks, and "When you've got one [song]"*: Richards interview.

38 *Studio and park*: Author visit to 4317 Romaine Street, former Motown studio that is now the West Hollywood Maintenance Building.

38 *"They just felt comfortable"*: Author interview with Russ Terrana.

38 *Jackson 5 royalty rates: Toriano Jackson vs. Motown*, March 5, 1976.

38 *"Just about everyone got ripped off"*: Posner, *Motown*, p. 212.

39 *Operation Crime Alert and 11 percent crime increase*: James B. Lane, *City of the Century: A History of Gary, Indiana* (Bloomington: Indiana University Press, 1978), p. 295.

39 *Tito held at gunpoint*: Katherine Jackson, *The Jacksons*, p. 65.

39 *"Everyone down!"*: Jermaine Jackson, *You Are Not Alone*, p. 85.

39 *"Joseph did rule"*: *The Jacksons: A Family Dynasty* (A&E, 2009).

39 *Dodge Maxivan, drive to LA, Santa Monica Boulevard, and Hollywood Motel*: Katherine Jackson, *The Jacksons*, p. 68.

39 *"Which was nothing special either"*: Joseph Jackson, *Die Jacksons* (Munich: Random House Germany, 2004), p. 110.

39 *1601 Queens Road: Toriano Jackson vs. Motown*, March 5, 1976.

39 *Fairfax High School and Susan and Sherry*: Author interview with Susan Jackson and Sherry Danchik.

39 *Gardner Street Elementary*: Ian Lovett, "Elementary School Reclaims Link to King of Pop," *New York Times*, October 31, 2010, p. A21.

40 *"We're from Gary"*: Susan Jackson and Danchik interview.

40 *Hippodrome, Hollywood sign, San Francisco, Disneyland, cannonballs, Gordy's home, "all white and bright," and Motown hype*: Jermaine Jackson, *You Are Not Alone*, pp. 100–2.

40 *"I Want You Back" at No. 90 and building to No. 1 in January 1970*: Adrian Grant, *Michael Jackson: A Visual Documentary 1958–2009: The Tribute Edition* (London: Omnibus Press, 1994/2009), p. 11.

40 *"People responded viscerally"*: Touré, "Black Super Hero: African-American artists and intellectuals, from Jay-Z to Henry Louis Gates, weigh in on Jackson's legacy," *Michael by the Editors of Rolling Stone* (New York: HarperCollins, 2009), p. 152.

40 *"Every host was a giant star"*: Author interview with William O. Harbach.

41 *"1-2-3," Richards's arguments with Gordy, and "Sit down, girl!"*: Richards interview.

42 *469 tracks and 174 released: Jackson vs. Motown.* Ikeda confirmed details of tracks, including lack of vocals and Lulu, Supremes, and Sly Stone covers.

42 *"God, Deke"*: Richards interview.

43 *Jackie playing tambourine*: Ikeda interview. (Sandra Crouch, who played tambourine on most Jackson 5 sessions, diplomatically begs to differ: "I did, but if it helps, it's okay.")

43 *Elgin Baylor, attendance figures, and $105,000 gross*: "The Jackson 5 Break Concert Attendance Records in Two Cities," *Soul*, July 27, 1970, p. 16.

43 *Hollywood Bowl attendance*: Leroy Robinson, "Jackson Five Performs at the Hollywood Bowl," *Los Angeles Times*, August 24, 1971, p. E10.

43 *Offers jumping from $2,000 to $25,000*: Gordy, *To Be Loved*, p. 287.

43 *March 1971 and eight thousand square feet*: Grant deed for 4641 Hayvenhurst Avenue, Encino, California, County of Los Angeles, March 1, 1971.

43 *$250,000*: George, *Michael Jackson Story*, p. 74.

44 *Earle Hagen, house description, and dogs*: Jermaine Jackson, *You Are Not Alone*, pp. 141–43.

44 *Birds and pets*: Walter Burrell, "Michael Jackson: Now 17, quietest J-5 plots his future," *Soul*, May 10, 1976, pp. 2–3.

44 *Johnny Jackson and Rancifer drifting away and Sunset Strip*: Author interview with Roderick Rancifer.

44 *"I came home one night"*: Ibid.

44 *"Anybody see my boa constrictor?"*: Pello interview.

44 *Walton School and "liberal attitude"*: Jermaine Jackson, *You Are Not Alone*, p. 143.

45 *Chevy Malibu, wax museum, skipping classes, "It was like we had a groupie," Schwab's Pharmacy, "All Michael did," and other Merkow quotes and vignettes*: Author interview with Mike Merkow.

45 *New van and Datsun 240Z*: Jermaine Jackson, *You Are Not Alone*, p. 142. (Jermaine refers to a "Ford Kombi," but the iconic Kombi vans were actually Volkswagens.)

46 *"I don't know" and "When you had a falling-out"*: Merkow interview.

46 *"As they got bigger"*: Susan Jackson interview.

46 *"And this one had to have"*: Danchik interview.

46 *Rehearsal rooms and "make it fat"*: Rancifer interview.

46 *Tom Jones and Jermaine as best singer*: "What's Jackie's Secret Ambition?," *Soul*, June 15, 1970, p. 1.

46 *Tito likes Ernie Banks*: "Toriano Jackson: His Many Moods," *Soul*, June 29, 1970, p. 1.

46 *"Sometimes he doesn't know"*: "Marlon Jackson: To Know Him Is to Love Him," *Soul*, July 27, 1970, pp. 1–3.

46 *"Good group" and "See, it's not copying"*: "Keeping Up with Michael Jackson," *Right On!*, November 1972, p. 23.

47 *Boston Garden, Pinto, and Blanket*: Rancifer interview.

47 *"When we got to the venue"*: Bill Dahl, *Motown: The Golden Years* (Iola, WI: Krause Publications, 2001), p. 89.

47 *Jermaine lost hair, MJ lost a shoe, rooftop concert, scarf, and "They were pulling"*: Rhetta Nickerson, "Hair-pulling, choking and knives: Europe greets the Jackson 5," *Soul*, January 15, 1973, p. 2.

47 *Roses in Japan*: "Japanese audience is thrilled with Jackson 5," *Chicago Defender*, June 23, 1973, p. 23; Judy Spiegelman, "Jackson family journeys to Japan," *Soul*, June 25, 1973, pp. 2–3.

47 *"We got a few nicks and cuts"*: Author interview with Walter "Clyde" Orange.

48 *Description of Jackson 5 show*: The Jackson 5, *Live at the Forum* (Motown/Hip-O Select, 2010) documents the band's June 20, 1970, concert; Robert Hilburn, "Jackson Five in Concert," *Los Angeles Times*, June 22, 1970, p. D19, describes the dance moves.

48 *"It's just like rock 'n' roll"*: Rancifer interview.

48 *"Man, why don't you go"*: Weldon McDougal interview, *Michael Jackson: The Life of an Icon*.

48 *"She's not here for you"*: Author interview with Samm Brown.

49 Playboy *Playmate story and "Suffice it to say"*: Ibid.

49 *"Feelin' Alright," "forgot," and "Nobody really liked Joe Jackson"*: Orange interview.

49 *"Stand still" and Suzee Ikeda's MJ memories*: Ikeda interview.

52 *"Berry wasn't even listening"*: Posner, *Motown*, p. 255.

52 *Jack Davis, "Bring him over here," Gordy meeting details, and "very much in control"*: Author interview with Arthur Rankin.

52 *Corporation songwriting royalties and "After 'I Want You Back'" got done*: Richards interview.

53 *"Bounced and kicked" and "I'll Be There" details*: Bill Dahl and Keith Hughes, liner notes, *The Complete Motown Singles, Vol. 10: 1970* (Motown/Hip-O Select, 2008), pp. 87–90.

53 *"I thought [Marlon] was a little bit 'under'"*: Richards interview.

53 *Marcellino-Larson background and "Berry Gordy was actually kind of pissed"*: Author interview with Mel Larson.

54 *$80,000 to $200,000 ceremony and details*: "Hazel and Jermaine say 'I do,'" *Soul*, February 4, 1974, pp. 1–5, 12, 15.

54 *Katherine Jackson divorce, reaction, and rescindment*: Taraborrelli, *Michael Jackson*, pp. 101–3.

55 *"They had really greasy skin" and dermatologist*: Author interview with Nancy Leiviska.

55 *"Mishmash of material"*: Richards interview.

55 *"Dancing Machine" story*: Author interview with James Gadson.

56 *"The music nurtured"*: Vince Aletti, "Discotheque Rock '72: Paaaaarty!," *Rolling Stone*, September 13, 1973, p. 60.

56 *"What was disco?"*: Gadson interview.

57 *"Without reading them"*: Toriano Jackson vs. Motown, March 5, 1976.

57 *"Sign it," "No," and "I was open to talk to them"*: Dennis Hunt, "Jackson 1 After the Feud," *Los Angeles Times*, July 6, 1980, p. O80.

57 *Jacksons seeking $1 million*: Ron Alexenburg interview, *Michael Jackson: The Life of an Icon*. In *Rhythm and the Blues* (New York: Knopf, 1993), Atlantic Records' Jerry Wexler says a Jackson contract was "awaiting signature, a done deal for $1 million," but label execs rejected it as "too expensive," leading the Jacksons to accept the CBS offer instead.

57 *One man talked him into it*: Former CBS A&R executive Sam Lederman says, "I think if you're going to give anybody the most credit for it, it's Ron Alexenburg."

CHAPTER 3

58 *Alexenburg background, Warwick Hotel, and "What's going on here?"*: Author interview with Ron Alexenburg; Jim Melanson, "Alexenburg turns Epic to gold," *Billboard*, April 27, 1974, p. 14.

59 *Nanuet Star Theatre*: Walter Yetnikoff, *Howling at the Moon* (New York: Broadway Books, 2004), p. 89, places this show at the Westbury Music Fair. Alexenburg disagrees.

59 *"He was in a state"*: Author interview with Rob Cohen.

60 *"It was a Vegas crowd"*: Author interview with Ronnie Rancifer.

60 *Description of Vegas shows and "a little of everything"*: Vince Aletti, "In Love with the Jackson Five," *Village Voice*, February 17, 1975, p. 109.

61 *"The brothers were older"*: Author interview with Damita Jo Freeman.

61 *The Robot and Robert Shields*: Author interview with Robert Shields.

61 *Importance of Clinkers*: Author interview with Rick Marcelli (Shields's manager).

61 *"I trained him"*: Shields interview.

62 *Davis and Keys backstage at* Soul Train: Stephen McMillan, "Diary of an Ex–*Soul Train* Dancer: Q&A with Former *Soul Train* Dancer Patricia Davis," soultrain.com, May 26, 2011.

62 *"It was a playtime"*: Freeman interview.

62 *"Michael, you don't need me"*: Stephen McMillan, "Diary of an Ex–*Soul Train* Dancer: Freddie Maxie," soultrain.com, November 1, 2011.

62 *Alexenburg show observations*: Alexenburg interview.

62 *"Less than spectacular"*: Yetnikoff, *Howling at the Moon*, pp. 89–90.

63 *" 'Ben' was a smash"*: Ibid.

63 *Motown contract details and $750,000 advance*: Toriano Jackson, et al., vs. Motown Record Corp., et al., Superior Court of the State of California, March 5, 1976.

63 *$500,000 recording fund, $350,000 guarantee, royalty details, and Yetnikoff agreeing to three songs per album*: J. Randy Taraborrelli, *Michael Jackson: The Magic, The Madness, The Whole Story 1958–2009* (New York: Grand Central Publishing, 2009), pp. 129–30.

63 *"One thing I'll tell you," "Michael, you haven't said," and "I want to write and produce"*: Author interview with Sam Lederman.

64 *"Ron basically had a lot"*: Ibid.

64 *Gamble and Huff background*: John A. Jackson, *A House on Fire: The Rise and Fall*

of Philadelphia Soul (New York: Oxford University Press, 2004), pp. 10, 14–20, 28–29.

64 *"Gamble and Huff were really adult oriented"*: Author interview with Charles Collins.

64 *"CBS offered them movies"*: Kenny Gamble interview, *Michael Jackson: The Life of an Icon* (David Gest Productions, 2011).

64 *8 to 10 percent*: Lederman interview. (Gamble and Huff turned down interview requests.)

65 *"It was the Jacksons"*: Collins interview.

65 *Entourage of ten and "associated people"*: Author interview with Joe Tarsia.

65 *Preparing twenty songs for a twelve-song album*: *Michael Jackson: The Life of an Icon*.

65 *"Lemme try"*: Tarsia interview.

65 *"Just watching Huff"*: Michael Jackson, *Moonwalk* (New York: Harmony Books, 1988), p. 123.

65 *Muhammad Ali*: Tarsia interview.

66 *Jermaine, Ali, and "what it took"*: Jermaine Jackson, *You Are Not Alone: Michael Through a Brother's Eyes* (New York: Touchstone/Simon & Schuster, 2011), pp. 187–88.

66 *"[Michael] had that breathy voice"*: Tarsia interview.

66 *Jackie Wilson encounter*: Author interview with Joyce McRae (Wilson's friend and nursing home companion).

66 *Jackie Wilson hospital details*: Tony Douglas, *Jackie Wilson: Lonely Teardrops* (New York: Routledge, 2013), pp. 234–35.

67 *"My staff was less than enthusiastic"*: Yetnikoff, *Howling at the Moon*, p. 100.

67 *"It didn't sell real well"*: Author interview with Pete Humphreys.

67 *"I just told Joseph"*: Rancifer interview.

67 *"I hated every minute"*: Michael Jackson, *Moonwalk*, pp. 118, 121.

68 *"Aw, he loved it," MJ commands, "That isn't a western saloon!," and "Michael hasn't wanted that series to surface"*: Author interview with Bill Davis.

69 *"Huge influence"*: Queen Latifah interview, *The Late Show with David Letterman* (CBS, July 2009).

69 *$2 million of Gordy's money, $500,000 for a black film, "This is not a black film," and Ross slapping Gordy*: Gerald Posner, *Motown: Music, Money, Sex, and Power* (New York: Random House, 2002), pp. 257, 261, 278.

69 *Rob Cohen on The Wiz potential and "darling sweetheart"*: Cohen interview.

70 *The Wiz details*: Quincy Jones, *Q: The Autobiography of Quincy Jones* (New York: Doubleday, 2001), pp. 218, 229.

70 *Employee statistics*: Quincy Jones, liner notes to *The Wiz: Original Soundtrack* (MCA, 1978).

70 *"It's like a war zone"*: Ed Harrison, "A Day In the Life of Quincy Jones: Veteran Composer's Main Project 'The Wiz' Keeps Him Busy 24 Hours," *Billboard*, July 15, 1978, p. 75.

70 *"Aw, Michael's great," "Michael Jackson's a Vegas act," "That boy is so sweet!," and $100,000*: Cohen interview.

71 *Perrier bath*: Ibid.

71 *"The gay side" and "He danced more like a tap-dancer"*: Author interview with Pat Cleveland.

71   *"Like ricocheting bullets all over the place"*: Cassette MJ recorded of Sidney Lumet, Nipsey Russell, Diana Ross, and others, during lunch on *The Wiz* set, marked September 23, 1977, provided by confidential source.

71   *Louis Johnson biography and "He had seen Charlie Chaplin"*: Author interview with Louis Johnson.

72   *"Feelings," windmill, and "Did you get that?"*: Cleveland interview.

72   *Costume details and "He was thrilled to have his nose covered"*: Author interview with Tony Walton.

72   *"He's our generation's Fred Astaire"*: Author interview with Tom Bähler.

72   *"Okay, Michael"*: Cohen interview.

73   *"He looked at Michael"*: Ibid.

73   *Socrates and "take a shot"*: Jones, Q, p. 231.

73   *MJ-Quincy Jones phone conversation, including "You know it's not talent, though"*: MJ cassette recording, circa 1978, provided by confidential source.

74   *"Everybody has a crying jag" and "Michael was the most high-spirited"*: Walton interview.

74   *"As big and as spectacular"*: Cohen interview.

74   *Bobby Colomby stepping in and "Hey, boss"*: Author interview with Bobby Colomby.

75   *"There was wonderful confusion everywhere"*: Author interview with Mick Jackson.

75   *Colomby on the Jacksons, "The plants would wilt," and "Tell him I'm the father!"*: Colomby interview.

75   *"Wait, wait, wait"*: Author interview with Rick Marotta.

76   *"I have to get this out," "That's not the way," Colomby meeting with the Jacksons, and twenty-minute groove*: Colomby interview.

76   *"It was a very strong"*: Author interview with Greg Phillinganes.

76   *"I would have said"*: Colomby interview.

77   *"If I could go back in time"*: Author interview with Mike Sembello.

77   *Quincy Jones background*: Jones, Q, pp. 1, 12, 30–31, 43, 48.

78   *Ella and Dizzy*: Ella Fitzgerald and Dizzy Gillespie interviews, *Listen Up: The Lives of Quincy Jones* (Warner Bros., 1990).

79   *"Lily"*: MJ-Quincy phone recording cassette.

79   *"It's about recycling energy"*: Jones interview, *Listen Up.*

79   *"Quincy does jazz"*: Steve Demorest, "Michael in Wonderland," *Melody Maker,* March 1, 1980.

79   *"I've got my boys," "There were a lot of problems," "A lot of it would start with Joe," and "It was very nasty"*: Author interview with Ron Weisner.

80   *"Too jazzy" and "I don't care what you think"*: Jones, Q, pp. 231–32.

80   *"Our underlying plan"*: John Moore, "Looking back on M.J.'s 'Thriller' at 30, a musical game-changer," *Denver Post,* November 23, 2012, p. 1C.

80   *"Part of the marketing"*: Weisner interview.

80   *"We tried all kinds of things"*: Jones, Q, p. 232.

80   *Seth Riggs on MJ's voice*: Author interview with Seth Riggs.

81   *"You don't have to do that"*: Ibid.

81   *"Quincy and Rod were like, 'Wow'" and "Michael would come in"*: Eckstine interview.

81 *"Braced and counterbraced" and "I absolutely love"*: Swedien, *In the Studio with Michael Jackson*, p. 10.

82 *Handclaps and Rolex*: Robinson interview.

82 *"Man, what is that?"*: Johnson interview.

82 *"She's Out of My Life" story*: Bähler interview.

83 *"Don't Stop 'til You Get Enough" songwriting details*: Robinson interview, Phillinganes interview, Colomby interview.

83 *"guitars chopping like kalimbas"*: Michael Jackson, *Moonwalk*, p. 161.

83 *MJ convinced Katherine the song wasn't about sex*: Katherine Jackson with Richard Wiseman, *The Jacksons: My Family* (New York: St. Martin's Press, 1990), p. 109.

84 *"Off the Wall" cover shoot and "Put a little attitude"*: Author interview with Mike Salisbury.

84 *Bud Rizzo jamming and "Why don't you come to rehearsal?"*: Author interview with Bud Rizzo.

85 *"Kind of these way-out talks" and Astaire on VCR*: Ibid.

85 *False Memphis Horns*: Author interview with Alan "Funt" Prater.

86 *Gym socks, "Wow, this guy is kinda nerdy-like," "I couldn't believe," "Hey hey hey, let's get it right," "Raise?," and women in the hotel room*: Ibid.

86 *"A symbol of what we are trying to say"*: Nelson George, *The Michael Jackson Story* (New York: Dell, 1984), p. 113.

87 *"It was the same thing over and over"*: Taraborrelli, *Michael Jackson*, p. 181.

87 *"You could feel"*: Rizzo interview.

CHAPTER 4

88 *James Ingram watching MJ sing "P.Y.T." and "universities of Berry Gordy and Quincy Jones"*: Author interview with James Ingram.

89 *"The Motown musicians"*: Author interview with Anthony Marinelli.

89 *"Sounds of how I want the bass"*: Michael Jackson deposition in Mexico City, November 8 and 10, 1993, *Smith, et al., vs. Jackson, et al.*, U.S. District Court for Central California, May 12, 1994.

89 *". . . And the piano be going 'da da da da'" and "I want the biggest drum sounds"*: MJ self-made cassette recordings, provided by confidential source.

89 *"Before Thriller"*: Confidential source.

90 *"It was kind of an orphaned, packaged studio," Hayvenhurst details, parrot and La Toya, and "We recorded in a hurry"*: Author interview with Brent Averill.

90 *"We had known Michael"*: Author interview with Oren Waters.

91 *"Bitch, you better leave my husband alone!"*: "One Big Unhappy Family: Despite a Feel-Good TV Reunion, the Jacksons Have Made Trouble Their Trademark," *People*, February 28, 1994, p. 62.

91 *"Graphically describing relations"*: Author interview with Joyce McRae.

91 *Joseph's affair with Terrell, Joh'Vonnie, Sprague's cuts and bruises, and hospital*: J. Randy Taraborrelli, *Michael Jackson: The Magic, The Madness, The Whole Story 1958–2009* (New York: Grand Central Publishing, 2009), pp. 193–94, 198. Joh'Vonnie Jackson turned down an interview request.

91 *Sprague's $21 million lawsuit*: Gina Sprague vs. Joseph Jackson, et al., Superior Court of California, July 21, 1983.

91 *"He didn't seem very happy"*: Leonard Pitts Jr., "'Thriller' was greatest triumph, greatest tragedy," *Miami Herald*, June 26, 2009, p. 1A.

92 *"Oh, no, I think I'd die"* and *"It may sound crazy"*: Robert Hilburn, "The Jacksons—Hail and Farewell?," *Los Angeles Times*, September 13, 1981, pp. K1–K61.

92 *First nose job in 1979*: J. Randy Taraborrelli interview, *Michael Jackson: The Life of an Icon* (David Gest Productions, 2011), p. 205.

92 *No memory of onstage accident*: Author interview with Bud Rizzo; author interview with Mike Mckinney. Tony Lewis, the Jacksons' Destiny drummer, has a vague recollection of "some kind of injury."

92 *"What in the hell"*: Jermaine Jackson, *You Are Not Alone: Michael Through a Brother's Eyes* (New York: Touchstone/Simon & Schuster, 2011), pp. 163, 189–90.

93 *"Offstage, our merciless teasing"*: Ibid.

93 *"Michael was doing plastic surgery"*: McRae interview.

93 *"Michael felt under pressure"*: Jimmy Ruffin interview, *Michael Jackson: The Life of an Icon*.

94 *"Hybridization"* and *"In short, he has been"*: Jean Baudrillard, *Cool Memories* (New York: Verso, 1990), p. 147.

94 *"Oh, hi!"* and *Terry George recollections*: Author interview with Terry George.

95 *Jermaine and Joe hired Michael Mesnick*: Author interview with Michael Mesnick.

95 *Mesnick asked Braun to extract MJ*: Mesnick interview; author interview with David Braun.

95 *"Suppose it sells this,"* royalty deal north of 25 percent, and *"We kept using arbitrary numbers"*: Braun interview; author interview with Dick Asher.

95 *"Michael was making equal to what CBS was making"*: Mesnick interview.

96 *"I left to make some money"*: Braun interview.

96 *Branca tried to help MJ move but he wouldn't leave Hayvenhurst*: Taraborrelli, *Michael Jackson*, p. 207.

96 *"Michael puts us to shame"*: Mesnick interview.

96 *Eight-track studio, recording equipment, Tito's house, and "Mike, what you doing today?"*: Mckinney interview.

96 *"There would be a lot of opinions"*: Author interview with Jerry Hey.

97 *Van Nuys office park, "The brothers had different ideas," "Bill, why you playing that?," "so they could present a unified front," and "Buy some for your friends!"*: Author interview with Bill Wolfer.

98 *"I can't eat this,"* colonics, and *"like a moth attracted to a flame"*: Ibid.

99 *Fiddling with new dance on Destiny tour*: Rizzo interview.

99 *"They cleared out the rehearsal space"*: Author interview with Reed Glick.

99 *MJ climbing back onstage after magic malfunction*: Author interview with Nick Luysterborghs (a crew member who oversaw the illusion for the Triumph tour).

99 *"This isn't working!"*: Glick interview.

100 *"Anytime they saw the name 'Michael'"*: Mckinney interview.

100 *Hayvenhurst renovation description*: Jermaine Jackson, *You Are Not Alone*, pp. 202–3.

100 *"Like a machine"*: Quincy Jones, *Q: The Autobiography of Quincy Jones* (New York: Doubleday, 2001), p. 237.

100 *"Michael rang me"*: Ray Coleman, *McCartney: Yesterday & Today* (Garden City, MI: Dove Books, 1995), p. 129.

101 *MJ and McCartney meeting*: Ibid.

101 *Westlake description*: Matt Forger, who guided a tour of the studio.

101 *"No matter what you do"*: Nelson George and Mark Rowland, "Michael Jackson's Perfect Universe: The Education and Execution of Total Victory," *Musician*, July 1984, p. 47.

101 *"I felt ignored by my peers"*: Michael Jackson, *Moonwalk* (New York: Harmony Books, 1988), p. 176.

101 E.T. *pushing* Thriller *crew back*: Author interview with Matt Forger.

101 *"Everybody was working"*: Author interview with Humberto Gatica.

102 *"Fuck off" and "Don't worry"*: Author interview with Steve Lukather.

102 *"Okay, guys"*: Bruce Swedien interview, "The Invisible Man: The Rod Temperton Story," BBC Radio 2, August 23, 2008, and December 12, 2009.

102 *"The Girl Is Mine" session description,* " 'The doggone girl is mine'—really?," "I Was Made to Love Her," "It was funkier," and guests: Lukather interview.

103 *six hundred or seven hundred songs and "When it was known"*: Forger interview.

103 *"I've never seen Quincy"*: George and Rowland, "Michael Jackson's Perfect Universe," p. 47.

103 *"It wasn't how most people" and film metaphor*: Marinelli interview.

103 *"Rod Temperton had that Quincy Jones sound"*: Wolfer interview.

104 *DiBango settlement for $25,000 to $50,000*: Confidential source.

104 *"There's a sound I want" and "We created this unusual"*: Author interview with Steven Ray.

105 *Cockatoo, "This guy is different," "that three-chord vamp," and "He couldn't play an instrument"*: Wolfer interview.

105 *"He knew what he wanted"*: Hey interview.

106 *"Dit dit dit dit!," "No, it's not gonna go," and "Billie Jean" bass description*: Author interview with Louis Johnson (not to be mistaken with the choreographer for *The Wiz*).

106 *"The girl in the song is a composite"*: Michael Jackson, *Moonwalk*, p. 191.

106 *"There was a story"*: Author interview with Ndugu Chancler.

106 *Theresa Gonsalves claim*: Author interview with Theresa Gonsalves.

107 *"He knew how to make"*: Forger interview.

107 *"Two records per household"*: Ray interview.

107 *"Hey, Quincy's guy" and "Human Nature" story*: Author interview with Steve Porcaro.

108 *"What's that sound?" and drum packaging*: Author interview with Bruce Swedien.

108 *"In its day"*: Author interview with Brian Banks.

109 *Van Halen's version*: George and Rowland, "Michael Jackson's Perfect Universe," p. 54.

109 *"Me and [drummer] Jeff Porcaro" and "It's too much"*: Lukather interview.

109 *Golden Bird, food details and "Bawk, bawk!"*: Ray interview.

110 *"There were always good meat/carnivore jokes"*: Chancler interview.

110 *"We thought at one point"*: Gail Mitchell, "How Michael Jackson's 'Thriller' Changed the Music Business," billboard.com, July 3, 2009.

110 *"I'd always envisioned this talking section"*: Peter Lyle, "Monster smash," *The Telegraph*, November 25, 2007, Seven supplement, pp. 12–19.

110 *Vincent Price story*: Temperton interview, "Rod Temperton: The Invisible Man."

111 *"Black Friday"* and Thriller *deadline concerns*: Mitchell, "How Michael Jackson's 'Thriller' Changed the Music Business."

111 *Champagne bottles*: Jones, Q, pp. 238–39.

112 *"It was a disaster"*: Ibid.

112 *"Oh my God," champagne, and bad feeling*: Author interview with Larkin Arnold.

112 *"You need big, fat grooves," "unreleasable," and "Smelly finally agreed"*: Jones, Q, pp. 238–39.

112 *"I'm not exactly sure," pumping up kick drum, and "There's more depth"*: Author interview with Bernie Grundman.

CHAPTER 5

113 *KDAY and "You've got to take it off!"*: Author interview with Jon Badeaux.

114 *"It was so electrifying"*: Author interview with Elroy Smith.

114 *Analysis of race and post-disco radio, including top-ten singles*: Steve Greenberg, "Michael Jackson's 'Thriller' at 30: How One Album Changed the World," billboard.com, November 29, 2012.

114 *"It wasn't any less racist"*: Author interview with T. C. Thompkins.

115 *Delicatessen meeting, Arnold's agreement, and "This was an attempt"*: Author interview with Larkin Arnold.

115 *"I had this idea"*: Author interview with Frank DiLeo, for Steve Knopper, *Appetite for Self-Destruction: The Spectacular Crash of the Record Industry in the Digital Age* (New York: Free Press/Simon & Schuster, 2009).

116 *"What are you doing?"*: Author interview with Fred Jacobs.

116 *Album-oriented rock, "Historically, the Michael Jackson sound," and "Can you play it again?"*: Author interview with Lee Abrams.

116 *$50,000 budget, "Billie Jean" video details, and "He burst into this incredible movement"*: Author interview with Steve Barron. MJ put the budget at $250,000, in *Moonwalk* (New York: Harmony Books, 1988).

116 *"Taking black people back" and MTV's attitude toward videos by black artists*: Robert Sam Anson, "Birth of an MTV Nation," *Vanity Fair*, November 2000, p. 72.

117 *"He called up Bob Pittman"*: Author interview with Ron McCarrell.

117 *"People ask me"*: Author interview with Les Garland.

117 *"If key CBS executives are lying"*: Rob Tannenbaum and Craig Marks, *I Want My MTV: The Uncensored Story of the Music Video Revolution* (New York: Penguin, 2012), p. 143.

117 *"He broke the boundaries"*: Author interview with will.i.am.

118 *"Look, here's what we're looking to do"*: Weisner interview for Knopper, *Appetite for Self-Destruction*.

118 *"Smacking each other around"*: Tannenbaum and Marks, *I Want My MTV*, pp. 150–51.

118 *"These people switched"*: Author interview with Popin Pete.

118 *Michael Peters background*: Daniel Chu and Barbara Rowes, "Michael Peters Is the Hot New Choreographer Who Makes Dancers Out of Video's Rock Stars," *People*, June 25, 1984, p. 119.

119 *"I worked with him totally"*: Michael Peters interview, *Great Performances: Everybody Dance Now* (PBS, October 2, 1991).

119   *Real switchblade and "That's illegal"*: Tannenbaum and Marks, *I Want My MTV*, p. 151.

119   *"Most of the gangbangers"*: Pete interview.

119   *"Back when MTV was in its music-video heyday"*: Author interview with "Weird Al" Yankovic.

120   *"As you back up"*: Chu and Rowe, "Michael Peters Is the Hot New Choreographer," p. 119.

120   *De Passe negotiations with Ross and Gordy begging*: Gerald Posner, *Motown: Music, Money, Sex, and Power* (New York: Random House, 2002), pp. 304, 306.

121   *"Nobody's asked my brothers," Gordy asking MJ to do "Billie Jean," "I don't think that's a good idea," "because they'll never get the groove," and lip-synching*: Author interview with Suzee Ikeda.

121   *"Nobody else worked with him"*: Ibid.

122   *Bill Bailey and Mr. Bojangles*: "Michael Jackson's Origins of the Moonwalk," youtube.com/watch?v=xH7VymwHLmo.

122   *Influence of Marceau and mime via Shields and Yarnell, Boogaloo Sam, Electric Boogaloos*: Author interview with Toni Basil.

122   *Damita Jo Freeman's claim*: Author interview with Damita Jo Freeman.

123   *MJ tracking down Cooley and Casper, "Where did it come from?," "I can't feel it!," and "I understood that"*: Author interview with Cooley Jaxson.

123   *"A break-dance step"*: Michael Jackson, *Moonwalk*, p. 210.

123   *"We kind of ended up"*: Jaxson interview.

123   *"I'm sure he was doing the moonwalk"*: Katherine Jackson testimony, *Katherine Jackson, et al., vs. AEG Live, et al.*, California Superior Court, July 19, 2013. For this case, the court does not provide original transcripts, attorneys on both sides refused to make them available, and a professional service, Alliance Court Reporters, did not to respond to repeated inquiries. I went with the transcripts posted by MJ fans, publicly available at scribd.com. A *Los Angeles Times* reporter who covered the trial told me: "I did find the transcripts the fans posted to be accurate. The only place they could have gotten them was from the court reporter." I attended a small portion of the trial and the transcripts match my notes.

123   *"I pretty much stood there"*: Michael Jackson, *Moonwalk*, p. 209.

124   *Ross, Courvoisier and stomach flu*: Posner, *Motown*, p. 306.

124   *"Now what Adams Ant had to do with Motown"*: Author interview with Valerie Simpson.

124   *Adam Ant, Motown, brocade jacket and "How the fuck do you follow that?"*: Author interview with Adam Ant.

124   *MJ's live microphone during Motown 25*: Author interview with Rus Terrana.

125   *Black jacket borrowed from Katherine*: Katherine Jackson testimony, *Katherine Jackson vs. AEG*, July 19, 2013.

125   *Other costume details, including 1,200 rhinestones*: Posner, *Motown*, p. 307.

125   *Speech by Buz Kohan*: Author interview with Buz Kohan.

126   *"He must have made me rehearse"*: Author interview with Nelson P. Hayes.

127   *"My crew just went"*: Terrana interview.

128   *"When everybody ran up"*: Simpson interview.

128   *Fred Astaire call*: Michael Jackson, *Moonwalk*, p. 213.

128   *"Oh, come on"*: Author interview with Seth Riggs.

128 *"You're a hell of a mover" and "It was the greatest compliment"*: Michael Jackson, *Moonwalk*, p. 213.

128 *"Our sales just exploded"*: McCarrell interview.

128 *twenty-two million copies*: Bob Cannon, "A Giant Step for Jackson: Michael Jackson moonwalks—the music icon seized the pop culture moment in March 1983," *Entertainment Weekly*, March 25, 1994, p. 68. Bill Wyman of *The New Yorker* has challenged the widely used 100 million number with regard to *Thriller* worldwide sales; Ron McCarrell, Epic's head of marketing from 1979 to 1987, tells me, "My gut feeling on that is 100 million is a pretty aggressive number. If somebody said to me 50 to 70 million, I could buy into that."

128 *"The* Thriller *phenomenon"*: Author interview with John Branca.

129 *MJ swung the ax and 2 million*: J. Randy Taraborrelli, *Michael Jackson: The Magic, The Madness, The Whole Story 1958–2009* (New York: Grand Central Publishing, 2009), p. 250

129 *Weisner received letter from attorney*: Author interview with Ron Weisner.

129 *expired contract, "There are a lot of leeches," and "I don't know what would make"*: Paul Grein, "Who Guides Jackson's Career: Singer's Father, Management Team in Power Struggle," *Billboard*, June 25, 1983, p. 3.

130 *DiLeo background*: DiLeo interview for Knopper, *Appetite for Self-Destruction*.

130 *DiLeo singing "Born to Run"*: *People*, May 9, 1988, pp. 42–43.

130 *Beverly Hills Hotel and "Gee, Michael"*: DiLeo interview for Knopper, *Appetite for Self-Destruction*.

130 *"Blocking back"*: Author interview with Jim Murray.

130 *"I think it should be 'Thriller'"*: DiLeo interview for Knopper, *Appetite for Self-Destruction*.

130 *"He lived in a room upstairs"*: Author interview with John Landis.

131 *$1.1 million, twenty times, $100,000, "Who wants a single," and MJ offering to make up the difference*: Nancy Griffin, "The 'Thriller' Diaries," *Vanity Fair*, July 2010, pp. 60–79. George Folsey Jr. confirmed the numbers in this article, although he says the $900,000 budget figure actually was "a few hundred thousand less than that."

131 *"Michael Jackson wanted to do 'Thriller'"*: Author interview with Bob Pittman.

131 *Folsey's idea*: Author interview with George Folsey Jr.

131 *$29.95 and $1 million*: "Top Videocassettes," *Billboard*, December 15, 1984, p. 30.

131 *MJ relationship with Landis*: Folsey interview.

131 *"The socks and the shoes" and "I have a shine on my nose"*: Griffin, "The 'Thriller' Diaries," pp. 60–79.

132 *"It was within what I would call reason"*: Author interview with Anthony Marinelli.

132 *"When you're a foot away"*: Author interview with Steve Jander.

132 *"I always felt he looked so good"*: David Gest interview, *Michael Jackson: The Life of an Icon* (David Gest Productions, 2011).

132 *"George, I'd like to introduce you"*: Folsey interview.

132 *"John, do you know"*: Landis interview.

133 *"What's the matter?"*: Ibid.

133 *"Do you know who I am?"*: Ibid.

133 *"This is not a glamour gig" and "It always makes me sore"*: Author interview with Kim Blank.

133   *Locking the canisters, "I feel so bad," and "No matter how wacky"*: Griffin, "The 'Thriller' Diaries," pp. 60–79.

134   *"Show the goddamn thing again!"*: Ibid.

134   *"We saw the ratings spike"*: Garland interview.

134   *thirty-three million copies*: Peter Carlson and Roger Wolmuth, "Tour De Force," *People*, May 7, 1984, p. 42.

134   *"After* Thriller *came out" and "The best offers coming in"*: Todd Gold, *Michael Jackson: The Man in the Mirror* (New York: Pan Books, 1989), pp. 132–33.

134   *"Only a fairly small sum" and Don King's attire*: Joseph Jackson, *Die Jacksons* (Munich: Random House Germany, 2004), pp. 146–47.

134   *"I found him extremely impressive"*: Ibid.

135   *Lawyers at meeting, "You know why you're not as big," eating chicken with Janet, and "Don's going to be the promoter"*: Author interview with Peter Paterno.

135   *$3 million and $500,000*: Michael Goldberg and Christopher Connelly, "Trouble In Paradise?," *Rolling Stone*, March 15, 1984, p. 27.

135   *"Would you get on a plane"*: Paterno interview.

135   *"A salesman is a salesman"*: Joseph Jackson, *Die Jacksons*, p. 149.

135   *MJ agreed after meeting with Katherine*: Katherine Jackson with Richard Wiseman, *The Jacksons: My Family* (New York: St. Martin's Press, 1990), p. 138.

135   *"Michael didn't want to do the tour"*: Gold, *Michael Jackson*, p. 145.

135   *"It was constant fights with Don"*: Paterno interview.

136   *Paterno and King hollering*: Ibid.

136   *"Had the Jacksons tour sponsorship" and King mentioning to Pepsi he'd spoken with Coca Cola*: Confidential source.

136   *"Nonetheless, we ended up doing a deal"*: Author interview with Roger Enrico.

136   *King's attorney chasing Jackie*: Confidential source.

136   *Coke and $4 million*: Glenn Collins, "Coke's Hometown Olympics; The Company Tries the Big Blitz on Its Own Turf," *New York Times*, March 28, 1996, p. 1.

136   *Pepsi and $5 million*: Bruce Horovitz, "Matchmaker Was First to Rock Ad World," *Los Angeles Times*, September 10, 1991, p. D1. Confirmed by Enrico.

136   *Pottasch and "You can shoot my feet"*: Enrico interview.

137   *MJ's borrowed military-style uniform*: Ant interview, Weisner interview, Marcelli interview.

137   *"Before the Victory tour"*: Gold, *Michael Jackson*, pp. 145–46.

137   *"Just very quiet but very determined" and other Enrico quotes*: Enrico interview.

137   *Glove, toilet, and "Oh, forget it"*: Taraborrelli, *Michael Jackson*, p. 280.

138   *"I want more!," "Why?," and "Because of the stuff he had in his hair"*: Author interview with Reed Glick.

138   *Details of Pepsi accident*: "Video: How Michael Jackson's Pill Addiction Began," usmagazine.com, August 31, 2009.

138   *"Get my glove" and "When they started skin grafts"*: Hayes interview.

138   *Hoefflin and "quite shaken up,"*: Discharge report, Brotman Burn Center, January 28, 1984; thesmokinggun.com, April 4, 2013.

139   *"palmed-size area" and "surrounding burned and singed hair"*: Ibid.

139   *MJ took sleeping pill but refused painkiller*: Taraborrelli, *Michael Jackson*, pp. 282–83.

139   *"You feel that?"*: Kohan interview.

139 *Taking painkillers after the hospital*: Brian Panish, attorney for Katherine Jackson, said during *Katherine Jackson vs. AEG* that MJ took Demerol after the Pepsi commercial accident. In 1993, MJ said in a statement: "I have been undergoing treatment for dependency on pain medication. This medication was initially prescribed to sooth the excruciating pain that I was suffering after recent reconstructive surgery on my scalp."

139 *"You don't understand"*: Enrico interview.

140 *"I'm done" and "I came back"*: Confidential source.

140 *"If you want to take this tour away from me"*: Jermaine Jackson, *You Are Not Alone: Michael Through a Brother's Eyes* (New York: Touchstone/Simon & Schuster, 2011), p. 248.

140 *Three percent of tour profits*: Ibid.

140 *Chuck Sullivan background*: John Steinbreder, "The $126 Million Fumble," *Sports Illustrated*, March 14, 1988, pp. 64–70.

140 *$41 million deal*: Sullivan interview.

140 *$12 million down, the rest within two weeks*: McDougal, "The Agony of 'Victory,'" p. AD60.

140 *61,000 seats*: Will McDonough, "Patriots' Records Show Debts Over $75 Million," *Chicago Tribune*, July 27, 1987, Sports p. 2.

140 *Sullivan Stadium as collateral*: Steinbreder, "The $126 Million Fumble," pp. 64–70.

140 *Roughly 83/17 percent split*: Dean Budnick and Josh Baron, *Ticket Masters: The Rise of the Concert Industry and How the Public Got Scalped* (Toronto: ECW Press, 2011), p. 205; confirmed by Sullivan.

140 *250 personnel*: McDougal, "The Agony of 'Victory,'" p. AD60.

140 *Riggers hanging kitchen sink*: Author interview with Ken Graham.

141 *"Ice sculptures, fuchsias, potted palms," $40,000 for traveling parlor, $196,500 for Sullivan's contract, and $500,000 for insurance*: Ibid.

141 *Bob Gurra meeting, Rolls-Royce, spider, "Michael came up with the idea"*: Confidential source.

141 *Hydraulics*: Author interview with John McGraw (stage designer); Roth interview.

141 *"We did fifty-five shows"*: Luysterborghs interview.

141 *"There was a whole system"*: Roth interview.

142 *Fifty-six thousand pounds of lights*: Ibid.

142 *"He struck me as sort of a kid"*: Jander interview.

142 *Jacksonville Picayune details*: Luysterborghs interview.

142 *"The power of a fifty-piece orchestra"*: James McBride, "The Glove Comes Off as Michael Goes to Work," *People*, June 11, 1984, p. 151.

142 *Rehearsal details and "It was like NFL training camp"*: Author interview with Gregg Wright.

143 *Kids moonwalking as the van went by*: Kaplan interview.

143 *"Oh, sir!"*: Luysterborghs interview.

143 *"Michael—Pepsi"*: Jander interview.

143 *Hoefflin eighty-minute procedure*: Gold, *Michael Jackson*, p. 145.

143 *$1 million a week*: McDougal, "The Agony of 'Victory,'" p. AD60.

144 *$500,000 Irving Azoff fee*: Michael Goldberg, "Behind-the-scenes confusion causing various delays: Wheeling and dealing continues as Jacksons tour approaches," *Rolling Stone*, June 21, 1984, p. 51. Confirmed by confidential source.

144 *Ken Graham and "front porch"*: Graham interview.

144 *375 security guards, 170 local police officers, and 70 metal detectors*: William Plummer and James McBride, "The Jackson Fireworks," *People*, July 23, 1984, p. 46.

144 *Pocket Redee and $160,000*: McDougal, "The Agony of 'Victory,'" p. AD60.

144 *Arrowhead road and Giant Stadium beam*: Graham interview.

144 *"It was like, turn it all on"*: Roth interview.

145 *$5,000 glove, "Really?," and Sharpie system*: Author interview with Tony Villanueva.

146 *"Pretty much each brother had their own session"*: Wargo interview.

146 *"Aptly named," $300,000 budget, Jackie was in charge, MJ had little interest, and $1 million costs*: Author interview with John Diaz.

146 *"I'm sorry, Perri"*: Author interview with Perri Lister.

146 *"It was the Heaven's Gate"*: Diaz interview.

147 *Meshulam Riklis's seven private jets*: Jermaine Jackson, *You Are Not Alone*, p. 266.

147 *"If there was jealousy"*: Author interview with Howard Bloom.

147 *"A Whitman's sampler" and $70 million in Jacksonville*: Plummer and McBride, "The Jackson Fireworks," pp. 44–47.

147 HOLD YOUR BREATH *and firefighters' convention*: Sally Kalson, "The Concert That Wasn't," *Pittsburgh Post-Gazette*, October 13, 1984, p. 7.

148 *$250,000 not going to Pittsburgh tax revenues*: Ibid.

148 *"Michael said it was going to be a drug-free tour"*: Graham interview.

148 *MJ rehearsed steps on a portable wooden platform*: Wright interview.

148 *"It didn't take anything"*: Luysterborghs interview.

148 *$20 million*: Gordon Forbes, "Sullivan family ties are broken," *USA Today*, April 1, 1988, p. 2C.

148 *$8 million*: Sullivan interview.

148 *"Jimmy, I'm gonna fly back"*: Murray interview.

149 *Sullivan spending the night in a luxury box*: Mark Farinella, "Jackson's part in Pats' history was real 'thriller,'" thesunchronicle.com, June 27, 2009.

149 *"I was not homeless"*: Sullivan interview.

CHAPTER 6

150 *Mr. Tibbs the ram, et al.*: "Jackson has new pet project," *Miami Herald*, September 28, 1986, p. 7K.

150 *OshKosh B'gosh, designer shirts, pajamas, dresser drawer, Häagen-Dazs, and prayers*: La Toya Jackson interview, *Michael Jackson and Bubbles: The Untold Story* (Animal Planet, 2010).

150 *Osaka mayor and green tea*: "Jackson & chimp visit Osaka mayor," *Chicago Sun-Times*, September 20, 1987, p. 17.

150 *Bubblesmobile*: Author interview with Steve Stevens ("Dirty Diana" video guitarist).

150 *"Bubbles became a human"*: La Toya Jackson interview, *Michael Jackson and Bubbles*.

151 *"If there was a box," tape machine story, "BUBBLES, NO!," and "like he would jump over his skin"*: Author interview with Matt Forger.

151 *"I saw Mike hit Bubbles with his shoe"*: Author interview with Chris Currell.

151 *"He hit that monkey so hard"*: Author interview with Brian Malouf.

152 *"We Are the World" origin details*: David Breskin, *"We Are the World"* (New York: Perigee Books, 1985).

152   *"He always gave to kids"*: Author interview with Hugo Huizar.

153   *Details of MJ-Lionel Richie "We Are the World" session, including "We didn't mention 'truth' yet"*: Cassette recording provided by confidential source.

153   *"Everybody came in there"*: Author interview with Louis Johnson.

154   *MJ's compact and touching his nose*: Author interview with Johnny Colla (of Huey Lewis and the News).

154   *"as his typical quiet self"*: Author interview with John Oates.

154   *"Ethiopians do not speak Swahili"*: Breskin, *"We Are the World."*

154   *"would go off by himself"*: Author interview with Kim Carnes.

155   *"How do you buy them?"*: Robert Hilburn, "The long and winding road," *Los Angeles Times*, September 22, 1985, p. 60.

155   *"You are now earning a lot of money," Northern Songs history, "too much money," and "I'm going to buy your songs"*: Ray Coleman, *McCartney: Yesterday & Today* (Garden City, MI: Dove Books, 1995), pp. 110–15, 132–40.

156   *The Long and Winding Road*: Hilburn, "The long and winding road," p. 60.

156   *"I think we hit the mother lode" and MJ–John Branca exchange about copyrights*: Author interview with John Branca.

156   *Gelfand, $46 million, and MJ's favorite Beatles songs*: Hilburn, "The long and winding road," p. 60.

156   *Kawashima background and "It became harder"*: Author interview with Dale Kawashima.

157   *Eisner background, "They hadn't made classics," "It was Michael Jackson doing something," and old-lady makeup*: Author interview with Michael Eisner.

157   *MJ arrived after Disneyland closed and "He knew his way around"*: Author interview with Rick Rothschild.

157   *"Where's Michael?"*: Author interview with Eric Henderson.

158   *Eleven-year-old friend*: Ibid.

158   *Jonathan Spence and Brotman Hospital*: *Jet*, August 19, 1985, p. 45.

158   *Boy holding cape and delivering drinks*: Author interview with Kevin Bender.

158   *Hyperbaric chamber as a plant*: Author interview with Michael Levine.

158   *"He was tabloid gold"*: Author interview with Tony Brenna.

158   *Currell Synclavier lessons*: Currell interview.

159   *"First, you take this floppy disk," MJ's low technical skills, and ten* A.M. *to seven* P.M. *at Hayvenhurst*: Ibid.

159   *Nineteen eighty-five demos and "He walked down twelve or thirteen stairs"*: Author interview with Bill Bottrell.

159   *"Wow, this is really cool"*: Currell interview.

159   *"He was very prolific"*: Forger interview.

159   *"He'd do it all himself" and "Michael would go to the ends of the earth"*: Currell interview.

160   *"Bad" bassline*: Ibid.

160   *"We wanted a tough album"*: Quincy Jones bonus-track interview, *Bad (Remaster)* (Epic/Sony, 2001).

160   *"They're so competitive"*: Quincy Troupe, "The Pressure to Beat It," *Spin*, June 1987, p. 43.

160   *"It would have been disastrous"*: Author interview with Russ Ragsdale.

161   *MJ, Prince, and James Brown*: "A Holy Trinity of Pop Music," newyorker.com, August 20, 2013.

161 *MJ and Prince in Vegas* and *"Why was Prince playing the bass in my face?"*: Author interview with will.i.am.

162 *$500,000 to $600,000* and *"We were certainly hoping"*: Author interview with Glenn Phoenix.

162 *Studio sizes*: westlakestudios.com.

162 *"Michael's room" and celebrity guests*: Ragsdale interview.

162 *"It was also unusual"*: Phoenix interview.

162 *"He would be in that room a lot"*: Author interview with Jolie Levine.

163 *"He was able to hear and see"*: Author interview with Cornelius Mims.

163 *"I grew up watching him on TV"*: Author interview with Eric Persing.

163 *"Michael was growing"*: Joseph Vogel, *Man In the Music: The Creative Life and Work of Michael Jackson* (New York: Sterling, 2011), p. 107.

163 *Jones background*: Quincy Jones, *Q: The Autobiography of Quincy Jones* (New York: Doubleday, 2001), pp. 237, 243, 273, 288, 233–34, 236–41, 243, 298.

163 *"There started to become a real problem"*: Currell interview.

164 *"It hit the fan"*: Ibid.

164 *"Either he goes or I go," "I just got fired,"* and *"Don't worry"*: Bottrell interview.

164 *"Michael had fantastic ideas"*: Author interview with Larry Williams.

164 *"They had every studio guitar player"*: Persing interview.

164 *eight hundred tapes*: Joseph Vogel, "How Michael Jackson Made 'Bad,'" theatlantic.com, September 10, 2012.

164 *3:30 A.M.*: Ragsdale interview.

164 *MJ's studio outfit and Bubbles*: Troupe, "The Pressure to Beat It," p. 45.

165 *Noon and 6 P.M. meals*: Ragsdale and Jolie Levine interviews.

165 *"When's Catherine coming?"*: Jolie Levine interview.

165 *"They're all happy"*: Author interview with Douglas Cooper Getschal.

165 *"Depending on the setting"* and *"It's like he really didn't want to be seen"*: Mims interview.

165 *Jimmy Smith and Run-D.M.C.*: Troupe, "The Pressure to Beat It," p. 45.

166 *"anthem that had a good feel to it"* and *Garrett-Ballard story*: Quincy Jones and Siedah Garrett interviews, *Bad 25* (Optimum Productions, directed by Spike Lee, ABC, 2012).

166 *"Make it sound like church"*: Author interview with Sandra Crouch.

166 *Mavis Staples and Shamone*: Chris Richards, "B-sides: Mavis Staples Talks Prince, Michael Jackson, Bob Dylan and President Obama," washingtonpost.com, September 3, 2010.

166 *100 MILLION*: Miko Brando interview, *Bad 25*.

167 *"He still had great momentum"*: Author interview with John Sykes.

167 *"Wow, this is great!"*: Jeffrey Daniel interview, *Bad 25*.

168 *"I always thought it was a little bit forced"*: Author interview with Nathan East.

168 *"When that video stopped," "This just can't happen," "I don't think you fucking understand,"* and *"We did our thing"*: Author interview with Larry B. Davis.

169 *"If you ever drop another"*: Ibid.

169 *"I felt the kiss was too corny"*: Joe Pytka interview, *Bad 25*.

169 *"I don't want to be in it"* and *DiLeo meeting*: Author interview with Larry Stessel.

169 *"the worst things that ever happened"*: Author interview with Don Wilson.

170 *"I can't film anymore"* and *Stessel-Pytka negotiations*: Stessel interview.

170 *"Let it talk to you" and "Smooth Criminal" choreography origins*: Author interview with Vincent Paterson.

171 *Lorne Michaels and Phil Hartman script*: Author interview with Jerry Kramer.

171 *$22 million budget*: Maria Gallagher, "'Moonwalker Glides In: Michael Jackson Video Hits Stores, 300,000 Strong," *Philadelphia Daily News*, January 10, 1989, p. 34. Confirmed by Kramer.

172 *"She's unbelievable!"*: Currell interview.

172 *"He was just gorgeous to look at"*: Author interview with Jennifer Batten.

172 *Sheryl Crow as a waitress*: Author interview with Darryl Phinnessee.

172 *"I guess they assumed"*: Sheryl Crow interview, *Larry King Live* (CNN, August 23, 2006).

172 *"She was really dedicated"*: Author interview with John Lobel.

172 *"I want this"*: Phinnessee interview.

173 *"When you sing the first 'Ooh!'"*: Confidential source.

173 *"We'd rehearse and rehearse and rehearse"*: Author interview with Allen Branton.

173 *Early Bad tour description*: *Michael Jackson: Live in Japan* (CineVu International/ Downtown Entertainment Inc., 2009).

173 *"The vicious challenge"*: Author interview with Greg Phillinganes.

173 *$40 tickets and $700 resale prices in Japan*: Michael Small and Todd Gold, "Michael's First Epistle," *People*, October 12, 1987, p. 103.

173 *$4.4 million and $125 million*: Paul Grein, "A New Stage for Michael Jackson," *Los Angeles Times*, January 27, 1989, p. E1.

173 *$500,000 payroll*: Steve Dougherty and Todd Gold, "All 'Bad' Things Come to an End, as a Tearful Michael Jackson Bids Bye-Bye to the Highway," *People*, February 13, 1989, p. 52.

174 *"During rehearsals, we all had access to him"*: Batten interview.

174 *Space Mountain*: Author interview with Eddie Garcia.

174 *Synclavier importance, "Oh yeah, I can do something like this," $1.5 million in equipment, and emergency repair to $500,000 synthesizer*: Currell interview.

175 *"The beauty of watching that thing"*: Paterson interview.

175 *"I just understood that I was designing a ballet"*: Author interview with Tom McPhillips.

175 *Mop-bucket story and "Michael didn't like it"*: Lobel interview.

175 *Bad show description*: Michael Jackson, *Live at Wembley July 16, 1988* (Sony Legacy, 2012).

176 *"I would use the tremolo bar"*: Batten interview.

176 *"Elizabeth Taylor, Princess Diana"*: Author interview with Rory Kaplan.

177 *"It was Michael's absolute"*: Ibid.

177 *Jolie Levine's son Yoshi, "the popular kid with Michael," "He didn't want [Safechuck] to have to feel," and "I don't think that's a good way"*: Jolie Levine interview.

178 *"I gotta talk to you, Mike" exchange*: Author interview with Sam Emerson. J. Randy Taraborrelli (*Michael Jackson: The Magic, the Madness, the Whole Story 1958–2009* [New York Grand Central Publishing, 2009], p. 402) has a variation of this conversation, in the context of MJ giving Safechuck's parents a $100,000 Rolls Royce. Safechuck's family did not return calls.

178 *"When he met adults"*: Jolie Levine interview.

178 *"There were these Australian kids"*: McPhillips interview.

179 *"On the back of the set, they were alone"*: Henderson interview.

179 *DiLeo responds to questions*: Cutler Durkee and Todd Gold, *People*, September 14, 1987, p. 93.

180 *"Frank was hard and pretty stern"*: Branton interview.

CHAPTER 7

181 *$2 million Neverland Cinema*: Michael Goldberg, "Michael Jackson: The Making of the 'King of Pop,'" *Rolling Stone*, January 9, 1992, p. 32.

181 Star Wars *and Gregory Peck*: Author interview with Will Vinton.

181 *"I stayed overnight"*: Author interview with Nathan Watts.

182 *"Woo! The Zipper!" and Aqil Davidson's Neverland recollections*: Author interview with Aqil Davidson.

182 *Neverland's $60 million price and MJ's $17.5 offer*: Author interview with John Branca.

182 *Neverland description*: Sycamore Valley Ranch brochure, p. 2.

182 *Stallion and pig details*: David Friend, "Michael in Wonderland," *Life*, June 1993, p. 52.

182 *MJ at the R-Country Market*: Author interviews with Karen Dittmar (store employee).

182 *Teens recalling MJ summoning their classes*: Author interviews with Bailey Adams and Jaisey Williams (Los Olivos shop employees).

183 *"I remember going to the recording studio"*: Michael Jackson interview, *The Oprah Winfrey Show* (ABC, February 10, 1993).

183 *"You know, Michael"*: Vinton interview.

183 *"Simply put, he wanted to be his own boss"*: Joseph Vogel, *Man In the Music: The Creative Life and Work of Michael Jackson* (New York: Sterling, 2011), p. 135.

183 *"Michael doesn't want to work with you" exchange*: Frank DiLeo interview for Steve Knopper, *Appetite for Self-Destruction: The Spectacular Crash of the Record Industry in the Digital Age* (Free Press/Simon & Schuster, 2009).

184 Moonwalker *and three hundred thousand copies at $24.98*: Dennis Hunt, "Music Video Makers Bet on 'Moonwalker,'" *Los Angeles Times*, January 6, 1989, p. E22.

184 *Yetnikoff spreading story*: Walter Yetnikoff, *Howling at the Moon* (New York: Broadway Books, 2004), p. 254.

184 *How Geffen, Mottola, and Grubman overthrew Yetnikoff*: DiLeo interview for Knopper, *Appetite for Self-Destruction*.

184 *"an instinct for recognizing talent" and Sandy Gallin background*: Claudia Eller, "Managing in Turbulent Times," *Los Angeles Times*, January 16, 1994, Calendar, p. 8.

185 *MJ asked Branca for biggest contract ever*: Confidential source.

185 *$18 million advance*: Randall Rothenberg, "Michael Jackson Gets Thriller of Deal to Stay With Sony," *New York Times*, March 21, 1991, p. C17.

185 *25 percent royalty rate and $5 million to $120 million per album*: Alan Citron and Chuck Philips, "Michael Jackson Agrees to Huge Contract with Sony," *Los Angeles Times*, March 21, 1991, p. A1.

185 *Grubman, new deal points, and added albums to contract*: Confidential source.

185 *"He admired Elvis Presley's career" and Creative Artists Agency*: Author interview with Rusty Lemorande.

186   Anton First and Angels with Dirty Faces: Ibid.
186   "He never starts an album": Author interview with Bill Bottrell.
186   "He was desperately searching": Author interview with Chris Currell.
186   Hummed the main hook for "Black or White" at Westlake: Bottrell interview.
186   "It was a melding of minds": Author interview with Thom Russo.
187   "I don't want to belittle Bill": Author interview with Bruce Swedien.
187   Early song titles and evolution of "Black or White," including rap and L.T.B.: Bottrell interview.
188   "We went out and set up camp" and MJ with Culkin at Can-Am: Author interview with Daryl Simmons.
188   Heavy D introduced MJ to Riley: Heavy D interview on Z104, July 10, 2009.
188   "Quincy's productions have a bit more": Author interview with Dave Way.
188   "I remember him saying, 'I want Teddy's beats'": Simmons interview.
188   "I came in with ten grooves": Jon Dolan, "On the Edge," in Michael by the Editors of Rolling Stone (New York: HarperCollins, 2009), p. 138.
189   Buz Kohan convinced MJ to record "Gone Too Soon" as a tribute to Ryan White: Author interview with Buz Kohan.
189   "You could make a lot of money": Author interview with John Chamberlin.
189   "He would set up independent teams": Author interview with Matt Forger.
189   $10 million, $4,000 a day at Record One, and $3,000 to $4,000 a day at Larrabee: Goldberg, "Michael Jackson: The Making of the 'King of Pop,'" p. 32.
189   "There was no deadline": Dolan, in Michael by the Editors of Rolling Stone, p. 140.
189   "I had a sense," Swedien as heroic figure, Swedien and Riley, and "Bruce would sit there": Chamberlin interview.
190   "I was feeling increasingly isolated," "On Bad, he could call me after dinner," "Hey, Billy," Sundberg picking up the Bad mixes, "I had no way of knowing," "screw you," and Sundberg placing the microphones under DAT racks: Bottrell interview.
191   Unexpected cable, Chamberlin called Bottrell, and "I thought it could've come from Bruce": Chamberlin interview.
191   "It was beyond not cool": Russo interview.
191   "Boy, that's great": Swedien interview.
191   "When the deadline came," MJ crying over "Keep the Faith," "Pull yourself together," and "That was scary": Goldberg, "Michael Jackson: The Making of the 'King of Pop,'" p. 32.
192   70,000 copies per day: Ibid.
192   seven hundred thousand in first two weeks: Michael Goldberg, "Fast start for 'Dangerous,'" Rolling Stone, January 23, 1992, p. 9.
192   "a messy grab-bag of ideas": Chris Willman, "Dangerous? Hardly," Los Angeles Times, November 24, 1991, Calendar, p. 3.
192   "Dangerous was all Michael": Author interview with Larry Stessel.
192   "It's not as cohesive": Forger interview.
193   "Michael as quirky crossover wunderkind": Susan Fast, 33⅓: Dangerous (New York: Bloomsbury, 2014), p. 17.
194   "Elvis is the King," MTV memo, and "It was laughed at": Rob Tannenbaum and Craig Marks, I Want My MTV: The Uncensored Story of the Music Video Revolution (Penguin, 2012), pp. 438–39.
194   "You just had to deal with unrealistic requests": Tommy Mottola, Hitmaker: The Man and His Music (New York: Grand Central/Hachette, 2013), p. 233.

194 *MJ meeting with Sighvatsson and* The Simpsons: Tannenbaum and Marks, *I Want My MTV*, p. 435.

194 *"You have a good relationship," "They'd blown through what the budgets were,"* and *Landis's request for money and paycheck:* Author interview with John Landis.

194 *"Trying to make something":* Ibid.

195 *" 'Black or White' is a mess," "Making shit up," and "That's so neat":* Ibid.

196 *"I said, 'I want to do a dance number' ":* Jocelyn Vena, "Michael Jackson's Video Legacy in His Own Words," mtv.com, July 2, 2009.

196 *"Sandy was a screaming queen":* Tannenbaum and Marks, *I Want My MTV*, p. 437.

196 *"violence like Jackson's":* Elizabeth Chin, "Michael Jackson's Panther Dance: Double Consciousness and the Uncanny Business of Performing While Black," *Journal of Popular Music Studies* 23, no. 1 (March 2011): 58–74. Fast's *331/3: Dangerous* pointed me to the Chin and Vena sources.

197 *"Very prescient":* Landis interview.

197 *Mayonnaise-commercial disguise, Jordan's dubbed dialogue, "Something about the presence," and President Bush meeting:* Author interview with David Kellogg.

198 *Golden Temple restaurant:* Ian Halperin, *Unmasked: The Final Years of Michael Jackson* (New York: Simon Spotlight Entertainment, 2009), p. 10.

198 *"fine-boned, delicate and dark like his mother":* Maureen Orth, "Nightmare in Neverland," *Vanity Fair*, January 1994, p. 70.

198 *"The parents had separate families":* Author interview with Larry Feldman.

198 *June gave MJ her number and MJ's call:* June Chandler testimony, *The People of the State of California vs. Michael Joseph Jackson*, California Superior Court, April 11, 2005.

199 *MJ and Jordie shared love for video games:* Ibid.

199 *MJ invited Jordan to his "hideout" but Jordan couldn't go:* J. Randy Taraborrelli, *Michael Jackson: The Magic, The Madness, The Whole Story 1958–2009* (New York: Grand Central Publishing, 2009), p. 452.

199 *"The feel was different":* Author interview with Eddie Garcia.

199 *thirty-foot wall with 350 lights and "Now can I get that all the way around":* Author interview with Peter Morse.

199 *"We can't have that" and "I need rocket man":* Author interview with Tom McPhillips.

199 *$20,000 for rocket man, Chuck Norris stunt double, and "Michael would step away":* Author interview with Ken Graham.

200 *Soviet An-124 jet:* Karlayne Parker, "M.J.'s Livin' Large in Russian Jet," *Tampa Tribune*, June 17, 1992, p. 2.

200 *Three jets:* Author interview with Benny Collins.

200 *"changed stuff according to his liking":* Garcia interview.

200 *Ten-by-ten-foot dance platform on Victory tour and "He'd have cameras":* Author interview with Sam Emerson.

201 *"Balloons":* David Gest interview, *Michael Jackson: The Life of an Icon* (David Gest Productions, 2011).

201 *Debbie Rowe background and discoid lupus diagnosis:* Debbie Rowe testimony, *Katherine Jackson, et al., vs. AEG Live, et al.*, California Superior Court, August 14, 2013.

201 *Vitiligo description and "You have a little spot":* Author interview with Endre Granat.

202 *"He didn't want to be spotted up"*: Katherine Jackson interview, *Michael Jackson: The Life of an Icon*.

202 *"I'd never seen skin that color before"*: Author interview with Sonya Saul.

202 *"Jackson emerges a casualty"*: Greg Tate, "I'm White! What's Wrong with Michael Jackson," David Brackett, ed., *The Pop, Rock, and Soul Reader* (New York: Oxford University Press, 2005). pp. 342–44.

202 *Nightly loss of eight or nine pounds of "water" weight*: Rowe, *Katherine Jackson vs. AEG*, August 14, 2013.

202 *"All I knew was that he wasn't eating"*: McPhillips interview.

202 *Doctor, protein, and Kentucky Fried Chicken*: Emerson interview.

202 *"He was eating cheese pizzas"*: Author interview with Johnny Ciao.

203 *"Can you please come and see Mike?"* and *"happy and working"*: Author interview with David Forecast.

203 *Barnes and von Thurn und Taxis*: Taraborrelli, *Michael Jackson*, pp. 452–53.

203 *"There was always this family around"*: Confidential source.

203 *"It's just uncomfortable"*: Author interview with Sonya Saul.

203 *MJ called Jordan while on tour*: June Chandler testimony, *People vs. Michael Jackson*, April 11, 2005.

204 *"What's he doing?"* and *"Some artists, with twenty dancers"*: Morse interview.

204 *Dangerous tour description*: *Michael Jackson Live in Bucharest: The Dangerous Tour* (Epic/Sony, 1992).

204 *"The revelation of his sculpted, made-up face"*: Susan Fast, "Difference That Exceeded Understanding: Remembering Michael Jackson (1958–2009)," *Popular Music and Society* 33, no. 2 (2010): 261.

204 *HBO had paid $20 million*: David Wild, "Jackson: $20 Million from HBO," *Rolling Stone*, October 1, 1992, p. 21.

205 *Phillinganes trying to meet with MJ, "No problem, we'll do it this time," and "I wasted a day"*: Author interview with Greg Phillinganes.

206 *"Hmm, let me think," "Why would I want to sleep in a chamber?," and other interview details*: Michael Jackson, *The Oprah Winfrey Show* (ABC, February 10, 1993).

206 *Chandlers at Neverland details*: June Chandler testimony, *People vs. Michael Jackson*, April 11, 2005.

206 *Fifty-six staff members*: Orth, "Nightmare in Neverland," p. 70.

207 *"sort of act like the place was hers"*: Wade Robson testimony, *People vs. Michael Jackson*, May 5, 2005.

207 *"First of all, it's a huge bed"*: Ian Halperin, *Unmasked: The Final Years of Michael Jackson* (New York: Simon Spotlight Entertainment, 2009), p. 15.

207 *"Jordie is having fun"*: June Chandler testimony, *People vs. Michael Jackson*, April 11, 2005.

207 *$12,000 Cartier bracelet*: Taraborrelli, *Michael Jackson*, p. 460.

208 *MJ crashing at the Schwartz house*: June Chandler testimony, *People vs. Michael Jackson*, April 11, 2005.

208 *"[Chandler] would go on and on"* and *"Hang on"*: Carrie Fisher, *Shockaholic* (New York: Simon & Schuster, 2011), pp. 62–63.

208 *Grand Floridian, May 1993, Lily-June and MJ-Jordan rooms, and "He was not wanting to be with Lily and I"*: June Chandler testimony, *People vs. Michael Jackson*, April 11, 2005.

208 *Description of Jordan's room*: Raymond Chandler, *All That Glitters: The Crime and the Cover-Up* (New York: Midpoint Trade Books, 2004), pp. 27–28, 34, 58.

209 *"Ruby red lipstick," "Are you fucking my son" exchange, and Memorial Day spooning*: Ibid.

209 *"Began to get jealous of the involvement"*: Mary Fischer, "Was Michael Jackson Framed?," *GQ*, November 1994, pp. 214–69.

209 *"I am prepared to move against"*: The Chandler-Schwartz transcript has been printed in numerous sources, including Halperin, *Unmasked*, p. 20.

210 *"nastiest son of a bitch"*: Ibid.

210 *Barry Rothman background and "done him in"*: Fischer, "Was Michael Jackson Framed?," pp. 214–69.

210 *Fields's $500 an hour, "If you're on the side he's against," Abrams's two-page letter, and "reasonable suspicion"*: Orth, "Nightmare in Neverland," p. 70.

211 *"Sodium amytal is a barbiturate"*: Halperin, *Unmasked*, p. 36.

211 *Pellicano questions, "Did Michael ever touch," "I'm sorry, Jordie," "I've missed you too," "I'm going to ruin you" exchange, and "Oh, my God"*: Taraborrelli, *Michael Jackson*, pp. 481, 486, 489–91.

211 *$20 million offer*: Orth, "Nightmare in Neverland," p. 70.

212 *$350,000 counteroffer, $15 million, three-script proposal*: Ibid.

212 *Custody battles*: Soni Nazario and Amy Wallace, "International Furor Stirred by Allegations on Jackson Inquiry," *Los Angeles Times*, August 26, 1993, p. 1.

212 *Jordan revealing masturbation details to Abrams*: Orth, "Nightmare in Neverland," p. 70.

212 *"I can't talk to you"*: Author interview with Conan Nolan.

213 *KNBC breaking the story*: Ibid.

213 *"Significant" pain*: Gordon Sasaki testimony, *Katherine Jackson vs. AEG*, August 13, 2013.

213 *Sasaki prescribed Percocet*: Rowe, Sasaki testimony, *Jackson vs. AEG*, August 13, 2013.

213 *"Filling" of acne scars and 100 milligrams of Demerol, Klein and Hoefflin competition, Diprivan through eyelid, Debbie brought soup to Neverland*: Rowe testimony, *Katherine Jackson vs. AEG*, August 13, 2013.

214 *Stuart Finkelstein, Demerol, scarring, and IV morphine drip*: Stuart Finkelstein testimony, *Katherine Jackson vs. AEG*, July 8, 2013.

214 *"led him down the path"*: Author interview with Eve Wagner.

214 *"He was exhausted"*: Emerson interview.

215 *"So we were behind"*: Author interview with Federico Sicard.

215 *LeMarque charges, Paul Barresi, $100,000 to $150,000 tabloid offers, Hayvenhurst Five details, Quindoys and "gay pedophile," $283,000 in "unpaid overtime wages," Hard Copy $20,000 payment, and Blanca Francia details*: Diane Dimond, *Be Careful Who You Love* (New York: Atria, 2005), pp. 76–77, 78–79, 108, 120–22.

216 *"It was frustrating," "They kept a diary," "we were just trying," and Jordan's description of the Mirage suite*: Sicard interview.

216 *National Enquirer's twenty reporters and knocking on five hundred doors*: Fischer, "Was Michael Jackson Framed?," pp. 214–69.

217 *"I just think Michael needs help"*: Jim Newton, "Jackson's Sister Says She Believes He Is a Molester," *Los Angeles Times*, December 9, 1993, p. B1.

217 *La Toya Jackson's rescindment and Jack Gordon abuse*: La Toya Jackson, *Starting Over* (New York: Pocket Star Books, 2011), pp. 1–10.

217 *"A lot of strange things happened"*: Feldman interview.

217 *"Watching Diane Dimond on TV"*: Author interview with Lauren Weis Birnstein.

217 *"Sorry!" and "He left us there"*: Phillinganes interview.

218 *"Things went belly-up"*: Forecast interview.

218 *"He was there, but he wasn't there"*: Collins interview.

218 *"head powers"*: Finkelstein testimony, *Katherine Jackson vs. AEG*, July 8, 2013.

218 *"We had a slight professional discussion"*: Forecast interview.

218 *"The pressure resulting from these false allegations"*: Chuck Philips and Jim Newton, "Jackson Ends World Tour, Cites Painkiller Addiction," *Los Angeles Times*, November 13, 1993, p. 1.

218 *MJ's entourage, 737 to Reykjavík, Liz's dog, Luton Airport, and John Reid's $3 million home*: Forecast interview.

219 *MJ on the sofa, "No one knew," and "Listen, we will send your kids"*: Ibid.

219 *"Okay, tour's over," "We didn't even know," and flying An-124s to Vegas*: Author interview with Anthony Giordano.

219 *"I went to a lot of different experts"*: Feldman interview.

220 *Chandler filing details and quotes*: "Declaration of J. Chandler," Los Angeles Superior Court, December 28, 1993; posted on thesmokinggun.com, November 18, 2003.

220 *"splotches," "a light color similar to the color of his face," and "He has short pubic hair"*: Deborah Linden affidavit quoted in Halperin, *Unmasked*, p. 46.

220 *"sharp-tongued and tenacious" and Sneddon background*: Martin Kasindorf, "Jackson's trial to open Monday," *USA Today*, January 28, 2005, p. 3A; Associated Press, "Prosecutor in Jackson trial denies personal grudge played role in case," June 14, 2005; and United Press International, "District Attorneys Back Toxic Waste Proposal," *San Jose Mercury News*, July 25, 1986, p. 2C.

221 *"We were pretty satisfied"*: Author interview with Ron Zonen.

221 *"hard-on for Michael"*: Author interview with David LeGrand.

221 *"People are getting ticked off," police arrival at Neverland, and harp music argument with Weitzman*: Author interview with Richard Strick.

222 *"Get out!" and MJ examination details*: Halperin, *Unmasked*, pp. 52–53.

222 *"He was whining and complaining" and "shut the fuck up"*: Strick interview.

222 *Forecast denial*: Forecast interview.

222 *examination details including discoid lupus erythematosus*: Strick interview.

223 *"It sure would appear"*: Ibid.

223 *"Get rid of this thing" and "I felt that paying any substantial amount"*: Author interview with Bert Fields.

223 *"Are you crazy, Michael?," MJ bringing Branca back, Branca's criticism of Fields, and Branca replacing Fields with Cochran*: Zack O'Malley Greenburg, *Michael Jackson Inc.: The Rise, Fall and Rebirth of a Billion-Dollar Empire* (New York: Atria, 2014), pp. 166–67. Fields told Greenburg and me that he believed in MJ's innocence and did not want to settle.

223 *EMI deal*: Andrea Adelson, "EMI to Pay Michael Jackson $70 Million to Manage Music," *New York Times*, November 25, 1993, p. D6.

224 *Settlement details*: "Confidential Agreement and Mutual General Release," Janu-

ary 25, 1994, signed by Jordan and Evan Chandler, Larry Feldman, MJ, Johnnie Cochran, and Howard Weitzman; thesmokinggun.com, June 16, 2004.

224 *Feldman wouldn't talk about settlement details*: Feldman interview.

224 *Jordan Chandler's $2.35 million home*: Taraborelli, *Michael Jackson*, p. 545.

224 *"He would've been better off," "Pandora's box," and "The word got out"*: Author interview with Thomas Mesereau Jr.

CHAPTER 8

225 *"You are Michael Jackson's newest favorite director"*: Author interview with Rupert Wainwright.

226 *HIStory "teaser" filming details*: Ibid.

228 *"He never touched New York City's dirt"*: Author interview with Tony Black.

228 *"It was really a simple formula" and "offering no personal opinion"*: Author interview with Dan Beck.

229 *MJ's trip to Minneapolis to work on "Scream"*: Author interview with Steve Hodge.

229 *"Mr. Sherman"*: Black interview.

229 *"a current immediately passed between us"*: Brad Buxer, *Black & White*, November/December 2009, pp. 74–75; posted at info.sonicretro.org.

229 *"Brad was his comfort-level guy"*: Black interview.

229 *"Brad was one of the most hyper people"*: Author interview with Trip Khalaf.

230 *"He had his own power"*: Author interview with CJ deVillar.

230 *Eleven months, twenty-three-hour days, "We were regularly handing in 220-hour time sheets," "I want it a little faster," and "We're going to need ten or fifteen hours"*: Black interview.

231 *$4,000 per day and "Everything costs and costs"*: Ibid.

231 *Bernie Grundman at the Pierre, $400-an-hour Sony mastering, MJ didn't want to stick around for cold NYC autumn, $200,000 in personal costs, and "HIStory was probably the most expensive album"*: Author interview with Bernie Grundman.

231 *"The crew, all these sound engineers"*: Confidential source.

231 *"Fiery and angry" and "soundscapes"*: Author interview with Chuck Wild.

232 *Four days on a panning effect and opening/closing a door*: Author interview with Gus Garces.

232 *hiring people to record LA sounds and "whoosh-vroom"*: Ibid.

232 *"They Don't Care About Us" and "Michael wanted the drums"*: Author interview with Rob Hoffman.

232 *"I've never seen so many people"*: Author interview with Trevor Rabin.

233 *"sat for days mixing"*: Ibid.

233 *"magnum opus," "It dropped into my lap" and "a much more inclusive, liberating understanding," MJ played the song for Buxer, and "It became quite the obsession"*: Joseph Vogel, *Earth Song: Inside Michael Jackson's Magnum Opus* (BlakeVision e-book, 2011).

233 *"I was pretty disappointed"*: Author interview with Bill Bottrell.

234 *"gravitas"*: Author interview with William Ross.

234 *Magic Johnson dropped by and "I'll see you guys tomorrow"*: Hoffman interview.

234 *"an unearthly pairing"*: Cheryl Levenbrown, "It Wasn't Just Their Imagination," *Wichita Eagle*, February 4, 1994, p. 2A.

234 *"If Elvis really were alive"*: Argus Hamilton, "Rumor Has Elvis Rolling in Grave," *Daily Oklahoman*, July 13, 1994, p. 2.

234 *Scientology theory*: Richard N. Leiby, "Harmonic Conversion? Ex-Scientologists Speculate on Why Michael and Lisa Wed," *Washington Post*, August 4, 1994, p. C1.

234 *Graceland value from low millions to $100 million*: "If His Wedded Bliss Ends Now, MJ Wins Pact Lets Him Off $ Hook," *Philadelphia Daily News*, December 2, 1994, p. 4; Michael Villano, "In Print," *Billboard*, October 17, 1998, p. 28.

235 *"In spite of what some people speculated"*: Lisa Marie Presley interview, *The Oprah Winfrey Show* (ABC, October 21, 2010).

235 *"I wouldn't change anything"*: Author interview with Lisa Marie Presley for the *Chicago Tribune*, 2013. Presley refused to answer questions about MJ.

235 *"My dad's family's from Hee-Haw"*: Author interview with Clif Magness.

235 *Livingston-Stone dinner*: J. Randy Taraborrelli, *Michael Jackson: The Magic, The Madness, The Whole Story 1958–2009* (New York: Grand Central Publishing, 2009), pp. 507, 510, 520, 542.

236 *"You and me," "He was freaking out," Lisa Marie encouraged rehab, and Lisa Marie encouraged Chandler settlement*: Ibid.

236 *"We're together all the time"*: Michael Jackson and Lisa Marie Presley interview, *PrimeTime Live* (ABC, June 14, 1995).

236 *"very hot"*: J. Randy Taraborrelli, "Lisa Marie Presley Said He Was a Passionate Lover. So What WAS the Truth About Jackson's Sexuality," *Daily Mail*, June 30, 2009, pp. 32–34.

236 *Sexual details with MJ and "There were other girls"*: Author interview with Theresa Gonsalves.

236 *ten-karat diamond*: Lisa Marie Presley interview, *The Oprah Winfrey Show* (ABC, October 21, 2010).

236 *MJ wearing lipstick and fifteen-minute ceremony*: Matthew McCann Fenton, "The Odd Couple," *Entertainment Weekly*, May 30, 2001, p. 94

236 *Lisa Marie in beige dress, MJ in black, gold bands*: Robert Dominguez and Joanna Malloy, "Judge Says He Married Jackson, Presley," *The Day*, July 13, 1994, p. 8.

237 *"They spent a full week"*: Author interview with Donald Trump.

237 *"The magazines were questioning whether it was a publicity stunt"*: Hoffman interview.

237 *"Wherever she walks, she's always in slow motion" and earthquake details*: Wainwright interview.

237 *"His hand was blue afterwards"*: Lisa Marie Presley interview, *The Oprah Winfrey Show* (ABC, October 21, 2010).

238 *"I don't know why I did it"*: Taraborrelli, *Michael Jackson*, pp. 609–10.

238 *"I love my family very much"*: Michael Jackson interview, *The Oprah Winfrey Show* (ABC, February 10, 1993).

238 *"The bottom line here"*: Chuck Philips, "Jermaine Jackson: 'Word to the Badd!!': A Call to Michael," *Los Angeles Times*, November 7, 1991, p. F1.

238 *La Toya receiving $500,000*: Taraborrelli, *Michael Jackson*, pp. 423–26.

239 *Jermaine's divorce and child support*: In re the marriage of petitioner Hazel Jackson and respondent Jermaine Jackson, Superior Court of the State of California, March 30, 1998.

239 *"I had been abused and humiliated" and Jackie Jackson, Paula Abdul, and Enid Jackson*:

Margaret Maldonado Jackson, "Jackson Family Values" (Dove Audio, 1995), pp. x, 29–30.

239   *"She sounded like a young Michael Jackson"*: Author interview with Bobby Watson.

240   *"Masterstroke" and "I don't want my daughter"*: Anthony DeCurtis, "Free at Last," *Rolling Stone*, February 22, 1990, p. 44.

240   *"If we did something she liked" and "I wanted her to sound like a rock queen"*: Author interview with Jesse "Jellybean" Johnson.

241   *"people would see that I'm holding my own"*: Steve Pond, "Janet," *US*, November 1995, p. 46.

241   *"working on that with Michael" and "She wanted to work really hard"*: Hodge interview.

241   *Janet predicted MJ would like "Scream"*: Chaz Lipp, "An Interview with Jimmy Jam of the Original 7ven, Part Two," themortonreport.com, April 19, 2012.

241   *$75,000 average Sony video and "much of what we were doing"*: Beck interview.

241   *Sony paid for up to $1 million and "It was like, 'Michael, write a check' "*: Confidential source.

242   *other videos were costlier, "I am annoyed," and shoot expanding from six to fourteen days, 2001: A Space Odyssey influence*: Peter Sciretta, "Interview: 'Never Let Me Go' Director Mark Romanek," slashfilm.com, September 10, 2010.

242   *Santiago Calatrava*: Author interview with Richard Berg.

242   *Janet insisted on using her choreographers*: Author interview with Sean Cheesman.

242   *"Make it magical," rolling on the floor and CGI*: Author interview with Tina Landon.

242   *Landon and Cheesman teaching the routine to Travis Payne*: Cheesman interview.

243   *"It wasn't a good vibe," MJ's behind-the-scenes footage, cameramen paying no attention, and dark curtains*: Landon interview.

243   *"When I first met him," and "You would see Janet"*: Ibid.

243   *"Everything gets worked out in the end"*: Ibid.

243   *"It was a dream"*: Berg interview.

243   *"When we subsequently found out"*: Author interview with Nick Brandt.

244   *"It was absolutely electrifying" and other* Earth Song *video details*: Ibid.

244   *Forty tracks, "On another budget, where every orchestra session," "[Songs] would come in and out," and "Much Too Soon" as an orphan*: Hoffman interview.

245   *Work expanding from sixteen to eighteen hours*: Ibid.

245   *"I'm sorry"*: Joseph Vogel, *Man In the Music: The Creative Life and Work of Michael Jackson* (New York: Sterling, 2011), pp. 181–82.

245   *"Michael was like, saunter"*: deVillar interview.

245   *Chuck Wild at Record One, MJ's sleep habits, and "It was a conscious decision"*: Wild interview.

245   *Finishing the album at three* A.M. *and Grundman's speedy mastering*: Vogel, *Man In the Music*, pp. 181–82.

245   *HIStory cost $10 million*: Jon Wiederhorn, "A Marketing Blitz of Epic Proportions," *Rolling Stone*, June 15, 1995, p. 24.

246   *"filled with deep emotions"*: Liner notes, *HIStory*, 1995.

246   *"never intentionally meant to be offensive"*: Abraham Foxman statement, "ADL Welcomes Michael Jackson's Decision to Remove Anti-Semitic Lyrics from Song," press release from Anti-Defamation League, archive.adl.org, June 22, 1995.

246 *Gallin views and "He tried to convince me to do it"*: Zack O'Malley Greenburg, *Michael Jackson Inc.: The Rise, Fall and Rebirth of a Billion-Dollar Empire* (New York: Atria, 2014), p. 177.

247 *How MJ cut the new lyric for "They Don't Care About Us"*: Beck interview.

247 *$30 million Sony budget*: Neil Strauss, "Michael Jackson's 'HIStory' shows the growing stature of global marketing," *New York Times*, November 25, 1996, p. D7.

248 *Two-hour special and "It was going to be the man"*: Damien Shields, "Inside the King of Pop's 1995 HBO special that never was," damienshields.com, December 27, 2014.

248 *MJ meeting with Jeff Margolis*: Author interview with Jeff Margolis.

248 *Sony sound stage and one hundred dancers*: Shields, "Inside the King of Pop's 1995 HBO special that never was."

248 *Marcel Marceau details and "It would have been one of those moments"*: Margolis interview.

249 *A Clockwork Orange version of "Dangerous"*: Shields, "Inside the King of Pop's 1995 HBO special that never was."

249 *"a futuristic, gritty, industrial feel" and MJ's choreography work with Barry Lather*: Author interview with Barry Lather.

249 *Marceau noticing no MJ illness*: Shields, "Inside the King of Pop's 1995 HBO special that never was."

249 *MJ seemed sick days before the show*: Lather interview.

249 *Broth and "You need to eat!"*: Beck interview.

249 *Heaters between door and trailer*: David Stout, "Michael Jackson Collapses at Rehearsal," *New York Times*, December 7, 1995, p. B3.

249 *"He is exercising regularly," Hoefflin, Vistaril and Ultram, and MJ more sensitive to pain*: Allan Metzger testimony, *Katherine Jackson, et al., vs. AEG Live, et al.*, California Superior Court, September 13, 2013.

250 *"He fell super-duper hard"*: Ibid.

250 *"My manager and I looked at each other"*: Author interview with George Duke

250 *Morey called 911 and paramedics details*: Shields, "Inside the King of Pop's 1995 HBO special that never was."

250 *"Abnormally low" and blood pressure*: Stout, "Michael Jackson Collapses at Rehearsal," p. B3.

250 *"Michael got himself into this shit"*: Khalaf interview.

250 *use of new "Thriller" steps in "Ghosts"*: Lather interview.

250 *"Who are all these people?" exchange*: Author interview with Benny Collins and John Lobel.

251 *"It was just a general feeling"*: Khalaf interview.

251 *MJ worked on his routines separately*: Author interview with Stacy Walker.

252 *German anesthesiologists, "enough equipment where it looked like a surgical suite," Diprivan, and "What happens if you die?"*: Rowe testimony.

252 *"Debbie Rowe says she'll do it" exchange*: Rob Tannenbaum, "Playboy Interview: Lisa Marie Presley," *Playboy*, July 30, 2003, pp. 59–63, 142–44.

253 *"He relied on her a lot"*: Author interview with Mick Garris.

253 *MJ-Rowe wedding details*: Karen S. Schneider, "What Friends Are For," *People*, December 2, 1996, p. 100.

253 *$10 million divorce settlement*: Maureen Orth, "Losing His Grip," *Vanity Fair*, April 2003, pp. 420–48.

254 *"I can tell on his face" and Prince Jackson at the vocal session*: deVillar interview.

254 *Grace Rwaramba scouting for locations and negotiating prices*: Author interview with Des McGahan.

254 *"Michael trusted her one hundred percent"*: Author interview with Dieter Wiesner.

254 *Early 1998, Marvin's Room, and Mottola and Rooney*: Damien Shields, "Xscape Origins: The Songs & Stories Michael Jackson Left Behind" (Modegy e-book, 2015).

255 *Forty tracks in ten days, "I may go here," and "Michael wastes a lot of money"*: deVillar interview.

255 *$1.54 million for Oscar, $5,000 an hour for plane, and $20 million for* Invincible *production costs*: Peter Wilkinson, "Is the King of Pop Going Broke?," *Rolling Stone*, April 25, 2002, p. 25.

255 *"Get anything you want" DVD-shopping exchange*: Author interview with Harvey Mason Jr.

256 *"Michael would believe somehow that Sony was paying"*: Randall Sullivan, *Untouchable: The Strange Life and Tragic Death of Michael Jackson* (New York: Grove Press, 2012), p. 123.

256 *$140 million debt in 1998, $11.2 million in* HIStory *tour losses, and* Dangerous *tour broke even*: William R. Ackerman testimony, *Katherine Jackson vs. AEG*, August 12, 2013.

256 *HIStory tour $165 million gross*: Jeff Gottlieb, "Lawyer Attacks Jackson Earnings Estimate," *Los Angeles Times*, July 17, 2013, p. AA1.

256 *"He was simply addicted"*: Tommy Mottola, *Hitmaker: The Man and His Music* (New York: Grand Central/Hachette, 2013), p. 288.

256 *$90 million*: Author interview with Michael Schulhof; in Greenburg, *Michael Jackson, Inc.*, p.174, Martin Bandier, Sony ATV's president, quotes a higher figure, $115 million, plus about $10 million annually.

256 *"He said it very explicitly"*: Schulhof interview.

256 *"vampires" and "spiders"*: Lisa Marie Presley interview, *The Oprah Winfrey Show* (ABC, October 21, 2010).

256 *"I was always scolding him"*: Author interview with Uri Geller.

257 *Aubrey cut SUV rental from $3,000 to $300 and "He didn't keep on top"*: Author interview with Henry Aubrey.

257 *Wayne Nagin and Anthony Giordano charged into the pit*: Author interview with Anthony Giordano.

257 *"Oh, no, we've killed the pop star!"*: Khalaf interview.

257 *"He suffered back pain"*: Karen Faye testimony, *Katherine Jackson vs. AEG*, June 28 and May 9–10, 2013.

258 *Teddy Riley in a bus, "I want you to go to your studio," and recording junkyard trash cans with DAT*: Shields, "Xscape Origins."

258 *Dr. Freeze production details, "We would all have our different planets," "Look what Teddy did" exchange, and "A lot of egos"*: Author interview with Dr. Freeze.

258 *"It was a lot of 'Do it again'"*: Author interview with Rodney Jerkins.

259 *"You Rock My World," rhythmic beginning, and beds in studio*: Shields, "Xscape Origins."

259   "It cost a fortune": Author interview with Robert "Big Bert" Smith.

259   "Most of the record could have been done," "way-too-expensive hotels," "If inspiration happens," and "[That] never really happened: Author interview with Brad Gilderman.

260   "Everything should be a key change," $50,000 for orchestral changes, and "Everything was one hundred percent over-the-top": Ibid.

260   "We were advancing Michael": Mottola, Hitmaker, pp. 348–49.

260   "Tommy was calling Rodney for days": Smith interview.

260   "He did not succumb to pressure": Mason interview.

261   "Butterflies" recording details: Author interview with Natalie "The Floacist" Stewart.

262   "By the time it came out, it was dated": Smith interview.

262   "good, but by no means Michael's best work": Mottola, Hitmaker, p. 349.

262   "There were some songs that we loved": Mason interview.

262   Twenty to thirty outtakes per album and "Every time that he recorded": Brian Hiatt and Steve Knopper, "Michael Jackson's Unheard Music," Rolling Stone, August 6, 2009, p. 49.

263   "Tommy said things" and "very inappropriate": Aubrey interview.

263   Billboards and bus-stop signs along MJ's route: Author interview with Mike Tierney.

263   "All you heard were radios," MJ in Sony's Santa Monica offices, and "Oh no, they're not videos" exchange: Author interview with Cory Llewellyn.

263   Favorite songs: MJ interview on Yahoo! and GetMusic, October 26, 2001.

264   "been through hell and back," "I spend a lot of time in the forest," and "There are these two sweet little kids": Ibid.

CHAPTER 9

266   "He was basically bankrupt": Author interview with Ron Konitzer.

266   $45 to $2,500 tickets: "Michael Jackson Gets All-Star Tribute in New York," Jet, October 1, 2001, p. 59.

266   MJ's $7.5 million cut: Randall Sullivan, Untouchable: The Strange Life and Tragic Death of Michael Jackson (New York: Grove Press, 2012), p. 17.

266   Elizabeth Taylor's $250,000 necklace and "requests and demands": Frank Cascio interview, Michael Jackson: The Life of an Icon (David Gest Productions, 2011).

266   $1 million for Marlon Brando: F. Marc Schaffel vs. Michael Jackson, Superior Court of the State of California, County of Los Angeles, February 16, 2005.

266   Jermaine and paparazzi: Author interview with Henry Aubrey.

266   "Good" and "It's like LeBron James": Usher interview for Rolling Stone, courtesy of David Browne.

266   MJ wasn't around by 8.30: David Gest and Cascio interviews, Michael Jackson: The Life of an Icon.

266   Karen Faye and "sleeping aid": Karen Faye testimony, Katherine Jackson, et al., vs. AEG Live, et al., California Superior Court, July 19, 2013.

267   "He's sleeping" exchange: Gest and Cascio interviews, Michael Jackson: The Life of an Icon.

267   "I could tell he's out of it": Cascio interview, Michael Jackson: The Life of an Icon.

267   "I usually come to the show": Adrian Grant, Michael Jackson: Making HIStory (Exclusive Distributors, 1998), p. 16.

267 *"Whenever he wanted to make a movie"*: Author interview with Howard Rosenman.

268 *Sony catalog paid $6.5 to $14 million, Mijac paid $2 to $9 million*: William R. Ackerman testimony, *Katherine Jackson vs. AEG*, August 12, 2013.

268 *"You couldn't just confront him"*: Konitzer interview.

268 *"Michael gave him all kinds of ability"*: Author interview with Zia Modabber.

268 *Myung-Ho Lee background*: Union Finance & Investment Corp. (Republic of Korea), et al., vs. Michael Jackson, et al., Superior Court of the State of California, County of Los Angeles, April 2, 2002.

269 *"cash poor," $90 million loan, $200 million in new loans, $7.4 million to MJ Net, "extremely interested," $10 million stake reduced to $2 million, Lee's 2.5 percent fee*: Ibid.

269 *$150,000 to the Mali bank for Baba*: Maureen Orth, "Losing His Grip," *Vanity Fair*, April 2003, pp. 420–48.

269 *Every Last Inch and Tomorrow Always Comes*: Schaffel's alter ego, Marc Frederics, listed on imdb.com.

270 *"Bag man," "difficult for Jackson to spend," and payments for custom cars*: Schaffel vs. Michael Jackson, February 16, 2005.

270 *Arby's bag*: Tanya Caldwell, "Jury Views Jackson Deposition in Lawsuit," *Los Angeles Times*, July 7, 2006, p. B6.

270 *"He liked his french fries"*: Author interview with Howard King.

270 *"We all had large amounts of cash on us"*: Author interview with Marc Schaffel.

270 *$2 million diamond watch and "Hello, sir"*: Frank Cascio, *My Friend Michael* (New York: HarperCollins, 2011), pp. 217, 222.

271 *"completely freaked out," $500,000 in escape money, and "go underground"*: Sullivan, *Untouchable*, p. 20.

271 *Aubrey's version*: Aubrey interview.

271 *"As we crossed the George Washington Bridge"*: Cascio, *My Friend Michael*, p. 222.

271 *"We all flew back on the plane"*: Schaffel interview.

272 *McDonald's deal for $20 million*: Gary Susman, "'Give' Out," ew.com, July 15, 2002.

272 *McDonald's 5-million copy estimate*: Sullivan, *Untouchable*, p. 20.

272 *$51 million on Invincible*: Ibid., p. 23.

272 *$75,000 exploding building*: Confidential source.

272 *"That was a crazy job"*: Author interview with Rubin Mendoza.

272 *MJ asked for $8 million for a video*: Sullivan, *Untouchable*, p. 23.

272 *"The problem for Michael Jackson"*: Author interview with Michael Schulhof.

272 *Sharpton didn't consider Mottola a racist*: Author interview with Al Sharpton.

273 *"sad and pathetic" and "It had nothing to do with race, heaven or hell"*: Tommy Mottola, *Hitmaker: The Man and His Music* (New York: Grand Central/Hachette, 2013), p. 7.

273 *MJ threw $11 to $15 million offer into the trash and "No way I'm gonna do that"*: Author interview with James Meiskin.

273 *$800 million for Marvel*: "Samia" estimate in *Union Finance & Investment Corp. vs. Michael Jackson*, April 2, 2002; confirmed by confidential source.

274 *MJ Universe details, "light and funny," "new, fresh, motivated people," and power-of-*

attorney documents: Konitzer interview (who provided documents and the Neverland video).

274 $10 million every ninety days, airline hangar, $80,000 debt to electronics store, and "He owed money to everybody": LeGrand interview.

274 Al Malnik and MJ background: Alvin Malnik and Stephanie Williams, "Behind the Mask," *Haute Living*, July 8, 2009, pp. 3–4, and almalnik.com.

275 Malnik denied being Blanket's father: Kelly House, "Remembering Michael," *Miami Herald*, June 23, 2010, p. 1E.

275 sky-high interest rates: Sharon Waxman, "Michael Jackson Faces Cash Crisis," *New York Times*, February 12, 2004, p. E1.

275 Prince's godfather and "bring up Blanket": Ibid.

275 "solidified all of Michael's assets" and "Michael was spending probably double": Author interview with Charles Koppelman.

275 Malnik loaned MJ $7 million to $10 million: Stuart Backerman, "Speaking for Michael: An Insider's Account of the Most Turbulent Period in Michael Jackson's Career," unpublished memoir used with permission, p. 69.

275 "Al personally wrote checks": Sullivan, *Untouchable*, p. 314.

275 Michael Clayton details, quotes, and money figures: Author interview with Michael Clayton.

276 two thousand reporters: Matt Taibbi, "The Nation in the Mirror," *Rolling Stone*, June 30, 2005, p. 69.

276 sixteen-pound tumor and chemotherapy: Davellin Arvizo testimony, *The People of the State of California vs. Michael Joseph Jackson*, California Superior Court, March 4, 2005.

277 Doctors told his family to prepare for his funeral: Author interview with Ron Zonen.

277 Laugh Factory background: laughfactory.com.

277 Gavin's list of Tucker, Sandler, and MJ: Jamie Masada testimony, grand jury, Santa Barbara, California, *People vs. Michael Jackson*, March 30, 2004, and March 29, 2005.

277 Quincy Jones's office number: Masada testimony, *People vs. Michael Jackson*, March 29, 2005.

277 "scripted": Jay Leno testimony, *People vs. Michael Jackson*, May 24, 2005.

277 Masada working his contacts: Masada testimony, *People vs. Michael Jackson*, March 30, 2004, and March 29, 2005.

277 MJ calls Gavin at hospital, Arvizos visit Neverland, guest room, and lake: Davellin Arvizo testimony, *People vs. Michael Jackson*, March 3, 2005.

277 David didn't want Gavin to ride on rides: Gavin Arvizo testimony, *People vs. Michael Jackson*, March 9, 2005.

278 Nicknames and "I'm going to put you in the movies": Ibid.

278 "Michael adored Princess Diana" and "my devastating mistake": Author interview with Uri Geller.

278 Bashir documentary description: *Living with Michael Jackson* (Granada Television), US airdate February 6, 2003.

279 "really, really bad questions": Author interview with Dieter Wiesner.

280 "For us, it was not something special": Ibid.

281 "We got information": Ibid.

281 "Dude, that documentary fucking sucked": J. Randy Taraborrelli, *Michael Jackson:*

The Magic, The Madness, The Whole Story 1958–2009 (New York: Grand Central Publishing, 2009), p. 604.

281   *"Michael, I love the way you are with children," "Get your ass in gear," and ABC, NBC, and Fox offers*: Backerman, "Speaking for Michael," pp. 38–43.

281   *$7.3 million, $4 million, and 20 percent: Schaffel vs. Michael Jackson*, February 16, 2005.

282   *Rebuttal-video lifeline*: Konitzer interview.

283   *$20,000 for Katherine's medicine*: Ibid.

283   *"I felt enough was enough" and "unfounded"*: Mike Taibbi, today.com, March 16, 2004.

283   *"shopping all the time"*: Konitzer interview.

284   *"Kids who fabricate"*: Author interview with Stan Katz.

284   *"Go away!," MJ Mirage rampage, $250,000 in damages, and "some berserk, out-of-control madman"*: Backerman, "Speaking for Michael," pp. 8–10, 122–23.

284   *"Everything fell apart"*: Konitzer interview.

284   *MJ mug shot preparation*: Backerman, "Speaking for Michael," pp. 8–10, 122–23.

285   *"wasn't even the Michael that I knew"*: Ibid.

285   *Malnik posted bail*: Backerman, Ibid., p. 69, confirmed by Schaffel interview.

285   *Discounted bail-bonds service and $300,000 up front*: Schaffel interview.

285   *Jesse Jackson on three times as much bail and "As soon as you get famous and black"*: Shawn Hubler, "Is Race Card in Jackson Deck?," *Los Angeles Times*, January 14, 2004, p. E1.

285   *"Dieter, the devil is listening"*: Backerman, "Speaking for Michael," p. 130.

285   *"And there was no access anymore"*: Konitzer interview.

286   *"the only D.A. in the nation"*: Gillian Flaccus, "Feud Between Jackson, DA Goes Back Years," Associated Press, November 20, 2003.

286   *"Was he eager to put him in prison?" and "aggressive sort of guy"*: Zonen interview.

286   *"Turn on your TV"*: Author interview with Linda Deutsch.

286   *"He's way over his head"*: Author interview with Thomas Mesereau Jr. Geragos did not respond to interview requests.

287   *Cochran to Randy while on his deathbed and "If it was me, I'd want Tom Mesereau"*: Sullivan, *Untouchable*, p. 316.

287   *Mesereau background*: Linda Deutsch, "Blake's New Lawyer Is Unlikely Choice," Associated Press, January 18, 2003.

287   *Mesereau meeting with Randy, MJ mansion, "I don't want the Nation of Islam," "This message of inclusion," and "on cloud nine"*: Mesereau interview.

287   *"I never felt it was in the bag" and "Okay, my life is about to change"*: Zonen interview.

288   *Mesereau in Santa Barbara County*: Mesereau interview.

288   *"They fought for copies"*: Rodney Melville speech at "Frozen in Time" panel, September 5, 2010.

288   *"A goddamn zoo, a freak show" and "fat white psychopath"*: Matt Taibbi, "Inside the Strangest Trial on Earth," *Rolling Stone*, April 7, 2005, p. 35.

288   *Sheree Wilkins background*: Author interview with Sheree Wilkins.

289   *"I believe the connection was pain"*: Ibid.

289   *Diane Dimond interviewed twenty "possible victims" and "I think Michael Jackson"*: Author interview with Diane Dimond.

289   *"A lot of people came there"*: Deutsch interview.

289 *Juror details*: "Jury Selected in Michael Jackson Case," billboard.com, February 23, 2005.

289 *Mesereau wanted female jurors*: Mesereau interview.

289 *"I like people who are businessmen"*: Zonen interview.

289 *"Humorless creep"*: Taibbi, "Inside the Strangest Trial on Earth," p. 35.

290 *"Like the sheriff and I are really into that"*: "Prosecutor in Jackson trial denies personal grudge played role in case," Associated Press, June 14, 2005.

290 *"On February the third of 2003" and other Sneddon opening-statement remarks*: Sneddon testimony in *People vs. Michael Jackson*, February 28, 2005.

290 *"Sneddon was much more abrasive"*: Author interview with Peter Bowes.

290 *"The way the state structured their case"*: Dimond interview.

290 *"He was a drug addict"*: Zonen interview.

291 *"Ladies and gentlemen, I have an* organized *opening statement,"* accusations *of Janet Arvizo exploiting and expenses, and "And guess what happens"*: Mesereau, *People vs. Michael Jackson*.

291 *"Very talkative" and other details from Davellin testimony, including 160 "I don't remember" references and 130 "I don't know references"*: Davellin Arvizo testimony, *People vs. Michael Jackson*, March 3, 2005.

292 *"I got dressed for this court date"*: Author interview with Tony Baxter.

292 *"Got milk?," "You're missing some pussy," and other Star testimony details*: Star Arvizo testimony, *People vs. Michael Jackson*, March 9, 2005.

293 *"[Michael] was like my best friend ever," "Daddy," and other Gavin testimony details*: Gavin Arvizo testimony, *People vs. Michael Jackson*, March 9, 2005.

293 *"You could see his health declining"*: Bowes interview.

294 *"close the book" and "most people thought anybody"*: Mesereau interview.

294 *"We wanted a cooperative witness"*: Zonen interview.

295 *"Michael wasn't paying him twenty million"*: Ibid.

295 *"Dressed impeccably" and "Gold digger"*: Aphrodite Jones, *Michael Jackson Conspiracy* (Aphrodite Jones, 2012), pp. 189–90.

295 *$7,000 gift certificate and other June Chandler testimony details*: June Chandler testimony, *People vs. Michael Jackson*, April 11, 2005.

295 *Janet Arvizo's testimony key to prosecution case*: Matthew Davis, "Profile: The Arvizo family," news.bbc.co.uk, June 13, 2005.

295 *Janet Arvizo testimony*: Janet Arvizo testimony, *People vs. Michael Jackson*, April 13, 2005.

295 *"It was just startling"*: Deutsch interview.

296 *"Why not Merv Griffin"*: Matt Taibbi, "The Nation in the Mirror," pp. 69–72.

296 *Shaplen narrating the verdict*: Author interview with Peter Shaplen.

297 *ABC coaxing six jurors onto a Disney jet and CNN locking out other networks*: Ibid.

297 *Wilkins on a stretcher and "I had given absolutely everything"*: Wilkins interview.

297 *"The one thing I really regret"*: Clayton interview.

CHAPTER 10

298 *Manama description, including prostitutes and movie theaters*: Yaroslav Trofimov, "Upon Sober Reflection, Bahrain Reconsiders the Wages of Sin," *Wall Street Journal*, June 9, 2009, p. A1.

298 *"baby Dubai, with its prenatal skyscrapers and tax shelters"*: Devin Friedman, "Where's Michael?," *GQ*, May 2006, pp. 175–77.

298 *DJ Whoo Kid flight and lost passport*: Author interview with DJ Whoo Kid.

299 *Sheik's palace pool, MJ with legs exposed, "Do you not understand?" exchange, and Abdullah paying*: Ibid.

299 *"It's difficult to explain to people"*: Author interview with Guy Holmes.

299 *"Where Have You Been?" and "It was like we'd already spent time together"*: Friedman, "Where's Michael?," 175–77.

299 *Sheikh loaned MJ more than $2 million*: Patrick Foster, "Sheikh's expensive duet with Jackson ends on a sour note," *The Times*, November 18, 2008, p. 5.

300 *"Michael was really, really ill"*: Holmes interview.

300 *Movies and Grace Rwaramba as manager*: Friedman, "Where's Michael?," pp. 175–77.

300 *Legend, Beckford, and other details of sheik dinner with MJ*: DJ Whoo Kid interview.

300 *Holmes pored over MJ's business papers and 76 to 80 percent of revenue*: Holmes interview.

301 *More than three dozen lawsuits*: Holmes's number is forty-seven, but another source close to MJ says that "seems high." Zack O'Malley Greenburg, *Michael Jackson Inc.: The Rise, Fall and Rebirth of a Billion-Dollar Empire* (New York: Atria, 2014), p. 225, identifies "the claims of dozens of creditors" upon MJ's death in 2009.

301 *$275 million in debt and overspending $15 to $20 million per year*: Ackerman testimony.

301 *"He knew he wasn't that fit"*: Holmes interview.

301 *"regain his health and overall stability"*: Author interview with Qays Zu'bi.

301 *Häagen-Dazs and a Ferrari and $7 million*: "Michael Jackson Sued By Sheik for $7M," Associated Press, cbsnews.com, November 22, 2008.

301 *$15 million per year and $24 to $45 million in spending*: Ackerman testimony.

302 *"No, I'm in trouble" exchange and $330 million cash flow*: Greenburg, *Michael Jackson Inc.*, pp. 200–2.

302 *"grossly disproportionate" and "It made a lot of sense"*: Author interview with Donald David.

302 *$9,000 suite at Burj Al Arab*: Timothy L. O'Brien, "Thriller: Rescuing a Sinking Pop Star: What Happened to the Fortune Michael Jackson Made?," *New York Times*, May 14, 2006, p. B1.

302 *Twelve advisers*: Author interview with Rob Wiesenthal.

303 *"He went through literally every key title" and Sony-MJ agreement details*: Ibid.

303 *6 percent Citibank offer and 20 percent Fortress rate*: O'Brien, "Thriller: Rescuing a Sinking Pop Star," p. B1.

303 *Branca gave up his 5 percent*: Letter from Ziffren, Brittenham, Branca, et al., to Michael J. Jackson, et al., March 29, 2006.

303 *"Mate, if you don't do" and "Thank you, and I appreciate your help"*: Holmes interview.

304 *"There's always going to be someone"*: Author interview with Thomas Mesereau Jr.

304 *Thirty thousand euros a week and Luggala Castle*: "King of Pop Stayed at Luggala for Months," independent.ie, January 7, 2009.

304 *Flatley encounter*: Confidential source.

304   *"pretty good health," "He had the body of a dancer," "dermal fillers in his face," two or three nose jobs, and extreme sensitivity to pain:* Confidential source.

305   *Propofol as "milk" and other European doctor–MJ details:* Ibid.

305   *"Because Michael always has leeches":* Author interview with will.i.am.

305   *"Nice rhythm," will.i.am-MJ collaboration details, and description of music:* Access Hollywood (November 2006); footage on accesshollywood.com.

305   *"I'm Gonna Miss You":* Brian Hiatt and Steve Knopper, "Michael Jackson's Unheard Music," *Rolling Stone*, August 6, 2009, p. 49.

305   *"You gotta turn the snare up!":* will.i.am interview

305   *Rwaramba doing most of the talking:* Author interview with Des McGahan.

306   *"You could have pushed me over," McGahan leaving the gate unlocked, "Oh, that's my dad," and Scarli's CD and Paris encounter:* Ibid.

306   *"What's up, Mr. Reid?" and Sharpton-Reid conversation:* Author interview with Al Sharpton.

307   *$100,000 and forty-six employees:* "King of Pop to Pay Neverland Workers," cnn.com, March 15, 2006.

307   *$91,602 and Martin Dinnes:* "Jackson Sued for Unpaid Vet Bills," billboard.com, January 7, 2006.

307   *Celine Dion's more than $500,000 per show, four thousand seats, $80 million per year, and 147 shows:* Pollstar.

307   *2785 South Monte Cristo Way mansion details and "absurdly oversized living room":* Bill Whitfield and Javon Beard, with Tanner Colby, *Remember the Time: Protecting Michael Jackson in His Final Days* (New York: Weinstein, 2014), pp. 32, 55, 57–58, 61–64.

308   *"You're probably one of those," Randy-Rebbie-Jackie exchange, and "Michael owe me money!":* Ibid.

308   *Alimorad Farshchian and four or five Naltrexone implants:* Alimorad Farshchian testimony, *Katherine Jackson vs. AEG*, July 24, 2013.

309   *Cascio suspicious but came around:* Frank Cascio, *My Friend Michael* (New York: HarperCollins, 2011), pp. 199–200.

309   *Aubrey's mistrust of Farshchian and "If certain things continue" exchange:* Author interview with Henry Aubrey. Farshchian did not respond to interview requests.

309   *Randy Jackson intervention attempts, Randy on Rwaramba, and "It was ironic":* Randy Jackson testimony, *Katherine Jackson vs. AEG*, played in court August 9, 2013.

309   *"Michael struggled with substance abuse":* Confidential source.

309   *Palms hotel and room service and "He was good at hiding":* Author interview with Zoe Thrall.

309   *"Clicked instantly" and other Akon details:* Jocelyn Vena, "Akon Won't Release Unfinished Michael Jackson Tracks," mtv.com, November 18, 2010.

310   *SoBe commercial:* Thrall interview.

310   *"I can't just be like the Osmonds":* Whitfield and Beard, *Remember the Time*, p. 114.

310   *Allgood meeting with Joe Jackson and RV with $50,000 in glove box:* Author interview with Patrick Allocco. Leonard Rowe did not respond to requests for comment. In Leonard Rowe's 2010 book, *What Really Happened to Michael Jackson: The Evil Side of the Entertainment Industry* (Linell-Diamond Enterprises), he makes some excellent points—why did MJ's manager Tohme Tohme receive $100,000

per month from promoter AEG when he was supposed to represent his client's interests? But he undercuts his arguments by obsessing about Jews in the music business.

311 *"a good amount of infighting," "This is a good deal for Michael," $9 to $12 million estimate, and "Michael could have walked away with $24 million"*: Ibid.

311 *$668,215 in cash*: Stevenson Jacobs, "Michael Jackson Said Net Worth $236M in 2007," Associated Press, July 3, 2009.

311 *"People would come up and drop these things"*: Whitfield and Beard, *Remember the Time*, p. 145.

311 *Thirty-seven thousand square feet on 99 Spanish Gate Drive*: Randall Sullivan, *Untouchable: The Strange Life and Tragic Death of Michael Jackson* (New York: Grove Press, 2012), p. 226.

311 *Raymone Bain and Peter Lopez met with Randy Phillips*: Randy Phillips testimony, *Katherine Jackson vs. AEG*, June 4–6, 10–14.

312 *They settled for $3.5 million*: Kim Masters, "Michael Jackson's Strange Final Days Revealed in Dueling Lawsuits," hollywoodreporter.com, July 19, 2012.

312 *"under the influence of drugs or alcohol" and "under the influence of prescription medication"*: Michael Jackson deposition, *Dieter Wiesner vs. Michael Jackson, et al.*, Superior Court for the County of Los Angeles, July 25, 2007.

312 *"You're surrounded by idiots again" and "alive and excited"*: Cascio, *My Friend Michael*, pp. 306–7.

312 *Fortress owned the note on Neverland*: "Re: $92,000,000 Senior Secured Loan Commitment and $3,000,000 Secured Purchase Option," Fortress Credit Corp. letter to MJ, April 18, 2005.

312 *$23 million mortgage*: Greenburg, *Michael Jackson Inc.*, pp 213–14

313 *Wizard of Oz–style "leisure kingdom," Tohme meeting, "Is there anyone you know," and "This guy"*: Jermaine Jackson, *You Are Not Alone: Michael Through a Brother's Eyes* (New York: Touchstone/Simon & Schuster, 2011), pp. 399–401.

313 *Tohme exercised "his extraordinary gift"*: Sullivan, *Untouchable*, p. 227.

313 *Barrack, Tohme, and MJ meeting details, "All of a sudden I got to this place," and "Are you willing to start down that line?"*: Greenburg, *Michael Jackson Inc.*, pp. 210–15.

314 *"He's a real nonstop salesman"*: Author interview with Arnold Stiefel.

314 *Phillips background and $1 million per show*: Phillips testimony, *Katherine Jackson vs. AEG*.

315 *Ninety-ten split, $5 million advance to MJ, of which $3 million went to settling with the sheik, $15 million line of credit, and $100,000 or $1.2 million*: Concerts West/ AEG draft of MJ contract, October 27, 2008, *Katherine Jackson vs. AEG* discovery documents.

315 *Gongaware tour sketch, including MJ net of $132 million and AEG fee of $27 million, "It's a big number," and "I do not recommend wearing suits"*: Paul Gongaware e-mail to Randy Phillips, et al., September 26, 2008, *Katherine Jackson vs. AEG* discovery documents.

316 *Promoters arranged MJ dates around other stars*: E-mails between Randy Phillips, David Campbell, John Meglen, Rob Hallett, and other AEG officials, November 4–6, 2008, *Katherine Jackson vs. AEG* discovery documents.

316 *Randy Phillips–Jeffrey Katzenberg exchange, "For you, for sure," and "You have a*

major AEG I.O.U.": E-mails between Phillips and Katzenberg, November 25, 2008, *Katherine Jackson vs.* AEG discovery documents.

316 *"One hopes that MJ will see the light"*: Timm Woolley e-mail, December 10, 2008, *Katherine Jackson vs.* AEG discovery documents.

316 *"He can have my lung later" and AEG executives passing around e-mails about MJ's health*: Dan Beckerman e-mail to Randy Phillips and others, December 23, 2008, *Katherine Jackson vs.* AEG discovery documents.

316 *"MJ is getting very real"*: Phillips e-mail to Gongaware and others, January 6, 2009, *Katherine Jackson vs.* AEG discovery documents.

316 *"Do you think he can pull this off?"*: Beckerman e-mail to Phillips, January 16, 2009, *Katherine Jackson vs.* AEG discovery documents.

316 *"He has to, or financial disaster awaits"*: Phillips e-mail to Gongaware and others, January 23, 2009, *Katherine Jackson vs.* AEG discovery documents.

316 *MJ meeting with Tohme, Hawk, and Lopez, with champagne*: Phillips testimony, *Katherine Jackson vs.* AEG.

317 *$17.5 million insurance policy*: Sue Zeidler, "Analysis: Jackson Case Will Change Tune for Concert, Artist Insurance," Reuters, October 4, 2013.

317 *"Passed with flying colors"*: Author interview with Randy Phillips, for *Rolling Stone*, 2009.

317 *Murray wanted $5 million, "This is the machine," and "Offer him one fifty!" exchange*: Paul Gongaware testimony, *Katherine Jackson vs.* AEG, May 28–31, June 3–4.

317 *MJ auction details*: "King of Pop: A Once in a Lifetime Public Exhibition Featuring Property from the Life and Career of Michael Jackson and Neverland Ranch," April 14–25, 2009, juliensauctions.com.

317 *"everything"*: Author interview with Darren Julien, for *Rolling Stone*, 2009.

318 *"That was the ultimate glove-wearer"*: Author interview with Jay Ruckel.

318 *125 visits to Neverland, "creative genius," condition of Neverland and rides, and "there was no question in our mind"*: Julien interview.

318 *Julien spent $2 million*: Ben Sisario, "Sales of Michael Jackson's Property Canceled," *New York Times*, April 14, 2009, p. A13.

318 *James R. Weller as fixer, MJ fired Tohme*: Sullivan, *Untouchable*, pp. 303, 376. Tohme Tohme did not respond to calls and e-mails.

319 *"We cannot be forced into stopping this"*: Gongaware e-mail to Phillips, et al., February 27, 2009, *Katherine Jackson vs.* AEG discovery documents.

319 *"We have a little issue"*: Phillips testimony, *Katherine Jackson vs.* AEG.

319 *"MJ is locked in his room"*: Phillips e-mail to Tim Leiweke, March 5, 2009, *Katherine Jackson vs.* AEG discovery documents.

319 *"Are you kidding me?"*: Leiweke e-mail to Phillips, March 5, 2009, *Katherine Jackson vs.* AEG discovery documents.

319 *"Alberto, you've got to let me in" and MJ on the couch*: Phillips testimony, *Katherine Jackson vs.* AEG.

320 *"I screamed at him so loud" and "an emotionally paralyzed mess"*: Phillips e-mail to Leiweke, March 5, 2009, *Katherine Jackson vs.* AEG discovery documents.

320 *"And when he went through that curtain" and other details of MJ's press conference preparation*: Ibid.

320 *Phillips talking MJ out of $93-million mansion and "When I'm on that stage"*: Phillips testimony, *Katherine Jackson vs.* AEG.

320 *"That's what motivated him"*: Phillips interview for *Rolling Stone*, 2009, courtesy of Claire Hoffman.

320 *Silver spacesuit, blue diamonds, and robot shoulder pads*: Zaldy Goco interview in *Michael Jackson's This Is It* (Columbia Pictures, 2009).

321 *Mirrored shoes and three million Swarovski crystals*: Ibid.

321 *6,600 crystals*: Ruckel interview.

321 *130-by-30-foot LED screen and "He had these great ideas," live-monkey idea, and $6 million budget*: Author interview with Bruce Jones.

321 *MJ paid 95 percent of Ortega's salary*: Gongaware testimony, *Katherine Jackson vs. AEG.*

321 *"MJ and I are already so in sync"*: Kenny Ortega e-mail to Gongaware, March 27, 2009, *Katherine Jackson vs. AEG* discovery documents.

321 *"He was thinner"*: Author interview with Stacy Walker.

322 *"He just walked in"*: Author interview with Chris Grant.

322 *Editing rehearsal clips, twenty-five rehearsals, "Michael asked to have the lights turned down," and general details of song-rehearsal dates*: Author interview with Tim Patterson.

322 *MJ-Bearden "It should be simpler" exchange* : *Michael Jackson's This Is It.*

323 *"He was very in charge"*: Grant interview.

323 *Ortega appearance*: *Michael Jackson's This Is It.*

323 *"Kenny never shows stress"*: Author interview with Erin "Topaz" Lareau.

323 *MJ's rehearsal schedule*: Patterson interview.

323 *Explosions, black widow spider, and cherry picker*: *Michael Jackson's This Is It.*

324 *"He would just fill the room up"*: Author interview with Tommy Organ.

324 *Cheering during "Billie Jean" and "At least we get a feel of it"*: *Michael Jackson's This Is It.*

324 *MJ's agreement on extra shows in exchange for "an English country estate"*: Phillips interview for *Rolling Stone*, 2009, courtesy of Claire Hoffman.

324 *MJ's agreement on extra shows in exchange for Guinness recognition*: Phillips testimony, *Katherine Jackson vs. AEG.*

325 *John Scher's 75 percent prediction*: Fred Goodman, with Steve Knopper, "Michael Jackson's Troubled Comeback," *Rolling Stone*, July 9, 2009, pp. 19–20.

325 *"I just believed in him"*: Phillips interview.

325 *"He can't do this" and "He might last a week"*: Faye testimony, *Katherine Jackson vs. AEG.*

325 *"I never noticed frailty" and "He looked like a cheetah"*: Author interview with Bashiri Johnson.

325 *"not in shape enough" and "Once he's healthy enough"*: Michael Bearden e-mail to Kenny Ortega, June 16, 2009, *Katherine Jackson vs. AEG* discovery documents.

325 *"It's a shame" and "I know why you're calling"*: Author interview with Ron Weisner.

325 *"Oh my God . . . I can see Michael's heart"*: Faye testimony.

326 *"Get him a bucket of chicken!"*: Ibid.

326 *"I've got to get a good night's sleep," "What if you don't wake up?," and other details about Cherilyn Lee's treatment of MJ*: Lee testimony, *Katherine Jackson vs. AEG*, August 28–29, 2013.

326 *MJ wrapped in blankets and "He just seemed he wasn't there"*: Ortega testimony, *Katherine Jackson vs. AEG*, July 8–10 and August 8, 2013.

327 *"He appeared quite weak and fatigued"*: Ortega e-mail to Phillips, June 20, 2009, *Katherine Jackson vs. AEG* discovery documents.

327 *"cold to the touch" and Karen Faye begged Ortega and others to intervene*: Faye testimony.

327 *"Stop trying to be an amateur doctor," "Please, tell the doctor," "Yes, that's what happened," "I am fine," and hug*: Kenny Ortega testimony, *People vs. Conrad Robert Murray*, September 27, 2011.

327 *"all the toys were coming out"*: Author interview with Abby Franklin.

327 *"He was pretty involved"*: Grant interview.

328 *"Earth Song" changes, "let it rumble!," and "Thank you, everybody"*: Michael Jackson's *This Is It*.

328 *"secure the proper route"*: Alvarez testimony, *People vs. Murray*, September 29, 2011.

328 *Faheem Muhammad drove MJ home, fan encounters, MJ rolled down window, bodyguards loaded gifts into car, Williams noticed Murray's BMW, Williams returned home, and perimeter check*: Michael Amir Williams testimony, *People vs. Murray*, September 28, 2011.

CHAPTER 11

329 *Six Carnival models, $1,200 a week, stabbing story, "No! You can't do it," "He is a pleaser"*: Author interview with Karen "Kalucha" Chacon.

329 *"He knew better"*: Author interview with Orlando Martinez.

330 *"Pissing contest over who could give the better drug"*: Debbie Rowe testimony, *Katherine Jackson, et al., vs. AEG Live, et al.*, California Superior Court.

330 *Scott David Saunders's relationship with MJ and watching Spider-Man at Neverland*: Scott David Saunders testimony, *Katherine Jackson vs. AEG*, July 25, 2013.

331 *PlayStation 2, popcorn machine, and Navigator drives*: Ibid.

331 *"innumerable occasions," MJ and Allan Metzger and aliases "For confidentiality"*: Allan Metzger testimony, *Katherine Jackson vs. AEG*.

331 *"hospital heroin" and ten times over twelve years*: Rowe testimony, *Katherine Jackson vs. AEG*.

331 *"He had different doctors in different places"*: Metzger testimony, *Katherine Jackson vs. AEG*.

331 *"He would be getting hundreds of injections," "So therefore he often needed to be sedated," Versed and propofol, and "He referred to it as 'the milk'"*: David Fournier testimony, *Katherine Jackson vs. AEG*, July 25, 2013.

332 *"You've done enough"*: Ibid.

332 *"to give a flatter appearance," anesthesiologist and propofol, "milk," and "Most people don't really"*: Stephen Gordon testimony, *Katherine Jackson vs. AEG*, August 21, 2013.

332 *Description of MJ hotel room incident and "wake up Daddy"*: Mike LaPerruque testimony, *Katherine Jackson vs. AEG*, August 1, 2013.

332 *"I'm not going to lie"*: Author interview with Henry Aubrey.

332 *"profound" and "Particularly when performing"*: Metzger testimony.

332 *"I don't usually go meet people in hotel rooms" and Christine Quinn procedure details*: Christine Quinn testimony, *Katherine Jackson vs. AEG*, August 28, 2013.

333 *"He told me that it's the best sleep"*: Ibid.

333 *"shot of Demerol for the road," "there's no way I'm doing that,"* and Conrad Murray accompanied MJ to Gordon appointment for Juvéderm: Gordon testimony, *Katherine Jackson vs. AEG.*

333 Murray had eight children with seven women: Orlando Martinez testimony, *Katherine Jackson vs. AEG*, April 30, 2013.

333 Murray met Sade Anding at Sullivan's Steakhouse: Sade Anding testimony, *People vs. Conrad Robert Murray*, October 4, 2011.

333 *"serial womanizer," "Had it not been for his voracious sexual,"* and Murray background, including parents' names, and Grenada birthplace: David Jones, "Dr. Conrad Murray: The sleazy Lothario Who Made for a Perfect Fall-Guy," *Daily Mail*, November 8, 2011, pp. 4–5.

334 *Zufan Tesfai*: Ibid.

334 Meharry Medical School and $45,000 in taxes: Mallory Simon, "Doctor Suffering Financially When He Decided to Work for Jackson," cnn.com, July 29, 2009.

334 Murray's father opened Acres Home clinic: Ruby Mosley testimony, *People vs. Conrad Robert Murray*, October 26, 2011.

334 Thirteen stents, Murray treated Dennis Hix for free: Dennis Hix testimony, *People vs. Conrad Robert Murray*, October 26, 2011.

334 *"desperate financial trouble"*: Martinez testimony, *Katherine Jackson vs. AEG.*

334 $1.6 million owed: "Michael Jackson's doc Conrad Murray in deep financial straits, paid $150,000 a month by MJ," Associated Press, August 1, 2009.

334 $71,332 in unpaid bills and $800,000 in total debts: Harriet Ryan, Kimi Yoshino, and Ashley Powers, "Michael Jackson's Death: Jackson Camp Says Concert Promoter Hired Doctor," latimesblogs.latimes.com, June 26, 2009.

334 *"He's not a businessman"*: Author interview with Miranda Sevcik.

334 MJ's kids with cough and runny nose: Los Angeles Police Department interview with Conrad Murray, June 27, 2009.

335 Michael Amir Williams call, *"very much like,"* and *"Well, I need more details"*: Ibid.

335 Murray's first visit to MJ home: Jeffrey Lee Adams testimony, *Katherine Jackson vs. AEG*, August 21, 2013.

335 London travel in chartered jet, guest house, and other AEG agreements with Murray, including $150,000 per month: Timm Woolley e-mail to Murray, May 8, 2009, *Katherine Jackson vs. AEG* discovery documents.

335 AEG house discussions with Brigitte Segal, Murray children details, and *"Make sure that the mattresses are in top shape"*: Murray e-mail to Brigitte Segal, June 15, 2009, *Katherine Jackson vs. AEG* discovery documents.

335 BMW Series 6 convertible: Martinez testimony, *Katherine Jackson vs. AEG.*

335 *"I was twelve"*: Prince Michael Jackson testimony, *Katherine Jackson vs. AEG*, June 26, 2013.

335 Shipments of ten 100-milliliter bottles and twenty-five 20-milliliter bottles, and *"clinic"* that was Nicole Alvarez's apartment: Tim Lopez testimony, *People vs. Murray*, October 4, 2011.

336 *"He liked his privacy"*: Michael Amir Williams testimony, *People vs. Murray*, September 28, 2011.

336 *"We have to be phenomenal"* and 45,000 milliliters in sixty-five bottles: David Walgren opening statement, *People vs. Murray*, September 27, 2011.

336 *Justin Burns requesting detailed medical records and "Anything less"*: Burns e-mail to Ian France and others, June 24, 2009, *Katherine Jackson vs.* AEG discovery documents.

337 *"Call me right away" exchange, "Hurry, turn around and go back"*: Williams testimony, *People vs. Murray.*

337 Speed up, *Williams on his cellphone, Alvarez running to the front door, Roselyn Muhammed let him in, Murray at the top of the stairs, Alvarez had only been in the house twice, "Alberto, come," MJ's position on pillow, "Daddy!," "Don't let them see their dad like this," "Everything is going to be okay," room details, and "some sort of, you know, medical device"*: Alberto Alvarez testimony, *People vs. Murray,* September 29, 2011.

338 *"I thought we were packing," pulse oximeter, "It's not looking good," and other details of MJ's death scene in his bedroom*: Ibid.

338 *"He's fifty years old, sir"*: "Michael Jackson: Transcript of 911 Call," telegraph. co.uk, June 26, 2009.

338 *Engine 71, 12:25 P.M., security men in front, MJ in pajamas and surgical cap, pale and underweight, hospice and DNR exchange, "Nothing," and MJ's lack of pulse and other medical details*: Richard Senneff testimony, *Katherine Jackson vs.* AEG, April 30, 2013.

339 *"a little bit of lorazepam," life-saving drugs, gurney, UCLA call, left house at 1:07 P.M.*: Ibid.

339 *Escalades*: Williams testimony, *People vs. Murray.*

339 *"It was madness at the hospital"*: Randall Sullivan, *Untouchable: The Strange Life and Tragic Death of Michael Jackson* (New York: Grove Press, 2012), p. 409.

340 *"Please, this is a private moment"*: Alvarez testimony, *People vs. Murray.*

340 *1:13 P.M., 1:21 P.M., and 2:26 P.M., Murray said he heard pulse, Cooper pronounced MJ dead*: Richelle Cooper testimony, *People vs. Murray,* October 3, 2011.

340 *"Well, I really shouldn't be telling you this"*: Phillips interview for *Rolling Stone,* 2009, courtesy of Claire Hoffman.

340 *"I almost fainted"*: DiLeo interview for *Rolling Stone,* 2009, courtesy of Claire Hoffman.

340 *Murray and Williams hallway exchange, "that he wouldn't want the world," "I am not giving him the keys," Williams refusing Murray's food request, and "make sure security"*: Williams testimony, *People vs. Murray.*

341 *"A star can never die"*: Michael Jackson, *Dancing the Dream* (London: Transworld/ Doubleday, 1992/2009), p. 15.

341 *Travis Payne heading to 2 P.M. rehearsal, mother's call, "I'm sure everything is fine," "No, we're rehearsing," rerouting to Staples, and "Smooth Criminal"*: Payne testimony, *Katherine Jackson vs.* AEG, May 13–14, 2013.

341 *"People say things" and twenty texts*: Author interview with Chris Grant.

341 *Tour accountant call from Gongaware and MJ in the hospital for heart attack*: Author interview with Abby Franklin.

342 *"Tell me something that will make me"*: Kenny Ortega testimony, *Katherine Jackson vs.* AEG, July 8–10 and August 8, 2013.

342 *Ortega collapsed, sobbing, Payne hauled him into a seat, friends held up Moffett, Bush in a similar state, and security closed building*: Franklin interview.

342 *Payne typed on his laptop, "No one knew what to do," and "So many deaths"*: Author interview with Stacy Walker.

342 *"Is it true?" and Grant getting calls*: Grant interview.

342 *"The room was dark"*: Author interview with Darryl Phinnessee.

343 *Mourners played "Heal the World" at hospital*: John Rogers, "Hundreds of Jackson fans converge on hospital," Associated Press, June 25, 2009.

343 *Sigma Alpha Epsilon cranking "Human Nature"*: Harriet Ryan, Chris Lee, Andrew Blankstein, and Scott Gold, "King of Pop Is Dead at 50," *Los Angeles Times*, June 26, 2009, p. A1.

343 *Teddy bears in Gary*: Michael McGuire, "Michael Jackson Mourned," examiner.com, June 25, 2009.

343 *Three hundred people at Hitsville*: "Fans gather where Michael Jackson's career born," Associated Press, June 25, 2009.

343 *"it's almost like Michael Jackson's last concert," Smokey Robinson devastated, "You try to find something"*: Larry King Live (CNN, June 25, 2009).

343 *Berry Gordy numb and "musical god"*: "Reaction to Michael Jackson's Death," CNN Wire, June 25, 2009.

343 *"Jackie Robinson of MTV"*: David Vigilante, "Commentary: Jackson Was the Jackie Robinson of MTV," CNN Wire, June 25, 2009.

343 *Four-thousand-word charity list*: Katie McKoy, "Thank You, Michael Jackson, for your Lifelong Charity Work," *Atlanta Examiner*, June 25, 2009.

343 *"Whatever else you might think"*: Craig Newman, suntimes.com, June 25, 2009.

344 *"We lost a hero"*: "From Sydney to Bogotá, Fans Mourn Jackson," cbsnews.com, June 25, 2009.

344 *Fans lining up at Forever Young*: Chris Hawes, "North Texans Mourn Death of Michael Jackson," WFAA, June 5, 2009.

344 *"Although we had always played"*: Author interview with Skip Dillard, for *Rolling Stone*, 2009.

344 *Thirty thousand sales before death, 1.8 million after*: Ed Christman and Antony Bruno, "Michael Jackson Sales Surge Expected to Last Months," billboard.com, July 3, 2009.

344 *8.2 million copies in 2009*: Nielsen Soundscan.

345 *Smith and Martinez interviewed Murray at the Ritz Carlton and other Murray claims about MJ's death*: LAPD interview with Murray.

345 *"We don't use it for rest"*: Alon Steinberg testimony, *People vs. Murray*, October 12, 2011.

346 *Times of Murray's calls*: Edward Dixon and Sade Anding testimony, *People vs. Murray*, September 27, 2011 and October 3, 2011.

346 *"I said, 'Hello, hello' "*: Ibid.

346 *"Michael made young men and women"*: Virginia Byrne, "Fans Gather for Apollo Theater's Jackson Memorial," Associated Press, July 1, 2009.

346 *Tito Jackson at Reggae Sumfest*: Author observation.

347 *$1.5 million memorial and AEG payment*: Patrick J. McDonnell, "AEG Announces Agreement to Pay $1.3 Million to Help Cover Cost of Michael Jackson Memorial," *Los Angeles Times*, June 19, 2010, p. AA1.

347 *"with orders that nobody was allowed onto the property," Talon locking down Hayvenhurst and Vegas homes, Ron Boyd, La Toya and Jeffre Phillips, and "took out whatever they wanted"*: Author interview with Ron Williams.

347 *"Grace, the children are crying"*: Maurice Chittenden and John Harlow, "Nanny Reveals Tragic Secret Life of Jackson," *The Sunday Times*, June 28, 2009, p. 1.

348 *Phillips gave Taj Jackson two computers and one went to the estate, Williams password, and Prince's bedroom closet*: Taj Jackson testimony, *Katherine Jackson vs. AEG*, July 11, 2013.

348 *"They backed up trucks"*: DiLeo interview for *Rolling Stone*, 2009, courtesy of Claire Hoffman.

348 *$400 million in debt*: Zack O'Malley Greenburg, *Michael Jackson Inc.: The Rise, Fall and Rebirth of a Billion-Dollar Empire* (New York: Atria, 2014), p. 227.

348 *Branca rehired June 17*: "Jackson's mother loses control of son's estate," Associated Press, July 6, 2009.

348 *DiLeo's request*: Johnnie L. Roberts, "A Superlawyer Returns, a Pop Icon Dies—a Will Is Discovered," thewrap.com, December 9, 2010.

349 *"full power and authority" and details of MJ will*: "Last Will of Michael Jackson," signed July 7, 2002.

349 *"The Scandalously Boring Truth"*: Zack O'Malley Greenburg, "The Scandalously Boring Truth About Michael Jackson's Will," forbes.com, August 17, 2012.

349 *Janet condo meeting, including McMillan on the phone and "big fraud," and Katherine Jackson backing off*: Author interview with Adam Streisand.

350 *Katherine saying Streisand talked her out of contesting the will*: Sullivan, *Untouchable*, pp. 471–73.

350 *Objections to MJ will, including "violations of fiduciary duties," and "in a fraudulent deceptive manner"*: "Joseph Jackson's Objection to Appointment of John Branca and John McClain as Executors of the Estate of Michael Jackson," Superior Court of California, County of Los Angeles, November 10, 2009.

350 *$24 million, including $15 million in advances*: Michael White and Adam Satariano, "Jackson's 'This Is It' May Make $400 Million in Sales," Bloomberg, October 26, 2009; Concerts West/AEG contract draft, *Katherine Jackson vs. AEG* discovery documents.

350 *"I don't think we've lost anything"*: Randy Phillips interview, for *Rolling Stone*, 2009, courtesy of Claire Hoffman.

351 *MJ's debts and legal claims, including franchise tax board and Erle Bonner*: Greenburg, *Michael Jackson Inc.*, p. 225.

351 *"Grab your camera and come in"*: Nancy Raskauskas, "On stage with the 'King of Pop,'" gazettetimes.com, November 1, 2009.

351 *Details of This Is It footage editing*: Author interview with Tim Patterson.

352 *"It's like the greatest show that never was"*: Ibid.

352 *Estate received 90 percent of the movie returns*: Associated Press, "Michael Jackson's Mother Sues Concert Promoter AEG Live for Fraud over Singer's Death," cleveland.com, September 16, 2010.

352 *"No one can ever watch 'This Is It' again"*: @wingheart tweet, May 22, 2013.

352 *$200 million gross*: Greenburg, *Michael Jackson Inc.*, p. 227.

353 *MJ recording at Bel Air Hotel, eleven different vocal lines, and other details from Michael songs*: Author interview with Michael Durham Prince, for *Rolling Stone*, 2010.

353 *"It should have all stayed in the vault"*: "Quincy Jones: Lady Gaga is 'Madonna, Jr.,'" usmagazine.com, November 22, 2010.

354   *DiLeo brought the songs to Doelp*: Author interview with DiLeo, for *Rolling Stone*, 2010.

354   *Impersonator accusations, "I'm disgusted," and estate response*: Steve Knopper, "Inside Michael Jackson's Return," *Rolling Stone*, December 9, 2010, pp. 13–16.

354   *Damien Shields investigation*: Author interview with Damien Shields.

354   Michael *selling 405,000*: Keith Caulfield, "Michael Jackson: Two Years Since His Death, How Much Has He Sold?," billboard.com, June 25, 2011.

355   *2.3 million copies worldwide*: Michael Jackson estate spokesperson.

355   *Estate earned $300 million and paid off MJ debt*: Mitchell Peters, "The Touring Afterlife of Michael Jackson," *Billboard*, November 16, 2013, pp. 24–34.

355   *Internal Revenue Service valuation conflict: Estate of Michael J. Jackson vs. Commissioner of Internal Revenue*, U.S. Tax Court, July 26, 2013.

355   *Branca's salary as Sony ATV adviser and "The Board is awkward"*: Internal Sony e-mail, April 1, 2014; posted at wikileaks.org/sony.

356   *"His passing—unfortunately—allowed a separation"*: Author interview with Matt Forger.

357   *"The most artistic was Paris"*: Author interview with Mark Lester.

357   *Prince as an extrovert, Blanket dancing, Paris as a daddy's girl, and "She is tough"*: Confidential source.

357   *Reasons for MJ family insisting kids look like him*: Sullivan, *Untouchable*, p. 441.

358   *"They are [Michael's] children"*: Martin Fricker, "Michael Jackson Is the Father of His Children—and Blanket Is Just Like Him, Says Tito Jackson," mirror.co.uk, July 16, 2009.

358   *"Once [I donated] to a sperm bank"*: Mark Seal, "The Doctor Will Sue You Now," *Vanity Fair*, March 2012, pp. 218–39.

358   *"I'm not interested in that"*: Lester interview.

358   Rolling Stone *and Sullivan reported MJ died without a nose*: Claire Hoffman, "The Last Days of Michael Jackson," *Rolling Stone*, August 6, 2009, p. 44; Sullivan, *Untouchable*, pp. 220–21.

358   *"Absolutely false" and tattooed lips and hairline*: Author interview with Ed Winter, and case report, Department of Coroner, Los Angeles County, June 26, 2009.

358   *"over-treating him to make money" and Demerol accusation*: Seal, "The Doctor Will Sue You Now," pp. 218–39.

359   *"He would put the time of the clocks forward" and twenty nose procedures*: Arnold Klein interview on tmz.com, November 5, 2009. Hoefflin has denied all the accusations. Hoefflin declined an interview request; Klein's representatives did not return messages.

359   *MJ's facial surgeries*: Joan Kron, "The Final Cut," *Allure*, September 2009, pp. 198–201.

359   *"My entire approach"*: Alan Duke, "Conrad Murray from Jail: 'I Was in the Wrong place at the Wrong Time,'" cnn.com, April 3, 2013.

360   *"I could not find a single shred"*: Ian Halperin, *Unmasked: The Final Years of Michael Jackson* (New York: Simon Spotlight Entertainment, 2009), p. 227.

361   *"People can admit it"*: Author interview with Henry Gradstein.

361   *"Jermaine's gonna be upset" and reality-show conflict: The Jacksons: A Family Dynasty* (A&E, 2009).

362 Hayvenhurst problems, including Joe "watching" Paris, and Rowe conditions: Sullivan, Untouchable, pp. 452, 488.

362 Alejandra Oaziaza, "Anytime Grace would say, 'Do your homework' ": Ibid.

362 "My dad didn't like her": Paris Jackson deposition, Katherine Jackson vs. AEG, March 21, 2003.

362 Jaafar's stun gun and Buckley School: Sullivan, Untouchable, pp. 452, 488.

362 "It's not like it was with her father": Author interview with Brian Oxman.

363 Katherine's $3,000-per-month stipend and $115,000 vacation: Sullivan, Untouchable, pp. 452, 488.

363 2002 will "fake, flawed and fraudulent" and "mini-stroke": Alan Duke, "Michael Jackson's Siblings Attack Estate Executors," cnn.com, July 19, 2012.

363 "I am going to clarify right now" and "hello dear FAMILY member": @parisjackson tweets, July 18, 2012.

363 Katherine Jackson at Miraval and Perry Sanders in Tucson: Author interview with Perry Sanders.

363 Calabasas tension: Sullivan, Untouchable, pp. 570–74.

364 Beau Rivage casino and "Hold On, I'm Comin'" in hallway: Author observations.

365 "One of the cruelties of stardom": Susan Fast, 33⅓: Dangerous (New York: Bloomsbury, 2014), p. 5.

365 "You got little kids that run around": Author interview with Ghostface Killah.

INDEX

Q&A WITH STEVE KNOPPER

When did you first hear Michael Jackson's music?
It was probably around 1974, when he and Roberta Flack sang "When We Grow Up" in that cartoonish kids' bedroom in *Free to Be . . . You and Me*. I was in high school in the eighties, and watched MTV all the time, so "Beat It" and "Billie Jean" were inescapable. Regrettably, back then, I was kind of a classic-rock snob, so I paid most attention to "We Are the World," because Bruce Springsteen and Bob Dylan were on it. In the early nineties, when I became a music writer, I made up for it and fell hard for *Off the Wall* and *Thriller*.

What is your favorite Michael Jackson song and why?
This question kind of depends on what day you ask it, but "Don't Stop 'til You Get Enough" is almost always Number One. I love the tension and release in Michael's opening monologue. It's a fantastic dance song, but it's also a rock 'n' roll song every bit as powerful as the punk and new wave coming out around the same time in the late seventies. It's so simple and droning, but also really complex and funky, and every time it ends, I wish it could have lasted twenty minutes longer.

In researching your book, which Jackson, other than Michael, did you find the most intriguing?
I'd say Randy, because he pops up intimately at crucial points in Michael's history. He observed Jacksonmania without being part of the original Jackson 5, then replaced Jermaine in the band during that really interesting phase when they were performing in Vegas, then recorded for Columbia and with Gamble and Huff, and so on, before Michael had broken out as a solo superstar. He's part of the Victory tour, then becomes one of Michael's most important confidants during his 2005 trial and handles his business affairs for a while. Then they have a dispute and Michael pushes him out, like he did most everybody in his life. Later, there's a point where Randy tries to bully his way onto Michael's property by smashing his car into a security gate, in what he later testified was an attempt at a drug intervention.

Do you have a favorite Michael Jackson performance?
I'm tempted to give some kind of not-so-obvious answer, like Michael's mind-blowing montage on the 1995 MTV Video Music Awards, or one of his robot moves to "Dancing Machine" on *Soul Train* or other seventies variety shows. But, come on, it's the moonwalk from *Motown 25*. When my daughter was four or five, she fell in love with "Goin' Back to Indiana," and we had to listen to it four hundred times a day, which eventually brought us to "Billie Jean," which we watched on YouTube together, over and over. It's just mesmerizing. How does he make his body do those things? How does he get his leg so high? How does he look like he's moving backward and forward at the same time? How does he manage to do all this so joyfully? And the speech at the beginning when he says "mostly, I like the new songs" is one of the great dividing-line moments of pop-music history. Everything used to sound like that and now it sounds like this.

What Michael Jackson album do you most relate to?
While I was writing this book, *Dangerous* was the album I returned to the most. It's all over the place and doesn't cohere as well as *Thriller* or even *Bad*, but I've come to appreciate its complexity and how it deals with sexual frustration, racism, absorbing the world's problems without driving yourself nuts, and other concerns for a thirty-three-year-old. It reminds me of Bruce Springsteen's *Tunnel of Love* or Prince's *Sign o' the Times* in this regard. The first few songs are just so funky, beginning with "Jam," then the album downshifts into sad and reflective hymns. He sings: "Somebody hurt my soul . . . I can't take this stuff no more." Somebody hurt Michael Jackson's soul! And there's that guitar riff in "Black or White," maybe the best in his career. As I grow older, I keep finding new things in it.

How do you think history will ultimately view Michael Jackson?
Even before "Wacko Jacko" and the child-molestation trials and all the terribly, unfairly mean press coverage via tabloids and cable news, I think the rock press had a weird suspicion of Michael. It was like he was just too weird, or childlike, or changed his appearance too frequently, or something, to be regarded in his time as respectfully as Prince or Springsteen. Or maybe people just saw him as a song-and-dance man. But to me his body of recorded work more than stands up to those guys—he made *Off the Wall* and *Thriller*! And *Bad* and *Dangerous*, and even *HIStory* and *Invincible*, are underrated and fascinating. Plus he was in the Jackson 5. Make a list of your favorite MJ songs, and you won't be able to stop. And he wrote a good portion of those and conceived dance routines for them at the level of Fred Astaire or James Brown. And there's the showmanship, the short films, and on and on. He's Mount Rushmore for me.